THE
GNOMES
OF
TOKYO

JIM POWELL

amacom
American Management Association

Library of Congress Cataloging-in-Publication Data

Powell, Jim.
    The gnomes of Tokyo : the positive impact of foreign
investment in North America / Jim Powell. — [Rev. ed.]
        p. cm.
    Includes index.
    ISBN 0-8144-7726-7
    1. Financial institutions—Japan. 2. Capitalists and
financiers—Japan. 3. Japan—Foreign economic relations—
United States. 4. United States—Foreign economic relations—
Japan. 5. Investments, Japanese—United States. I. Title.
HG187.J3P68 1989
337.52073—dc20   89-6730
                                                                       CIP

Originally published by Dodd, Mead & Company.

Printing number

10 9 8 7 6 5 4 3 2 1

CONTENTS

ACKNOWLEDGMENTS

When I started this project in 1986, I was well aware how reserved Japanese people tend to be. Some friends doubted that I'd have much luck persuading Japanese financial executives to talk about their businesses, much less their personal lives.

Well, I did encounter reticence—somewhat more than with the hundreds of American business people I've interviewed over the years.

But the Japanese I met turned out to be surprisingly cooperative. Many, like executives at Dai-Ichi Kangyo Bank, the world's largest bank, responded more quickly than most Fortune 500 companies, arranging interviews with the top people here and in Japan.

While I often needed proper introduction before an interview could proceed, generally a cold call letter was enough. I found Japanese executives much easier to get on the phone than their American counterparts. They apologized for their English, which was far better than my limited Japanese.

By the time I was through, I had interviewed almost two hundred people, most of whom you'll meet in these pages. They covered the gamut—commercial banks, trust banks, securities firms, insurance companies, leasing companies, consulting firms, trading companies, real estate and construction companies.

Among the most helpful people from Japanese companies: Kazuhiko Takano, Koji Yoshii, Asahi Shimbun,. Minoru Inouye, Takeo Shinde, Eiichi Yoshimura, Eiichi Matsumoto, Hiroshi Hayashi, Haruo

Kimura, Toshio Asakai, Bank of Tokyo; Mutsuo Murai, Nobuhiro Fukaya, Bank of Tokyo Trust Company; Tetsuya Ota, BOT Leasing; Nobuya Hagura, Yasuhiko Ikeuchi, Yuko Oana, Katsuji Minato, Taka Murai, Masanori Ebihara, Keiyu Kitagawa, Masahiro Sakaguchi, Haruo Kawano, Dai-Ichi Kangyo Bank; Takuro Isoda, Yutaka Onda, Paul Aron, Jiro Yamana, William Brachfeld, Yukio Hosoi, Elwyn P. Wong, Daiwa Securities; Masanobu Nakamura, Daiwa Securities Trust Company; Kaoru Abe, Diamond Lease Company; Ko Uemura, Takao Oishi, Kazuhiko Kasai, Yutaka Komatsu, Tominori Otsuka, Ryoji Hirabayashi, Fuji Bank; Kunitake Nomura, Hiroaki Suzuki, Yoshihiro Sawada, Fuji Bank & Trust Company; Tatsuo Takamizu, Hitachi Leasing; Hirokichi Mizutano, Hokkaido Takushoku Bank; Hideo Ishihara, Norihide Yoshioka, Hidetsugu Usui, Satoshi Hiroshawa, Fumio Norimatsu, Takeshi Kawano, Industrial Bank of Japan; Hiroshi Morita, J. W. Chai, Masanori Kitano, Albert Ping, R. Kenneth Merkey, C. Itoh & Co.; Tsutomu Karino, Japanese Chamber of Commerce, New York; Seiji Ishibashi, Kajima International; Hiro Saito, KG Land; Shuji Irisawa, Yukio Fujishima, Hiroaki Isozaki, Kumagai Gumi Co., Ltd.; Yoshio Iwashita, Kyodo Leasing; Rikuichi Yoshisue, Yoshihisa Kitai, Long-Term Credit Bank; Yuji Kage, President, LTCB Trust Company; Sueo Adachi, Tsuneo Dainaka, Hiroshi Kobayashi, Osamu Yamamoto, Marubeni America; Kanji Tanaka, Hiroshi Ohnishi, Tsuneyasu Nakano, Mitsubishi Bank; Katsuhiko Hiyama, Mitsubishi Heavy Industries America; Minoru B. Makihara, Takashi Iwamura, Mitsubishi International Corporation; Kazue Naganuma, Mitsubishi Motors Sales of America; Takuji Shidachi, Michihiro Sekiya, Masami Hinata, Tateo Nagano, Masaru Masumoto, Noriyoshi Yamaguchi, Ryutaro Shidehara, Mitsubishi Trust & Banking; Hisao Kondo, Mitsui & Co; Yoshisuke Mohri, Chitoo Bunno, Mitsui Bank; Yukio Furuta, Kitaro Onishi, Yukinobu Takiyama, Mitsui Fudosan; Hiroshi Aoki, Mitsui Leasing of America; Yoshihisa Hamabuchi, Mitsui Life Company; Yoshima Tanaka, Shuichi Nagayama, Nichimen Corporation; Susumu Ohara, Nihon Keizai Shimbun America; Toshio Mori, Steven Axilrod, Hirofumi Saito, Nikko Securities; Yoriyuki Nagao, Kozo Nogami, Masatoshi Nishikawa, Nissei Life Insurance Company; Hideki Akamatsu, Nissei Realty; Setsuya Tabuchi, Masaaki Kurokawa, Katsuya Takanashi, Yoshi Terasawa, John Niehenke, Robin S. Koskinen, Sumiko N. Ito, Steven M. Looney, Michio Katsumata, Nomura Securities; Hirosuke Sato, Norinchukin Bank; Yasushi Iwai, Shinetsu Hamada, Takashi Koizumi, Orient Leasing; Kenji Kawakatsu, Kichirou Yamamoto, Shuhei Sato, Takeo Sakai, Ryuzo Okuto, Soichi Tatsuta, Toshihide Mizuno, Sanwa Bank; Tadao Komatsu, Shimizu Construction Co.; Takaji Kobayashi, Shuwa Investment Co.; Masaaki Tezuka, Sony Corporation of America; Akira Tominaga, Sumisho Leasing Corporation; Tokuyuki Ono, Tomoyuki Kato, Morikuni Uchigasaki, Sumitomo Bank; Tadahi Fukatsi, Takashi Kano, Sumitomo Corporation; Saburo Miura, Kazu Washizu, Sumitomo Life Insurance Company; Hiroshi Ohashi, Sumitomo Trust & Banking Corporation; Osamu Nishimura, Taiyo Kobe Bank; Saburo Shinoda, Tokai Bank; Takao Matsumoto, Kenji Takagi, Tokyo Leasing USA; Koichi Yanagita, Tsugio Kambara, Tokyo Forex; T. Morita, Tokyo Tanshi Co.; Richard W. P. Magee, Peter J. McLachlan, Neil Humphreys, Kimotoshi Yasui, J. C. Okazawa, Tullett & Tokyo Forex; Takeshi Naito, Yamaichi International; Masayoshi Miyake, Yasuda Fire & Marine Insurance Co.; Norikazu Okamoto, Yoshikazu Takase, Kyosaku Sorimachi, Yasuda Mutual Life Insurance Co.; Toshio Hiratsuka, Yasuda Trust & Banking.

I also talked with people at American companies which work with and compete against the Japanese, and they're in this book, too. For instance: Timothy Harte, Cross & Brown; Stephen Siegel, Kevin Haggerty, James Montanari, Cushman & Wakefield; David Sexton, First Boston Corporation; Arthur I. Frankel, Manhattan attorney; John L. Weinberg, Roy C. Smith, Thomas J. Healey, Christian McCarthy, Michael McCarthy, Hideki Mitani, Goldman, Sachs; William Hedman, Edward S. Gordon Company; Harry Helmsley, Scott Coopchik, Helmsley-Spear, Inc.; Tetsundo Iwakuni, Merrill Lynch; Paul Reichmann, Patricia Goldstein, Camille Douglas, Olympia & York; William Rutherford, State of Oregon; Arthur M. Mitchell 3rd, Yoshinori Takagi, Pacific Investment Partners (Japanese-American joint venture); John W. Robinson, Pivco Group; Neil P. Benedict, J. Steven Manolis, Salomon Brothers; Francois de Saint Phalle, Ruggero Magnoni, Susan Levine, Akio Aoki, Shearson Lehman Brothers; Jack Shaffer, Sonnenblick-Goldman; Jerome M. Cohen, Williams Real Estate; William Zeckendorf, ZCW Associates.

Also, Leland Yeager, Auburn University; Murray Weidenbaum, Center for the Study of American Business; Paul Craig Roberts, Center for Strategic & International Studies; Mary Alexander, Citizens for a Sound Economy; Joe Cobb, Congressional Joint Economic Committee; George Benson, Emory University; J. Peter Grace, W. R. Grace & Company; Milton Friedman, Hoover Institution; John Higham, Johns Hopkins University; Stephen Marris, Institute for International Economics; Norman Ture, Institute for Research on the Economics of Taxation; Robert O. Quinn, Federal Reserve; Lawrence J. Kotlikoff,

National Bureau of Economic Research; Gregory Ballentine, Peat Marwick Main; Alan Reynolds, Polyconomics Inc.; Robert Z. Aliber, David Hsieh and George J. Stigler, University of Chicago; Max Hartwell, University of Virginia.

For the help of these and many others whose names escape me right now, I'm grateful.

Introduction to the Revised Edition:

THE NEW THREAT OF XENOPHOBIA AND ECONOMIC DECLINE

Are foreign investors really buying up everything in America? Are they destroying our jobs? Do they threaten our sovereignty? Will they turn this nation into a colony? Should we stop foreign investment before it's too late?

These are the kinds of provocative questions a lot of people are asking amidst news that American companies, Treasury securities, Hawaiian homes, New York office buildings, and other assets are being acquired by foreigners, especially by the very visible and wealthy Japanese.

Well, contrary to all the xenophobic headlines, foreign investment is a great thing for America. It's great for reasons that have nothing to do with our federal budget deficit. The more investment that takes place here—whether from foreign or domestic sources—the more American jobs will be created, the better those jobs will pay, and the stronger our nation will be.

During the 1980s, Japan and Europe have exported a tremendous amount of capital, while the United States has imported capital. And in this decade, the United States has created more than two-and-a-half as many jobs as Japan and Europe combined. What's more, according to the U.S. Bureau of Labor Statistics, American jobs are being created fastest in the top third of the wage scale.

Foreign investors contribute two ways. Directly, they met $70 billion of payrolls annually for about 3 million American people. A lot of these jobs are in rural areas that, for one reason or another, haven't been able to attract U.S. employers, and consequently living standards there have lagged below the national average. By injecting capital into these areas, foreign investors expand opportunities and help raise living standards.

We gain directly, too, from better ideas which often come in with the foreign capital. For example, a decade ago, before Lee Iacocca and other U.S. industrialists challenged the Japanese to invest in more manufacturing operations here, a lot of Americans thought Japanese management techniques could work only in Japan, because its culture was unique. Well, subsequent Japanese investment has enabled people to see firsthand how the techniques work in America. Japanese employers have eliminated many executive perks and improved employee morale. They've given more responsibility for improving quality to assembly line employees who can actually do something about it. Japanese managers introduced a policy of low inventories that simultaneously cuts costs and pressures suppliers to deliver reliable components on time. Across the country, U.S. companies have implemented these policies, too.

In a 1988 survey of American opinion about Japanese investment, the University of Miami discovered that people who have the most direct experience—those who actually work for a Japanese-owned company—report the most favorable ratings. For example, 79 percent believed that Japanese-owned companies provide job opportunities that otherwise wouldn't exist, 51 percent believed that Japanese-owned companies are more attentive to employee concerns than U.S. companies, and 90 percent believed that Japanese investment spurs American manufacturers to become more competitive.

The indirect contribution of foreign investment is equally important. However investment capital comes into America, it recirculates far from the initial entry point. For example, when a Japanese investor buys a Hawaiian house, the seller—probably American—gets money. This may go toward a new house, in which case another seller gets money. Some money may be deposited at a local Hawaiian bank that participates in business loans originated by an Atlanta bank, helping the economy there. Perhaps some money from the Hawaiian house sale is spent on an appliance, benefiting people in Ohio, Pennsylvania, New York, or wherever the appliance and its components are manufactured.

Thus, whenever a foreigner invests in the U.S., they make our pie bigger and frequently they make it better. Contrary to what some xenophobes suggest, we aren't giving anything away. CBS, for example, didn't give away CBS Records to Sony; they received $2 billion for it. American shareholders didn't give away Federated Department Stores, either; they received $6.8 billion from the Canadian entrepreneur Robert Campeau. Foreign investors cannot increase their U.S. holdings without increasing the total assets available here.

How much do foreign investors actually own in America? The highest estimates are around $1.5 trillion, about 5 percent of U.S. assets. This is less than the total assets Americans own in a number of other countries. Foreign investors own an estimated 6 percent of U.S. corporate equities and about 1 percent of U.S. land.

According to the Treasury Department, foreign investors hold only about 13 percent of U.S. government securities, and this percentage is declining. It was higher a decade ago. More than a century ago, after the Civil War, foreign investors held about 12 percent of U.S. government securities, so not much has changed.

What's the danger of foreign influence in America? The biggest foreign investors are our friends and allies. Britain heads the list with about $80 billion in new investment in 1988. The Dutch are next, with about $50 billion. Then come the Japanese, with $44 billion. They're followed by the Canadians, West Germans, French and Swiss.

Moreover, there isn't any evidence that foreign investors have objectives fundamentally different from our own. We don't see foreign investors promoting higher taxes, higher inflation, crime in the streets, or poor education. On the contrary, foreign investors come to America for the same reasons that most American investors keep their capital close to home: this is a politically stable, low-tax, low-inflation, dynamic market. As long as America maintains these competitive advantages, both domestic and foreign capital are likely to stay here.

When a government pursues policies which threaten savings, we see both American and foreign investors seek safer havens. It makes much more sense to preserve capital for future opportunities than to leave it in harm's way.

How about the influence of foreign companies on our society? We have decades of experience with foreign-owned companies such as Nestle (Swiss), Shell Oil (Dutch), Bic Pens (French), and Sony (Japanese). Generally, they seem to maintain a discreet, low profile to avoid a xenophobic backlash against foreigners. When such companies do become politically active, it's almost always because they're threatened. California's unitary tax is an example. With this measure, California asserted its prerogative to tax income earned out of state, in Illinois, New York, Tokyo, and elsewhere—in other words, taxation without representation. All kinds of companies with operations out of state, American as well as foreign, worked to overturn this outrageous law.

It's useful to keep in mind that politically active foreign investors don't defend their interests in a vacuum. Altogether, there are more than 4,100 political action committees registered with the Federal Election Commission and 7,000 lobbyists registered with the clerks of the House and Senate. Foreign investors aren't outshouting the legions of American companies, unions, health associations, environmental groups, and others who crowd the Capitol's corridors. In any event, we shouldn't deny a voice to the three million Americans employed by foreign-owned firms.

Our best protection against abuses by Americans or foreigners is the availability of alternatives. As long as consumers are free to switch products for any reason, they can avoid high cost as well as poor quality products, regardless of the seller's nationality. If employees become dissatisfied with compensation, working conditions, opportunities for advancement, or anything else, they are best protected in a dynamic economy that generates job alternatives. Suppose a landlord demands above-market rent or fails to properly maintain the elevators, heating, or other services: regardless of the landlord's nationality, tenants are free to go elsewhere when the lease expires.

In addition, of course, Americans as well as foreigners are subject to the laws of the United States. Contract laws, anti-discrimination laws, environmental protection laws, worker's compensation laws, you name it—they apply to everyone. We're all free to seek remedy in court when our rights are violated.

Some people object to foreign investment on grounds of national security, but this rarely ever becomes an issue. The Defense Department isn't obliged to deal with any particular contractor, domestic or foreign. For years, the Defense Department has had a standard clause in its contracts that provides the department must be notified before management sells the role of contractor to a foreign buyer. The Defense Department reviews the affected contracts, evaluates the sensitivity of information, and decides whether to terminate or continue the contracts. In any case, very few employees of foreign firms are eligible to enter a secured facility. No foreigner can gain unrestricted access to classified information.

While foreign investment doesn't pose a threat to America, restrictions against foreign investment do. A policy of self-sufficient isolation may sound like the kind of thing that would help protect America against a hostile world, but paradoxically, like trade and immigration barriers, investment restrictions would actually promote stagnation and decline.

- Restricting the amount of capital here would exert upward pressure on U.S. interest rates. This, in turn, would discourage companies here from investing in American growth and jobs.

- Investment restrictions would make it harder for American companies to tap lower-cost capital that foreign competitors—notably the Japanese—already use.

- Investment restrictions would lower the value of American assets by excluding potential bidders. This would make it harder for ailing American companies to finance a turnaround, as when Fujitsu was forced to withdraw its $250 million bid for Fairchild Semiconductor, enabling Fairchild to grab the company for half as much ($122 million).

- Investment restrictions would encourage foreigners to make their capital available in nations other than the United States. Consequently, jobs would be created overseas.

- American exports would be displaced as foreign investors built manufacturing plants in other countries, which would serve those markets.

- Investment restrictions would help cut off the United States from the world's fastest-growing region: the Pacific Basin. To appreciate the ominous possibilities, consider that Los Angeles has become the largest U.S. port and manufacturing center, as well as the third largest U.S. financial center, principally because of its Asian ties. Overall, the United States does about 50 percent more investment business with East Asia than it does with Western Europe.

- Investment restrictions would reduce the stake that foreigners have in a strong U.S. economy. Look at the oil industry. When the United States was just another market, oil sellers didn't particularly care whether we got oil or not, as long as they sold their oil some place. In recent years, the Saudis have bought U.S. gas stations, while the Kuwaitis bought an oil refinery here. Consequently, they now have a strong incentive to see that oil continues flowing through those gas stations and the refinery.

• Investment restrictions would probably trigger retaliation against American interests abroad. We have more money at risk than anyone else: over $1 trillion of international investments at book value and several times that at current market value. Exxon, for example, has three-quarters of its assets abroad. IBM earns more than half of its profits from overseas operations. Coca-Cola makes more money in Japan than in the United States. Americans would be the biggest losers from escalating economic warfare.

When you review the experience of nations which substantially obstruct foreign investment and other contact with the outside world—nations such as Russia, Poland, Peru, Argentina, Tanzania, Uganda, Indonesia, Burma, and North Korea—you find not prosperity but depressing decline and debt.

Historically, the most dramatic failures of economic isolationism occurred when xenophobic rulers seized control of Japan and China during the 17th century. Both countries lost touch with advances taking place elsewhere. Both stagnated. Two hundred years later, China easily fell prey to Western imperialists; Japan avoided this fate by aggressively re-establishing contact with foreigners.

Throughout human history, people have prospered to the degree that they could shop for the best the world had to offer. From Athens, Rome, and Byzantium to Venice, Amsterdam, London, New York, and Tokyo—the world's greatest cities have thrived on peaceful contact with the outside world. Interdependence has proven to be a dynamo for higher living standards. We should welcome it.

1

THE NEW KINGPIN OF GLOBAL FINANCE

It's in America's self interest to have other people prosper, and that includes the controversial Japanese.

When a nation is prosperous, its people are more likely to enjoy personal liberty and peace. This was the case, for example, in the Netherlands during the 17th century. It was a thriving commercial center that became a safe haven for persecuted Protestants, Jews, and others. During the nineteenth century, private entrepreneurs ushered in the Industrial Revolution, which led to an unprecedented rise in living standards and an expansion of human freedom. It's no coincidence that the nineteenth century was also the most peaceful period in modern history.

Liberal democracies rarely ever emerge from an economic crisis. On the contrary, it's the classic breeding ground for xenophobia, dictatorship, and war. Adolph Hitler couldn't attract much support in the 1920s as long as Germany enjoyed a modest prosperity; he seized power during the Great Depression, when millions of unemployed people were desperate for a strong man to "do something" about their problems. Similarly, it wasn't until economic nationalism in the United States and other countries cut off Japan from its major markets—thereby giving credibility to the Japanese military—that a policy of empire-building was successfully promoted.

The prosperity of other people also benefits us because the better off they are, the more of our goods they can buy. About three-quarters of our trade is with people in prosperous nations; impoverished people in the Third World simply can't afford to buy much. A century ago, the European quest for overseas empires was touted as a strategy for securing markets, but the new markets turned out to be mirages. Prosperous Europeans continued to trade mostly with each other.

In addition, as people become more prosperous they're likely to accumulate investment capital, some of which may be deployed in our country, helping to raise our living standards. This book is about the impact of foreign investment—especially Japanese investment—on the United States.

By now, most people must be aware that in many respects the Japanese have become very prosperous indeed. World War II left the Japanese amidst ruins, with a meager standard of living equivalent to primitive Indians in the Andes, but four decades of toil and thrift have built a mighty money machine. The Japanese gross national product is almost as big as that of the Soviet Union—with less than half the population; double that of West Germany; and more than triple that of Great Britain.

A visitor to Tokyo is astonished at the signs of prosperity all around. The two-hour ride from Narita International Airport affords a panorama of new cars and neon signs. Tokyo's buildings aren't as densely clustered as in Manhattan, but the number of high rises is overwhelming—they extend to the horizon. Tokyo is perhaps the world's largest major city in terms of geographical area, with several buoyant business districts. It has one of the liveliest retail scenes, including a couple dozen department stores, huge underground arcades and small shops almost everywhere. Fashions and electronic wonders are commonplace.

If Tokyo isn't picturesque like London, Paris, or New York, it's richer than all these. There's far less crime. A vast metropolitan belt stretches from Tokyo southwest to Kawasaki, Yokohama, Nagoya, Kyoto, Osaka, and Kobe. Probably it's the world's greatest concentration of people and industry.

The Japanese have emerged as the most powerful financiers, and their financial markets have become the world's largest. A single Japanese company, Nippon Telegraph & Telephone, has a greater market value—about $300 billion—than all the stocks in West Germany. The total market value of stocks traded on the Osaka Stock Exchange surpasses the combined total of stocks on the London, Frankfurt, and

Paris stock exchanges. In 1987, for the first time, the total market value of 1,500 stocks listed on the Tokyo Stock Exchange surpassed the market value of 2,250 stocks on the New York Stock Exchange.

Consider real estate. In downtown Tokyo, a compact umbrella will cover a spot worth about $75,000. Recently, a four-hundred-fifty square-foot soba (buckwheat noodle) shop closed downtown, and the delirious owner pocketed $14 million from a developer who hoped to assemble enough parcels for an office building. Office rents downtown are about 140 percent higher than in London and 280 percent higher than in New York. Largely because of steep land prices, a membership in Tokyo's exclusive Koganei Country Club hit $3.5 million. Green fees are extra.

According to the Federation of Economic Organizations, average land prices in Japan are thirty-five times higher than in the United States. *Forbes* calculates that the total market value of property in Japan exceeds the value of all U.S. land.

Although the Japanese still tend to think of their country as poor, there's enormous personal wealth. *Forbes* named twenty-four Japanese believed to be worth more than $1 billion. They come from the most unexpected places.

Konosuke Matsushita, ninety-three, was the youngest son of a rice farmer who worked fields near Osaka. Though the family was prosperous at one time, they lost everything as they became caught up in a wild stock speculation and subsequent crash. Matsushita left primary school to work as an apprentice in a charcoal brazier shop and a bicycle wholesale house. He learned about electricity while working at Osaka Electric Light Company.

When, in 1918, executives told Matsushita they weren't interested in his idea for a new kind of electrical socket, he began a little business to make it himself. He raised capital by borrowing from friends. His wife Mumeno pawned her kimonos. From a single rented room, the business grew into the world's largest consumer electronics manufacturer, with some six hundred companies and familiar brands like Panasonic. Konosuke Matsushita's major stock holdings are worth $2 billion. He's revered as a god of modern management methods.

Masatoshi Ito, sixty-three, opened a Tokyo clothing store after World War II. He expanded gradually into a chain of general-merchandise stores. Noting the remarkable success of American chain stores, he secured licensing agreements from 7-Eleven convenience stores and Denny's family coffee shops. Now Ito presides over Japan's second-largest retail chain with, among other things, more than three thousand 7-Eleven stores. His family's holdings are estimated to be worth $1.8 billion.

Taikichiro Mori, eighty-three, was an economics professor who inherited a hundred thousand square feet of Tokyo land from his father. In 1959, he decided that Minato Ward, where many government buildings are located, would prosper. So he sold his properties elsewhere and bought as much as he could in Minato Ward. He built office buildings, numbering each one. As you walk around the ward's tangled streets, especially at night, you can orient yourself by illuminated green and white circular signs saying "Mori No. 7," "Mori No. 35," "Mori No. 15." Now Mori is the biggest private landlord in Tokyo, with an empire of sixty-five office towers, hotels, and apartments—7.7 million square feet of space altogether. Mori is reportedly worth more than $16 billion.

Yoshiaki Tsutsumi, fifty-three, is worth about $2.5 billion and controls more than $20 billion of assets. His father, Yasujiro Tsutsumi, bought as much land as he could from impecunious aristocrats. This business evolved into the Seibu Group, which owns retail stores and real estate. Now the Seibu Group is Japan's largest private landowner, with train lines, the Prince chain of over thirty hotels, twenty-four golf courses, resorts, ski slopes, a professional baseball team, and 2.4 million square feet of commercial property in Tokyo.

While these wealthy Japanese may make the headlines, lesser-known chief executives of Japan's financial institutions wield more global clout. Nine of the world's ten largest banks and securities firms are Japanese. The highest-ranking securities firm on the list and number two overall is Nomura Securities—with a market value ten times greater than Merrill Lynch. The lowest-ranking company on that list is Mitsubishi Trust & Banking, which is worth three times more than Citibank, the largest U.S. bank. Citibank ranks only twenty-ninth worldwide.

That's not all. Tokyo's giant Orient Leasing has more than $14 billion of assets. Mitsui Fudosan is among the world's largest real estate companies, controlling over $50 billion of property. The world's largest life insurance company, Nippon Life, is Japanese. This and other Japanese insurance companies are the most powerful investors, with the deepest pockets.

Japan arrived as a financial superpower only in recent years, thanks to mounting export surpluses and diminished prospects for investment at home. By the end of 1981, Japan had $10.9 billion of net overseas assets. Now Japan has about $200 billion, more than any other country. Japan's wealth dwarfs that of the Saudi oil sheiks during their heyday.

Says Fred Bergsten of the Institute for International Economics: "This stunning speed, combined with the size of the Japanese buildup, is unique in human history. Within a decade, Japan will have piled up a net international creditor position of half a trillion dollars, rising very rapidly."

Meanwhile, the United States, which had $140 billion of net assets in 1981—an all-time high—has become the world's largest debtor. Net foreign obligations now exceed $263 billion, the result of the Japanese and others stepping up their investing in the United States while American lenders and investors cut back their activities abroad, particularly Third World loans. Never before has a country gone so deep in debt.

The Japanese have unprecedented impact on world money markets, influencing capital flows, interest rates, exchange rates, economic growth, and jobs. The Bank for International Settlements reports that the Japanese control 25 percent of international banking assets, more than anyone else. The United States is in second place.

The frugal Japanese have preferred to invest and lend money rather than accumulate consumer goods. An estimated 94 percent of Japan's wealth has been recycled back through the financial markets via Japan's banks and securities firms.

The Japanese are also making their presence felt in the international art market. Tokyo real estate billionaire Seijiro Matsuoka, ninety-three, has stormed art auction rooms in Hong Kong and London, amassing a $210-million collection that includes Ming porcelain and Greek and Indian sculptures. Part of it is on display at his Matsuoka Museum.

On March 31, 1987, Yasuo Goto, the sixty-four-year-old chairman of Yasuda Fire & Marine Insurance, made headlines worldwide when he bid the equivalent of $36.22 million for Vincent Van Gogh's bright, agitated canvas called *Sunflowers*. Auctioned at Christie's in London, it set a record for a painting. *Sunflowers* joins a corporate collection of some four-hundred-fifty paintings and sculptures, including two Renoirs, two Picassos, a Chagall, and a Rodin. Many of these are displayed in Yasuda Fire & Marine's museum on the forty-second floor of their Shinjuku, Tokyo, headquarters.

The Japanese are especially interested in the United States, the most stable and competitive international market. Financial companies can operate in a substantially deregulated environment. After-tax return on investment is higher here than in Japan and other countries. Largely because of the 1981 and 1986 income tax rate cuts, after-tax returns continue to improve. U.S. inflation and unemployment have remained at lower levels than almost anywhere else in the industrialized world. Massive Japanese financial commitments are a dramatic vote of confidence for America's relatively open-market economic policies.

As if to bow before the almighty yen, more and more Americans are calling on the gnomes of Tokyo, who control the huge cash flows. The ultimate high-powered international gathering place is the graceful 910-room Okura, Tokyo's most prestigious hotel—across the street from the American embassy and about a fifteen-minute cab ride from the Marunouchi business district. Financier David Rockefeller, California governor George Deukmejian, secretary of state George Schultz, Bankers Trust chairman Alfred Brittain III, Shearson Lehman Brothers chairman Peter Cohen, Merrill Lynch chairman William Schreyer, and hundreds of American industrial barons have all stayed at the Okura. "One of the world's finest hotels," says former secretary of state Henry Kissinger. President Ronald Reagan stayed in the six-room Imperial Suite, surrounded by a Japanese-style rooftop garden. It runs ¥320,000—about $2,300—a night.

There's a Japanese tea ceremony room and art museum at the Okura, but most people come to talk money. American governors vie with one another, seeking Japanese direct investments that will help bring jobs to their states. They promote their locations and special advantages, address Japanese concerns about high taxes, obstructive unions, and capricious regulations.

M. Danny Wall, chairman of the Federal Home Loan Bank Board, asks pension fund and insurance company portfolio managers to buy bonds that will help bail out the Federal Savings and Loan Insurance Corporation. It ran out of money as hundreds of American savings and loan associations failed. Wall hopes to sell $10.8 billion of these bonds over the next three years.

Wall Street investment bankers pitch Japanese investors on American companies that need to raise money or seem like good acquisition candidates. Trust bankers call on Japanese pension administrators whose funds they hope to manage. American real estate brokers bring lists of American buildings on the market.

The Japanese may take what seems like an impossibly long time to make decisions, and most Americans return home empty-handed. The Japanese aren't always familiar with places like Arkansas, just as few Americans can point to Kagoshima on a map. Before the Japanese even consider the merits of a potential investment, they spend time learning more about these visitors who are so kindly disposed toward their savings.

Deals are happening faster, though. The Japanese make some $10 billion of direct investments annually in manufacturing facilities, which helps give American customers greater choice, better quality, and lower prices. Asahi Glass built a plant in Ohio, Kawasaki Steel built one in California, and Nissan Motor has a facility in Arizona. Among the other Japanese companies that made commitments to America are Sekisui Chemical (Massachusetts), Kinugawa Rubber (Tennessee), GMF Robotics (Michigan), Fujikura Ltd. (South Carolina), Mori Seiki (Texas), Sony (Indiana), Isuzu Trucks (Kentucky), Hitachi Chemical (Georgia), Matsushita Communications (Illinois), and Mitsubishi Heavy Industries (Pennsylvania).

These investments in manufacturing facilities mean the Japanese are creating jobs here. An estimated two hundred fifty thousand Americans work for Japanese-owned companies now. They're among the fastest-growing employers, expected to generate a million jobs within a decade.

In many cases, the Japanese are helping to salvage beleaguered American companies. Nippon Kokkan Steel, for instance, injected $300 million into troubled National Steel. Fuji Bank spent more than $1.1 billion acquiring and turning around Walter Heller, an asset-based lender with a portfolio full of bad loans. This is among the biggest Japanese commitments to a single American company.

Many Japanese dare to go where American executives failed. RCA closed a Memphis TV-manufacturing plant that employed as many as forty-two hundred workers during the late 1970s. Yet Sharp Corp. came to Memphis and built a new five-hundred-thousand-square-foot plant that produces thirty thousand TV sets and thirty thousand microwave ovens a month now. About 85 percent of managers and all assembly-line workers are American. In Forrest City, Arkansas, Sanyo Manufacturing Corp. took over a factory about to lose its contract with Sears because the TV sets were of poor quality. Sanyo achieved high quality and boosted employment from five hundred to twenty-five hundred. Toyota took over a closed General Motors factory in Fremont, California, hired about twenty-five hundred American auto-workers, and made this among the most productive auto plants in the country. Thus, the Japanese are helping to reinvigorate the vital manufacturing sector of the U.S. economy.

Japanese commercial bankers have loaned an estimated $270 billion to American companies. Because these loans represent the most competitive financing available, they help secure millions of American jobs and keep consumer prices lower. Many projects would not go forward without Japanese financing.

Bank of America Chairman A. W. Clausen asked major Japanese banks for help so that stumbling institution could survive all the bad loans he and his people made during the go-go years. In October 1987, Dai-Ichi Kangyo Bank, Fuji Bank, Sumitomo Bank, Mitsubishi Bank, and others bought $250 million of twelve-year, floating-rate notes, plus $100 million of preferred stock. But Bank of America will need a lot more money than this, which is probably why American institutions didn't exactly clamor for the risky securities.

Because of Japanese investments in American financial companies, they're more competitive. The venerable investment banking firm Goldman, Sachs has $500 million more to deploy against global competitors, thanks to Osaka-based Sumitomo Bank, which will get a 12.5 percent cut of profits. Shearson/Lehman Brothers boosted its war chest by $538 million after Nippon Life Insurance Company bought a 13 percent stake. Benjamin V. Lambert sold half-interest in the $3 billion mortgage banking firm Eastdil Realty Inc. to Nomura Securities so he could gain capital needed for expansion.

Japanese leasing companies take on risks that most American lessors avoid. The Japanese provide low fixed-rate equipment financing for more than ten years. This enables United Airlines, American Airlines, Northwest Airlines, TWA, Texas Air, and others to get the aircraft they need, so they'll remain competitive. None of these companies has terrific credit ratings.

Japanese investment bankers have raised billions of dollars for American companies by helping them issue Euromarket bonds. The savings realized contribute to the continuing competitiveness of IBM, General Electric, Exxon, Dow Chemical, Texaco, Sears, General Motors, and many more.

Japanese eagerness to buy American stocks and real estate helps make these markets more liquid. Because of Japanese participation, it's easier to sell even large positions without disrupting a market. Often, sellers benefit from higher prices, too. Proceeds are available to reinvest in other projects.

To help raise lower-cost capital from stock offerings, American companies tap Japanese equity markets via a listing on the Tokyo Stock Exchange. IBM, ITT, Chrysler, General Motors, McDonald's, Du Pont, Eli Lilly, RJR Nabisco, Bell Atlantic, Proctor & Gamble, Philip Morris, Eastman Kodak, 3M, and Walt Disney Productions are among those listed. Major American banks, too, like Citibank, Chase Manhattan, and First Chicago are Tokyo-listed so they'll be more competitive.

Japanese bankers guarantee bond issues by state and local governments in Arkansas, California, Florida, Illinois, Maryland, Massachusetts, Michigan, Missouri, New York, Ohio, Oregon, Pennsylvania, and other states—to help finance schools, sanitation systems, health facilities, rapid transit, and other projects. The Japanese get the business because they're willing to do the job for less than American banks. Most major Japanese banks have triple-A credit ratings (only one major U.S. bank is triple-A), so the Japanese enable U.S. states and municipalities to borrow money at lower interest rates, saving taxpayers hundreds of millions.

Similarly, Japanese investors buy a small percentage of U.S. Treasury bonds. This translates to lower interest rates than would otherwise be the case. American taxpayers save billions. If the Japanese pulled out of the Treasury markets, interest rates would spike upward, threatening a serious U.S. recession.

Furthermore, because mortgage markets are now closely linked to Treasury bond markets, lower rates for Treasuries mean lower monthly mortgage payments for homeowners and renters across the country. When the Japanese have bought fewer Treasuries, mortgage rates jumped as much as a couple of points in a single week.

If it weren't for the tremendous commitments by Japanese and other foreign investors, American companies would be crowded out of the credit markets by the huge demand for government and home mortgage funds. "Our foreign borrowing alone," explains investment banker and former commerce secretary Peter G. Peterson, "will fund all our net housing investment and a good 40 percent of our declining level of net business investment."

The Japanese presence is quite evident in the business districts of our major cities. Some sixty thousand Japanese work and live in the New York metropolitan area alone. A couple decades ago, the Nippon Club was about the only place in Manhattan serving an authentic Japanese meal. Now there are some six hundred Japanese restaurants. "Their country is half a world away," says Michael P. Huerta, New York commissioner of ports, international trade and commerce, "but the Japanese are the single biggest foreign influence in the city's business community."

The Japanese are more involved in Hawaii than anywhere else. Japanese investors own three-quarters of the oceanfront hotels along Waikiki Beach, including almost all the famous properties, like the Royal Hawaiian Hotel. The Japanese own resorts, shopping centers, golf courses, restaurants, office buildings, and residential developments throughout the Hawaiian Islands. They bought an estimated $1 billion of new property during 1986 alone.

As the Japanese have become more visible, however, many Americans have become more hostile. Despite the benefits of Japanese lending and investment, alarmed Japan-bashing American politicians are pushing protectionist schemes harder than at any time since the Great Depression.

More self-assured because of their prodigious success, the Japanese speak up more than they used to. "The United States is adhering to the idea that it remains a creditor nation," Sony Chairman Akio Morita told a recent gathering of the Japan Society in New York. "Japan continues with the attitude of a debtor nation. Somehow, both nations are finding it difficult to see the world as it is now.

"From the American standpoint, I believe this is because people have always been able to buy anything they wanted with U.S. dollars. They never felt the need to export and earn other nations' money.

"Japan's experience was the exact opposite. Japan had to buy practically all its energy, raw materials, and food. No trading partner would accept our yen for payment. They wanted dollars, and the only way Japan could earn dollars was to export. If Japan earned dollars, we could survive. The dollar taught us we had to export. Now a lot of our savings are coming back to the United States as investments."

How did Japan become the world's greatest financial powerhouse in less than five years? Who are the most powerful Japanese moneymen? What kinds of stocks, bonds, and real estate are they interested in? How well are they actually doing with their investments? How do certain American financial companies work successfully with the Japanese? How will the United States be affected by mounting pressures for more protectionism? What does all this mean for U.S. interest rates, inflation, and the economy? How can America be more competitive?

These are some of the key questions I address in this book. Which direction our policymakers go will have a tremendous impact on our future competitiveness and vitality.

2

PRELUDE TO POWER

Recently, Nomura Securities chairman Setsuya Tabuchi visited President Jose Sarney of Brazil, and Sarney asked what could be done about his country's immense debt load. "There's a traditional approach and an approach which would require a miracle," Tabuchi replied. "The traditional approach would involve visiting Japan and asking the prime minister to pay off Brazil's debts."

Sarney seemed stunned. "What's the other approach, which you say would take a miracle?" Sarney asked.

"If the Brazilian people worked harder, saved money, and paid their debts themselves," Tabuchi said.

Not very tactful, perhaps, but Tabuchi was describing obvious things anyone must do to prosper. The Japanese do these things, and they're puzzled that Brazilians, Americans, and others have such a hard time. It all seems so straightforward.

Japan's financial success is rooted in the hard work and thrift of people like Masatoshi Takahashi, twenty-six, who works in the marketing section of J. Osawa, a Tokyo-based trading company.

Takahashi earns the equivalent of about $14,000 a year. He rents a cramped room in a house, spending a paltry $120 monthly for room and board. He budgets about $400 a month for his car, clothing, and other pleasures. Every year, he manages to save about $2,700—19 percent of his earnings.

On average, the Japanese earn about as much as Americans and they save almost a fifth of their paychecks. In Japan, household savings average $43,000. By contrast, Americans save only 6.5 percent of their earnings. The French save 13 percent, West Germans 12.7 percent, and the Canadians 11.5 percent. "The dedication of the Japanese public to savings is as important as anything ;e to Japan's success," says Takuji Matsuzawa, former chairman of Fuji Bank.

Mieko Tanaka sees a lot of Japanese savers. She's branch manager at the Daiwa Securities counter on the fourth floor of Mitsukoshi department store, Yokohama. "Most people in this store," she says, "should have savings about three times the national average, which means we should sell the average customer about 10 million yen— $70,000—in securities." She talked about one man, unknown to her, who put $700,000 on the counter and asked about securities.

All these savers contribute over $1 billion a day to Japan's savings pool. This is why Japan can devote 16 percent of its gross national product for investment, triple the rate of investment in the United States. During 1986, the Japanese made about $300 million of net investments, compared with $270 million by the United States. They spend more than we do on factories, laboratories, roads, and nondefense research and development. Just think of it: Japan, with half the population of the United States, invests more total resources for the future. No wonder Japanese are so much more productive than Americans.

The Japanese save partly because they don't have room to put many things. With about half the population of the United States, Japan covers an area about the size of California. Some 85 percent is mountainous. Farms, industries, and homes must make do with the rest.

Though Japan's actual population density is comparable to that of Massachusetts, laws intensify the pressure on land by valuing it according to present use. That's why, incredibly, there are rice farms within metropolitan Tokyo. Despite all the urban pressures, rice farms continue to be economical in Tokyo, because they're taxed at low rates as agricultural land, rather than at the much higher rates one would expect for a high-rise building. Similarly, there are many single-family homes in metropolitan Tokyo, because they, too, are taxed at low rates. Often, the only way developers can assemble enough land for a major building is to buy up small parcels as their owners die. With comparatively little land available for more intensive development, many Tokyo city dwellers must squeeze their families into housing units the size of a suburban American living room.

Japanese laws discourage consumption. Income tax rates go up to 70 percent. There aren't any tax breaks for home mortgage interest or consumer borrowing. Income taxes and the equivalent of Social Security taxes take 36 percent of Japan's gross national product— about the same as in the United States and decidedly less than in Britain, France, and West Germany, where these taxes wipe out half the gross national product.

On the other hand, the Japanese government gives tax breaks for savers. There are four popular benefits, generally known as *maruyu*. The Japanese were permitted to deduct from taxes the interest earned on bank deposits up to ¥3 million (about $20,000). Similar exemptions applied to deposits at postal savings banks. As an account approached the limit, people commonly opened additional accounts in other names. It wasn't legal, but neither was the law enforced. Also exempted were dividends from government and corporate bonds. Finally, wage earners could have their employers deduct savings from their paychecks, and up to ¥5 million was tax-free.

Overall, the interest on an estimated 70 percent of Japanese personal savings is tax-free. This compares with 11 percent in Britain, and zero in West Germany and the United States.

Although abolishing these tax breaks reduced important incentives for savers, the legislation was part of a complex package. It included: a cut in the top national tax rate, from 60 percent to 50 percent; the lowest national tax rate was cut from 10.5 percent to 10 percent; and the highest local tax rate was cut from 16 percent to 15 percent. Corporate tax rates are coming down from 42 percent to 37 percent. Also, a 3 percent consumption tax was introduced; it's applied to most goods and services.

To be sure, taxes aren't the only influence on the savings rate. Japanese also save to buy their own home. Down payments average a whopping 32 percent of the purchase price. Typically, Japanese can't afford a home until age forty, a decade later than Americans.

The Japanese save for many other reasons, too. They spend more than Americans on education. About a quarter of Japanese elementary and secondary school children attend *juku*, after-hours cram schools intended to help children pass entrance examinations for prestigious schools.

The Japanese save to pay for weddings, which may cost several million yen.

Providing for old age is another powerful incentive to save. More than 95 percent of Japanese employers set mandatory retirement by age sixty, but there are limited old-age benefits in Japan. The modest Japanese equivalent to Social Security is being reduced, to help keep it solvent. Moreover, few companies provide a pension. Historical practice favors a single lump-sum payment when people retire, and it can go quickly. "Most Japanese think of themselves as middle class," says novelist Shusaku Endo, "but when they retire, they're poor." Surely Americans would save a lot more, too, if they knew that when they quit work, they'd be substantially on their own.

Finally, the Japanese save for emergencies. Frequently since World War II, the Bank of Japan has run surveys to determine why people save. Providing for emergencies has always elicited at least a 75 percent response, and in the 1986 survey the figure was 79 percent.

Consider how vulnerable the Japanese are. Dependent on imports for a wide range of basic commodities, including food and energy, the Japanese would be hard hit by escalating war in the Mideast, a trade war with Western countries, or upheavals in East Asia, Latin America, or elsewhere. Soviet Russia controls territory just a few miles north of Japan, and they're building up their Pacific naval fleet. The Japanese never forgot they're the only country to have been bombed with atomic weapons. Most of Japan is in an earthquake zone, and an earthquake has already leveled Tokyo once during this century. Understandably, Japanese don't share the sunny optimism of Americans who see little reason to save for the future.

Japanese Money Barons

Japanese saving is channeled through a protected, compartmentalized financial system. During the past century, since the Meiji Restoration ushered feudal Japan into the modern world, banks have dominated the scene. The biggest ones are in Marunouchi and Nihonbashi, Tokyo's most prestigious business districts—and probably the most valuable chunk of real estate on earth.

There are a dozen major commercial banks, called city banks, which are based in cities and do business nationwide. Providing medium-term financing for Japanese industry and agriculture, they gather savings via interest-bearing deposits with a maximum three-year term. City banks, together with smaller regional banks, control 29 percent of Japan's savings, the largest share among financial institutions. Although the city banks are powerful, they aren't permitted to manage trust or pension portfolios.

The city banks got underway during the early years of the Meiji Restoration. Dai-Ichi Kokuristu (First National) Bank was among the first, opening its doors in 1872. It was the forerunner of Dai-Ichi Kangyo Bank, now the world's largest bank, with $240.7 billion of assets.

Most of the other major banks trace their roots to Japan's then family-owned conglomerates known as *zaibatsu*. Mitsui Bank ($132 billion of assets) incorporated in 1876, an adjunct of a two-centuries-old merchant house. Fuji Bank ($213.4 billion of assets) started in 1880, as did Mitsubishi Bank ($204.7 billion of assets). Sumitomo Bank ($206.1 billion of assets) opened in 1895.

The city banks dominate Japan's financial scene, though gradually they're losing clout to the securities firms. Until recent years, the city banks were able to keep corporate borrowers on a short leash, as they were dependent on banks for virtually all their financing. The stock market was undeveloped. Almost everything, including long-term projects, were financed with three-month loans that could be called at the bank's discretion. In practice, these loans were rolled over continuously, but the control was always present. As world capital markets were deregulated, Japanese companies have raised funds more cheaply by issuing bonds—a business which the Japanese government restricts to securities firms.

Besides the city banks, Japan has a network of smaller banks. There are sixty-three deposit-rich regional banks which derive more than half their deposits from individuals, typically a more stable source of funds than corporations. About two-thirds of the lending is done in a bank's prefecture. Moreover, there are seventy-one savings and loan institutions which lend primarily to small wholesale, retail and construction firms. To provide some protection for these smaller banks, the big city banks aren't permitted to open more than one branch a year.

The Industrial Bank of Japan is among the most influential, blue chip Japanese financial institutions. It sits astride $205.2 billion of assets. The Japanese government created it in 1902 to provide long-term capital for heavy industry like steel, coal, metals, cement, shipbuilding, oil refining and utilities. City banks couldn't do the job, since their deposits had terms under three years. The Industrial Bank of Japan raises funds by issuing debentures—debt instruments commonly with a five-year term.

After World War II, it became a private institution, and two competitors were started: the Long-Term Credit Bank of Japan ($142.6 billion of assets) and Nippon Credit Bank ($114.2 billion of assets). All these long-term banks collect fees as lead-commissioned banks on bond issues, whether government or corporate, thereby gaining influence over the terms of a bond issue.

Seven Japanese trust banks are licensed to issue two- and five-year trust certificates, which account for more than half their funds. The balance comes from demand deposits and income earned managing trust and pension portfolios. Japan's trust banks provide medium-term loans to heavy industry. They have real estate licenses, too, so they broker and finance properties. The biggest of these institutions are Mitsubishi Trust & Banking ($238.8 billion of assets) and Sumitomo Trust & Banking ($225.5 billion of assets).

Government officials granted a monopoly on foreign exchange and trade finance business to the Yokohama Specie Bank, which opened in 1880. The government provided a third of its start-up capital, approved the appointment of top executives, and established a special relationship with the Bank of Japan. After World War II, the name was changed to Bank of Tokyo. Though it doesn't have a monopoly anymore, it still handles more foreign exchange business than any other Japanese bank, and it has far more international branches. It's a major institution, with $145.1 billion of assets.

The Norinchukin Bank, owned by some eleven thousand farm and fishery cooperative workers, was chartered to serve as the bank of last resort for Japan's farmers—about 10 million at last count. Norinchukin Bank has the largest private yen base, with assets of $233.5 billion. It's the largest supplier of short-term funds to Japan's city banks, and it's one of the biggest buyers of U.S. Treasury bonds.

Not to be overlooked is the $500 billion Postal Savings Bureau of the Ministry of Posts and Telecommunications. The world's largest savings institution, it competes with all the city banks, trust banks, and mutual savings banks for private capital, claiming about a third of individual deposits in Japan. One advantage it has is that transactions can be handled by any of Japan's twenty-three thousand post offices—in many villages, the only deposit-taking facility. Postal savings officials want to offer deregulated accounts for small savers, and this has stirred bitter opposition among private bankers.

Recognizing that asset-based financing requires expertise that few commercial bankers seem to have, Japanese banks, manufacturers, and trading companies started the Japanese leasing industry during the 1960s. Leasing companies finance office equipment, computers, airplanes, industrial machinery, and more.

Securities firms, along with the Tokyo Stock Exchange, are headquartered in Kabuto-cho, a nondescript section northeast of Tokyo's banking district. The name comes from the word for an ancient war helmet. Unlike Wall Street's canyon of skyscrapers, Kabuto-cho has few buildings more than eight stories high.

The Tokyo Stock Exchange, a private joint-stock company, opened for business in 1878. For years, though, it didn't do much trading, since about two-thirds of stock remained in the hands of a company's main banks and associated companies. Despite its prodigious volume now, the Tokyo Stock Exchange remains a surprisingly thin market for many stocks. Besides Tokyo, there are exchanges in Osaka, Nagoya, Kyoto, Hiroshima, Fukuoka, Niigata, and Sapporo.

The Big Four securities firms—Nomura, Daiwa, Nikko, and Yamaichi—tower over the business. The market value of the four firms is greater than that of most banks. Nomura alone has more assets in custody than any bank in the world. All securities firms are booming, and their offices are overcrowded with rows of desks jammed next to each other. In fact, because of the shortage of adequate office space in Kabuto-cho, several firms are expected to move into larger quarters elsewhere in Tokyo.

Japanese securities firms enjoy a sheltered life, thanks to friendly government officials. While the firms aren't permitted to take deposits, they have the exclusive franchise to underwrite stocks and bonds. This is because Japan, in 1948, adopted Article 65 of their securities law, adapted from the U.S. Glass-Steagall Act. It bars banks from entering the securities business. Brokerage firms also benefit from commissions fixed at high levels.

Japanese life insurance companies, located principally in Tokyo and Osaka, serve the world's largest life insurance market. More than 90 percent of Japanese buy life insurance, and they have 50 percent more coverage per person than is the case in the United States. Life companies aren't allowed to offer non–life insurance products, just as non–life companies are restricted to their licensed fields, like fire and marine insurance. The Ministry of Finance limits their capacity to seek returns from overseas investments.

Byzantine Bureaus

For all its incredible might, Tokyo is a highly restricted, unimaginative, comparatively slow-moving financial center. It can't compare to the dynamism of New York or London.

There's nothing wrong with the Japanese, of course. They can work wonders anywhere. But you can't expect energy and innovation in a protected environment.

The Bank of Japan, or Nippon Ginko as it's called, is the central bank, and funds government operations, issues bank notes, determines monetary policy, and serves as lender of last resort to commercial banks.

Started in 1882, the Bank of Japan occupies an old Roman-style building, entrances flanked by imposing columns, that could pass for a bank in any western country. The Bank of Japan governor, one of the most powerful people in the country, is always either a former finance minister or retired city bank chief executive, appointed to a five-year term by the Diet, Japan's national legislature.

The Bank of Japan exercises its most visible power through the discount rate, the fee it charges banks that come to its loan window. Most interest rates in Japan—from bonds to commercial bank loans—are pegged to the discount rate. Lowering it may help stimulate economic growth, and raising it may help curb borrowing and inflation. U.S. government bureaucrats continually pressure the Bank of Japan to move the discount rate in a way that they believe will favor American interests.

The Bank of Japan has an uneasy relationship with the Ministry of Finance. Officials at these institutions don't always agree on what should be done. Bank of Japan bureaucrats cherish their independence as an institution 55 percent owned by the government and the balance by private investors. Ministry bureaucrats tend to view the Bank of Japan as a branch office that should carry out their policies.

The Ministry of Finance is located in a gray brick building near other government offices in Tokyo's Kasumigaseki district. It's enormously powerful, concentrating functions that the United States has dispersed among the Treasury Department, Commerce Department, Federal Reserve, Internal Revenue Service, and Securities and Exchange Commission.

A Japanese finance minister is almost always a leading candidate to be the next prime minister. Even if one doesn't make it to prime minister, there's *amakudari*—descent from heaven. Amakudari describes the practice of Ministry bureaucrats who retire and join private firms they developed relationships with, for more money than they ever dreamed of. Their employers buy connections that are good for business.

The Ministry is actually a catacomb of bureaus. There are nine altogether, one for each of the basic functions. Most politicized is the Budget Bureau, which drafts the national budget, determining who gets what. The Banking Bureau licenses banks, the Tax Bureau administers taxes, the Finance Bureau is Japan's biggest borrower, and so on. Each bureau is further divided into divisions—the International Finance Bureau, for instance, has nine. Each grouping has a constellation of lobbyists.

To the outside world, the Ministry may be a model of harmony, but behind their dingy walls, bureaus struggle with one another for influence. The International Finance Bureau is commonly referred to as "the mafia," because officials in competing bureaus resent its concessions to foreign demands. Internal wrangling is a major reason why decisions seem to take forever at the Ministry.

Ministry bureaucrats do work to maintain stability, and they've been successful. The financial system has endured wars, depressions, soaring oil prices, and other shocks virtually intact. From World War II until 1986, there was only one bank failure: the Heiwa Sogo Bank, a Tokyo mutual savings and loan institution.

Many Ministry bureaucrats stoutly resist efforts to deregulate the system, fearing it will imperil inefficient institutions. If interest rates for small savers are freed, the bureaucrats argue, then city banks, which have access to big corporate borrowers, will be able to offer higher rates than those of shaky rural banks. They'll lose depositors, and quite a few rural banks will have to merge or go out of business. So interest rates for small savers continue to be set at a low level, which will help those banks survive.

But stability comes at a cost. Small savers—the backbone of Japan's financial strength—suffer. They get less return than they deserve for their toil and thrift. After calculating the effects of inflation, small savers have actually had a negative real rate of return.

At least you don't stand in line at a major Japanese bank: the lobby is filled with sofas, and you sit in one until a teller calls your number.

Investors generally suffer from regulations that limit financial market competition and customer choice. Brokerage commissions are much higher than in deregulated markets like New York and London. Those markets offer investors vastly more alternatives to help improve return as well as hedge risks.

Because the Ministry restricts what portfolio managers can do at life insurance companies, trust banks, and pension funds, portfolio performance is mediocre. Many Japanese fund managers report their holdings at cost only, so it isn't evident whether the actual market value soared, crashed, or did nothing. American and European fund managers abandoned this oblique practice more than a decade ago.

The Ministry reviews proposed life insurance company real estate investments, one by one. This is why typical purchase agreements contain a provision that says "subject to review and approval by the Ministry of Finance." Months can pass without a decision. Many good deals are lost.

Securities firms must submit proposals for new financial instruments to the Ministry. If these instruments aren't offered in other countries, the proposal probably will be rejected on the grounds that it is premature. But since the proposal will be circulated among securities firms if it has merit and is approved, soon competitors will introduce their own versions, reducing the possible gain and increasing the risks of innovation.

Political factors influence the selection of top people at Japanese financial companies. It's crucial to cultivate good relationships at the Ministry. It helps if an executive graduated from Tokyo University— Todai—the Harvard of Japan, which was started more than a century ago to groom government officials. Protocol involves endless courtesy calls and informal consultations with Ministry bureaucrats.

As a consequence of all this bureaucratic interference, there's a dramatic contrast between the way Japanese financial people perform at home and abroad. At home, they're relatively unsophisticated, since they aren't permitted to work with a lot of financial instruments commonplace abroad. Things move slowly. Though Japanese financiers are intensely competitive within their compartmentalized sectors at home, they're shielded from a wide range of domestic as well as international competition. They don't seem sharp, because of the self-inflicted shackles that are holding them back.

How different the situation is abroad! In America and especially Europe, where almost any kind of financial transaction can be done, the Japanese are dramatically expanding their capabilities. They're adapting their slow, consensus decision-making system to the rigors of volatile markets. They're shrewd traders and resourceful deal makers. They're introducing financial innovations. They're coming on strong and are not to be underestimated.

The contrast between Japanese financiers at home and abroad parallels the situation in scientific research. Medical researcher Susumu Tonegawa, for instance, worked for twenty-four years in Japan's research community, but he was frustrated by bureaucratic restrictions. So, in 1963, he left for the United States. In 1987, while a biology professor at the Massachusetts Institute of Technology, he won the Nobel Prize for developing techniques that help reveal how the human body produces antibodies to fight disease. His findings should help in treating victims of acquired immune deficiency syndrome. "Had I stayed in a Japanese university," he says, "I may not have been able to do this kind of work."

Adds Akiyoshi Wada, a molecular biophysics professor at the University of Tokyo: "It's often said the Japanese aren't creative people. That isn't true. It's just that when creativity emerges, it isn't allowed to grow. It's the system. But when you send Japanese to a place where creativity is fostered, it does grow."

Shoku

Regulations are being eliminated in Japanese financial markets, and the pace of these markets is picking up. But the Japanese are changing reluctantly, as *shoku*—a succession of jolts—has rocked the compartmentalized system and forced Japanese financiers into the international arena.

The so-called Bretton Woods international monetary system, established by the Allies following World War II, pegged the U.S. dollar at $35 per ounce of gold, and other currencies were assigned a fixed value in terms of dollars. The Japanese yen was set at 360 per dollar.

This was cheap enough to help fuel Japan's phenomenal boom—output soared twentyfold in two decades.

A lot of people look back with nostalgia at this smoothly functioning fixed-rate system. But really it had no magic. Like a thermometer, exchange rates register what's going on in the world. As long as international economies are relatively stable, currencies are relatively stable. Central banks can buy or sell currencies to help maintain fixed exchange rates. The system collapses when there's instability in the world.

President Lyndon Johnson doomed Bretton Woods when he escalated federal spending both on the Vietnam War and welfare programs. The resulting flood of dollars—inflation—depreciated their value. The Federal Reserve, even with its hoards of gold and foreign currencies, couldn't afford to maintain fixed exchange rates by buying dollars. As long as the dollar depreciated, the Fed lost money on every transaction.

So on August 15, 1971, President Richard Nixon closed the gold window. The U.S. government would no longer stand ready to exchange the dollar at official rates. This opened the era of freely floating currencies. As a consequence, the yen appreciated, Japanese exports weren't so cheap anymore, and the fabled "Japanese miracle" stalled. Japanese recall this sobering experience as "the Nixon shoku."

Japanese officials resisted change as best they could. "Probably the greatest lesson we learned," recalls Toyoo Gyohten, vice minister of finance for international affairs, "was the appalling gap between domestic and international perceptions of the strength of the yen. We had lots of international discussions about appreciating the yen by fifteen percent, twenty percent. Those kinds of arguments were absolutely unacceptable at home, where the almost unanimous view was that appreciation of more than ten percent would definitely kill the economy.

"So when Finance Minister Mikio Mizuta had to accept yen appreciation by 16.77 percent to 308 yen, he thought that upon his return to Japan, he'd be really treated as a traitor! As we expected, questioners accused him, asking, 'Why did you accept this kind of humiliating result?'" Within months, the yen appreciated to 254, and Japanese products lost ground in the U.S. market.

To stimulate the economy, wheeler-dealer Prime Minister Kakuei Tanaka, who took office in 1972, announced extravagant public works projects purportedly to relocate Japanese industry away from populated regions. Results were mixed on this score, but government spending escalated, and inflation hit 18 percent in 1973.

Then came the oil shoku. The Middle East war, which broke out in October 1973, triggered a 450 percent hike in oil prices. This hit Japan especially hard, because 80 percent of its oil was from the Middle East. There were fears that other imports might be jeopardized—Japan imported all its iron ore, wool, rubber, soybeans, and other raw materials.

Prices of scarce commodities jumped 30 percent, and the economy skidded into a recession. The gross national product fell for the first time in the postwar era.

Shoku unleashed two powerful forces. First, the dynamics of Japanese business changed. Faced with recession, Japanese companies had to slash their costs. Long dependent on banks to finance rapid growth, companies cut back their bank borrowings and terminated lines of credit.

By the late 1970s, the Japanese economy recovered, but heavy industries like steel, shipbuilding, chemicals, and textiles didn't. They were losing business to such newly industrialized countries as South Korea, Taiwan, Singapore, and Hong Kong. Japan's sunset industries became cash cows that could finance most of their needs internally, without much help from banks.

Second, recesssion brought lower government revenues, and the national budget incurred deficits. Rather than cut politically popular social spending, the Ministry of Finance issued a large volume of ten-year bonds at below-market interest rates. The banks had to perform their traditional function and buy these bonds.

In the past, bank executives could count on the Bank of Japan to provide a secondary market, buying back the bonds. But taking back bonds would mean giving the banks cash and increasing the money supply—inflation. Officials announced they would take back fewer than usual. Stuck with ever-increasing amounts of below-market assets, the banks' financial situation deteriorated. By 1980, they reported losses over ¥441 billion.

Bank executives became desperate to offset their losses on government bonds. With corporate loan demand down, they contemplated opportunities overseas. But regulations restricted overseas lending. So bank executives pressured the Ministry of Finance to begin deregulation.

Deregulation Begins

Concerned that banks would have a hard time handling all their bonds, the Ministry of Finance finally took steps to nurture the secondary market. The minimum required holding period for government bonds was cut from a year to a hundred days, and banks were allowed to sell bonds in the secondary market. The Bank of Japan stopped rigging interest rates in the interbank markets, where regional banks with surplus funds lend to city banks, which handle the bulk of corporate loan business. The Ministry of Finance began permitting city banks to raise funds by issuing yen certificates of deposit.

Deregulation proceeded at a painfully slow pace, because each proposed change involved intense lobbying among affected interest groups. Still, the Ministry of Finance pushed ahead, because the government was chronically in the red. It depended more than ever on further bond issues. In the decade from 1975 to 1985, Japanese government indebtedness soared eightfold, to ¥134 trillion. If Japanese capital markets didn't develop enough to handle this debt, there could be chaos. It would be very difficult for the government to sell more bonds to finance its perennial deficits.

A major break came in 1980. The Foreign Exchange and Foreign Trade Law suspended most foreign exchange controls. Capital was largely free to flow in and out of Japan. The following year, Japanese banks were permitted to act as securities dealers, selling Japanese government bonds to the public. This cut into the business of Japan's brokers, who demanded and got the right to sell money market funds like those in the U.S.—high interest deposits linked to government bonds.

As the U.S. dollar gained strength during the early 1980s, U.S. exporters had a harder time, and they lobbied Washington for help. The Reagan administration responded by complaining about Japanese controls limiting the use of the yen in international dealings. If restrictions were lifted, there would be a greater demand for yen, strengthening it against the dollar and improving the price-competitiveness of U.S. exporters.

The Japanese accelerated deregulation, more because of their preoccupation with the ten-year bonds than a desire to please Washington. In May 1984, the Ministry of Finance dropped some restrictions on Japanese and foreign companies that wanted to raise inexpensive yen funds in the unregulated Euromarkets. However, there was a caveat: a 20 percent withholding tax on earnings by nonresident holders of Euroyen bonds issued by Japanese. Naturally, this made Euroyen bonds unappealing. The withholding tax was dropped, and a booming new market developed. "We accept that the yen will become more of an international currency," says Toyoo Gyohten, vice minister at the Ministry of Finance.

Deregulation gained momentum during 1985. In March, for the first time, the Japanese Ministry of Finance allowed Japanese banks to make short-term Euromarket loans denominated in yen. By May, Japanese banks were extending medium- and long-term Euromarket loans in yen. The Ministry of Finance removed barriers to a market in bankers' acceptances—short-term bearer notes facilitating international trade. It also permitted a bond futures market, so institutions dealing in bonds could hedge their risks.

Meanwhile, maturing Japanese companies scaled back their capital investments. As a result, they amassed cash, which had to be invested somehow. Since regulations limited their choices, they joined the chorus for deregulation. In October 1985, the Ministry of Finance announced a scheduled phaseout of interest rate ceilings on certificates of deposit, starting with those over ¥300 million.

Long-suppressed interest rates went up on bank deposits, and banks had to charge more for loans. Borrowing from a bank became decidedly more expensive than tapping capital markets directly with bond issues. Corporations with good enough credit ratings did just that. Banks faced not just a loss of business but also deterioration of their loan portfolios, since the corporate customers they retained had weaker credit ratings.

Therefore, Japanese bank executives pushed bureaucrats to relax regulations, so they could take on new business. They got permission to form syndicates and loan money to resource-rich countries like Iran and Brazil. As long as monetary inflation helped keep commodity prices high, this seemed like solid business.

Noting that securities firms boomed by underwriting corporate bond issues, banks hungered for a cut of the lucrative underwriting fees. This was more complicated, since banks were barred from securities underwriting by Article 65 of the Japanese constitution. Banks have lobbied to repeal it, but thus far the securities firms have prevailed, arguing that they need protection. A similar debate is going on in the United States, over the Glass-Steagall Act, and if proposals to repeal that go through Congress, competitive pressures will build for the Japanese to repeal Article 65 and keep their banks competitive.

"The liberalization of deposit rates has accelerated the entire process and is putting profit pressures on banks to expand the range of their operations and move into businesses previously excluded," says Yoshiro Araki, chairman of Fuji Bank. "Competition is tough."

In coming years, the Ministry of Finance probably will permit a free market in short-term government securities, particularly Treasury bills, expected to be the most attractive liquid short-term financial asset for overseas investors holding yen.

Deregulating Equity Markets

As global bond markets were deregulated, the volume of bond offerings soared, and more companies reached the limits of their borrowing power. They couldn't handle additional interest payments. To be competitive, they had to raise equity capital, since management can adjust dividends according to profitability. So pressures mounted to deregulate stock markets and make equity financings easier.

Japanese securities firms fought deregulation as best they could, lobbying bureacrats in the Ministry of Finance. But the Ministry ruled that high fixed brokerage commissions should be lowered gradually. A half-dozen foreign securities firms were admitted to membership on the Tokyo Stock Exchange in 1985, including four U.S. firms: Merrill Lynch, Goldman, Sachs, Morgan Stanley International, and a subsidiary of Citibank. Two years later, more than a dozen additional foreign firms became members.

In June 1986, the Osaka Securities Exchange opened for trading of stock futures contracts. The initial offering was Stock Futures 50, a basket of fifty blue chip stocks. More contracts are expected to follow, so portfolio managers can better protect themselves against adverse fluctuations.

After decades of dismal experience with nationalized industries, it became evident that government bureaucrats aren't very attentive about the way they spend other people's money. So, in recent years, more and more governments have sold off nationalized industries, notably through public offerings. They raise money for governments, and the enterprises are better run, since the participants are more at risk. Britain's Prime Minister Margaret Thatcher is the outstanding leader of this policy, which has caught on throughout Europe, Africa, and Asia. In 1986, Japan began privatizing the Nippon Telephone & Telegraph Company, Japan Airlines, and other government enterprises. Their stock issues proved immensely popular and drew more investors into the equity markets.

An Opening Door

Foreign firms are being allowed to participate in Japanese money markets for the first time. In June 1985, the door was opened for three U.S. banks to go after Japanese trust business: Bankers Trust, Morgan Guaranty Trust, and Chase Manhattan.

In December 1986, to reduce the loss of financings to other markets, the Ministry of Finance created an offshore financial market comparable to the International Banking Facilities, which has operated in the U.S. since 1981. With this new Tokyo-based market, financial institutions create special accounts exempt from many domestic regulations.

In just a few months, it garnered more than $100 billion of deposits. This compared with $260 billion in New York's offshore facility, $140 billion in Singapore, and $130 billion in Hong Kong. However, trading and management functions, essential for the long-term success of such a facility, haven't yet developed.

Though plenty of nettlesome regulations remain, Japanese financial markets are already about as open in many respects as those in the United States or West Germany. Moreover, the trend is unmistakably toward further deregulation, while politicians in the United States and Europe wave the banner of protectionism, threatening to restrict markets there.

Global Expansion

Spurred to seek growth overseas, Japanese financial companies opened new offices and expanded existing ones. Forty-two Japanese banks have offices in New York, and more offices are across the United

States. The Bank of England reports forty Japanese banks are in London, and fifty-two Japanese companies are licensed securities dealers.

Japanese financial companies operate in more than fifty major cities, from Abu Dhabi to Zurich, in every major country. Japanese financial companies offer more services than ever, including many financial instruments still not permitted in Japan. "The time will never come back when banks can make a living from straightforward deposit-taking and lending," says Roy Takata, Jr., managing director of the Bank of Tokyo. "Now it isn't funds we can offer customers, since there's an oversupply of funds in Japan. We have to offer our know-how and technology, by arranging all kinds of complex financial transactions."

As competition has intensified in world financial markets, profit margins have tumbled. But the major Japanese financial companies are well-financed, lower-cost operations with higher credit ratings than those of competitors in the United States. The Japanese have staying power.

A New World Financial Capital

Although Tokyo financial markets lag behind New York's and London's, the city has leaped onto the world stage. Tokyo is where major industrial companies and the richest financial companies are, so foreigners must come calling. At last count, 211 foreign banks and securities firms maintained offices there.

Major American investment banks are spending tens of millions of dollars to expand their Tokyo offices. "These days, you can't be a global player without an important presence in Japan," says Neil P. Benedict, director of finance at Salomon Brothers.

Paradoxically, though Americans and Europeans in their own self-interest are pushing Japanese officials to further deregulate their financial markets, the result is sure to be leaner, stronger, far more sophisticated and versatile Japanese competition that will force other financial companies to improve their service or withdraw from the business. Customers everywhere should cheer.

3

T-BONDO FEVER

There isn't anything new or worrisome about foreigners buying U.S. government bonds. They've been doing it for more than a century. Throughout history, in fact, foreign investors have bought bonds from many different governments wherever rulers couldn't resist spending more money than their citizens were willing or able to pay—provided that the investors were confident they'd get their money back.

It's easy for us to forget that the foreigners are the ones at risk when they invest here, just as Americans are at risk investing abroad. First, there's currency risk. Since February 1985, the U.S. dollar has lost approximately 50 percent of its value in terms of yen. A Japanese investor who bought a $10,000 Treasury bond back then would get only about $5,000 if they sold it now and converted it to yen. Interest income doesn't make up for these losses.

That's not all. Capital markets are so sensitive that any sign of higher inflation translates to lower bond prices immediately. Moreover, new tax laws may devalue investments. And it's always possible that in some unexpected emergency, the United States government might reimpose capital controls, restricting the ability of investors to liquidate their positions—thereby prolonging their exposure to unwanted risks.

What about the alleged control foreigners may gain over us if they buy "too many" government bonds? No one seriously claims that buying government bonds will give foreigners control of the U.S. Armed Forces. Nor will holding government bonds enable foreign investors to dictate who our judges, congressmen, senators, or President will be. Holding government bonds probably won't even enable a foreign investor to fix a parking ticket.

The only thing foreign investors can do is take their money elsewhere, if they decide that the United States isn't competitive or safe enough. For spendthrift U.S. politicians, this may mean having to make unpopular budget cuts, but that's about all.

Meanwhile, foreign investors are helping to relieve the upward pressure on U.S. interest rates. It's an important contribution to our standard of living.

Cautious Giants

The biggest Japanese investors are the life insurance companies. There aren't many—twenty-four versus over two thousand in the U.S.—but they're big. The industry is second only to that in the United States, controlling more than $2.9 trillion of assets. The largest Japanese life company is Nippon Life, followed by Sumitomo, Dai-Ichi, Meiji, and Asahi.

The life companies dominate Japanese financial markets. They hold 13.3 percent of the outstanding stock in publicly traded Japanese corporations. They're major buyers of Japanese government bonds and government-guaranteed bonds, which finance bridges, highways, and other public projects. They own 75 million square feet of real estate.

Industry leader Nippon Life reports $103 billion of assets—up 85 percent during the past five years. Osaka-based, the company has 75,900 people, mostly women, who sell its policies door-to-door across Japan. It has more than $1.4 trillion of life insurance in force.

Nippon Life is Japan's largest institutional investor. It holds more than $13 billion of Japanese bonds, and it's a backstage power at the Tokyo Stock Exchange, with more than 10 billion shares, worth over $17 billion. It's the biggest stockholder in sixty-nine listed companies and among the top five stockholders in another 432 major companies. Nippon Life has $39 billion of outstanding loans to Japanese companies. There are 333 Japanese buildings in its real estate portfolio.

According to President Gentaro Kawase, the company has limited objectives overseas. It serves the life insurance needs of Japanese companies operating internationally and advises foreign insurance companies about doing business in Japan. Though there are few legal restrictions on foreign insurers in the United States, Nippon Life isn't pushing to compete directly with U.S. life companies. Its New York office, which opened in 1984, has fewer than three dozen people. They monitor U.S. Treasury, stock, real estate and other financial markets for the company's portfolio managers back in Japan, and they execute many transactions.

During the past two years, the company's foreign securities portfolio has surged 104 percent. It holds $400 million of Australian government bonds, $2.45 billion of Canadian government bonds, and $5.46 billion of U.S. government bonds. The company has also loaded up on U.S. stocks.

Since the life companies control so much wealth, some reporters have portrayed them as capricious potentates who make markets rise and fall seemingly on a whim. After all, by shifting funds into Australian government bonds, they help bid up bond prices there, putting downward pressure on interest rates. When they cut back their purchases of U.S. Treasury bonds, home mortgage payments across the United States jump.

Yet this would be an utter misreading of the situation. None of the vast Japanese life insurance wealth is in the hands of dynamic entrepreneurs. Perhaps incredibly, Japanese life company investment portfolios are handled by middle-level managers without special expertise. Typically, they're generalists rotated through different career assignments. For a while, they happen to run money. Inexperienced, they tend to be fearful as they contemplate huge, volatile world money markets. Their primary drive is to avoid risk. They favor cautious, conventional investment strategies.

The Japanese compensation system underscores this aversion to risk. "Seldom do companies provide performance bonuses for exceptional achievements," explains Richard C. Koo, senior economist at the Nomura Research Institute, "but there may be severe punishment for big failures. Consequently, making small mistakes in succession is preferable to one big mistake, even if the cumulative losses from small mistakes become larger." The life companies are cautious giants.

In recent years, they've incurred stupefying losses. Since February 1985, the U.S. dollar depreciated 40 percent against the Japanese yen, but Japanese life companies continued to buy U.S. Treasury bonds. The idea of selling these seemed unpatriotic, since it would help push down the U.S. dollar further against the yen, and Japanese exports would become more expensive on world markets. The Japanese government pressured the life companies against selling Treasuries.

Eventually, though, the life companies had to cut their losses. For the year ended March 31, 1987, they reported a ¥2-trillion hit—about $13.8 billion. That the life companies could endure it was dramatic testimony to their immense strength. It isn't surprising that the life companies reduced their purchases of Treasuries.

"If the Japanese had sold their dollar assets earlier," says Koo of Nomura Research Institute, "dollar interest rates would have shot sky-high—a blow to the United States as well as Third World countries with dollar-denominated debt. The willingness of Japanese fund managers to buy and hold dollar assets helped keep the world economy together during the past two years of dramatic, changing economic relationships."

Mounting Pressures

Life company executives face powerful pressures to improve their results. As the Japanese population ages—faster than any major Western country—people have become more concerned about the yield on their investments. They recall the ruinous double-digit inflation of the 1970s. They're restless for investments offering better yields than life insurance.

It isn't easy to stay competitive with banks and securities firms. Regulations permit the life companies to pay policyholders only from investment yield, not capital gains. Japanese government bonds, now a staple of life company portfolios, offer mediocre yields. The stock and real estate markets are priced so high that yields are negligible there. For years, the Ministry of Finance severely limited what the life companies could invest in overseas.

In 1977, the Ministry of Finance allowed the life companies to extend *samurai* loans—yen-denominated loans to foreign borrowers. Because these were in yen, the life companies didn't incur a currency risk. They were attractive investments that yielded about 1 percent over the corporate prime rate. Samurais were often for terms longer than ten years, corresponding with the life companies' long-term source of funds.

Many of the samurai loans were for multinational agencies or governments. Since inflation generated a bull market for natural resources, many of the loans involved energy plays in the United States, Britain, Canada, Australia, and Mexico. In December 1977, for instance, Nippon Life participated in a ¥2-billion financing for PEMEX, Mexico's nationalized petroleum company.

Though the life companies provided funds, the loans were lead-managed by Japanese banks, which collected lucrative 1/2-percent to 1-percent fees. The life companies wanted in on these, but the banks resisted, arguing that the life companies lacked experience finding overseas borrowers, evaluating their creditworthiness, and producing proper documentation. While the banks and life companies wrangled with one another, the Ministry of Finance blocked further samurai issues in October 1979, because of their concern about Japan's balance-of-payments deficit.

Expansion Overseas

The samurai experience convinced Japanese life company executives that they had to expand the investment side of their business overseas. They'd train people who could perform all the needed functions, collect lead-management fees, and cut banks out of the deal, as soon as samurai loans could be made again. Now they are able to lead manage samurai loans.

To explore the possibilities of investing in foreign bonds, the life companies opened information-gathering representative offices abroad. The U.S. looked interesting not only because of its political stability, but also because bond yields were about 8 percent—about 2 percent more than in Japan.

In 1981, a new law put more pressure on the life companies. It allowed Japanese banks, for the first time since World War II, to sell government bonds. Suddenly, banks could compete directly with securities firms, who countered by pressuring the Ministry of Finance for permission to offer the public money market funds with high rates based on medium-term government bonds. Permission was granted not only for securities firms, but also for trust banks and long-term credit banks. The life companies had to offer better yields or lose a lot of business.

The huge size of Japanese life insurance portfolios presented severe limitations. They needed highly liquid markets where large positions could be sold quickly on attractive terms. In a small market, substantial purchases would push up the price against the buyer, and sales would depress the price against the seller. Frankfurt really wasn't big enough. Nor was London or Hong Kong, Singapore or Sydney.

Stampede for U.S. Treasuries

The biggest, most liquid market in the world is U.S. Treasury bonds, with daily turnover estimated to exceed $100 billion. They're an easy investment, requiring no credit analysis, backed as they are by the full faith and credit of the U.S. government. They're considered the world's safest investment during times of low inflation like the early 1980s. Because of enormous volumes and intense competition, brokerage commissions are the lowest anywhere.

For a number of years, the U.S. Treasury had required that bank custodians collect a 30-percent withholding tax before remitting interest payments to foreign investors. Naturally, this made Treasuries unappealing. By 1984, however, it was apparent that runaway U.S. government spending must be financed with ever-larger Treasury bond issues. Interest rates might spiral upward, imperiling the U.S. economy—unless the market for Treasury bonds could be expanded. The obvious solution was to exploit the potential market overseas. First step: repeal the 30-percent withholding tax. This was done in July 1984.

The rush into Treasury bonds began. Since the Japanese life insurance companies had long-term obligations to policyholders, they were primarily interested in longer-term Treasury bonds, particularly ten-year bonds, and there was some interest in thirty-year bonds.

In March 1986, the Ministry of Finance announced that the life companies could invest as much as 25 percent of their assets overseas. This was lifted to 30 percent in August 1986.

Now, according to Nippon Life president Kawase, the Japanese life insurance companies have about 46 percent of their overseas bond portfolio in U.S. dollars. About 22 percent is in Canadian dollars, 5 percent in Australian dollars, 5 percent in British Sterling, and 22 percent in other currencies, including the yen, deutsche mark, Dutch guilder, French franc, and European currency unit.

$300-Million Debacle

Gyrating currencies and interest rates increased uncertainty about what the life companies should do. Other major players in the market were reading the tea leaves, too. In 1986, many guessed wrong.

Since the most liquid Treasuries are the most recently auctioned, investors, including the Japanese, rolled over their Treasuries. They sold old ones as they acquired new ones. At the February 1986 Treasury auctions, the Japanese life companies had sold many of their previously purchased bonds and bought an estimated $5.65 billion of 9¼-percent bonds—almost two-thirds the issue—which would mature in 2016. Since then, bond markets rallied, and interest rates fell a couple points.

The Japanese were widely expected to sell the 9¼-percent bonds and buy new 7¼-percent bonds at the May 8, 1986, Treasury auction. That would keep their holdings as liquid as possible and register a capital gain resulting from the bond market rally.

This pattern set up a traditional arbitrage opportunity. When investors sell their old bonds, the prices decline relative to newly auctioned bonds. Accordingly, American securities firms made futures commitments to sell the 9¼-percent bonds, expecting to buy those bonds cheaper when the Japanese unloaded, then turn around and sell at their committed, higher price.

But the Japanese didn't sell nearly as many 9¼-percent bonds as they were expected to. Moreover, they bought about $5 billion of the new 7¼-percent bonds. To make good on their commitments, securities firms scrambled to bid for whatever 9¼-percent bonds they could find. Prices for the bonds were up a point, while other bonds were off a half a point. This doesn't sound like much, but billions' worth of bonds was involved. Because the securities firms financed their operations on a lot of borrowed money, losses were perhaps ten times greater than the actual investment. Altogether, Wall Street was believed to have lost as much as $300 million.

What happened? There was speculation that the major Japanese securities firms, who handled much of the business for Japanese life companies, pulled a squeeze play. Market leader Nomura Securities was the prime suspect. A capital markets expert at a major New York bank reports: "I had lunch with a Nomura executive and asked him a few questions. All he did was give me one of the inscrutable Japanese smiles. I think they felt they were given bad service and rotten prices by U.S. dealers. Nomura wanted them to know they wouldn't put up with it."

New York congressman Charles Schumer, many of whose constituents are in the securities business, was angry at the Japanese and believed they contributed to the debacle. He wrote New York Federal Reserve Bank president E. Gerald Corrigan, asking for an investigation.

"From our point of view, and that of the Treasury," Corrigan responded, "it would be shortsighted to criticize investors for purchasing and holding significant amounts of U.S. government debt. I am aware of no evidence that there was any concerted effort to 'corner' the market or otherwise purposely cause price distortions in these issues."

To many Japanese, what the life companies did was obvious. Since they could pay policyholders only out of current income like bond interest or stock dividends, it didn't make any sense to sell a 9¼-percent bond for one paying less—despite the potential for a capital gain.

But the magnitude of buying surprised even savvy Japanese securities firms. "The Japanese economy is much cooler than most people realize, so there's a lot of idle money," says Yoshitoki Chino, chairman of Daiwa Securities.

"Anything beyond the ten-year Treasury has become a foreign security," says John Mann, head trader at Manhattan-based Diversified Hedge Fund, "and I am not authorized to trade in foreign securities."

Will the Japanese Boycott?

By the spring of 1987, the U.S. dollar had plunged on world currency markets, interest rates edged upward, and bond prices fell. There was widespread concern that the Japanese might boycott the Treasury auctions rather than risk further losses with dollar-denominated assets. Wall Street analysts reported that Japanese investors were diversifying into bonds of other major countries and into U.S. stocks.

Some Japanese investors voiced optimism. "If we held back because of concern about foreign exchange or other risks," says Kozo Nogami, chief representative of Nippon Life's New York office, "we'd never invest at all. We just have to accept the ups and downs of the marketplace. With the long-term outlook favorable, we'll continue to make investments here."

Between March and early May 1987, bond prices tumbled more than 12 percent, the biggest drop since 1980. Yields jumped more than three-quarters of a point in a single day. Twenty years ago, bonds might move an eighth of a point over an entire year.

"There's no reason for anyone, American or Japanese, to buy bonds right now," said Lawrence A. Kudlow, chief economist at the brokerage firm Bear, Stearns & Co. "Economic activity is picking up, the inflation rate is rising, and there's no clear evidence that the U.S. is prepared to defend the dollar at its current level. For a foreign investor, there's a currency risk as well as an inflation risk in buying bonds."

Decline in Treasury markets continued on the eve of the seven-year note auctions, Monday, May 4. Traders were disappointed over meager results of meetings between President Reagan and Japan's Prime Minister Yasuhiro Nakasone. As they met, the U.S. House of Representatives voted to approve a protectionist amendment sponsored by Representative Richard Gephardt (D, Mo.). A trade war, if it got started, would surely jolt financial markets.

On Wednesday, May 6, when ten-year Treasury bonds were auctioned, bond prices tumbled about 1½ points, or $12.50 for each $1,000 face amount, as the Japanese seemed to pull back from the market. The average yield was 8.52 percent, up sharply from the previous auctions on February 4 and the highest in more than a year. "We don't see much demand," reported William M. Brachfeld, head of fixed-income securities at Daiwa, a leading Japanese securities firm. "Customers aren't even calling us to see what we think, let alone buying."

Robert A. Brusca, senior vice president of Nikko Securities Co., another major Japanese securities firm, added: "Interest from Japan was virtually nonexistent. Nearly every single investment the Japanese have made in U.S. bonds has turned to fertilizer, and that's not the sort of thing which leads your investing to grow."

There was some relief on Thursday, May 7, when it became apparent that the Japanese had bought a substantial amount of thirty-year Treasury bonds. The average yield of 8.69 percent compared with 7.49 percent at the February auction. "Those of us in the domestic market have been sitting around waiting for the Japanese to show their hand," remarked William Budd, a money manager at the New York investment firm Favia, Hill Associates.

The unexpected buying patterns of Japanese investors contributed to market volatility and horrendous losses for Wall Street firms during the second quarter of 1987. Salomon Brothers, perhaps the leading dealer in Treasury bonds, reported $100 million of trading losses. First Boston, another $100 million. Merrill Lynch lost $250 million.

The partial Japanese pullback from the Treasury markets hit American consumers as well. According to Federal Reserve Board estimates, consumers have some $57 billion of variable-rate installment debt. Moreover, there are some $335 billion of adjustable-rate mortgages whose rates are set according to indexes that respond to money market rates and other factors. Within days of the auctions, all this consumer and mortgage debt became significantly more burdensome to carry.

Hedging Risks

As so often in their history, the Japanese are learning to adapt. They're starting to restructure their portfolio management operations. Enormous bond losses are spurring Japanese investors to become sophisticated at hedging interest rate and currency risks.

This has accelerated since the Ministry of Finance opened the door to financial futures and options trading on May 22, 1987. Eligible to use futures are the banks, life insurance companies, property/casualty insurers, investment trust companies, securities firms, and government institutions.

Futures enable investors to hedge a portion of their risks and lock in their profits by taking a futures position opposite their cash position. For instance, if a life company wants to buy Treasury bonds several months from now, they could lock in the price with a "long" position in the futures market, agreeing to take delivery for a specified amount of Treasuries at a specified price by the contract date. Alternatively, if they have securities that won't be sold until several months from now, they could cut their price risks by taking a "short" position equal to the volume of the planned sale. Then they'd profit from a price decline, offsetting the portfolio loss.

Futures contracts tend to be traded up to eighteen months ahead. The most liquid markets, though, are contracts that expire in several months. Investors needing to hedge for longer periods use forward contracts, typically arranged through a bank.

Many Japanese are using options, too. A call option confers the right—but not the obligation—to purchase a futures contract at a guaranteed price anytime before the option's expiration date. Similarly, a put option confers the right—but not the obligation—to sell a futures contract at a guaranteed price. Options are an enormously versatile insurance against market fluctuations and a tool for planning cash flow.

According to Takuro Isoda, chairman of Daiwa Securities America Inc., Japanese investors are most interested in U.S. Treasury futures, Eurodollar futures, Standard & Poor's 500 index futures, Nikkei 225 index (Tokyo Stock Exchange) futures, and currency contracts.

The very day the Ministry of Finance approved futures trading by Japanese firms, the Singapore International Monetary Exchange (SIMEX) was flooded with orders. SIMEX had introduced a Nikkei 225 index futures contract. Trading volume tripled over the previous day's session. Futures exchanges in Hong Kong, Sydney, Auckland, London, Paris, New York, and Chicago prepared to handle larger volumes. In Chicago, a seat on the Chicago Board of Trade sold for a record $470,000. Board of Trade chairman Karsten Mahlmann attributed it to the impact of nighttime trading sessions, which accommodate the Far East market and the coming of the Japanese.

In some markets, reports Chet Brauch, senior vice president in Chase Manhattan Bank's Tokyo office "the Japanese will likely phase in gradually over the next three to six months. Even the tremendous Chicago futures market isn't big enough to handle what the Japanese need."

At this point, the Japanese are learning how best to take advantage of futures and options. Firms are sending trainees to the United States. They've set up "paper trading" accounts to test computer-modeled hedging strategies before they actually put their money on the line. They're preparing their back-office capabilities. "Our main concern is how to handle these orders," acknowledges Yuji Shibuya, a manager of quantitative analysis at Nomura Research Institute.

Although the October 1987 stock crash had its greatest impact on stock futures and options, it jolted all the futures and options markets. It provided a warning that they have limits. They don't always reflect the underlying markets closely enough to provide an effective hedge against risks, and they may not have enough depth to handle huge volumes of transactions in a financial panic.

$39 Per $1 Million

If U.S. Treasury bonds have proven to be a mixed experience for the Japanese life companies, they've been a bonanza for Japanese securities firms. Because the Treasury market is so competitive, it's the easiest financial market for newcomers to enter. They don't have to break through established relationships that tie corporations to their bankers. Newcomers need only offer an important advantage like a little finer pricing, faster execution, or market intelligence.

But margins are perilously thin. The spread between what a buyer and seller pay may be only $150 per $1 million worth of Treasury bonds. In some cases, competition drives the spread down to just $39.

The four major Japanese securities firms—Nomura, Daiwa, Nikko, and Yamaichi—have the financial strength to handle large transactions, and they have the marketing network to place huge volumes of Treasuries in Japan.

When, in 1984, Japanese investors got serious about the Treasury market, the Japanese securities firms became a force to reckon with on Wall Street. Japanese investors were believed to have bought $4 billion of Treasuries in 1984 and nearly $27 billion just two years later. Although the Japanese securities firms expanded into virtually the whole range of securities and investment banking services, as much as 90 percent of their volume came from marketing Treasury bonds.

These firms are ideally positioned to offer American investors advice about what Japanese buyers may do next. Many American investors deal with a Japanese firm for a window on that market. Accordingly, business has skyrocketed. Two years ago, less than a third of their volume was with American clients. Now three-quarters of it involves clients like Northern Trust Company and pension funds for the states of Ohio, Kentucky, and Minnesota. The four Japanese securities firms report that daily Treasury trading volume in their New York offices alone often hits $20 billion.

Key Player

The pioneer and biggest Japanese securities firm is Nomura Securities. Its $10.7 billion of equity capital is far more than any competitor. Nomura reports an estimated $1.7 billion of profits. The firm has 11,000 employees in 155 offices and handles more than $320 billion of assets for 4 million customers.

Some Nomura executives come across with the imperious arrogance of self-made tycoons who recall years of hardship and slights. They're proud that Nomura makes more money than Britain's mighty Barclay's Bank and America's blue-blooded J.P. Morgan combined. Nomura has more capital than Merrill Lynch, and does more international bond underwritings than prestigious Morgan Stanley.

Nomura executives fancy themselves as investment bankers, but they don't compare with Western investment bankers, who orchestrate corporate restructuring, mergers, acquisitions, and divestitures. When Japanese corporate executives need strategic business advice, they still tend to consult their traditional bankers.

In Japan, Nomura is primarily a sales machine. What they offer is placement power, the ability to gather vast funds by placing securities with Japanese savers. Nomura's saleswomen go door-to-door, offering a "stock of the week," mutual funds, and other investments to housewives who control family finances.

Nomura handles about 30 percent of stock underwriting in Japan. It's the biggest participant in the Japanese bond market, underwriting about 20 percent of Japanese corporate bonds, a quarter of medium-term government bonds, and 40 percent of short-term government bonds. This placing power is the foundation of Nomura's strength overseas. Perhaps half the Eurobonds they underwrite are placed in Japan. With the so-called *sushi* bonds, Nomura anticipates that 100 percent of buyers will be Japanese and negotiates terms accordingly.

Nomura is headquartered in Kabucho-cho, the mélange of modest shops and office buildings near Tokyo's main business district. Despite its immense wealth, Nomura doesn't spend money for opulent American-style corporate palaces. Their people work in several seven-story brick buildings on a narrow side street by Metropolitan Expressway No. 5. The lobbies are plain. Most employees work amidst Spartan surroundings—linoleum floors, concrete walls, and standard-issue steel desks.

Nomura chairman Setsuya Tabuchi and president Yoshihisa Tabuchi (no relation) are on the second floor. Their wood-paneled offices are nice, accented with paintings by Chagall and other Western artists, but they aren't plush executive suites with panoramic views.

Chairman Tabuchi, sixty-three, is a charming gray eminence with global connections. He knows the leading Japanese politicians. He's on a first-name basis with the world's principal central bankers and finance ministers. He's consulted by top officials at the World Bank and International Monetary Fund. In France, he's known as the King of Money. He started as a retail salesman and claims to have worn out a pair of shoes a week. A consummate corporate operator, he relishes Go, the ancient Japanese board game of strategy.

Though Nomura has a reputation as a monolithic organization, Chairman Tabuchi cites examples that show how adaptable it is. "I think it was 1974," he recalls, "when Merrill Lynch chief executive Don Regan visited Nomura. During a meeting, he pulled out a credit card and told us that, through it, Merrill Lynch delivers new services to its customers. Until then, I wasn't aware of credit cards or money market funds offered by securities firms. Regan's visit encouraged Nomura to developing new services."

Chairman Tabuchi is a devoted Nomura man who believes in the traditional system of consensus decision-making. "I have made lots of wrong decisions, but always someone would appear and tell me when I was wrong. Such people give me a lot of chances to reflect. The only decision I made entirely on my own was to step down from the position of president, in 1986. Some Nomura managers advised me this was wrong, but I didn't even listen to their advice. My strong belief is that a business needs young blood."

President Tabuchi, fifty-three, is a tall, chain-smoking whirlwind. He had only two years' part-time experience on the international side of the business before he became president in 1985, and he's working to catch up. His schedule takes him to New York, Toronto, London, Paris, Frankfurt, Sydney, Seoul, and Beijing. "My basic philosophy," he says, "is that you must see the on-site developments. Otherwise, you won't be able to form correct strategy or make the right decisions on a daily basis." Back in Tokyo, President Tabuchi works ten-hour days, then entertains clients and associates at karoake bars.

Tabuchi's father was a liquor store owner in Okayama City, between Kobe and Hiroshima near the Inland Sea. Tabuchi recalls being disciplined early on with a bamboo rod. In 1956, he graduated from respected Waseda University and joined Nomura, though the securities business was considered disreputable at the time. Brokers were derided as *kabuya*, or stock peddlers. Tabuchi proved himself to be a supersalesman. "To work your utmost, make money, win fame, and beat the competition—I realized just how great those things are," he says.

He and his wife Yokyo live in Shibuya, southwestern Tokyo. They have two sons, twenty-nine and twenty-six, neither of whom can work for the company, because of its rule against nepotism. Tabuchi plays a lot of golf, mostly for business. When he goes to a golf course outside Tokyo, he'll travel on the *shinkansen* bullet train with everyone else, rather than take a corporate helicopter or limousine.

Nomura operates with a strict, disciplined corporate culture. The atmosphere is more like the Pentagon than American Express. These people have a mission to be number one in the world, and they're working very hard at it. There's hardly a financial front where they aren't on the offensive. At headquarters, executives confer about their growing investment trust business, new venture capital commitments, deals in China, a banking license in Britain, and forays into leasing and real estate. Above all, they seek supremacy in the huge international securities markets, like U.S. Treasuries.

Nomura trades Treasuries around the clock, as positions are passed from one office to the next. If, for instance, the firm wants to sell $125 million of Treasuries, but the market doesn't hit the desired price by the time New York closes, that position would be passed to Tokyo. Perhaps most of the positions are sold there. The remainder might be handled after Tokyo closes, in Nomura's London office.

Meanwhile, they may have picked up some buy orders that can't all be filled in London by the close of trading there. They'd be passed to New York.

T-bondo in Kanazawa

A visit to the Nomura branch in Kanazawa reveals the passion many Japanese have for U.S. Treasury bonds, known as T-bondo. Kanazawa, in Ishikawa prefecture, is an appealing city of four hundred and thirty thousand people, about 180 miles northwest of Tokyo. From a nearby hill, you can see the mountains and the Sea of Japan. Kanazawa was an important cultural center during the feudal era, and samurai mansions still survive. The people, who earn their livelihood farming and manufacturing textiles as well as machinery, have about $26 billion of financial assets. Banks, credit unions, insurance companies, farm cooperatives, and securities firms compete to trade and manage these funds.

Kazumasa Kuze, forty-four, manager of the branch, is doing well. He says the firm has some thirty-five thousand customers in the area and manages ¥300 billion—about $1.8 billion. If things continue the way they are, he says, he'll pick up another ¥400 billion of business within three years.

"Thanks to the U.S. budget deficit, Kanazawa is enjoying prosperity," he exclaims. Treasury bonds are a surprisingly popular item. Some people buy one day and sell the next for small gains. Others may hold as long as three weeks.

Kuze generates some business by personal calls. Recently, he got a ¥9 billion account—about $65 million—from the local Hokkuku Bank. Then there's drop-in business from people who stop at the office to check the quote board and maybe make a trade. About thirty women in blue Nomura uniforms solicit business, aiming for their monthly quota of ¥4.5 billion, about $30 million. On the second floor, about twenty men solicit wealthy customers. The third floor has twenty-seven women, part-time saleswomen who call on housewives. For now, anyway, a lot of Japanese have T-bondo fever and want to make money in the U.S. Treasury market.

An Osaka Money Changer

Company founder Shinnosuke Nomura was born the son of an Osaka money changer in 1878—the same year the Tokyo and Osaka stock exchanges were started. The monetary system was chaotic, with some fifteen hundred varieties of gold, silver, copper, and paper money circulating. Money changers like Tokushichi Nomura made a market in these. They also handled the finances of the landed aristocracy, particularly their debts. Osaka was Japan's business capital, and it's still a key commercial center.

When Shinnosuke Nomura was eighteen, he apprenticed to a small stock-trading house called Yashiro Shoten. It was tiny, for the Japanese stock market was in its infancy. Major industrial companies of the Meiji era were funded with government bonds. When this wasn't enough, the government encouraged private ventures. Joint-stock companies were used to develop railroads, mining, and textile industries. But the market was limited, because stock served mainly as collateral for loans provided by the banks.

Stock traders were a disreputable lot. Protecting investors wasn't one of their guiding principles. When the monetary system was reformed, substantially reducing the need for money changers, the major ones became bankers. Small money changers joined pawnbrokers, rice merchants, and pickle dealers in the stock market.

Shinnosuke Nomura joined his father's firm, Nomura Shoten, which evolved from money changing to stock dealing. The market boomed in 1907, after Japan defeated Russia and gained control of Manchuria. He proved himself to be a shrewd trader who made money on the way up and, somehow sensing that it would peak soon, sold out before it crashed. His father retired, and as a gesture of respect, Shinnosuke changed his name to Tokushichi Nomura II.

In 1908, when he was twenty-nine, Nomura decided to see the world. He joined a tour, sponsored by a major Japanese newspaper, that took him through Europe and the United States. He visited Wall Street firms, noting their efforts to develop investment research. The experience abroad convinced him that his firm must develop international capability, especially since the Japanese government was issuing bonds abroad, where interest rates were cheaper. Nomura began hiring an English-speaking staff, and he prepared to enter the bond business, then controlled by the banks.

Challenging the Banks

His opportunity came in 1910, when the government announced a ¥520-million refunding of 5-percent bonds. This was bigger than a single bank could handle, so a syndicate of sixteen Osaka and Tokyo banks was formed. Recruiting a half-dozen Osaka securities firms, Nomura formed another syndicate and negotiated with government and bank representatives to secure a role as secondary underwriters.

Soon he astonished the banks by gaining mandates as primary underwriters. His syndicate of four securities firms handled a bond issue for the Mino-Arima Electric Railway Company. Then he formed a syndicate to underwrite bonds for Osaka Mercantile Steamship Company.

During World War I, Japanese trading ships entered markets in Asia, Africa, and Latin America, long dominated by the Europeans. The Japanese merchant marine doubled between 1915 and 1920, and Nomura's profits multiplied tenfold. During this period, the number of manufacturing workers doubled. Japanese companies required larger and larger amounts of capital for expansion, and Nomura gained a big chunk of the underwriting business—stocks as well as bonds. For the first time, Japan became a creditor nation.

It wasn't apparent that the boom would last, though. Many thought it was a wartime phenomenon. But Nomura believed that Japanese companies would become larger, more sophisticated, and need more capital than banks could provide. So he prepared for expansion. In 1918, he started the Osaka Nomura Bank to specialize in underwriting government and corporate bonds. To run the operation, he hired a chief lender named Otogo Kataoka away from the mighty Industrial Bank of Japan. Kataoka traveled to the United States and called on an acquaintance who was president of National City Bank. He was allowed to observe how a premier bank ran a securities department.

As wartime inflation ended in 1920, Japan's economy crashed. The stock market was a disaster. The government encouraged disillusioned investors to buy their bonds as a more secure investment. Banks were reluctant to serve as bond brokers, but Nomura seized the opportunity to concentrate on bonds and establish a commanding position in the market. In 1922, he formed Nomura & Co. as a holding company for his expanding ventures. Three years later, this became Nomura Securities Co.

Depression, Nationalism, and War

The next two and a half decades, though, were tough on business. In 1923, Tokyo was devastated by an earthquake, which killed a hundred and thirty thousand people. Though the need for reconstruction brought on a building boom, which was financed with bond issues, the stock market didn't recover. Generally, Japanese business was depressed through the 1920s, then hit hard by a banking crisis in 1927 and the Great Depression in 1930. Nationalist fervor brought government control of business by the late 1930s.

Though Nomura's corporate business faded, the company managed to hang on. Continuing to handle bonds in some volume, it opened a downtown Manhattan office in 1927, the first Japanese securities firm to expand overseas. As in the United States and elsewhere, the Japanese government attempted to stimulate business with subsidies and public works projects, all of which required more money than could be raised from taxes. Government bond issues soared, and, once past the initial jolt of the Great Depression, Nomura prospered for a while.

Military adventurism escalated government expenditures and inflation, which depressed the bond market. Nomura continued to handle some government bonds, but investors were interested mainly in stocks. Nomura introduced forty-two investment trusts, with a guarantee to make good 20 percent of any losses. The stock market boomed, until it became clear that Japan would lose World War II. Since the government had a powerful impact on financial markets, Nomura moved its offices from Osaka to Tokyo.

Defeat rocked the company. Nomura lost half its offices and employees. Documents were destroyed, financial markets were dead. Tokushichi Nomura II died in January 1945. In November, General MacArthur ordered the fifteen largest *zaibatsu* dissolved, and that included the Nomura Group. Assets were frozen. Family members had to resign their positions. Officers of Nomura Securities weren't permitted to serve on the boards of other companies. A forty-two-year-old bond salesman and longtime Nomura employee named Tsunao Okumura became president.

About the only business they could do was private trading of non-defense-related stocks. Since many Japanese needed to liquidate their holdings and raise cash, it was a growing business. Inflation stimulated some demand, but about the only companies prospering were textiles and entertainment.

Aggressive Rebuilding

Nomura rebuilt their network of branch offices, so they'd be in a good position to grow if the stock market recovered. In 1948, U.S. President Harry Truman announced a policy of rebuilding rather than punishing the former adversaries. Many restrictions on business were lifted. Companies proceeded with their plans, which included raising substantial amounts of capital. While continuing inflation and rigid bond regulations kept the bond market in limbo, the stock market recovered. Nomura handled about a third of the stock underwritings for electric power companies and banks.

When, in 1948, the Securities and Exchange Law was amended to separate the securities business from bank lending, Nomura was suddenly the biggest Japanese securities firm.

The company addressed a lingering issue: what to do about those forty-two investment trusts issued during the war. About fifteen reported red ink, and the company had guaranteed to make good 20 percent of the losses. Rather than disclaim responsibility due to an act of God, Nomura honored its original agreement and paid the shareholders. Undoubtedly, this contributed to the eagerness of Nomura's customers to participate in future investment trust offerings.

Nomura didn't wait for things to happen. They expanded aggressively. The company grew to fifteen offices plus nineteen investment centers in high-traffic locations like department stores. The company established six hundred twenty "service stations," where customers could apply for investment trusts and subscribe to bond issues.

Army of Saleswomen

Nomura devised clever gimmicks to draw people into the stock market. For example, "I'd like to make a million *ryo*" was a common expression, meaning that a person wanted to get rich—the ryo was an ancient currency unit. To help persuade the public that securities were a valid way of saving money, some resourceful Nomura marketing person suggested offering "Million Ryo Savings Chests," small cash boxes. Nomura retained the key, so once money was deposited, it was reasonably secure from temptation. When the box had five thousand yen, a saver would take it to a Nomura office and buy an investment trust certificate.

Since the boxes were usually brought in by women, Nomura hired one hundred fifty women to collect the money. This worked so well that not only did Nomura continue the Million Ryo Savings Chest scheme for almost a decade, distributing more than a million chests, but also the company hired several dozen women to sell securities across the country. It conducted investment seminars and more than ten thousand women attended.

Stocks took a dive in September 1949 as companies flooded the market with shares and Occupation authorities released shares they had frozen. The Nikkei Stock Average was ¥176.21. But the market rebounded in 1950 with the outbreak of the Korean War. Japan became a vital base, and business expansion began.

Gradually, the Japanese approached their prewar standard of living. Food and clothing became readily available. New refrigerators, sewing machines, and radios appeared in many homes. The gross national product was about a fifth that of the United States. But per capita annual income was still only about $220.

An American Presence

In 1953, Nomura reestablished a New York office, which had closed sixteen years before during the Depression. It was the first Japanese securities firm to return. Its aim was to facilite foreign investment in Japan, since the country desperately needed capital for growth. When the Japanese government announced an issue of U.S. dollar bonds,

Nomura joined major American securities firms in the underwriting syndicate.

Nomura invested in sophisticated teletype communications to link its scattered operations. In 1955, it became the first Japanese private enterprise to buy a true computer, a Univac 120. It was needed to handle the surging volume of stock transactions—stock averages tripled during the 1950s.

The Japanese government relaxed a wide range of trade barriers, touted to protect companies from foreign competition and control balance-of-payments deficits. With lower barriers, Japanese companies had to become more competitive or die. Most accelerated capital investment, funded largely with bond issues. Nomura handled the biggest share.

In June 1961, Nomura participated in a U.S. syndicate that handled a 2-million-share offering for Sony Corporation on the New York market. It sold out in an hour, raising ¥100 million. Buy orders outnumbered sell orders by thirty to one. Nomura stood shoulder-to-shoulder with the giants of Wall Street. This pioneering deal helped gain wider acceptance for Japanese stocks and stimulated the flow of foreign capital into Japan.

In September 1962, Nomura comanaged a Japanese convertible bond offering in the American market: $10 million for Mitsubishi Heavy Industries. That same year, to handle the growing volume of international transactions, Nomura opened a London office. It cultivated contacts among merchant banks, underwriters, and institutional investors throughout Europe.

Recession and Crash

In 1963, the Kennedy administration pushed through Congress the interest equalization tax, which penalized foreign investors buying U.S. securities. Foreign buying, a significant amount of which had come from Japan, evaporated immediately. By 1965, the Japanese economy skidded into a recession, and stocks declined 44 percent from their peaks.

Securities firms that emphasized stock transactions were hit especially hard. Market leader Yamaichi Securities nearly went bankrupt, saved only by cash infusions from the Bank of Japan.

Nomura was in better shape, since most of its business involved bonds. But it was shaken, too. "This was really a major problem," recalls Chairman Tabuchi, "and it caught me by surprise. The only precedent I could think about was the Great Depression in the U.S. I began reading many books on the subject. In the unlikely event of a repeat, I'm ready."

→ The crash revived the notion that buying stocks was crazy speculation. For several years, few stock issues came to market.

Resourceful Promotion

Nomura, however, continued to be relentless in promoting securities. Brokers pushed a "Stock of the Week" and sponsored *juku*, nationwide investment seminars that often drew more than a hundred thousand people a month. The company published a magazine, *Second Income*, which promoted securities investment to the general public and distributed more than two-hundred thousand copies of investment books.

After studying employee stock-ownership plans developed by Merrill Lynch, Nomura adapted plans that satisfied the requirements of Japanese corporate and tax laws. Intended to help reduce employee turnover and stabilize a company's share prices, they started to catch on in 1969.

Until about 1970, Nomura had concentrated on raising capital for the Japanese government and private companies. But business had become so competitive that Japan reported trade surpluses. The country was in a position to export capital. In July 1971, the Ministry of Finance permitted Japanese investors to buy foreign securities.

Nomura lead-managed samurai bonds and cut into traditional banking business by issuing unsecured bonds for Mitsubishi Corporation and Marubeni Corporation, two leading trading companies. The Nikkei Stock Average continued climbing until it passed ¥5,000, and Nomura was making money every step of the way.

Bond Markets Go Boom

The 1974 oil shock resulted in government budget deficits, covered by record amounts of bond issues. Nomura was required to underwrite

¥80 billion of government bonds in 1975. The next year, Nomura's commitment jumped to ¥380 billion. The company opened "Government Bond Corners" in all its offices and promoted government bonds to individual investors throughout Japan. This enormous volume of primary bond issues led inevitably to an active secondary market where investors could sell their issues.

All these government bonds drained the Japanese market of funds, so companies had a hard time raising what they needed. They looked abroad. Nomura turned to lead-managing Eurobonds, beginning with an issue for Marui Co.

By 1981, the Japanese had adjusted, and they were capital exporters again. That year, Nomura became a registered member of the New York Stock Exchange. Japanese financial markets were jumping, and the Nikkei Stock Average soared past ¥10,000. Nomura as well as the other Japanese securities firms handled record volume at fixed commission rates, which helped propel them to leadership in international money markets.

A Tough Time Adapting

Adapting to American ways isn't easy for the Japanese. To help accelerate their growth in the U.S., Nomura and other Japanese brokerage firms began hiring more Americans, paying about 5 percent more than employees at similar levels of U.S. firms receive. But many of these American employees became convinced that the high-ranking positions would always be held by Japanese, and they have quit. William J. King, a top stock trader at Nomura, left over a dispute about bonuses. The Japanese, he says, exasperated, "never deal directly with a problem. At Salomon Brothers, you have your fight, executives handle it, and it's over. But at Japanese firms, the problems simmer, never reaching the surface."

Many Japanese quit Japanese financial firms in the U.S., because they're paid a fraction as much as their American counterparts. American traders, for instance, earn $100,000 to $300,000 at a Japanese firm, while the firm's Japanese traders earn only $50,000 to $60,000. The departures cause anguish among Japanese executives steeped in a tradition of loyalty and lifetime employment.

Nomura's top executives have insisted on a strict application of successful Japanese business methods with a rigor that some observers have likened to the discipline of U.S. Marines. Any departure is considered a sign of weakness. This is frustrating for many American employees.

The company's consensus decision-making, for instance, contributes to internal turmoil. Consider the dynamics of meetings. In Japan, they're for exploration. There's no agenda. Never any decisions. No action plan. There are endless meetings, each of which may be a small step in the decision-making process. This frustrates American employees who believe there should be an agenda, that everyone should vote, and that a meeting should close with an action plan.

Sometimes, Nomura seems paralyzed with indecision. In November 1986, only a day after they won a mandate to lead-manage their first underwriting in the United States—$250 million of twenty-five-year notes for giant GE Credit Corp.—Nomura turned down an opportunity to lead-manage a $300-million underwriting for J.P. Morgan & Co. Morgan is the most profitable U.S. money-center bank, the only one with a triple-A rating; any Wall Street firm would be ecstatic at the prospect of gaining the bank as a client. Morgan's notes were priced at forty basis points over five-year Treasury securities, versus eleven basis points for the GE Credit deal. A basis point is one-hundredth of a percentage point.

Nomura was unable to make a decision by the appointed deadline. "It was an embarrassing and upsetting turn of events," a Nomura executive acknowledged. Marc Silverman, an assistant vice president at Morgan, says, in the bank's typically low-key manner: "We were surprised." The deal was managed by Merrill Lynch and the Union Bank of Switzerland.

Many American clients are put off because Nomura and other Japanese companies hire generalists who are rotated through a succession of career assignments. The representative responsible for an account may change a half-dozen times in a few years. While Japanese clients don't seem to mind, since they consider that they're doing business with Nomura, American financial companies do business more on the basis of individual relationships, and they definitely prefer specialized expertise—someone who knows their account. There's no benefit to educating a succession of Nomura people.

Nomura executives have insisted that their representatives make protocol calls on American money managers, because this is traditional practice in Japan. Dedication to a major client is demonstrated by the enthusiasm with which a representative pursues him. A good client may be called eight or ten times a day, to show one's sincerity. But this drives American money managers crazy. They don't want to be bothered unless someone is offering new information. Several American money managers declared they wouldn't do any more business with Nomura if those protocol calls continued. When representatives reported this reaction, superiors criticized them for making excuses.

Nomura's assembly-line retail style has turned off many American money managers. They laugh when they're offered a stock of the week. Some Nomura representatives seem to think that they are talking with unsophisticated housewives in Yokohama.

To be sure, some American money managers like dealing with the company. S. Lawrence Prendergast, AT & T treasurer, says: "Nomura has called on us for about fifteen years, and they didn't get any business for the first decade. Their persistence and the wealth of Japan are paying off for them."

Nonetheless, Nomura's U.S. operations have lagged. They depend primarily on U.S. Treasury bond sales, selling U.S. stocks mostly to Japanese clients. During 1986, Nomura's U.S. operations contributed only $30 million to the company's profits.

That year, Nomura reportedly was wracked by a power struggle as Tokyo executives demanded stronger, more hands-on leadership to make the vital New York operation more profitable. This, apparently, was why the New York chairman, Yoshio Terasawa, and president Akira Shimizu—both Wharton School graduates—were summarily transferred back to Tokyo in November. It's unusual for the two top executives of a financial firm to be transferred at the same time. Terasawa, an elegant international man and a former Fulbright Scholar, was perhaps the best-known Japanese financial executive in the United States.

Although Shimizu had expressed his hope that he or Terasawa would be succeeded by an American, the latter was succeeded by Masaaki Kurokawa, fifty-three, a tall, austere, tough corporate infighter. Soon after taking over, Kurokawa reportedly trashed a press release prepared by Terasawa, reviewing his achievements. Kurokawa issued a brief release announcing simply that Terasawa had returned to Japan. For president, Kurokawa chose Katsuya Takanashi, fifty-one, widely respected for his expertise on bond financings. The duo had worked together in London several years before.

Normally in Japanese companies, the chairman performs more honorary functions, while the president runs the operation. But clearly Kurokawa is in charge here. He has extensive international experience, and—perhaps more important—he has the confidence of top executives back in Tokyo.

Kurokawa is a formidable personality who learned American ways when he was a Nomura man attending the University of Wisconsin during the early 1960s. Though company rules forbade an employee from owning a car or bringing his wife to the United States, Kurokawa did both. He didn't earn his master's degree, either. "Rather than go to the classroom," he recalls, "I found it better to play golf in the summer and follow the Green Bay Packers in the winter." He refers to himself as "a Wisconsin dropout."

Kurokawa relishes Nomura's power and remembers the slights he experienced when the company was much smaller. Salomon Brothers chairman John Gutfreund, he says, treated Nomura executives with condescension. "I reminded him, 'Ten years ago, I was a nice little boy. I'm still nice, but not a little boy.' "

Though Tabuchi, Kurokawa, and other top Nomura executives remain supremely confident in their traditional business methods, they seem to be adapting more to the American market and resolving many difficulties. Robin Koskinen, forty, is firmly in charge of government bond trading in the New York office, with about seventy people, virtually all American. John J. Niehenke, former deputy assistant secretary for federal finance at the Treasury Department, runs the government-bond sales force.

Primary Dealers

Nomura and its nearest Japanese rival, Daiwa Securities, celebrated in 1986 when they were designated primary dealers of U.S. Treasury securities, joining an elite of forty firms that deal with the New York Federal Reserve Bank. This status puts Nomura in a position to get business from investment funds whose charters require that they use primary dealers.

Now Nomura is one step away from the Fed's inner sanctum.

Perhaps fifteen of the primary dealers have a trading wire that enables them to handle transactions directly with the Fed. They're the ones who actually see its daily transactions. Becoming a primary dealer is like gaining a badge to join the club, but you still want a key to the bathroom.

Naming Nomura and Daiwa primary dealers triggered considerable controversy among American securities firms trying to gain entry to the Tokyo market. "They've closed their internal market to foreign firms in industry after industry until they've developed a completed lock on it, and then used it as a base with which to expand," declared Congressman Schumer. He and thirty-seven others on the House Banking Committee asked New York Federal Reserve Bank president Corrigan to deny the Japanese applications until U.S. financial companies "are accorded full reciprocal treatment in the Japanese securities markets."

It was a tough call for the Fed, since Japanese securities firms are such big buyers of U.S. securities—helping to finance the U.S. deficit and keep interest rates lower than they would be otherwise. But there was concern that if the Fed didn't use this leverage, U.S. firms might never gain equal footing in the Japanese market.

Corrigan stated his intention of treating all applicants equally, noting that among primary dealers in U.S. government securities are Canadian, British, and Hong Kong firms. "By any of the Fed's traditional standards, the Japanese firms would easily pass muster," concedes a U.S. brokerage executive. Daiwa is bigger than Shearson Lehman/American Express, and Nomura towers over everyone. But Corrigan may be overruled by a trade bill making its way through Congress.

Outlook for Treasuries

Undoubtedly, the Japanese will continue buying U.S. Treasury securities, because there are few markets big enough to absorb their wealth. But the volumes seem likely to decline. Remember that the Japanese plunged into Treasuries partially because they were unsophisticated. Buying Treasuries didn't seem to require much knowledge about credit. As Japanese investors learn more about the many alternatives in international investment, they're bound to diversify. Already, they've put billions of dollars in U.S. stocks and real estate.

In the future, Japanese life insurance companies are less likely to incur the risk of exchange rate losses for the gain of current interest income. Almost certainly, they will invest according to expected total return—which includes capital gains or losses. They will compete more aggressively for investments that offer good prospects of capital gains.

Portfolio managers probably would move huge chunks of money among financial markets more quickly, as foreign exchange rates change. This would increase market volatility in the years ahead. It would become more important for individual investors to master the intricacies of hedging risks.

Unexpected declines in the value of the dollar have shocked many Japanese investors. Major insurance companies have curtailed their purchases of dollar-denominated assets like Treasuries. When market conditions point to further dollar depreciation, the Japanese could substantially withdraw from the market. Even interest rates well into double digits may not compensate for the risk of loss due to volatile currency markets.

If the Japanese do substantially withdraw, there will be strong upward pressures on interest rates. Businesses will curtail borrowing, homeowners will struggle to meet higher mortgage payments, and the federal budget—with its high built-in interest costs—will soar farther into the red. Yet another gentle reminder to cut federal spending.

4

GUARANTEED IN JAPAN

Japanese banks provide almost half the letters of credit guaranteeing municipal bonds in the United States. In scaremonger parlance, they "control" the market.

What do such market share numbers mean? Many U.S. state and local governments have mediocre credit ratings, because they live beyond their means. Investors—overwhelmingly American—aren't willing to accept the higher risks involved without higher interest rates, which, in turn, would require higher taxes on those who presumably benefit from municipal bond issues.

As is often the case, the letter of credit market share numbers by themselves have little significance, because municipalities have many alternatives. They aren't forced to rely on Japanese banks—or anyone else—in the marketplace.

Aside from reducing expenditures—as a lot of municipalities have—there are three main ways to lower investor risks and taxpayer costs for municipal bonds.

First, provide or expand a government-funded program to guarantee municipal debt. For example, many states guarantee bonds by municipalities. If a school district, for example, defaults on a bond, the state may simply withhold enough state education aid so that the bondholders continue to be paid. In addition, states may set up bond funds to ensure payment of debt service, or they may authorize special appropriations for the same purpose. Based on such programs, Standard & Poors rates about $11 billion of municipal debt in California, Indiana, Kentucky, Michigan, New Jersey, New York, Pennsylvania, Texas, Virginia, and West Virginia.

The interest rate spread between the highest-rated and lowest-rated investment grade municipal bonds is 80 to 100 basis points (a full percentage point). The spread for non-rated municipals is even greater. When a bond issue involves millions of dollars over five years, ten years, or longer, the savings from credit enhancement can be substantial.

The second way to enhance credit (if a municipality isn't in bad shape) is to find an insurance company willing to underwrite a bond offering. Insurance extends for the term of an issue, with premiums paid from proceeds of the bond sale; premiums vary according to the issuer's credit rating and the size and term of the bond issue. The bonds carry the credit rating of the insurance company. During the 1980s, the number of bond insurers has increased significantly. In 1988, 24 percent of municipal bonds were enhanced with private bond insurance. This is expected to increase to over 30 percent within a few years, as individual investors—who rely on ratings more than institutions—come to dominate the market.

Generally, it pays to obtain credit enhancement if a municipality is rated Baa-1 or lower. Higher-rated municipalities are likely to find that the additional benefit of an insurance company doesn't offset the premium cost.

The third way is when a municipality seeks a bank willing to provide a letter of credit. For a letter of credit, a bank will estimate the default risk and decide how much of a bond obligation it will guarantee. In effect, a municipality's mediocre credit rating is replaced with the better credit rating of an insurance company or bank on a specific offering. The result is that investors are willing to accept lower interest rates. In 1988, 14 percent of municipal bonds were enhanced with letters of credit.

Japanese banks get half the municipal letter of credit business, not because their officers have more appealing personalities than American bankers or give away free toasters (they don't). They get half the business because they're willing to assume the risks at lower costs than anyone else. How can they do that? Mainly because they have better credit ratings than most major U.S. banks. U.S. banks have portfolios loaded with bad loans to energy companies, real estate developers, and Third World dictators. Since these banks tend to be riskier, their cost of raising funds is higher, and they have to charge higher fees for issuing a letter of credit—which means they aren't as competitive in this business as they used to be.

Mitsubishi Bank, for instance, has backed more than $3 billion of U.S. municipal bonds. It has helped the City of Chicago with $100 million to $300 million of its general financings annually. The State of Louisiana has increased its borrowings since oil revenues went down, and it used a $250 million letter of credit from Mitsubishi Bank. The bank helped fund $25 million for New York's Metropolitan Transit Authority, $100 million for a resource recovery plant in Florida's Broward County, $150 million for student loans in Mississippi, $150 million for student loans in California, $250 million for various municipalities in Texas, and $500 million for public projects in Puerto Rico.

Thus, Japanese bankers hardly "control" the market. They can't force municipalities to use their services. Nor can they prevent municipalities from spending less money and operating more efficiently. If Japanese bankers increase their fees or demand unattractive terms, more municipalities would take advantage of the alternatives. The seeming Japanese "control" would dissolve as their market share declines.

Japanese letters of credit are one way to relieve a little of the endless upward pressure on taxes—and thereby make a modest contribution to the American standard of living.

Worry About Default

Credit enhancements like a letter of credit are relatively new. Until recent years, municipal bonds were bought mainly by banks and property/casualty insurance companies, which have in-house expertise to assess the creditworthiness of a municipality. But dwindling profits as well as changes in the tax law made municipal bonds a less advantageous investment for these institutions.

Along came a new breed of buyers: wealthy individuals. If yields are high enough on tax-free municipal bonds, they make more sense than taxable bonds. Now people earning over $280,000 buy half the municipal bonds issued. But few individual investors have the capability to analyze the creditworthiness of a municipality.

This is important information, because many municipalities have defaulted. During the nineteenth century, Chicago, Detroit, New Orleans, and Philadelphia defaulted. So did the states of Alabama, Arkansas, Florida, Michigan, Minnesota, Tennessee, and Virginia. There were defaults during the Great Depression—Chicago, Cleveland, Detroit, Miami, New York, and Toledo. In the 1970s, New York experienced another financial crisis. Cleveland defaulted on its bonds, and many more rust belt cities were in bad shape.

The Washington Public Power Supply System was a shocker, because it was unexpected. In 1980, the major rating companies, Moody's and Standard & Poor's, had given it their highest ratings, and accordingly it sold more than $8 billion of bonds. Yet it defaulted, and by 1986 Moody's declined to rate the bonds. Standard & Poor's gave the defaulted Project 4 and 5 bonds a D rating. Even sophisticated investors, including Omaha billionaire Warren Buffett, lost money.

Insurance is one way to enhance the creditworthiness of a bond issue. It's primarily used for long-term, fixed-rate financings, as long as thirty years. Bond insurance premiums are paid up front.

Letters of credit are available for short-term, variable-rate financings under ten years. They're appealing, since fees are paid over the term of a bond. Such short-term financings became the standard during the early 1980s, because so many investors were burned by double-digit inflation. They had bought fixed-rate bonds, only to be repaid in depreciated dollars without offsetting higher interest rates. Since interest rates could rise above a municipality's capacity to pay, the risk of default was higher than with fixed-rate bonds, and they could only be sold with credit enhancement.

To help gain more acceptance and lower rates, municipalities agreed investors could "put back" their bonds at the par price before maturity. In this way, the issuer supported the secondary market. If a high volume of bonds came back, the issuer would face an unusual cash drain. It would need the liquidity protection afforded by a letter of credit. Bond insurance doesn't provide liquidity protection.

A letter of credit from a triple-A bank lowers the risk for investors, and so they're willing to accept fifteen to one hundred basis points less interest. On a $500-million financing, annual savings would be as much as $5 million.

Good Timing

In 1982, the timing was right for Japanese banks, since they were starting to pull back from Latin America. They had followed U.S. banks there during the 1970s, but it was becoming apparent that countries like Brazil, Mexico, Peru, and Argentina were having trouble handling all their debt. Mexico shocked investors by devaluing the peso in August 1982.

The Japanese serviced those Latin American loans from New York. So, by pulling back, suddenly they had a lot of people in New York with little to do. The Japanese banks came to the United States decades ago, providing trade finance for Japanese companies, but they hadn't served American companies. Few newcomers were able to challenge traditional relationships between American executives and their bankers.

One day in 1982, Masamichi Yamada, senior deputy general manager of Mitsubishi Bank, was commuting from his Bronxville, New York, home into Manhattan. Along the way, he encountered Douglas Hamilton, a friend and managing director of Merrill Lynch. Hamilton mentioned that Michigan needed to raise $500 million, but probably investors wouldn't buy their municipal bonds, because the depressed auto industry had undermined the state's finances. Investors were worried about default.

Yamada discussed the conversation with his colleagues, and they recognized a great opportunity to establish themselves in a new market. Mitsubishi Bank could arrange a syndicate of Japanese banks, whose short-term notes were triple-A rated, to provide a letter of credit guaranteeing interest payments on Michigan's general obligation bonds. The syndicate included Dai-Ichi Kango Bank, Sanwa Bank, Fuji Bank, and Long-Term Credit Bank of Japan. By offering needed reassurance for investors, the bonds would be salable.

This idea made sense to everyone concerned, and they did the deal. It was the first time foreign banks provided a letter of credit for a U.S. municipal bond issue. The bonds went to market successfully in October 1982.

With the Latin American situation in limbo, and a major American state government willing to work with Japanese bankers, it made sense to canvass other states and municipalities that might be interested in letters of credit. The Japanese were comfortable with American sovereign entities. "We think municipals are generally safer than corporates," says Mitsubishi Bank's Shinshite, "because private companies may disappear if they go bankrupt. Cities may go bankrupt, but they won't disappear."

Kenneth Gibbs, of the investment banking firm First Boston Corp., adds: "The municipal market has a value to them beyond dollars and cents. Part of the Japanese strategy is to increase their profile by associating themselves with prominent state and local governments. This helps them build a level of trust in this country. Certainly they help generate goodwill in regions hit by competition from Japanese manufacturers."

Most major Japanese banks have triple-A credit ratings, so they can raise funds cheaper than almost all American banks and quote cheaper letter-of-credit fees. Only one American bank, Morgan Guaranty Trust, has the advantage of a triple-A rating, and the letter-of-credit business doesn't have enough profit margin for their requirements. Many other major American banks have had their credit ratings downgraded as a result of bad loans for Latin America, real estate, energy companies, and agriculture.

Japanese bankers concentrated on major states and cities among the approximately thirty-five thousand municipal bond issuers rated triple-B to single-A. Below triple-B, the risks were too great. Above single-A, a triple-A letter of credit might not lower financing costs enough to be worth the cost of arranging the transaction, which ran about twenty-five basis points—less than half what American banks charged.

While many municipal officials may have preferred dealing with American bankers, they owe taxpayers the best deal. Across the country, the best deals came from Japanese banks. "If your name is not well known, finer pricing is one way of getting the deal. Japanese banks will continue to expand in this kind of public finance," says Masanari Ebihara, assistant general manager of Dai-Ichi Kangyo Bank, New York.

More Competition

More and more Japanese banks entered the market. Sumitomo Bank, for instance, issued its first municipal letter of credit in August 1984. Ten more Japanese banks followed after that.

Competition forced letter-of-credit fees down. Williams College, in Williamstown, Massachusetts, issued a $22.8-million bond issue to finance new construction. Sumitomo Bank provided the letter of credit, charging only twelve and a half basis points.

In 1984, Boston paid Morgan Guaranty Trust seventy-five basis points for a $70-million letter of credit. A year later, the city sought competitive bids on a $100-million issue. Two Japanese made bids, but neither won. A participant, Sanwa Bank, upgraded its Boston office to a branch. Next time around, Sanwa won the mandate with a bid of nine basis points.

"I suspect Boston officials would be reluctant to buy a fleet of Hondas for their police force," remarked a Boston banker who submitted a losing bid. "But they don't have any qualms about Japanese letters of credit. Police cars are visible. You don't see letters of credit."

Hideaki Yamazaki, general manager of Sanwa Bank's Boston office, says: "Other bankers are mad. They are unhappy. I tell them, 'Boston is a good credit. Maybe U.S. banks are charging too much.'" Boston treasurer George Russell estimates that Sanwa Bank's lower fee saved the city $130,000 to $400,000.

Some issuers expressed surprise that there wasn't a public outcry against having water works, sewers, airports and other facilities guaranteed by Japanese banks. "There was one member of the City Council who served in World War II, and I'm near that age myself," reported Ruth Stalter, auditor for the city of Findlay, Ohio. "I wondered if there would be severe criticism, but I haven't heard any. I guess people are more concerned about their pocketbooks than whether we use a foreign bank."

Rush to Issue

Meanwhile, there were rumblings of tax reform in Washington. Some proposals discussed during 1985 would cut individual income tax rates to their lowest point in a half-century, reducing the value of tax-exempt municipal bonds accordingly. Officials recognized that if they were considering any major bond issues, this was the year to do it.

Some proposals would restrict the ability of municipalities to issue bonds. President Reagan proposed that a municipal bond would lose its tax-exempt status if more than 1 percent of funds benefits

private parties—for instance, a waste-treatment plant where a corporation used more than 1 percent of its capacity. Illinois congressman
Dan Rostenkowski, chairman of the House Ways and Means Committee, proposed raising that limit to 5 percent or $5 million, whichever
is less. Both of these proposals, to take effect January 1, 1986, would
mean the end of industrial revenue bonds, issued by states and municipalities for private corporations pursuing locally valued projects.
These accounted for more than half the municipal bonds issues.

By August 1985, it became clear that the ability of states and
cities would be severely restricted in some fashion after January 1.
The proposals had a powerful impact even before they were enacted
into law, because the marketability of a bond issue depended on the
opinion of bond attorneys. They had to be able to certify compliance
with pending as well as present tax laws. Officials scrambled to prepare bond issues so they could be brought to market by year end.

In 1986 and 1987, Japanese banks provided more letters of credit
than anyone else to American municipalities. Dai-Ichi Kangyo Bank,
for instance, guaranteed a $42.7-million bond issue by the City of New
Orleans, and a $50-million issue by the California Student Loan Cor-
poration. Long-Term Credit Bank of Japan guaranteed a $23.5-million
bond issue by the City of Baltimore and a $90-million bond issue by
the Boston Transit Authority. Sumitomo Bank guaranteed a $200-
million bond issue by the New York State Job Development Authority.
Mitsubishi Bank, Fuji Bank, and Sanwa Bank formed a consortium
that guaranteed a $230-million bond issue by the City of Philadelphia.

In December 1985, the House of Representatives passed a com-
prehensive tax package with 154 pages of new restrictions on municipal bonds. In a compromise, Congressman Rostenkowski agreed that a
municipal bond would retain its tax-exempt status if up to 10 percent
of funds or $10 million, whichever is less, benefited private parties.
There were some exceptions, like water and housing bonds, but they'd
be constrained by state-by-state caps.

Blockbuster Deal

The biggest letter-of-credit deal nearly missed the December 31 deadline. Sometime in mid-1985, financial analysts in the Oregon treasurer's office, Salem, realized that their state's Department of
Veterans' Affairs was spinning out of control. Because recent adminis-

trations had offered these mortgages at below-market rates, the department would go into deficit in a little over a decade. Solvency of the program was at stake, and politicians who mishandled the crisis would probably be voted out of office. A solution came from the Japanese.

It seems a bit ironic that the Japanese would bail out a program to help U.S. veterans, but U.S. banks, recently enthusiastic about loaning money to spendthrift Third World regimes, were notably absent from the bidding.

Oregon's Department of Veterans' Affairs had $5.6 billion of debt, and a staggering $5.2 billion was for veterans' mortgages. The issues floating these issues were derisively known among financiers as "belly button bonds," because everybody seemed to have one. If the situation weren't taken care of soon, it would require potentially ruinous tax increases. More than $700 million needed to be raised.

William Henderson, chief financial officer of the Department of Veterans' Affairs, issued a request for a proposal to major New York investment banks. A half-dozen responded, including Lazard Freres, First Boston, Shearson Lehman Brothers, Smith Barney, and Salomon Brothers.

People at Goldman, Sachs seemed to have the most experience and ideas, and they got the nod. Two of the firm's municipal bond specialists, Michael McCarthy and Christian McCarthy, contacted almost twenty banks. Half were Japanese.

The deal was most likely to succeed if about half the funds were raised via bonds that could be "put back" weekly to the state. This meant the state would support the secondary market by agreeing to buy any of these bonds investors wanted to sell. Thus, the state suddenly might have to pay out some $365 million in the event investors presented their bonds because of sagging bond prices.

To price their issue competitively, Oregon officials needed a triple-A-rated bank. No American bank stepped forward. European banks didn't see U.S. municipalities as a worthwhile opportunity, either.

Japanese Consortium

Eight of the Japanese banks had triple-A ratings, and they decided to make a proposal as a group, led by Takatsugu Murai, vice president and head of merchant banking and planning at Dai-Ichi Kangyo Bank's New York branch.

Murai, forty-four, is an urbane Japanese who's comfortable working in the American market. His father Masaharu was an English teacher who pushed the value of a good education. While Murai was a student at Hitotsubashi University, a respected institution that trains people for business, he made a lot of extra money tutoring. "Competition is so severe among students hoping to attend a major university," he explains, "that parents are generous in spending money for preparatory education. Tutoring is the best side job. Two hours a night, I'd visit a student's home and teach English, Japanese, mathematics, whatever, and earn the equivalent of about $100 a month. At the time, this was enough to pay more than half my living expenses in Tokyo. Forget about waiting on tables—too cheap."

Then in 1975, Murai visited the United States to learn about American business. The following year, he earned an MBA degree at the Wharton School.

Now Murai and his wife Noriko live in Scarsdale, an affluent community about a thirty-minute train ride north of New York, with their fifteen-year-old daughter, Sachiko, and their thirteen-year-old son, Takahito. Education is a concern. "My headache is that my daughter likes American school too much. I'm nervous about that. If she goes back to Japan, nobody will want her. My son transferred from American school to Japanese school, so he'd have a little easier time adjusting when we return to Japan. It's a more intense environment, and he has lost a fair amount of weight, which concerns me."

Murai is a typical bank trouper. He has spent his entire career at Dai-Ichi Kangyo Bank. He expects to be rotated around various assignments, with little say about where he'll go. "It's up to the personnel department," he says offhandedly. Sometimes he works until one in the morning, but he's still due back at his desk by 9:00 A.M. the next day. Generally, his first concern is to gain market share for the bank. Profits come later. "However," he adds, "Dai-Ichi Kangyo Bank places a somewhat higher priority on profits than other Japanese banks."

The Oregon letter-of-credit deal appealed to Murai and other Japanese bankers because it would be the largest general obligation bond issue ever done. It would be far and away the largest veterans' loan program. Consequently, it promised high visibility, which would help the Japanese further penetrate the American market.

Concerned about local sensitivities, Murai asked more than a dozen American banks if they wanted to participate in the deal. All declined, without disclosing the reason why. He attempted to form a syndicate of European banks, but they weren't interested either.

On November 4, Murai and his associate, Keiyu Kitagawa, submitted a proposal for a ten-year, $740-million letter of credit. Each participating Japanese bank would provide about $96 million. The fee would be 5/8 percent annually.

A competing offer came from another Japanese bank, Mitsui, which lacked a triple-A rating but had the highest short-term credit ratings. They hoped to do the deal by offering a line of credit if Goldman could find municipal bond insurance. A line of credit would provide short-term funds in the event Oregon encountered a cash squeeze, while insurance would provide ultimate backing for the credit. Mitsui's line of credit would cost 1/8 percent annually. Add the expected insurance premiums, and the total cost would be well below the letter-of-credit proposal.

Accordingly, Chris McCarthy invited the major municipal bond insurance companies to submit a proposal for underwriting Oregon in this deal. Three responded: FGIC, Bond Investors Guaranty, and the Municipal Bond Insurance Association. McCarthy arranged a meeting to present the deal and answer questions anyone might have.

Tight Negotiations

While McCarthy waited for the insurance companies to reach a decision, he pushed Murai to offer better terms. Murai had a tough task, for every point had to be discussed with the New York representative and home office executives of each bank. There was always somebody who objected to a proposal. Despite the fabled Japanese quest for consensus, it was apparent that some of the Japanese bankers were stubborn, autocratic characters.

Murai accommodated Oregon on most points. On November 12, Murai submitted a revised proposal for a letter of credit which would extend for twelve years instead of ten. Accordingly, it would cost more: 11/16 rather than 5/8 percent. This made the proposal decidedly more expensive than Mitsui's line of credit plus municipal bond insurance.

McCarthy was about to reject the proposal when he heard from the insurance companies. Two decided they weren't satisfied with Oregon as a credit and declined to make a proposal. The third insurance company offered to cover about $100 million of the deal. Since this wasn't nearly enough, McCarthy had no choice but to tell Mitsui their deal wouldn't go.

Suddenly, there was just one proposal. After consulting with Oregon officials, McCarthy called Murai and reported that they wanted to proceed with the eight Japanese banks. Murai was elated.

Then, with the clock ticking, the tough negotiations began. One Japanese bank objected to almost everything, and Murai spent a tremendous amount of time talking with them. "When we have somebody who won't play ball," Chris McCarthy recalls saying, "we kick them out. Why do you need these people?" But Murai explained that he wanted to do things his way and maintain the *wa*—harmony.

Apparently, there was considerable behind-the-scenes battling within the Japanese banks, for each branch is set up as a profit center. Dai-Ichi Kangyo Bank's practice, for instance, is that if a piece of business originates in New York, the New York branch can pursue it anywhere in the country, competing with branches in Los Angeles, San Francisco, Seattle, and elsewhere. Goldman had invited the Seattle branch of Sumitomo Bank, for instance, because it was closest to the credit—in Oregon—but the officers at Sumitomo's other U.S. branches felt they should have gotten the business. Similarly, the Los Angeles branches of Fuji Bank and Long-Term Credit Bank were in the deal rather than their New York branches.

With less than a month to do the deal, almost every negotiating point involved conflict. There were covenants, financial reporting requirements, endless details. "I've got six banks which will agree to this," Murai would explain to McCarthy, "but two are against it. How badly do you need it?" Or: "Three banks say yes, five say no. Could you help me out and let this one go by the boards?"

The banks followed traditional practice and didn't issue a letter of credit for longer than ten years. But in this case, Oregon officials anticipated their problem would occur in eleven to twelve years, and obviously a letter of credit wouldn't do them any good if it had expired. After considerable back-and-forth, the Japanese banks agreed on a twelve-year letter of credit that would be converted to a line of credit.

Another major sticking point was an interest rate cap. Oregon had a law that made it illegal for the state to pay banks more than 13 percent. According to Howard Rankin, the state's legal counsel, a quirk in the law could be interpreted to mean 14 percent, but still there had to be a cap. But the Japanese didn't make loans with a cap, since, in the event of renewed inflation, they'd bear the entire risk of market rates going above 14 percent. The solution involved extending the payment period to cover additional interest due. But the details were complicated.

Murai and the people at Goldman worked virtually around the clock, inching the deal forward among Japanese bankers in Los Angeles, Seattle, Osaka, and Tokyo. "Whenever I called Murai," says McCarthy, "he was in the office. I remember reaching him eleven at night and six-thirty in the morning.

Deal-Breaker?

Meanwhile, with interest rates rising, Oregon officials announced that monthly interest payments would be due from veterans holding state-sponsored mortgages. About a thousand veterans objected. They insisted that while the state could collect more interest, it didn't have the right to increase monthly payments and disrupt family finances. The dispute resulted in a lawsuit that Associated Oregon Veterans filed November 1 in Marion County Circuit Court.

The prospect of litigation alarmed the Japanese on two counts. First, they prefer to resolve conflicts privately with the harmonious *wa*. Litigation exacerbates conflict. Second, if Oregon couldn't increase monthly payments to reflect current interest rates, the cash flow would be squeezed. In some cases, loan terms would be extended from thirty years to fifty-seven years. This would make the state a significantly riskier credit.

Goldman consulted State Counsel Howard Rankin, and he issued an opinion that the lawsuit was without merit. There was no way the veterans could win, he declared. The Japanese still weren't happy, but they resumed negotiations.

But on December 12, the unthinkable happened: the veterans won. Howard Rankin's opinion turned out to be worthless. The Japanese were in an uproar. With the scheduled closing less than a week away, suddenly the whole deal was in jeopardy. The courtroom defeat, if upheld, would mean the state's financial position would weaken, bond-rating agencies would downgrade the Oregon issue, and the Japanese banks would face risks they hadn't bargained on.

"I apologized to Mr. Murai," recalls Chris McCarthy of Goldman, Sachs. "We got the best legal advice we could, and we were wrong. But we were so far into the deal, we had to do it. Couldn't wait. I asked him: Are you going to continue with us? He said yes.

"He had a terrible time explaining the situation to senior officers at Dai-Ichi Kangyo Bank and representatives of the other banks. None of them liked surprises, particularly involving something as un-Japanese as litigation. There was a lot of embarrassment before bank superiors. With anybody else, I believe, the deal would have collapsed."

Murai adds: "I shared with my colleagues a distaste for litigation, but I explained this is part of the American way. Over here, being sued doesn't involve loss of face. I didn't believe the creditworthiness of the bonds would be seriously threatened. I emphasized the benefits of going ahead with this, the biggest deal of its kind. Eventually, all the banks agreed."

After Dai-Ichi Kangyo Bank got the mandate for this letter of credit, Murai persuaded the United States National Bank of Oregon to participate in the deal. "It isn't easy," he says, "because American banks want to make more money than we're willing to accept."

On December 18, there was a dinner celebrating the successful negotiations at New York's Pierre Hotel. It was like a Japanese bankers' convention, for each bank had invited several representatives. Perhaps half the forty people attending were Japanese. There was a lot of bowing and Japanese conversation. The deal closed the next day.

On December 28, the Oregon Supreme Court upheld the decision in favor of Associated Oregon Veterans. But by then, the Japanese had anticipated the setback and moved on to other business. Oregon officials were relieved, for this deal saved the state $30 million to $40 million.

Gaining Market Share

Nineteen eighty-five was an all-time record year in the muni business. Securities Data Co., a Manhattan firm that tracks the industry, reported that more than $200 billion of municipal bonds were issued—double the volume recorded for 1984. Japanese banks provided letters of credit for more than 70 percent of bonds requiring credit enhancement.

In 1986, interest rates came down, and the volume of municipal issues declined. More municipal issues were done on a fixed-rate basis, so they required fewer letters of credit. But on variable-rate issues, the Japanese boosted their share of the letter-of-credit business to 80 percent. Sumitomo Bank, for instance, provided a $160-million letter of credit to the Arkansas Development Finance Authority. Reported savings over the next three years: $1.8 million in lower fees and interest costs.

Competition is forcing the Japanese to do even better. Kyowa Bank offered Oklahoma not only a low fee but a "friendly agreement" letter promising to help promote the state as a location for direct investment. "This isn't our first Japanese letter of credit," says Mike Martin, an Oklahoma City bond attorney working on the transaction, "but it's the first bank which offered to give us more than just the letter of credit. Kyowa has identified about seventy of their clients who are thinking about locating new plants in Oklahoma. With our troubled economy, we need outside capital."

The ever-adroit Japanese banks have begun offering yen-based financing to municipal treasurers—a new twist. Since U.S. municipalities obviously don't need yen, the yen would have to be swapped into dollars, a task that the eager Japanese would be happy to take care of.

As long as major U.S. banks are overwhelmed by their bad loans to farmers, real estate operators, and Third World governments, they won't be able to compete in the municipal finance business. Japanese bankers are willing to accept paper-thin profit margins. Almost surely, the Japanese will increase their share.

If, in the future, profits are squeezed at Japanese banks, or their credit ratings are downgraded, the prices for these municipal guarantees will go up sharply, approaching the levels demanded by American bankers. Taxpayers will then face higher bills or will have to curtail their appetite for costly government projects.

5

MEN FROM MARUNOUCHI

As Japanese banks have made acquisitions in the U.S., especially California, their share of the U.S. banking market has gone up. It's now around 20 percent. Many people claim this shows the diabolical Japanese are gaining a stranglehold.

How about this claim? It's yet another charming misuse of market share numbers. Japanese bankers can pay as much as they wish for acquisitions in the U.S., but they can't force anyone to do business with them. They can't force you to open a checking account. They can't force you to buy their certificates of deposit, or take out a car loan, home mortgage, business loan, or any other type of financing. No one is loony enough to claim that Japanese banks will maintain their market share if they offer less interest to depositors, charge borrowers more, offer slower service, or stay open fewer hours. Obviously, people are free to seek better alternatives.

There are more alternatives now than ever before. Deregulation is ending traditional bank fiefdoms created by regulations that used to block competition from other banks as well as nonbank financial services companies. Now it's easier than ever for banks to compete across state borders. Within a few years, any bank will be able to bid for business anywhere in the U.S.

Moreover, hundreds of nonbank companies have entered the banking market. During the past decade, for example, Merrill Lynch, Prudential-Bache, and many other brokerage firms began offering in-

74

terest-bearing checking accounts. Money-market funds attracted hundreds of billions of dollars of deposits away from miserly banks. The booming mortgage-backed securities market has converted formerly illiquid home mortgages into easily traded instruments, and this, in turn, has enabled pension funds, insurance companies, and others to enter the market for home mortgages. Consumer finance companies such as General Motors Acceptance Corporation have also entered the home mortgage market.

Corporations have more financing alternatives, too. Securities have displaced conventional loans as a key component of corporate finance, because securities are cheaper and often more flexible. Investment banks, of course, have long dominated the securities business. Commercial banks compete for leasing business with the financing arms of major manufacturers such as Ford and General Electric.

There are even alternatives for the most basic of banking businesses: processing payments. General Motors' Electronic Data Systems and American Express' First Data, for example, handle a substantial portion of this business. As credit cards and electronic-funds-transfer technologies become more widely used, they're expected to expand the range of nonbank payment systems.

So it's absurd to claim that foreign banks generally—or Japanese banks in particular—have any power to command business. Bank customers have plenty of choices. What foreign banks actually do is make more capital available here, contributing to wider choice of services and lower loan rates.

Essentially, Japanese bankers provide U.S. borrowers with an important safety valve of choice. When U.S. bankers encounter problems, as they have with delinquent loan portfolios, borrowers needn't suffer along with them. Thus, Japanese bankers help American companies be competitive.

U.S. banks are improving, too. Although they aren't as large as Japanese banks at current exchange rates, they're substantially more profitable. Citicorp, for example, earns more money than Dai-Ichi Kangyo Bank, the largest bank in Japan. U.S. banks are responding to dissatisfied shareholders by selling their poor-performing businesses, concentrating their resources on what they do well, streamlining their back-office operations, and taking other measures. It's the improved profitability at U.S. money-center banks that has enabled them to survive their terrible loan portfolios. Meanwhile, surging U.S. super-regional banks seem likely to become the money centers of the future—and that will be tougher for the Japanese and other competitors.

Better Deals

Generating business in the United States is difficult, because until a few years ago hardly any corporate treasurers had ever heard of a Japanese bank. They were brand-new names in the marketplace, though they had maintained offices here for decades to serve Japanese companies.

Treasurers were, however, at least willing to consider a Japanese bank, because back in the 1970s, British, German, and Swiss banks had expanded here, so they knew that foreign banks could offer better deals—lines of credit without compensating balances, for example. Traditionally, a loan agreement required that the borrower maintain a certain percentage of the loan amount, perhaps 10 percent, on deposit at all times. The bank would invest it to boost its profit. But the Europeans offered to earn their money entirely by charging a fee. They agreed to let borrowers minimize their idle balances. This was irresistibly appealing when inflation and interest rates hit double digits.

Often, Japanese bankers got introductions to American financial executives because of assistance they had provided a company's subsidiary in Japan. "For a while, the only major U.S. company where we got some business was United Technologies, a result of the good job we did handling their Otis Elevator subsidiary in Japan," recalls Tomoyuki Kato, joint general manager and chief credit manager of Sumitomo Bank, among the most aggressive Japanese banks in the United States.

Japanese bankers had extensive dealings in Latin America, so they could offer to help there. "The first thing we'd discuss with a U.S. multinational client was whether they had any needs in Latin America," Kato explains. "We offered to provide a revolving line of credit structured to yield lower-cost financing than was available from U.S. sources. How much cheaper depended on the country, since tax rates differed. I was in Mexico where the tax was 15 percent. So the difference in taxes might be several percent, which amounts to a considerable amount of money saved. That's the way we began establishing ourselves in U.S. corporate finance with companies like General Foods, Pepsico, Sperry, Becton Dickinson, Kodak, General Electric, Bausch & Lomb."

Some Japanese banks like Mitsubishi have pursued a slow, cautious strategy of internal expansion in the United States. Mitsubishi is considered a conservative bank, a result of their links to the Mitsubishi zaibatsu. However, things are starting to change under Mitsubishi Bank's new president, Kazuo Ibuki. He's a decisive man who cultivates orchids and is pushing his people to be more aggressive. In 1986, for instance, Mitsubishi Bank got the mandate to lead a $500-million syndicated financing for Northwest Airlines. It used the funds to acquire Republic Airlines.

Dai-Ichi Kangyo Bank has relied on internal expansion, though they forged a strategic alliance with Citicorp. In January 1988, the customers of each bank started using automatic-teller machines of the other bank. Moreover, Dai-Ichi Kangyo Bank will issue Citicorp's Mastercard credit card in Japan and earn fees from the billings. The banks will exchange credit information, so that customers of one bank can borrow money in the other's country quickly. "You wouldn't have to have an established relationship with us before borrowing," says Nobuya Hagura, president of Dai-Ichi Kangyo Bank.

A number of Japanese banks have accelerated their expansion into the United States by acquisition. For instance, in December 1985, the Industrial Bank of Japan paid $110 million for a 75 percent interest in the J. Henry Schroder Bank & Trust Company. Started in 1923, Schroder serves an international clientele including U.S. subsidiaries of European companies, U.S. middle-market companies, and high-networth individuals. After the deal was done, Hideo Ishihara, IBJ's managing director for international operations, shook hands with almost every Schroder employee, from secretaries to the executive chairman.

Schroder has about $2 billion of assets, but perhaps more important are its connections. "They have well-established relationships with European central banks and U.S. regional banks," says burly Norihode Yoshioka, general manager of IBJ's New York branch.

Many Japanese banks have established extensive branch banking networks in California, both to attract deposits and get lending business. Mitsubishi acquired the Bank of California for $250 million. Mitsui Manufacturers Bank has twelve offices. Sumitomo Bank of California has forty-eight offices and $2.8 billion of assets. The Bank of Tokyo owns California First Bank, with one hundred thirty-four California offices, four overseas branches, and assets over $5.4 billion. In 1986, Sanwa Bank paid $263 million for Lloyds Bank California, then integrated it with Sanwa Bank California. The combined operation has one-hundred sixty-six offices and reports $4.5 billion of assets.

How Sound?

For years, Japanese banks have had capital ratios around 3 percent, compared to capital ratios between 5 percent and 6 percent for U.S. banks. This means the Japanese have had to set aside less money as idle reserves, a cushion to help assure adequate liquidity. With a little more of their funds earning money, the Japanese are able to offer loans and other services for lower rates.

Demanding a "level playing field," American bankers have pressured the Japanese Ministry of Finance to hike the required capital ratios of Japanese banks. The Ministry responded with an announcement that Japanese banks must report capital ratios above 4 percent by 1990.

Japanese bankers have resisted going much higher, arguing that they have extensive "hidden" reserves that should be counted when determining the soundness of a bank. Hidden reserves are the difference between book value and market value of their common stock and real estate holdings. Many of these assets were purchased years ago, and both real estate and the stock market have skyrocketed since.

When calculations are done using 70 percent of market value rather than original cost, Japanese bankers argue, their capital ratios are 9 percent to 11 percent. American and British bankers counter that 70 percent is too high, considering the volatility of Japanese financial markets. "We can't accept zero, but we are flexible," says Mitsuaki Yahagi, deputy general manager of Mitsui Bank.

Moreover, argues analyst Hideki Mitani of the U.S. investment banking firm Goldman, Sachs, "Japanese banks have virtually no potential loan loss risk. Dai-Ichi Kangyo Bank, for example, recorded loan losses of only $12.54 million in 1985 on its financial statement, approximately 1 percent that of Citicorp, which recorded $962 million in net loan losses for the same period. This low loan loss proves the high quality credit control capability of Japanese banks." One reason for this is a high percentage of Japanese corporate loans are backed by collateral. Most U.S. corporate loans are unsecured.

In any event, at least ten major Japanese banks have proceeded to boost their capital via new issues. Starting in 1986, they've issued more stock in Japan and convertible bonds abroad. The offerings, when they're done, are intended to realize ¥1 trillion—about $6.7 billion.

Financing Acquisitions

More and more Japanese companies are doing the unthinkable: acquiring other companies. This was rarely done, partly because Japanese companies nurtured distinctive corporate cultures. Also, it was presumed that any company for sale must have problems, so internal growth was a more prudent policy. "In Japan, selling a company is like surrender to your enemies," says Shuhei Sato, senior vice president at Sanwa Bank, New York.

Only about a thousand acquisitions a year are consummated in Japan. Most involve small companies, and until recently all were friendly. This compares with about three thousand acquisitions annually in the United States, typically much larger and often hostile.

Accelerating overseas expansion is often easier via an acquisition. "It's becoming more important for Japanese companies to have strategic international alliances for technologies, marketing, and management," adds Koji Hirao, general manager of Long-Term Credit Bank's New York branch.

An increasing number of Japanese banks are financing acquisitions. In recent months, Long-Term Credit Bank handled four acquisitions, including Toshiba Ceramics' purchase of Quartz International Corp. The Industrial Bank of Japan helped finance Nitto Boseki's acquisition of a U.S. biotechnology firm. Mitsui Engineering & Shipbuilding turned to the Bank of Tokyo when it wanted to purchase a U.S. engineering company.

In 1983, Sanwa Bank became the first Japanese bank to establish an international mergers and acquisitions group. Since then, Sanwa's Sato has helped negotiate twelve transactions between Japanese buyers and primarily American sellers. "You've got to have a manufacturing operation in the United States," he tells Japanese firms.

Sato, forty-one, graduated from Keio University and Stanford Business School. The first member of his family to travel outside Japan, he married an American, Jeanne Carreau, and they gave their children international names: Yuhei Matthew and Kaoru Camille. He's quite self-assured as he moves from boardrooms to television interviews.

He reports that Sanwa Bank is handling about $100 million of mergers and acquisitions a year—small by U.S. standards, but ahead of other Japanese firms and growing. Thus far, most acquisitions have been small. Fujisawa Pharmaceutical, for instance, acquired a 22.5-percent stake in LyphoMed, a Chicago drug company. Toyo Bearing, an auto parts supplier, bought research facilities in Illinois and Michigan for $35 million. Hitachi Zosen paid $70 million for Cleary Co., a Chicago sheet metal manufacturer.

Now deals are getting bigger. Sanwa Bank represented Kokusai Motors when it spent $319 million to acquire the Hyatt Regency Hotel, Hawaii, the largest hotel transaction ever.

"Traditionally," Sato explains, "we never charged for advice. But with squeezed margins from lending, we've had to expand into new fields and be compensated for our value added."

Coming next, it would seem, are hostile takeovers by Japanese companies. In 1986, Dainippon Ink & Chemicals corralled Sun Chemical's graphics-art division for $550 million, and in 1987 launched a $473 million hostile takeover of Reichhold Chemicals Inc., of White Plains, New York. "Many Japanese managers are realizing that a hostile takeover doesn't stigmatize you in the United States," says Sato. "It's an acceptable way of doing business."

But the Japanese are sure to proceed cautiously after the controversy following Fujitsu's attempted acquisition of Fairchild Semiconductor. "The Japanese became painfully aware of American sensitivities," notes Robert Reich, professor of political economy at the John F. Kennedy School of Government, Harvard University.

Swap Boom

Japanese bankers, like their American counterparts, cultivate fee business to help compensate for the corporate finance business they're losing to securities firms. The $300 billion swap market is an increasingly important source of fees. With interest rate swaps, companies reduce their interest rate risks.

For example, a Japanese banker may bring together an American savings and loan association and a Japanese bank. The American S & L pays variable rates on money market accounts to attract depositers and receives fixed-rate income from mortgage holders. The S & L is exposed to the risk that interest rates—the payments it has to make—might go up, exceeding its fixed-rate income. On the other hand, a Japanese bank might borrow fixed-rate funds in the European market and extend variable-rate loans to corporations. Its risk is that interest rates might decline below its fixed cost of funds. So the Japanese banker who did the deal would collect perhaps a 0.5-percent fee for bringing these two parties together. The S & L's fixed-rate mortgage income would be passed along to the Japanese bank, paying its fixed-rate cost of borrowing. The Japanese bank's variable-rate income would be passed to the S & L, covering its variable-rate cost of borrowing.

Swap counter-parties exchange only their income flows. They keep their original loan agreements and remain responsible for repayment of principal. The risk in a swap is that if one participant defaults, the counter-party may face higher interest rate costs.

Currency swaps offer similar advantages. Even though an American company may need U.S. dollars, it may issue a yen loan to take advantage of low interest rates. The company goes to a bank, which arranges a swap with a counter-party who needs yen. When the transaction is done, each party has the currency it wants for less than would be the case if it borrowed direct. Currency swaps are a $40-billion market now.

Brokering Loans

As relative newcomers to the United States, Japanese bankers lack the advantage of established connections, but they're doing the next best thing. They're buying other people's loans.

For example, when Philip Morris prepared to acquire giant General Foods in 1985, the company's treasurers arranged $6 billion of credit with the largest American banks. They couldn't handle that amount by themselves, so they obtained commitments from many more banks, including seven Japanese banks.

The American banks gained by selling off the loans. First, the American banks collected a percentage of the loans, which they passed on to other banks. Second, they minimized the effect on their reserve situation. If they handled the entire $6-billion deal themselves, they would have had to raise more than $300 million for their reserves.

Altogether, about fifty banks participated in the deal. About 70 percent of the funds came from foreign banks, particularly the Japanese. Many of these, in turn, sold part of their deal to others—Dai-Ichi

Kangyo Bank, for instance, brought in three middle-sized Japanese banks it regularly does business with.

Thus, Philip Morris loans found their way to lesser-known institutions like Kyowa Bank and Hokkaido Takushoku Bank. "We are aggressive about buying loans, because we have few lending opportunities with prime U.S. borrowers," says Akaishi Narikazy of Hokkaido Takushoku Bank. Providing funds serves both to generate immediate interest income and gain the best of corporate introductions, setting the stage for future blue chip relationships.

Philip Morris is delighted. "Loan sales didn't concern us," says Philip Morris treasurer Hans Storr. "They worked to our advantage, because we couldn't have done the deal in the U.S. market alone."

Leveraged Buy-outs

Japanese bankers have ventured into riskier kinds of loans, like leveraged buy-outs. A leveraged buy-out commonly occurs when a company wants to sell a subsidiary. Managers of the subsidiary may want to buy it, but they lack the funds. If the company is mature, with stable cash flows, the managers may be able to borrow almost all the money. These loans would be secured by the subsidiary's assets, and the interest payments are covered by the cash flows. Since, after a deal is done, the new entity is overloaded with new debt, almost always the managers anticipate selling some assets and paying down the debt.

Leveraged buy-outs are riskier than conventional loans, because a deal could sour if interest rates take off, the acquired company experiences unexpected declines in cash flows, or managers can't sell off assets as they planned.

But as interest rates declined during the early 1980s, leveraged buy-outs boomed. Merrill Lynch Capital Markets reports that more than $36 billion of leveraged buy-outs took place in 1986, up about eighteenfold in five years, and account for 20 to 25 percent of all corporate restructurings. There have been multibillion-dollar leveraged buy-outs involving such companies as Macy's, Beatrice Foods, and Safeway Stores.

Leveraged buy-outs are difficult deals for anyone to get, because they arise suddenly. You don't tell the boss you'd like to buy the subsidiary you run, since that indiscretion could cost your job. But once top management has announced a subsidiary is for sale, then interested managers scramble for financing. Usually, they'll go to the banks where they have established relationships. An American bank that takes the initial call may invite other banks, like the Japanese, to share the risks of a large deal. Banker's Trust, for instance, syndicated the Beatrice Foods leveraged buy-out to many participants, including Sumitomo Bank and the Bank of Tokyo.

Real Estate Finance

Japanese commercial banks, trust banks, and leasing companies are coming on strong as real estate lenders in the United States. Commercial banks, for instance, are reporting real estate loan volume up about 35 percent compared to the previous year. Altogether, these lenders are expected to finance more than $8 billion of U.S. property annually—about 10 percent of the U.S. market. Japanese lenders had a negligible presence a few years ago.

The $8 billion estimate doesn't include Japanese life insurance companies, which are prevented by the Ministry of Finance from writing straight loans. They buy properties. They take convertible mortgages and participating mortgages. Whatever they do must have predominantly equity characteristics.

In broad terms, the move by Japanese lenders into U.S. real estate is comparable to the boom in commercial paper. Banks were long accustomed to charging their corporate customers about the same rates for loans. They didn't give much of a break for the strongest credits. So when, during the 1970s, it became apparent that investors would accept significantly lower rates for commercial paper issued by corporations with the strongest credit, these corporations relied more on capital markets for short-term funds. Banks were stuck with poorer credit risks that couldn't go into the capital markets. The credit quality of commercial bank loan portfolios continues to deteriorate—one reason why commercial banks are anxious to generate fee business and get into underwriting.

Similarly, until the last couple of years, long-term real estate financing was a lender's market. The U.S. life insurance companies priced their real estate loans pretty much the same, as if every property were a triple-B credit. That's a middling investment grade—top rating would be triple-A. Financing that involved a B building in a B city would be on terms similar to an A building in an A city, because the life companies didn't have much competition. Entrepreneurs lacked viable alternatives for projects, say, over $100 million.

Now Japanese lenders like Sanwa Bank, Sumitomo Bank, Sumitomo Trust & Banking, and Mitsubishi Trust & Banking, are targeting the top 10 percent of real estate properties and offering significant price breaks. The U.S. real estate market is huge, of course, and the Japanese aren't about to take it over anytime soon, but they're definitely gaining top-bracket clients whom the U.S. life companies seem to have taken for granted. The biggest real estate entrepreneurs on the continent, like Albert and Paul Reichmann, Trammell Crow, Gerald Hines, John Tishman, and others, turn increasingly to the Japanese.

In most cases, Japanese lenders go for straightforward, low-risk, low-wrinkle transactions over $50 million. The Japanese use somewhat more conservative underwriting criteria than U.S. real estate lenders. Generally, they favor finished class-A office buildings. Their typical loan-to-value ratio is 70 percent to 80 percent, which is common among U.S. lenders. The Japanese prefer a coverage ratio—cash flow to mortgage payments—of 1.2 or higher. U.S. life insurance companies tend to accept 1.1. Because the Japanese are so conservative, it doesn't seem likely that they'll trigger a wild building boom.

Japanese real estate loans are floating-rate, because they have floating-rate liabilities. Typically, they lend at fifty to seventy-five basis points above the prevailing rate major London banks charge each other for funds. These loans are converted to fixed-rate via interest rate swaps. The total cost, for prime buildings, is fifty to two hundred basis points cheaper than what's widely available from U.S. lenders.

Big differences come in the loan agreements. For instance, the Japanese don't require yield maintenance agreements, as do U.S. insurance companies. An owner may want to sell a property before the term of the loan, or, with substantial appreciation, refinance a property and raise cash. In these cases, a typical U.S. financing becomes quite costly. Because the Japanese are more flexible on prepayment terms, their loans can be 30 to 50 percent less expensive.

The strongest trend in long-term real estate finance is securitization. Instead of relying on banks to provide mortgage loans, a securities firm will design a debt instrument backed by one or more buildings. Usually, they're office buildings in a major city. Their appraised market value will help secure the principal, and interest payments must be covered by rent payments.

Like other notes or bonds, securitized commercial mortgages, as these debt instruments are called, appeal to investors such as savings and loan associations, pension funds, and insurance companies. Securitized commercial mortgages offer much more liquidity than traditional real estate investments, one of the reasons why they're popular among investors. Property owners like them because they raise money directly in the capital market, cheaper than can be borrowed at a bank.

Now we're seeing more and more commercial real estate mortgages being packaged for capital markets—especially Japanese lenders. Goldman, Sachs alone has raised $1.7 billion in eleven transactions, according to Vice President Thomas J. Healey. "By applying corporate finance techniques to real estate and combining them with the technology of swaps," he explains, "the Japanese get the floating-rate assets they want, while real estate entrepreneurs get fixed-rate liabilities matching their fixed-income stream from rent rolls."

Often, Japanese banks back securitized mortgages with letters of credit, to lower the risks for investors and lower the interest cost for borrowers. Recent transactions include the $85-million refinancing of San Francisco's Transamerica Building, in which Sumitomo Trust & Banking participated, in December 1986. Since then, Sanwa Bank has provided a letter of credit for the $290-million financing of Southland Corporation's Cityplace Center East, a Dallas office complex. The Industrial Bank of Japan led a group of Japanese banks to help refinance the Marriott Marquis Hotel in New York, for $375 million. Mitsubishi Trust & Banking participated in $278.6 million of twelve-year rated commercial mortgage bonds, which are financing IBM's new eight-hundred-thousand-square-foot manufacturing facility in Southbury, Connecticut. According to Healey, who helped arrange the IBM deal, the company saves about $9.5 million over a conventional mortgage.

The Japanese are affecting more than just long-term real estate finance. They're moving into the market for short-term construction loans, too, taking business away from U.S. commercial banks. Some major U.S. real estate companies use Japanese commercial banks to finance construction with commercial paper, short-term unsecured IOUs widely issued by major corporations. In an unusually complex case, Olympia & York raised $750 million for two buildings at Manhattan's World Financial Center. It's the largest construction financing ever done.

Each time the commercial paper matures, O & Y has the option of exchanging it for new paper when the old expires or switching to a short-term loan, whichever is cheaper at the time. If they go for a loan, they can switch back to commercial paper next time around, and so on. Fourteen Japanese banks are involved, including Sumitomo, Dai-Ichi Kangyo, Mitsubishi, Sanwa, Mitsui Trust, Nippon Credit, and the Bank of Tokyo.

Satisfied with the results, the Reichmanns are financing two more Manhattan buildings with Japanese lenders—another building at World Financial Center and one on Lexington Avenue next to the Chrysler Building.

Plain Vanilla Lending

Some Japanese bankers court smokestack industries. This is a strategy of the Long-Term Credit Bank of Japan, traditionally a lender to heavy industry. LTCB has about a hundred people in New York managing an $8-billion loan portfolio.

"For us, the United States is still a frontier," says Rikuichi Yoshi-sue, vice president and deputy general manager of the bank's New York branch. "We have to prove ourselves with growth, and that means finding a community or company or industry where we can add long-term value. I try to look beyond a particular transaction to the future. On occasion, that may mean offering a deal for ten or twenty basis points below market. I wouldn't flinch at that.

"There's hardly any profit lending money to triple-A-, double-A-, or single-A-rated companies, because they can get money by going directly to capital markets in the U.S. and Europe. Usually we can make money only as an intermediary—originating a loan, then syndicating it among Japanese institutional investors who are seeking higher yields than possible just with government securities. We try to forecast interest rates a couple months ahead and price the deals right. If we don't, we may be stuck with a loan yielding a below-market rate.

"Among these Japanese institutional investors are insurance companies, regional banks, leasing companies, agricultural cooperatives. They aren't worried about foreign exchange losses if the dollar continues to go down against the yen. They'll just keep rolling over their dollar loans—keeping a portion of their portfolio in dollars. They're primarily concerned about raising their interest rate yields. As long as interest rates remain higher in the U.S. than Japan, they'll continue to roll over their money here.

"We focused on some capital-intensive industries, like utilities, because we feel more secure with asset-rich companies. We don't feel comfortable with service businesses, where the principal assets are people, who can always walk out the door. Lending isn't like buying stock, where you can easily sell out when you want. You may be stuck with loan for a while if it turns sour.

"We concluded that despite financial pressures, construction delays, and other problems, utilities had to be there. If a utility were operated reasonably well, it would be a good credit serving a public purpose as far as you can see into the future. We learned about American regulations, how regulatory commissions are set up, what the political climate is like, how the rate-relief recovery process works. Even though rate relief may come a little at a time, it will come, since customers have to pay for the service. Stockholders might suffer, but lenders ought to remain secure.

"Of course, some utilities such as Lilco and Seabrook are in trouble, but many are strong. So, during the past few years, we have helped finance major utilities across the country, $50 million to $100 million at a time in private placements, letters of credit, pollution-control bonds, first-mortgage bonds. For example, Northeast Utilities, Niagara Mohawk, New York State Gas & Electric, Philadelphia Electric, Ohio Edison, American Electric Power System, Iowa/Illinois, Public Service of Northern Indiana, Kansas City Power & Light, Union Electric, Southern California Edison, Puget Sound Electric, San Diego Electric, El Paso, Houston Lighting & Power, Duke Power. This isn't a glamorous niche, but it's important.

"Or take a case like the steel industry. It's ailing, just breaking even, but then, we don't just look at the balance sheets. We consider the underlying necessity of an industry. We believe steel is so basic, it will continue to be manufactured here. We became successful funneling our money into basic Japanese industries, and we're trying to do the same thing here. We've completed three financings for U.S. Steel—about $150 million altogether.

"The company may close a lot of factories, but they'll keep operating the most modern ones. They're still the largest producer of steel.
They have a lot of people who produce steel efficiently. They have a
hundred years of history, which would be difficult to give up easily,
because their people were brought up in the business of making iron
and steel. Maybe this is a Japanese way of feeling more sympathetic
with lifelong employment."

Toyota and General Motors

Long-Term Credit Bank is among the few banks that extended long-
term loans to Toyota during its early, difficult days. But as the company prospered, it ceased to borrow from any bank. Occasionally, it
would raise money via a stock offering, but it didn't take on any debt.
Toyota had a $4-billion mountain of cash and securities, and people
referred to it as Toyota Bank.

Toyota's management is conservative, and in the early 1970s it
didn't want to tackle the risks of U.S. manufacturing—high costs,
difficult labor, and poor quality—all at once. But the company was
under pressure from its competitors, particularly Honda and Nissan,
which were developing U.S. operations.

General Motors, like the other Detroit automakers, was taking a
bath. During 1980 and 1981, the company had lost $5.5 billion. Hun-
dreds of thousands of autoworkers were laid off. Four out of five auto-
manufacturing plants in California were closed. More and more
American customers preferred Japanese cars, because they were much
higher-quality, and they cost $1,500 to $2,000 less per car. GM management figured out that maybe they could learn something from the
Japanese.

So GM chairman Roger Smith and Toyota chairman Eiji Toyoda
agreed to an historic joint venture. They signed a letter of intent in
September 1983.

GM would contribute its shuttered plant in Fremont, California,
a monument to the failure of American manufacturing. Though GM
put many more man-hours than Toyota into each car, quality was
decidedly worse. The work force was about sixty-five hundred, with
absenteeism over 20 percent. The plant was littered with beer bottles.
When it closed in 1982, there were about a thousand grievances pend-

ing with the National Labor Relations Board, plus about sixty disputed firings. "We'd been trained to fight with management," says United Auto Workers Local president Tony DeJesus. "And GM's management guys were trained to fight the union. Both sides were good at it. We fought like hell."

Toyota would contribute management know-how and operate the new plant to produce about two hundred fifty thousand cars a year. They'd do it with about twenty-five hundred workers, about 30 percent of General Motors' work force when the plant closed.

Toyota wanted to participate in this joint venture to gain firsthand experience with American ways, and thus could be more likely to succeed with its own U.S. manufacturing plant. General Motors wanted to see just how the Japanese worked their miracles of productivity.

This joint venture was exempted from antitrust laws because its term was limited: it would be liquidated in ten years. Consequently, both Toyota and General Motors looked for ways to minimize their investment. It made sense for them to use borrowed money as much as possible to equip the plant.

Though Long-Term Credit Bank was unable to establish contact with Toyota back in Japan, it could build on a relationship with General Motors. In 1982, LTCB had provided a letter of credit for GM's Mexican subsidiary, which manufactures Chevrolet engines. This displayed a certain amount of courage on the part of LTCB, because by then Mexico's financial situation was deteriorating, and bankers didn't want to take on additional risks in Mexico. But LTCB reasoned that more than 80 percent of the Chevrolet engines were exported, so the subsidiary generated quite a bit of cash. It should remain solvent even as the national government flirts with bankruptcy.

Yoshisue called on Jay Chai, a Korean who's the automotive expert at C. Itoh, a giant Japanese trading company. Itoh had a relationship with Isuzu, a smaller Japanese auto manufacturer that shared dealers with General Motors. Chai encouraged LTCB, even though Isuzu had worked for years with Dai-Ichi Kangyo Bank and Industrial Bank of Japan. The Industrial Bank of Japan didn't figure in the joint venture, because it was also the lead banker for Nissan, Toyota's chief rival, and Toyota wouldn't approve financing the deal through the Industrial Bank of Japan.

So Yoshisue arranged a $175-million financing with Chase Manhattan Bank. He brought in Mitsui Bank, Tokai Bank, and Golden

State Sanwa Bank. "The NUMMI deal was the beginning of our investment banking activity, which involved very competitive pricing," Yoshisue says.

NUMMI has become a stunning success. Overall quality rivals that of Toyotas produced in Japan. Worker attendance on the factory floor is about 98 percent, and unexcused absences are under 0.5 percent. During the past two years, fewer than twenty grievances were filed by the union.

"In the U.S., Long-Term Credit Bank will grow by identifying the special needs of other industries like auto parts," says Yoshisue. "To avoid losing market share, Japanese auto parts firms are moving to the U.S., where they're serving their clients, like Toyota and Nissan, who have established manufacturing operations here. Meanwhile, a number of U.S. auto parts manufacturers are discussing joint ventures with Japanese firms. We're knocking on a lot of doors, to see if we may be of help."

Making of a Japanese Banker

Yoshisue was born in the village of Hofu, Yamaguchi prefecture, the western tip of Honshu island, fifty miles west of Hiroshima. This whole region is a big industrial base, except Hofu, where traditional-minded people have resisted extensive industrialization.

"My father Matuhisa was a teacher," Yoshisue explains. "Over several generations our family had acquired fifteen to twenty acres of farmland, which was worked by other people. The government confiscated it after World War II—MacArthur believed that land under absentee ownership, worked by poor peasants, would lead to Japanese militarism.

"After World War II, my father became more pessimistic about the future. That's the way I was brought up. He encouraged me to visit the United States. I first came here as an exchange student from 1962 to 1963. I lived with a family in Massachusetts and finished high school there.

"That was risky, because normally you need to graduate from a good Japanese high school to gain admission to a good Japanese university, and without that it's hard to get a job with a big Japanese company. But life is full of risk. It took me an extra year to study and gain admission to Hitosubashi University in western Tokyo. It's a business administration–type college.

"I thought about becoming a government bureaucrat after I graduated in 1969, because it's a tradition in our prefecture. It has produced an unusual number of prime ministers, like Virginia and Massachusetts have produced U.S. presidents. But I realized that becoming a bureaucrat would involve so many restrictions I wouldn't care for. I realized that money is going to be needed forever. If you follow the money, you can go anywhere in the world. I applied for a job at Long-Term Credit Bank, and they accepted me.

"After a while, I decided to get an M.B.A. in the United States. So from 1973 to 1975, I was at the Massachusetts Institute of Technology's Sloan School, which emphasizes computers and mathematics. My father thought this was the direction the banking business should go in the future.

"I had a hard time adapting to American ways. It was especially difficult for my wife Yukiko and our son Tomoyuki, who was about three back then. Returning to Japan involved another adjustment. Not everybody accepted Tomoyuki, because of the foreign ways he had picked up.

"Our second son, Hiroshi, who's seven, had to learn the ways of a Japanese classroom. For instance, he was seated in a corner and couldn't see the blackboard very well, so he asked the teacher if he could move somewhere in the middle. Well, in Japan, you cannot say that. What you have been assigned is your permanent place until somebody tells you to move. In Japan we would be concerned that the person moved may suffer, but Hiroshi wanted to see clearly. Why not ask? Maybe somebody else wants to sit in the back next to a nice girl. He ended up switching seats.

"I came to New York about four and a half years ago. I felt that, as a Japanese, I couldn't be any use if I just tried to be like an American banker. Yet whenever I tried to do something international, I faced tremendous competition. The big multinational companies were fully banked, didn't need any more banking services—it's so hard competing with other companies already well established. What to do? I struggled through this dilemma almost two years. I asked myself: Can't you do anything without relying on your being Japanese? Of course, I couldn't forget I'm a Japanese banker, but couldn't I do it my own way?

"I just didn't understand the structure of the deals. It took us so much time. Maybe we didn't really know what we were doing at that point. We'd spend a lot of time considering the most basic questions, like whether IBM was going to survive the next five years. I made a lot of mistakes, which means I lost a lot of deals.

"It was difficult learning how to compete for corporate business against and sometimes in cooperation with powerful competitors like Salomon Brothers and Morgan Stanley, because I was afraid of making deals by phone. The traditional Japanese way is to cultivate relationships in person. But here in America, you pick up the phone. Would you be interested in this? Okay, fine. Huge commitments are made in five or ten minutes. It's a gentleman's game.

"I treat people a bit differently than typical Japanese managers. I try to create a sort of tension, and I let everybody be more individualistic. I don't like conformity. If he or she knows what he is supposed to do, let them do it. Because you don't impress a competitive New York client if you can't make a move until you get advice from somebody else. I hope I can give our people good direction.

"I've found it easy to get along in the United States, because people are tolerant. As long as you are a decent citizen and work hard. On Wall Street, people accept you if you talk plain language, make a deal in an honest way. Deal is done over the phone.

"Come Monday morning, I'm up early, ready to go until Friday. During the week, I do whatever I have to for business. Sometimes, I work until two A.M., sacrificing my family. But not on weekends.

"I live in Stamford, Connecticut, about an hour from New York by train. I like to spend as much time as possible with my wife and children. We work on a small vegetable garden. It's tough to get good tomatoes! We volley on a tennis court together.

"My wife, a daughter of a successful Japanese corporate executive, is a very strong Japanese person. She hates all the time I spend on company work. She doesn't enjoy company entertaining. She says it's not the company but your own ego drive which requires you to do this and that. The company is just your excuse. Maybe she's right.

"We have a three-year-old daughter, born here—Mayuko Poly Yoshisue. I'm proud to have her with middle name. Japanese don't have middle names. But she is born here, an American citizen."

Number 1

Genial Nobuya Hagura, president of Dai-Ichi Kangyo Bank, comes from a long line of Shinto priests who served at Kyoto's eighth-century Fushimi Inari Shrine. He notes that one ancestor, Itsuki Hagura, was a prominent seventeenth century scholar responsible for reviving classical Japanese studies at a time when most scholars were absorbed in Chinese philosophy.

Hagura, sixty-eight, departed from this proud tradition and started a new family line of bankers, joining Nippon Kangyo Bank after graduation from Keio University, April 1941. Hagura and his wife Toshiko have a son, Nobuaki, who's deputy managing director of Mitsubishi Bank's Australian operation. Their daughter, Yoshiko, is an officer at Barclay's Bank, Tokyo.

Hagura acknowledges the role of luck. "As a student, I had gone mountain climbing in Nagano prefecture, and after we came down, we wandered through the streets of Matsumoto. We saw a magnificent stone building which turned out to be a branch of Nippon Kangyo Bank. I decided I wanted to work in an impressive place like that."

Although most bankers started their careers in commercial lending, Hagura pursued research on international as well as domestic business. He kept the bank informed about the American economy, because he was fluent in English. "I had read Chaucer's *Canterbury Tales* and Charles Lamb's *Essays*," he recalls, "and before I knew it, I was hooked on the language." Hagura continues to read widely on philosophy, Japanese history, and economic history.

During World War II, collateral for many of the bank's loans was destroyed by bombings. All they had left was raw land. "We felt it was our duty to put Japan back on its feet," he says. "We had lost something like a quarter of our classmates and war buddies, and we had a sense of obligation as the survivors. We worked hard." Hagura displayed managerial talent and was assigned to run some of the bank's most important branches.

By the 1960s, he was managing the New York branch. "We had a hard time raising funds, because we were not very well known," he says. "They wouldn't even accept us as members of the Wall Street Club, on the top floor of Chase Manhattan Plaza. Just a decade ago, officers at major New York banks like Chemical, Citicorp, and Chase Manhattan were reluctant to loan us much, and demanded that we maintain large compensating balances. Now, of course, many American bankers ask us for funds."

International travel gave Hagura and his wife an opportunity to pursue their interest in opera. "We've been to the Metropolitan Opera, Vienna State Opera, the Opera in Paris, and the Teatro Colon in Buenos Aires. I saw a magnificent performance of *Aida* on the outdoor stage of Rome's Baths of Caracalla."

When Nippon Kangyo Bank merged with Dai-Ichi Bank in October 1971, creating one of the largest Japanese banks, Hagura reached the front ranks of Japanese finance. He became president in June 1982. "Usually the press spots prospective bank presidents when they're still new managing directors," he laughs, "but in my case nobody noticed me even after I became deputy president.

"I remember *Time* magazine called for my views on banking, because they were publishing a feature about the economies of Asia. I was amazed when I saw the article a month later. There I was together with electronics entrepreneur Konosuke Matsushita representing big business and Ministry of Finance officer Kiichi Miyazawa talking about politics. I showed the article to my wife, and she commented that *Time* must have goofed! I wouldn't have agreed to the interview, if I had known I'd be outclassed like that!"

But he proved himself a formidable manager. Together with Chairman Tetsuo Fujimori, he united the bank which had been split between people loyal to the original Nippon Kangyo Bank and those from Dai-Ichi Bank. Rather than promote people on the basis of their prior affiliation, Hagura and Fujimori made merit the operating principle. Hagura reorganized the bank to better handle rapid growth. He substantially upgraded their computer system and delegated more authority to local branch managers. Hagura favored aggressive growth from within rather than acquisitions, and the bank blanketed Japan with three hundred sixty offices, plus fifty-seven offices abroad.

Hagura set his sights on making Dai-Ichi Kangyo Bank the world's biggest bank, a rank it attained in 1986. Now there isn't any Japanese financier better connected than Hagura. He has served as chairman of the Tokyo Bankers Association, financial director of the Japan Federation of Employers' Associations, executive director of the Japan Federation of Economic Organizations, and chairman of the Federation of Bankers Associations of Japan.

Dai-Ichi Kangyo Bank has made one of the biggest commitments to the United States, and its New York operation is the largest of any foreign branch bank, with about two hundred people.

The bank's top man in New York now is Yuko Oana, a gregarious, forceful man who gestures continuously as he talks. Oana, fifty-six, is from northern Tokyo. "When I was born," he jokes, "bond quotations were at their lowest point in Japan and the United States."

His father Fujio was an engineer who became a sake brewer in Kyoto. When Oana was a young man, he learned to play the violin and piano. On occasion, he still plays these instruments, especially sonatas by Mozart, Beethoven, or Chopin.

Oana attended Tokyo University, where, he says, he worked hard and played hard. He dabbled at billiards, dancing, and mah-jongg, like many Japanese. He liked contract bridge best. That and golf are lifelong passions.

"When I graduated in 1953," he recalls, "Tokyo was still in ashes from World War II. Industry wasn't rebuilt yet. It seemed to me finance would be vital regardless what happened, so I applied to Nippon Kangyo Bank, the Bank of Japan, and Ministry of Finance. I decided, though, that the Ministry of Finance was just a government office, and I preferred the private sector. So, of these three, my only choice was Nippon Kangyo Bank."

Oana was rotated around the major departments of the bank—corporate lending, foreign exchange, investments, domestic branch offices. By 1961, he was in London, when the unregulated Euromarket was in its infancy. "It was exciting to see a brand new market develop," he says.

On a subsequent assignment, Oana managed the Ginza Branch, amidst Tokyo's famous retailing district and adjacent to the Marunouchi business district. It's one of Japan's most important bank branches, and an assignment there is an important point en route to the top.

Oana worked in the bank's securities division when the samurai bond market opened up. Until the late 1970s, these bonds were only for foreign governments or international agencies like the World Bank. The Ministry of Finance imposed requirements, which made it difficult for a private company to qualify. But Oana helped persuade Jack Kincannon, chief financial officer of Sears, Roebuck, that his company could benefit from lower total financing costs via the samurai market. Kincannon appointed Dai-Ichi Kangyo Bank the lead-commissioned agent to handle the administrative work involved, and in March 1979 Nomura Securities did the underwriting for ¥10 billion.

The Euromarket expanded, and Dai-Ichi Kangyo Bank co-lead-managed yen bond issues for Dow Chemical, Proctor & Gamble, and other companies.

Oana became a director of the bank in 1983, and he was appointed New York general manager two years later—a step up. His most exciting days are right now. "There's so much change," he says, "with banks moving into new businesses like leveraged buy-outs and mergers and acquisitions. Growth of the Euromarket. All the new financial products coming out, to suit different client needs."

Oana and his wife Kazuko do their best to take in the concerts and museums and charitable affairs of New York. She loves art, and follows auctions at Sotheby's and Christie's. "I tell her not this time, on the very expensive paintings," he smiles.

They have two sons: Yuichi, thirty, who graduated from Keio University and now works for Sebu department store, Tokyo; and Shinji, twenty-six, a graduate of Chiba University, who practices as a pediatrician in Matsudo.

On Saturday nights, when the week's work is done, Oana and his wife retire to the Nippon Club, on Manhattan's West Fifty-seventh Street, where they gear up for an evening of contract bridge. He established the Dagood Bridge Club, but he readily admits he's not the best player. His opponents may include Takeshi Nozaki and his wife, of Tokio Fire & Marine Insurance Company; or Yoshio Mizoe and his wife, of Zenshinren Bank; or Jiro Ishizaka of Nippon Life Insurance Company. "I am enjoying," Oana says.

"Typical Japanese"

Tokuyuki Ono, senior managing director of Sumitomo Bank and general manager of its New York branch, is among the two or three highest-ranking Japanese bankers in the United States. But he certainly didn't start out to become a banker.

He's reluctant to talk about himself, saying: "In large Japanese corporations, we don't like to have a situation where one individual helps himself too much. His duty is to serve the company."

The trim, taciturn Ono was born in Osaka, where his father Keitaro was an officer at Kanebo, a large textile company. For three centuries, his family financed the *daimyos*, or regional lords. But they went bankrupt during the upheaval of the Meiji Restoration.

Ono loved early-nineteenth-century romantic German literature by Heine, Schiller, and Goethe, and he dreamed of becoming a novelist. He studied literature as long as he could. He went to Kobe University, then transferred to Tokyo University, where he spent three more years. To help pay his expenses, he worked as a laborer, fixing streets and doing construction jobs. "I could have done more intelligent work, like teaching young students," he reflects, "but I wanted to do real work."

After graduation, he realized that novel writing would be a financial struggle, so opted for a more practical career. "At that time banks had their entrance examinations first," he explains, "and then other companies followed. I took a test for Sumitomo Bank. Quite strangely, they accepted me."

In 1956, he started as a bank clerk back in Osaka, tending account books, calculating interest, and other chores. Next, he wrote loan applications for four years. He believes his most important education came in the corporate research department, where he came to understand the workings of major companies.

By 1968, he was learning how European bankers syndicated loans. "The traditional Japanese practice was for a bank to originate a loan and take the entire amount, holding it until term," he says. "We didn't have any concept of syndication. This involved a number of banks participating in a large transaction with foreign borrowers—the whole idea was new. I arranged some syndicated loans at our headquarters and our London office, which served Japanese companies over there. The first loan syndication we managed ourselves was a $500-million deal for the Electricity Board of London."

How did he learn English? "I was a late starter. In the universities, I learned only German. I didn't study much English. Up until 1968, I couldn't study any at all. Then I took a private teacher in English conversation. I had to catch up fast with my colleagues on the international side, who had spent several years overseas."

Over the years, he has displayed impish American humor. At a recent reception following a major transaction, for instance, he spoke a few words about each member of the Sumitomo Bank team. He introduced one man simply as "typical Japanese." When an American staffer stepped forward to make his bow, Ono smiled: "Here's Mr. Smith—not from home office."

He and his wife, Akiko, live in Manhattan. Their twenty-two-year-old daughter, Yoko, is attending the Royal Academy of Music, London. Their daughter Kyoko, two years older, is working in Tokyo after having graduated from Amherst College. He skis, and plays golf and tennis. They attend light operas. Akiko Ono is studying classical guitar.

"Sometimes my wife and I feel we have a couple strangers," he says a bit ruefully. "Our daughters' mentalities seem more American than Japanese. When they talk, we feel we are listening to American minds speaking Japanese. They're more independent than daughters would be in Japan. There, they'd ask for money and advice. Here, they earn their own money and make their own friends. Maybe after ten years, we might think we made a great mistake. Or we could be pleased." In the summer of 1987, Ono was diagnosed as having liver cancer, and he returned with his wife to Japan.

Prospects

Japanese bankers seem sure to expand their presence dramatically in the United States.

Except in California and Hawaii, where a number of Japanese banks have retail branches, most Japanese bankers will probably stick to wholesale banking—large transactions with Fortune 1,000 corporations. Relatively small numbers of people in money centers like New York and Los Angeles can handle this business.

As Japanese bankers gain market share, U.S. funds that would have gone to the Fortune 1,000 will be available for middle-market American companies, with sales from about $25 million to $500 million. So a huge chunk of the U.S. market benefits from Japanese participation.

A few Japanese bankers will undoubtedly serve the middle market directly. Profit margins are greater here.

Since this market requires a branch network with people who can evaluate the creditworthiness of many smaller, privately held companies, Japanese entry is likely to come via acquisition. In some cases, they'll wait to be asked in by a management that needs capital. Unfriendly acquisitions are almost out of the question.

Japanese bankers will expand the number of services they offer.

Expect to see some start to innovate and lead the market, rather than adopting what others have introduced.

As time goes on, Japanese banks will become a familiar, accepted part of the financial landscape. More high-ranking officers will be American. Clients will deal with American representatives. They'll be international institutions. This process will take a number of years, since the Japanese are a homogeneous people with strong traditions, but it will happen. In the process, the Japanese will assure their lasting success. People will tend to forget they're Japanese banks and will focus exclusively on the caliber of service.

Thanks to competition from the Japanese, the cost of banking services, especially for companies, will be lower than they otherwise would be. Terms will be more accommodating. Competition will force American banks to find niches where they can add value, or they'll see their market share dwindle further. Either way, customers win.

6

RISKIEST BETS

Japanese leasing companies are among the most agile, adaptable, entrepreneurial competitors in global finance. Primarily, they help finance equipment, for an estimated 80 percent of U.S. companies lease equipment to stay competitive. Leasing is the biggest external source of equipment finance, providing more funds than bank loans. It's credited with helping to create almost 1.5 million jobs a year. Worldwide, some $250 billion of equipment is being leased. This is growing about 20 percent a year.

Japanese leasing companies started by serving market niches that other Japanese companies, such as the banks, ignored. Now that they're expanding in the U.S. market, they're filling niches vacated by U.S. companies. At one time or another, they have bumped heads with most financial services companies—substantially expanding the options available for corporate borrowers.

Although Mitsui Leasing, for example, has only three people in their Manhattan office in the Pan Am Building, they help channel hundreds of millions of dollars to a wide range of clients. They helped Pemex, Mexico's oil company, finance a $5.1 million oil-drilling platform. They participated in a $100 million refinancing of 1345 Sixth Avenue, a Manhattan office tower. Mitsui Leasing provided some of the funds used in the $667 million leveraged buy-out of Burlington Industries.

Despite their successes, Japanese leasing companies haven't been able to establish primary relationships with many American clients; these relationships seem securely in the hands of sophisticated American lessors such as GE Capital Corporation, commercial banks such as Citicorp, or investment bankers such as Goldman Sachs. The result is that American firms originate almost all transactions in the United States—and collect the often lucrative origination fees.

Mainly what the Japanese leasing companies do is provide lease financing—an $85 billion market in the United States. The Japanese help finance equipment—an estimated 80 percent of U.S. companies lease equipment to stay competitive. Leasing is the biggest external source of equipment finance, providing more funds than bank loans. It's credited with helping to create almost 1.5 million jobs a year. Some $250 billion of equipment is being leased worldwide. This is growing about 20 percent a year.

Leasing is crucial for transportation companies. About half the U.S. commercial aircraft fleet is under lease. Texas Air, United, American, TWA, Northwest—they all lease aircraft. Buying airplanes is exceedingly expensive, and few airlines can take full advantage of the depreciation deductions generated by outright ownership. About 30 percent of ships and 40 percent of railroad cars are leased, too.

Heavy industry finances about a third of its capital equipment with leases—printing presses, machine tool production equipment, drilling rigs, computers, and computer-aided manufacturing systems, for instance. About a quarter of computers are leased.

Traditionally, lessors financed only things that could be moved to another market when they came off lease, but now they're taking the risk of financing power plants and manufacturing facilities. A $540-million lease deal is financing the Chrysler-Mitsubishi joint-venture auto plant in Flat Rock, Michigan. The $575-million Nissan auto plant in Smyrna, Tennessee, is leased, too.

That's not all. More and more service industries lease equipment like telecommunications systems, word processors, medical equipment, and computer-aided design systems. Many companies use vendor leasing programs, which help customers finance their purchases.

"Often, leasing is the least expensive form of financing available," says Takao Matsumoto, president of Tokyo Leasing USA. "Partly this is because a lessor gains depreciation deductions on the equipment and anticipates the residual value of equipment when it comes off lease. Also, many lessors have a higher credit rating than their lessees, enabling them to borrow funds at cheaper cost. Consequently, the monthly payments tend to be lower than payments on a conventional bank loan.

"Leasing affords valuable flexibility. If the needs of a business change, usually a lessee can switch to different equipment for a modest additional charge. Similarly, a lessee can upgrade to more productive equipment when it becomes available.

"Many companies like contractors do short-term projects, and they lease almost all of their equipment. They'll choose terms coinciding with the time required to complete a project."

The 1986 Tax Reform Act provided a powerful spur for the leasing industry: the Alternative Minimum Tax. This imposes a 20 percent tax on a substantial chunk of depreciation deductions, making it less attractive to buy, more attractive to lease for many companies.

A Long-Term Niche

The Japanese have identified a clear niche in the marketplace: they supply low-cost, long-term funds to lessors, participating in other people's deals.

Of all lenders, Japanese lenders may make the riskiest bets. They assume the financial risks of long-term transactions up to twelve or fifteen years, occasionally twenty. Only the biggest, most sophisticated American lessors dare provide fixed-rate financing for more than ten years. Anything can happen. It's difficult to hedge so far in the future against the risk that interest rates will go up. The risk seems especially high in light of uncontrolled federal spending, which is likely to trigger renewed inflation.

Long-term lease financing is even more risky, because the U.S. airline industry—perhaps the leading taker of long-term funds—is in turmoil. It isn't always apparent which companies will emerge stronger or go under with deregulation. Pan American and Eastern, once stalwarts of the industry, are in trouble. Several regional airlines have filed for bankruptcy. People's Express is gone.

The best credits in the airline industry are Delta and USAir, which have single-A ratings. United is a triple-B. Texas Air, a single-B. Because the Japanese take long-term financial risks in U.S. airlines, travelers enjoy lower air fares in the latest airplanes.

While the Japanese have access to low-cost yen, this doesn't give them much advantage when they lend U.S. dollars. They must raise dollars like other companies and institutions, in the United States as well as European capital markets.

When they can, the Japanese will borrow matching fixed-rate funds to cover their fixed-rate lease commitments. But there are few takers for periods over ten years. That's the risky period, when they earn their money. The Japanese limit their risks by syndicating a large portion of deals they originate to other companies. A large deal may involve more than a dozen Japanese leasing companies.

"We're almost by ourselves taking the long-term credit risks," says Takashi Koizumi, president of Orient Leasing USA Corp. "Our policy is matching fixed-rate funds to cover our fixed-rate commitments. No need for us to handle short-term transactions, since many American companies do that."

Leasing Goes Boom

Chroniclers report that leasing originated at least a couple of thousand years ago in ancient Babylon, but it developed as a modern industry only after World War II. U.S. equipment makers started "captive" leasing companies to help customers finance their purchases. Later, some of these captives expanded to finance purchases from other manufacturers.

U.S. Leasing Corporation, launched in 1954, was the first general leasing company. It offered what are called net leases, where it arranged the financing. The lessee paid maintenance, insurance, taxes, and other related costs.

The 10-percent investment tax credit, passed in 1962, provided an important incentive to order equipment, since the deductions reduced tax liabilities dollar for dollar. A lot of leasing companies were started to provide the tax-advantaged financing.

Some Japanese financial executives noted this leasing boom and began forming their own leasing companies during the early 1960s. Shinji Ueda, who headed the New York office of the Nichimen trading company, was a pioneer of the Japanese leasing business. He asked executives at Sanwa Bank if they'd be willing to back such a venture, to be called Orient Leasing.

"Twenty years ago, lease financing was practically unknown in Japan," recalls Yoshihiko Miyauchi, president of Orient Leasing. "The option of leasing didn't occur to a manufacturer about to install a new production system or a company in need of office equipment. Therefore, lenders questioned our commercial prospects and were reluctant to provide ample funding."

Sanwa Bank would help, but their officers wanted to reduce the risks. They talked to many other banks about the possibility of becoming partners in the venture. Toyo Trust Company, Taiyo Kobe Bank, and Nippon Kangyo Bank agreed, and these banks provided a ¥50-million line of credit. The Nissho and Iwai trading companies became partners, too, since lease financing could help customers buy more from them. U.S. Leasing became a stockholder. Orient Leasing got underway in April 1964.

From the start, Orient Leasing was a cultural novelty, drawing people from diverse Japanese companies. The first chairman, Keizo Fujui, was president of Nichimen. Orient's first president, Tsuneo Inui, headed the New York office of Sanwa Bank. Many of the other people were drawn from the trading companies and banks.

Things were a little unsettled at first. Many people remained loyal to the companies they came from, which competed aggressively with one another. Furthermore, the companies had rather different operating styles. Some people at Orient felt competitive with each other. They'd be on the phone, reporting to their former associates. It took about five years before Orient developed a distinct corporate culture people felt loyal to.

Initially, the company leased mainly office equipment. The first contract financed four cash registers for a supermarket in Kanazawa. Then trading companies helped by bringing in orders for factory machinery. Orient would borrow funds from their banks and provide leases to finance the purchases.

As Japan's exporters expanded, they needed more and more factory machinery. Orient's revenues grew from ¥644 million to ¥100 billion in a decade. Success, though, encouraged some discontent. Nippon Kangyo Bank pulled out of the venture, so they could help form their own competitive leasing company.

Japanese trading companies, city banks, regional banks, insurance companies, and savings and loan institutions all got into the game. The Bank of Tokyo helped launch BOT Leasing Co. Ltd. Sumitomo trading company started Sumisho Leasing. Mitsubishi trading company helped launch Diamond Lease Co. The number of Japanese leasing companies jumped from 33 in 1970 to 280 by 1987.

As might be expected, competition for customers cut profit margins. Japan's Ministry of International Trade and Industry surveyed twenty-three major leasing companies and reported that profits dropped from 4.89 percent in 1978 to 1.8 percent by 1985.

Orient expanded into less crowded markets, where profits might be higher. They leased freighters, medical equipment, aircraft. These were appealing as high-ticket markets, where a comparatively small number of people could write a substantial volume of business.

Japanese companies hit the international market in 1978 with the so-called samurai lease. The Export-Import Bank of Japan loaned low-cost funds to the leasing companies, which purchased aircraft mainly from Boeing, McDonnell-Douglas, and Lockheed. The aircraft were leased back to British Airways, Air France, Olympic Airlines, and Singapore Airlines. Within a year, resourceful Japanese leasing executives had financed thirty-one aircraft for $930 million.

The program ended after a year, but Japanese leasing executives gained valuable experience. Subsequently, they, together with eager American investment bankers, devised resourceful ways to provide long-term financings that complied with complex regulations. Many transactions were referred to as *kagonuke*—the word for a stunt where a magician escapes from a locked cage.

One maneuver was conjured by Phillip J. Adkins, Citicorp vice president in Tokyo. A Citicorp office in Britain's Channel Islands bought a car fleet and sold it to a group of Japanese leasing companies that paid cash. Then they sold the fleet back to Citibank, taking a twenty-year note. Citicorp brokered the deal to the government of Malaysia, which is making the car payments. Bankers and leasing companies reportedly have done about $4 billion of such transactions.

Such transactions were possible because Japanese leasing companies are regulated not by the obstructive Ministry of Finance but by the Ministry of International Trade and Industry, which is more inclined to encourage new ventures. "Since banks take deposits from the public," says Osamu Nagano, an associate director of Japan Leasing Corp., "they should be closely regulated. But the leasing companies don't take deposits. So they shouldn't be subjected to the same regulations."

The 1980 reform of Japan's Foreign Exchange Control Law gave leasing companies more latitude in international transactions. Still, there are regulations to contend with. Interest rates and loan periods, for instance, are restricted on yen-denominated syndicated loans.

To avoid losing major financings, resourceful Japanese lessors devised what's called the "Musashi lease," referring to a master swordsman in Japan's feudal era. It cuts through the bureaucratic thickets by structuring a lease as an installment sale that is unregulated. In one Musashi lease, Japan Leasing lead-managed a syndicate of Japanese leasing companies that provided $61.2 million, the cost of three DC9-82s, to American Airlines. The airline will repay the debt representing 55 percent of the transaction, in twenty-year installment payments. Institutional investors provided equity.

The biggest markets for Japanese leasing companies are, in order, Asia, Europe, and the United States. "Most of our overseas expansion has come via joint ventures with local parties," says Miyauchi of Orient Leasing. "Timely low-cost funds are crucial to establishing a competitive position, and we select local partners, usually banks or other financial institutions, to ensure ready access to competitive funding. These partners also bring close ties to the local business community that are essential for effective marketing of the joint venture's leasing services."

Japanese leasing companies scrambled to line up joint venture partners. Tokyo Leasing teamed with Manufacturers Hanover Holding Corp., IBJ Leasing with Boston Overseas Financial Corporation, and Fuyo Lease with Citibank. Most deals were on a deal-by-deal basis— Chase Manhattan, for instance, worked both with Orient Lease and Diamond Lease.

Two dozen Japanese leasing companies are active in the United States now. They've carved out a niche in the long-term segment of the market, generally providing funds for more than ten years. Few American companies do this. The Japanese are major providers of funds for U.S. airlines, railroads, manufacturers, and real estate developers.

The 1986 Tax Reform Act made leasing transactions uneconomical for many U.S. lessors, and a lot more of the business is going to the Japanese. "When the volume of deals we gather exceeds what our tax situation enables us to absorb, we sell the deals to other companies," explains Robert O'Reilly, manager of leasing services operations at GE Credit Corporation. "The Japanese are high on our list of people to call."

By now, the dozen largest Japanese leasing companies reportedly derive a quarter of their income from overseas transactions. During the past five years, they've done more than $15 billion of transactions with overseas customers, particularly in the United States.

Orient Lease reported that its net income has grown an average of almost 12 percent annually for the past five years. Now it's a giant with more than $23 billion of assets. In 1987, it bought the shares held by U.S. Leasing, while retaining the largest stake in that company.

To fund all this activity, Orient Leasing has become a familiar name in capital markets. In 1987, it had $250 million of commercial paper outstanding, making it among the top five Japanese companies in the U.S. commercial paper market. Orient Lease has issued about $450 million worth of Eurobonds.

High-ticket Specialist

Perhaps more than most Japanese firms, Diamond Leasing concentrates on high-ticket financing as opposed to financing small office equipment or machinery. "About 70 percent of our deals involve aircraft," says Kaoru Abe, president of Diamond Leasing USA, a joint venture with Mitsubishi Bank. The parent company has $4.7 billion of assets and is listed on the Tokyo Stock Exchange.

While Abe solicits business, he spends most of his time evaluating proposals submitted by American investment bankers. Diamond Leasing has worked with Chase Manhattan, Shearson Lehman Brothers, Salomon Brothers, Citibank, and Goldman, Sachs.

To limit their risks of a high-ticket default, Abe helps arrange syndicates, so that each company has only a small percentage of funds at risk in any deal. As if to make the task easier, Orient Leasing and Tokyo Leasing are also located in the same Midtown Manhattan building, 780 Madison Avenue. The brass nameplate on the brown granite outside says "Wang," but many people know this as the Japanese leasing building.

"Our company started with medium-size regional aircraft," Abe explains. "America West, for instance, a Phoenix-based airline which is about four years old. We managed the syndication of a $120-million financing where they bought a dozen Boeing 737-200 aircraft from an Australian airline.

"We've helped arrange $90 million for Delta Airlines—with a reasonably good credit like that, we may have to be satisfied earning only a forty-basis-point spread over our cost of funds. With lesser credits, the spread may be fifty to sixty basis points, even a hundred basis points. We consider the aircraft, too, since something like a 737-200 has a history of maintaining its value, and there's steady demand for it."

It was at Kobe University that Abe first became interested in international finance, inspired by professor Hiro Shinjo, who was an expert in the field and adviser to the Bank of Japan. After graduation in 1957, Abe joined Mitsubishi Bank so he could pursue the subject.

He spent four years in Malaysia, learning how to adapt in that Moslem, nationalistic environment. He was two years in the Philippines, where everything seemed to depend on personal relationships.

"This is my second time in the United States," Abe says. "When I first came over, my wife Makiko and I associated mainly with other Japanese, particularly my associates at Mitsubishi International and Mitsubishi Bank. Now we see mostly local people."

They live in Greenwich, Connecticut, where he plays golf at the Burning Tree Country Club. During the winter, he plays tennis at the Greenwich Racquet Club. Their twenty-one-year-old daughter, Machido, is attending Oberlin College, an hour northwest of Tokyo. His son, Nirihiko is in the tenth grade at Greenwich High School. Though they attend an occasional lecture and art exhibit at Manhattan's Nippon Club, he isn't involved with the Japanese Chamber of Commerce.

Middle-market Ambitions

In some cases, Japanese companies have expanded into leasing with joint ventures. Nomura International formed a joint venture with San Francisco-based lease broker Babcock & Brown. Nomura provided 80 percent of the 300-million yen equity. Nomura's rival, Yamaichi Securities, formed a joint venture with Equitable Life Leasing, called Consortium Leasing.

Other cases involve acquisitions. Sanwa Bank was looking for a good U.S. leasing company, since the leasing market was growing rapidly, and they didn't believe they could develop the needed capabilities in-house. In 1985, they acquired the leasing division of Continental Illinois Bank, which, hit by bad energy and real estate loans, had to raise funds quickly. Sanwa Bank is believed to have paid about $50 million and refinanced about $500 million of debt. They retained the American president, Bernard McKenna, and changed the name to Sanwa Business Credit Corporation.

McKenna praises Sanwa for giving him considerable latitude. "They're letting me do things Continental wouldn't allow," he says. He has expanded the number of fields where the company operates.

Meanwhile, during the early 1980s, as Japanese banks competed ferociously for market share in the United States, executives at Fuji Bank considered their prospects. With $162 billion of assets, Fuji Bank was one of the world's three largest Japanese banks. Major corporations, both in Japan and the U.S., were raising funds directly from capital markets. What corporate lending business remained was done on thin profit margins. Because of the Glass-Steagall Act, banks couldn't expand into securities underwriting.

But if somehow they penetrated the higher-risk, higher-margin business of lending to middle-size companies—who lacked the credit ratings needed to tap capital markets—Fuji Bank might make a lot of money in the United States and gain decided advantages over its Japanese competitors. Because middle-size companies seldom have great credit ratings, their loans are often secured by assets. Many middle-size companies are growing rapidly and use leases to finance their equipment purchases. Fuji Bank executives doubted that they could develop the expertise in-house to handle asset-based financing and equipment leasing.

In 1983, Fuji Bank's senior managing director, Ko Uemura, fifty-seven, was dispatched to head their operations in the Americas and explore possible acquisitions. Fuji Bank considered the mission so important that Uemura wasn't on the customary executive rotation of three to five years. He was to stay indefinitely, until significant expansion was well underway. Nothing like this had happened before in the bank's history, which went back more than a century. Uemura became the highest-ranking Japanese banker in the United States.

Uemura is a solid, distinguished-looking man from Tokyo. He has a formal manner, and his conversation reveals a lively interest in culture. His grandfather was among those who rallied around the Meiji Emperor in 1867, after the revolution that ended three centuries of the medieval Tokugawa Shogunate. Uemura was awarded a Rhodes Scholarship while attending the University of Chicago back in the early 1950s. Somewhere along the way, he became an ardent Mozart lover, and he reports attending over 550 Mozart performances.

He's a thoughtful man much concerned about Japanese-American relations. "People tend to talk about the trade friction between our countries in terms of economic analysis," he says, "but I believe the cause is cultural friction. Economics is important, but it's only one part of life and culture."

Three days after his arrival in 1983, Uemura suffered two severe heart attacks. He stopped smoking and began taking regular walks along Central Park. He appears to be in good health now.

Uemura quickly narrowed the field of possible acquisitions. Chicago-based Walter E. Heller & Co., with more than $442.4 million of annual revenues, stood out as the most likely choice. Started in 1919, it's one of the largest asset-based lenders to middle-market U.S. companies. It leases equipment, buys receivables, and provides working capital and other loans secured by the assets of the borrowing company.

Heller incurred major losses on real estate loans, as developers were hit by an overbuilt real estate market. Losses led to a lower credit rating. As a result, it had to pay higher interest rates when issuing commercial paper, its chief source of funds. Unable to compete as effectively as it used to, Heller's management put it up for sale in 1982, and in February 1983, Heller management agreed to be acquired by Security Pacific Corporation, a Los Angeles bank. They would pay $400 million.

Uemura thought the game was over, but his investment banking advisers at Morgan Stanley told him that if he was still interested, he should top Security Pacific. He offered $425 million. By January 1984, Fuji Bank had acquired Heller.

Uemura knew very well that Heller was in trouble. "Why else would it have been up for sale?" Uemura asks. "If Heller were a healthy company, why would they sell themselves? How come a foreign institution like ourselves could buy a healthy, growing, no-trouble company on a reasonable price? They had to sell themselves. There was a disease within them. We considered the price a foreign tax."

Uemura recognized that Heller was an American firm. It had a widely recognized name in its field. Almost all the employees were American. So it wouldn't do to bring in a lot of Japanese as top executives. After an intensive search, he hired Norman P. Blake, Jr., forty-five, an ambitious man who was executive vice president of GE

Credit Corporation, the largest U.S. diversified financial services firm, to become president.

Blake got an $800,000 bonus for signing and $600,000 in salary—more than Uemura is paid. Uemura doesn't seem to mind, since he's a proud, lifetime Fuji man. He receives generous fringe benefits, and when he retires, he expects to be accorded respect as a wise business leader. "If you just considered the money, I'd die of shame!" Uemura laughs.

Soon Blake learned the ways of dealing with the Japanese. When he has a request for Mr. Uemura, he has a junior executive make the phone call. This arrangement means Uemura isn't in the position of telling Blake no directly. Neither man loses face. Blake also hired Yukihiko Chayama, an associate of Fuji Bank's two top officers, who helps keep Blake informed about the latest doings in Tokyo.

In early 1984, Uemura, Blake, a number of colleagues he hired from GE Credit, and some transplanted executives from Fuji Bank assessed the magnitude of their task. Previous management had carried millions worth of delinquent loans they made to troubled carpet manufacturers. Perhaps inspired by freewheeling New York banks, Heller's Latin American office wrote off $35 million of loans that turned bad. Somehow the company's Florida office lost money lending on Palm Beach mansions.

Under Uemura and Blake, Heller wrote off hundreds of millions of dollars in bad deals. They transferred $350 million of delinquent loans to a subsidiary, because this put Heller in a position to expand without violating loan covenants—restrictions in loan agreements Heller signed when it borrowed from banks. They raised credit standards and centralized the credit approval process. Staff was cut 15 percent to sixteen hundred—as gracefully as possible, Uemura urged. Blake's people closed twenty-eight of the company's sixty-eight offices. They discontinued real estate financing. To keep Heller going, Fuji Bank injected $725 million of additional capital—Heller represented the largest Japanese investment in a single U.S. company. Fuji was in deep.

Though they were preoccupied with damage control, Uemura, Blake, and their associates recognized that to stay competitive, they had to expand their business. Equipment leasing, for instance. Heller did $350 million annually, and it had the potential of growing 50 percent to sixteen hundred—as gracefully as possible, Uemura urged. Blake's people closed twenty-eight of the company's sixty-eight offices.

tion deductions it would earn as lessor, owning equipment.

They wanted to expand their participation in leveraged buy-outs, too. While Heller did well in this business, they had more than their share of nervous moments. They had $3 million of financings out to Hall Motor Transit Company, a Mechanicsburg, Pennsylvania, truck line, when top management wanted to buy it. In 1985, Heller agreed to help, increasing its loan exposure to $11 million. A year later, Hall filed for protection from creditors under Chapter 11 of the bankruptcy code.

In a close call, Heller loaned $75 million to Harley-Davidson Motor Co., the embattled motorcycle maker. Management took it over, but the future looked grim as the company was hit by high interest rates as well as Japanese competition, particularly from Honda and Yamaha. Harley-Davidson cut costs, then pulled strings in Washington and got a special tariff. It hurt motorcycle customers by restricting price competition, but the company was able to hang on and make their loan payments.

Turnaround

Though Heller was in deep trouble, it turned around within a couple years. In their 1986 10-K filing with the Securities and Exchange Commission, which reports financial details often unavailable in an annual report, Heller Financial Inc., the company's biggest unit, reported their first profit since their financial crisis began. It was even a respectable 9-percent, $39-million net on $413.9 million of gross income.

"The most important thing about our Walter Heller acquisition is time," Uemura says serenely. "Nothing can be done within a year. Three years has passed, and that's not enough for such a big project. But three years are better than two years.

"Second important thing is we have met and employed the right person for CEO post of Heller—Norman Blake. He's a wonderful man. He is a man of integrity. He's a young man. He has an American spirit—frankness, vitality, energy. He's a rare person who can understand something new quickly. Not all Americans or Japanese can do that.

"Third, we have autonomy. Since it is on the soil of the United

States, which is very important to Japan and Fuji Bank, I believed we must treat the company separately from the rest of the Fuji Group. In the press announcement of this acquisition, we stated that we would give Walter Heller autonomy, and we have."

Assuming Heller continues to improve: was it good for the Japanese to take over this company? Well, it was undeniably in terrible shape. Fuji Bank was willing to pay the top price. No one else stepped forward with the cash infusions needed to keep the company going. Maybe someone else could have done a good job. But they didn't. Uemura and his compatriots at Fuji Bank deserve credit for what they accomplished.

Because Heller is profitable again, it's able to continue providing hundreds of American companies with cash they need to grow—even companies like Harley-Davidson, anxious to keep Japanese competitors away from American customers. Now Heller executives are eyeing possible acquisitions.

"We foreigners can't do anything short-tempered," Uemura says. "We should behave like Japanese do. Patience. Longsighted. Don't be moved by temporary things. We must have historians' eyes.

"Economic change involves social change, and it comes slowly. Our bureaucracy goes back three hundred years, and it's not going to change overnight. But I believe it must change. It's our destiny. Japanese are very provincial people. An island mentality. We confined ourselves mainly to four islands until one hundred twenty years ago. Like Americans, we had a strong tradition of isolation. Also like Americans, we've had to learn how to be international. That means adapting to things which are totally new and different. As you can see, we are adapting."

What's Next?

In the United States, leasing is widely considered a technique for minimizing tax bite. But it has proven to be a versatile financing tool quite apart from taxes. Although during the past two decades, the U.S. Congress has enacted many measures expected to throttle leasing activity, companies just adapted their leasing techniques. They're a good bet to continue providing substantial funds for business and industry.

In Japan, leasing has thrived without offering any tax benefits, and the industry seems to have more room for growth. The Japanese Leasing Association reports that leases provide 6.36 percent of Japan's private capital investment. This compares with 8.4 percent in France, 20 percent in Britain, and 31 percent in the United States.

With profit margins meager on traditional finance leases, probably some major Japanese lessors may expand into operating leases. These would involve hiring a lot of people with the expertise to appraise and remarket used equipment.

Japanese leasing companies, like many companies in the United States, are diversifying beyond leasing. "Now our loans are 54 percent of new business, and leasing is less than 30 percent of total volume," says Orient Leasing president Yoshihiko Miyauchi. The company has expanded into consumer finance, mortgage-backed securities, venture capital, and securities brokerage. In August 1987, it acquired a 23.3 percent stake in Rubloff Inc., a major Chicago commercial real estate brokerage firm. This followed Nomura Securities' December 1986 purchase of a 50 percent stake in Eastdil Realty Inc. Look for more acquisitions to come.

Consequently, even when leasing becomes a less advantageous financing technique, Japanese leasing companies can be expected to gain a greater presence in the American market. This Japanese competition will help maintain steady, downward pressure on American financing costs, especially for companies in need of very long-term money. Thus, Japanese leasing companies are helping to support the riskiest kinds of investments that so many American jobs depend on.

7

EUROMARKET ULCERS

As the most wide-open and free-wheeling financial center, the Euromarket provides vital alternatives for companies that are restricted in their local markets. It enables borrowers to cut their costs and to use financial instruments that are often unavailable anywhere else.

The very existence of the Euromarket helps curb the power of government bureaucrats in Japan, West Germany, the U.S., and other countries. These bureaucrats are increasingly aware that if they impose more burdensome regulations, borrowers as well as lenders will simply conduct their business with someone else. Funds can be transferred anywhere in the world electronically within seconds.

The Euromarket is much bigger than the most powerful financial firms, and leadership in the market is precarious. British firms were surpassed by U.S. firms during the 1970s and although Japanese firms are the high-fliers now, everyone has trimmed operations following the October 1987 stock crash and after a volatile period in certain Euromarket sectors. As the European Community deregulates financial markets, the resulting mergers are creating new financial powerhouses.

Square Mile of Money

"Tokyo is supplying the funds," says Koichi Kimura, managing director responsible for Daiwa's international operations. "New York is supplying the product. London is where a lot of deals get done."

According to Securities Data Company, New York, over $180 billion of bonds were issued in the London-based Euromarket during 1986.

The "Euromarket" includes any dealings where currencies are traded outside their country of origin—yen in Europe, dollars in Japan, and so on. Institutions, particularly Japanese, buy about 60 percent of the Eurobonds issued. The balance go to individual investors.

Principal borrowers include governments and international agencies like the World Bank. When interest rates are cheaper on the Euromarket than in the United States, U.S. corporate treasurers flock to London, borrowing from Japanese and other lenders. Internationally known names like American Express, RCA, Mobil, Sears, AT & T, Atlantic Richfield, McDonnell Douglas, Burroughs, GTE, Campbell Soup, Hertz Corp., Du Pont, Aetna Life & Casualty, and General Motors Acceptance Corporation are eager borrowers on the Euromarket. At times, the market can absorb bond issues in the $200-million to $750-million range.

Japanese borrowers use the Euromarket, too. Among Japanese financiers, there's a new buzzword: *kudoka*. It's commonly used to mean the "hollowing out" of Japan's industrial capacity as companies transfer production offshore, where costs are lower. Increasingly, kudoka refers to Japanese companies that seek lower-cost funds on the Euromarket rather than in Japan, thereby undercutting the domestic Japanese capital market. More than half the funds raised by Japanese companies come from overseas, chiefly the Euromarket. Usually the lenders are Japanese.

The square-mile City of London is the primary center of the Euromarket, handling three-quarters of Euromarket stock and bond issues. It's an international center, having little to do with Britain's domestic economy—a dramatic contrast with New York and Tokyo, where domestic markets are vitally important. The City of London contributes more to Britain's gross national product than all its oil in the North Sea.

London thrives as a financial center because traditionally foreign banks and securities firms are permitted to operate here with little interference from the Bank of England. For foreign banks, there are no reserve requirements that improve the safety of a bank but reduce profits. Moreover, they're free to underwrite securities, even though banks can't do this in Japan or the United States. Securities are traded for freely negotiated commissions rather than for fixed rates still prevailing in Japan and other countries. Because of the wide-open competition, financing costs are about a third lower than in the United States.

London offers a tremendous concentration of financial expertise. Japanese, American, British, German, and Swiss securities firms and banks compete for business. The City is convenient for communication with other financial centers—five hours ahead of New York and eight hours behind Tokyo.

Rapid growth of the Euromarkets has stretched London's formidable resources to the limits. Financial services firms are expanding so fast that they're having a hard time finding enough people. Compensation has jumped 30 percent to 50 percent annually in recent years. A bond trader, for instance, may get $150,000 a year plus bonus.

Adequate office space is scarce, and rents have soared. A decade ago, they were as high as £20 per square foot. Now they're up to £60—decidedly more than in Paris or New York. Now in the City of London and beyond, there's a tremendous building boom.

League Table Rivalry

Any securities firm or bank with global ambitions must stake out a position in London. In 1980, 335 securities dealers were licensed by London's Department of Trade and Industry. Forty were Japanese. By 1987, 691 securities dealers were licensed, of which fifty-eight were Japanese.

The major financial firms compete fiercely for rank on the so-called league tables. These record the volume of Eurobond offerings each firm has lead-managed. Having gained a mandate to lead-manage an issue for a borrower, a firm negotiates the deal, sets up the syndicate of financial firms that will distribute the bonds, and collects the biggest fee.

Until recently, the league tables were dominated by old-line American and European firms. Credit Suisse First Boston was at the top for years. In 1984, only one of the top ten lead-managers was Japanese. Altogether, Japanese firms generated under 5 percent of total new issue volume.

But as the U.S. dollar declined, dollar-denominated securities became less appealing for investors. Firms with roots in non-U.S. currencies gained the upper hand, because they had established relationships with lenders and borrowers. The mighty Deutsche Bank profited, as did the French firm Paribas.

The biggest gainers were the Japanese. In 1987, five of the top ten lead-managers were Japanese. Total new issue volume for Japanese firms skyrocketed to 22 percent.

Nomura tripled the pretax profits of their London-based European operation to £54 million—so much for criticism from competitors that they buy market share with money-losing deals. In 1986, Nomura jumped into second place on the league tables, and it reached the number-one spot the following year. Nomura's rival Daiwa Securities moved from thirteenth place in 1985 to fifth place and then second in 1987.

Well-known American firms are having a hard time keeping up. Morgan Stanley, for instance, almost doubled its worldwide earnings in 1986, but it remained in sixth place. Merrill Lynch slumped from second place to ninth. Salomon Brothers slipped a notch and lost money. Morgan Guaranty Trust dropped three places. They reported losses, too. Other U.S. merchant banks have become minor players, though Citicorp still makes markets in Eurocommercial paper. Kidder, Peabody virtually abandoned efforts to make the league tables, preferring to trade Eurobonds in the secondary market after they're issued.

Understandably, many competitors see the Japanese as a threat. "My concern is that the Japanese will use their balance sheets in Tokyo to buy firms in New York and London, and they'll become so big we can't compete with them," laments Archibald Cox, Jr., managing director of Morgan Stanley's London office.

But many observers express a broader perspective. "There's a notion the Japanese are going to take over the City," says Andrew Large, managing director of London-based Swiss Bank Corporation International. "That's a crude distortion of what is basically a normal, competitive situation."

Beginnings of the Euromarket

For more than three centuries, London has served as a nerve center of global finance. Many British financial institutions like the Bank of England and Lloyd's of London, born in London coffeehouses, became financial arbiters of the British Empire. The British pound sterling— at one time redeemable for a pound of silver—was the key currency of international trade.

The Euromarket as we know it began in the 1950s. But since World War II, British Labor governments pursued inflation and nationalization, which triggered a relentless decline of the pound. An increasing volume of business was conducted in dollars. Then, in 1967, the British government limited use of the pound among non-Commonwealth countries.

The dollar emerged as the dominant currency. During this, the Cold War era, Russia and other communist governments needed dollars to finance their imports, but they feared that balances held in the U.S. might be blocked by Washington. So they kept their dollar accounts in London and elsewhere.

It was a sleepy banking business. "You would have drawn a fair number of glazed looks in the City if you mentioned Eurodollars back then," recalls Rodney Leach, who helped pioneer the Euromarket when he was at N.M. Rothschild. Now he's a director of Matheson & Co.

Companies didn't issue bonds, because the British had almost forgotten how to do it. Markets withered after decades of depression, war, and exchange controls. "When we started on the internationalization of the securities markets, there was little experience at raising money," says Rolf Hallberg, senior general manager at Skandinaviska Enskilda Banken and the first chairman of the Association of International Bond Dealers. "We turned to people like Sigmund Warburg and Julius Strauss, who had experience before World War II. We learned a lot from Americans, since they were the most experienced."

Peter Spira, vice chairman of Goldman, Sachs International, recalls the pioneering days at S.G. Warburg: "Sir Sigmund took the view that, since most foreign U.S. dollar bonds were sold in Europe, why not re-create London as the center of the capital markets."

Spira, with his associate Ian Frazier, put together a $15 million

Eurobond issue for the Italian motorway operator Autostrade. Under-written by S.G. Warburg, Banque de Bruxelles, Deutsche Bank, and Rotterdamsche Bank, it was issued June 17, 1963. Though rival merchant bankers claim they did earlier Eurobonds, this is the one credited as the first by *Euromoney*, a leading magazine chronicling the Euromarkets. It helped get the market going.

The Euromarket got a lift during the 1960s, when Washington, attempting to curb U.S. balance-of-payments deficits, imposed a series of controls. The Interest Equalization Tax (1964) and Foreign Credit Restraint Program (1965) penalized Americans who bought foreign securities. As a result, they didn't buy as many, and foreign companies that had borrowed in the U.S. market did their deals in London.

During these early years of the Euromarket, the typical investor was widely caricatured as a Belgian dentist, much as U.S. stockbrokers used to describe safe, boring telephone bonds as going to widows and orphans. Belgium is a small economy where people have thrived as international traders. They're accustomed to investing beyond their borders. Next door is Luxembourg, where bankers still tend to honor the confidentiality of their clients' accounts. So a Belgian dentist, a self-employed professional paid in cash, could buy high-interest bearer Eurobonds, and tax collectors wouldn't be any the wiser. Times have changed, since it became common to pay dental bills with health insurance.

A breakthrough came in 1966, when London banks began offering negotiated, U.S.-dollar, fixed-rate certificates of deposit. These were the first negotiable bank instruments introduced under British law since 1896. Central banks, with their vast resources, were attracted into the Euromarket, because CDs made U.S.-dollar bank financing much easier. Previously, central banks parked their assets in gold, U.S. Treasury bonds, and gilts (as British government bonds are known). Negotiable certificates of deposit prepared the way for dramatic expansion of banks in the Euromarket.

The Foreign Investment Program, formed in 1968, forced U.S. companies to borrow what they needed for overseas operations in overseas financial markets. They, too, flocked to London. In 1968, U.S. companies raised $2 billion in the Euromarket, four times more than the year before.

In 1970, floating-rate notes came along, enabling investors to protect themselves somewhat against inflation losses. These attracted more investors into the market.

When the Organization of Petroleum Exporting Countries hiked oil prices in 1974, the Euromarket slumped. But within a year, when it was evident that most of the petrodollars would be deposited with London firms, the Euromarket took off again.

As it expanded, the traditional British merchant banking firms lost share of market. Only S.G. Warburg remained a significant player. "The big European banks asked themselves why they shouldn't play a more important role, because of their power to place bonds," explains Damien Wigney of Kredietbank SA Luxembourgeoise.

Large institutional investors increased their participation in the Euromarket, but they demanded liquidity. This put a premium on deep-pocket trading firms that could make markets even in difficult times. Enter the major U.S. banks and securities houses.

Meanwhile, France, West Germany, Switzerland, and other countries continued to regulate their financial markets heavily, protecting entrenched interests. But this accelerated the loss of business to London.

Responding to regulations and financial needs in major countries, the Euromarket has developed its own distinctive character. It's mostly for fixed-rate bonds with five- to ten-year terms. The variable-rate markets are erratic. For longer-term funds, generally borrowers must go to the United States or Japan.

"In the U.S. market," explains Peter Ogden, Morgan Stanley International vice president of corporate finance, "investors look only at the yield. But Europeans necessarily look at the currency situation, too."

Japanese Challengers

Osaka-based Daiwa Securities led the dramatic expansion of Japanese firms overseas, particularly into Europe. The practical attitude of Daiwa executives is evident in their unremarkable eight-story headquarters building on the edge of the Kabuto-cho district, central Tokyo. Before you reach the fifth-floor executive offices, you may pass rows of commonplace steel desks on drab open floors. Looking at this no-frills operation, it's easy to understand why Daiwa's profits are about triple those of Merrill Lynch.

But the company does what it must to make a suitable impression on international clients. Daiwa's handsome, urbane, sixty-four-year-old chairman, Yoshitoki Chino, wears English-tailored suits and French shirts. The firm's subsidiary, Daiwa America, occupies plush, wood-paneled offices at Manhattan's World Financial Center, overlooking the Hudson River. "We Japanese," says Chino, "have an obligation to spend money on foreign manufactures."

He urges his people continuously to adapt. When he discovered managers in the New York office had Japanese prints on their walls, he ordered them replaced with American prints. His advice for Americans who really want to be competitive: learn Japanese, as his people learned English.

During his six years as chairman, Chino has pushed for rapid expansion of Daiwa's international operations. He's convinced that the company can't be a world-class firm based on success in the Japanese market alone. Daiwa had about a hundred people abroad when he started, and there are more than five hundred now.

Chino's sophisticated cadre of executives includes Takuro Isoda, fifty-one, chairman of Daiwa America. Isoda has lived outside Japan for nineteen years. Two years after he joined Daiwa, following graduating from Hitosubashi University, he was assigned to Honolulu, where he married Judy Miura, a Japanese-American. Their first son, Kurt, twenty-three, was born in Honolulu and carries two passports. Over the years, Isoda has worked in New York, London, and Frankfurt, as well as Japan.

Daiwa has adapted more to the American market than any other Japanese securities firm. Vice Chairman Paul Aron, sixty-six, who used to manage the Dreyfus Fund's huge investment portfolio, is the highest-ranking American at a Japanese securities firm. Back in the 1960s, he was among the first Americans to recognize Japan's economic potential, channeling tens of millions into Japanese stocks. During recent years, he has played an important role helping American companies raise capital in Japan. "At Daiwa I have real authority," he says. "If I think a certain line of business is too risky, we don't go into it, period. I approve all trading limits for our people. I monitor our daily cash position. I'm one of three people on Daiwa America's board of directors, and we can meet almost any time to make decisions."

Makoto Kasui, fifty, is the aggressive chairman of Daiwa Europe whose mission is to challenge American dominance of the Euromarket business. "This is a game of survival," he says. "If we try a safety-first policy, we'll lose." Kasui looks a little like a sumo wrestler, because, he says, he must dine out all the time with clients and prospective clients.

Though Daiwa has advanced smartly in the Euromarket league tables to second place, from sixth in 1986, intense competition has shaved profit margins. Customers in deregulated markets pay a fraction as much as those in Tokyo, where commissions are fixed at high levels. Only about 15 percent of Daiwa's after-tax income comes from international operations. If related activities are included, like trading U.S. Treasury bonds in Tokyo, the international operations contribute about a quarter of after-tax profits. Daiwa claims these are higher figures than those of any other Japanese firm.

"I don't know how profitable Eurobond underwriting is," says Kasui, "but there's good reason to lead the league tables. Leadership has a powerful impact on Daiwa's reputation. It helps in the second-ary market."

Nonetheless, the pressure is mounting to boost profits. Daiwa's president, Sadakane Doi, was a salesman who came up through the ranks of domestic operations, where profits are protected by regulations. Reportedly, he wants to deploy resources from international back to domestic, so total profits will be higher. There are ongoing backstage power struggles at Japanese securities firms, so the long-term outlook may be uncertain. For now, anyway, Daiwa is a shooting star in the Euromarkets.

Entry in the Euromarket

Daiwa was started in 1902 by a man named Fujimoto Kiyobe. His fledgling firm, Fujimoto Billbroker, was the first dealer facilitating transactions among banks. It handled both government and corporate bonds. By 1924, it established a New York-based subsidiary to serve Japanese clients.

The firm merged with Japan Trust Bank and Matsunaga Yoshi-kawa Shoken in 1943, becoming one of the Big Four Japanese securities firms. The new name, Daiwa, means "growth with harmony."

Somehow, it survived the virtual destruction of Japanese securities markets during World War II. It expanded through the 1950s, acquiring the most sophisticated computer system of any Japanese securities firm. By the 1960s, Daiwa was doing good business in New York, Los Angeles, and London. The Dreyfus Fund became the first major U.S. institutional investor to buy Japanese stocks on a large scale, and the transactions, handled through Daiwa, helped establish Daiwa in the United States.

By 1970, Daiwa's top executives noted that their clients, major Japanese companies, were being approached by international firms, particularly the British merchant banks. These firms handled the underwriting of bond issues. They got the big fees.

A Japanese securities firm might be invited to comanage a financing, but that didn't mean much. Though the comanager got copies of all the documents, the firm wasn't involved in putting together the deal. Daiwa executives realized that until they lead-managed an international deal, they would never learn how to do it. They decided the time had come to expand abroad and establish a reputation among non-Japanese firms. No Japanese securities firm had raised funds abroad.

Who could Daiwa get as issuer? The company lacked contacts and experience. They had few people who could even handle English, the language of international finance. It didn't make sense to start in the United States, since major firms were entrenched there. The London-based European market was in its infancy, so that seemed the logical place to try selling bonds.

They decided to look for issuers close to home. During the late 1960s, Bank of America reportedly had tried to develop a market for short-term debt instruments in Hong Kong, but nothing happened. The Hong Kong government didn't issue any bonds, and there wasn't much support from local companies.

Bank of America had better luck in Singapore. Lee Kuan Yew, the strongman of that island country, was eager to help diversify the economy. Singapore had broken away from Malaysia a half-dozen years earlier, and no one was sure how it was going to survive. It didn't have any natural resources. There were about 2 million hardworking people and a harbor. Assisted by Bank of America, Singapore began a short-term capital market.

"In 1970, Toshio Karigane and I traveled to Hong Kong, Thailand, and Singapore looking for opportunities," recalls Yukio Hosoi, sixty-one, who headed Daiwa's international operations. He's a compact, intense man who has never lived outside Japan. The son of a liquor distributor, he graduated from Tokyo University. Though he wanted to become a government finance officer, he decided to join Daiwa, because it offered ¥700 a month plus a quarterly bonus, and the government paid only ¥4,000 a year.

"The most receptive person we encountered," Hosoi continues "was Singapore finance minister Goh Kensui. I saw him without introduction; he was very kind. It seemed we were the first Japanese investment bankers to call on him.

"We suggested that they develop a Singapore market for long-term bonds, and they were enthusiastic. They were concerned, though, because Daiwa had never lead-managed an international bond issue. They were reassured that the firm did a lot of securities business in Japan and had representative offices in New York and London. So they gave Daiwa the mandate to underwrite a $10 million bond issue for the Singapore Development Bank. We set up a bond issuance facility which would help protect prospective bond buyers against adverse changes in the Singapore tax laws."

The Singapore government insisted on an 8.5 percent interest rate, about the same as internationally known, quality bonds. The government didn't want to offer a premium interest rate and have the issue viewed as a junk bond. But without a premium, the bonds were hard to sell, because Singapore was a place few investors knew much about.

Masanobu Nakamura, then the thirty-four-year-old chief representative in Daiwa's London office, was called to help put together the deal. "The first challenge was the documents, which were written in English," he says. "English is always a difficulty.

"We had never done anything like this before," he continues, "so we approached Dallas Bernard, an investment banker with Morgan Grenfell, an old, established London firm. He was a tall, slim, quiet, decisive man who never raised his voice. They were knowledgeable about Singapore, since it used to be a British colony. Mr. Hosoi took charge of negotiations.

"We needed Morgan Grenfell's help, but we were concerned about losing control of the deal. We were very poor at English. We didn't know the business. So it was hard to take the initiative. The Morgan Grenfell people were very professional. They spoke the Queen's English, and they had a good relationship with people in the Singapore government. One of my functions was to maintain the stance that we were the lead manager. We repeated to the Morgan Grenfell people that it was our deal. It was very difficult.

"We got a lot of help from Kunio Hamada, a Tokyo attorney. He was educated in the United States, so he spoke American English. Each evening, after a day's negotiations were through, we'd talk in our hotel. He criticized the way we handled things and suggested what I should do next.

" 'Don't be so timid!' he'd say. 'You are a lead-manager! You should lead the meeting! You should have a particular opinion! You should insist! Behave like a lead-manager!'

"I forced myself to pretend I knew what I was doing. Somehow we got through the negotiations okay, and the next step was to sell the bonds in Europe.

"I asked Tokyo how to do it, but they didn't have any idea. They didn't know who might be interested in bonds from Singapore. Currency controls limited the funds which Japanese companies could send abroad, so there wasn't much the home office could do to help. Our London office consisted of four people, including myself.

"Actually, I doubt that any of the big merchant banks knew much about selling Singapore bonds, either. If it were easy, they would have done it already.

"Switzerland was a famous money center, so I decided they would be my test market. Just as I did selling bonds in Tokyo, I visited banks one by one in Zurich, Basel, and Geneva. I told each person that Daiwa was new, but maybe we'd get stronger, because the Japanese economy was growing stronger. I urged them to look ahead ten years. Buy a few bonds as a contribution to a new friend.

"Later, I sold Singapore bonds in Britain, West Germany, and Italy. I remember placing some in the Middle East, especially Kuwait. I never sold anything in France. The prime customers were banks.

"Most bankers weren't interested, as you might expect, but occasionally someone would buy. I sold $50,000 of bonds here, $100,000 there. Gradually, I accumulated a little experience.

"I remember the Christmas season, 1971, and all the staff was away. I was by myself in the office, struggling with the telex machine, sending confirmations to Tokyo and Singapore. I was nearly crying, because it was frustrating and I was alone. But finally we sold all those bonds."

Life of a Japanese "Business Soldier"

Daiwa's Nakamura, now fifty-one, defies the conventional notion that Japanese are conformists. He's outspoken about what it's like to be a Japanese "salaryman" doing business overseas.

He was raised in Utsunomiya, a town about sixty miles north of Tokyo. His father, Chikahira, had various jobs with the government-run postal service. Two of his brothers were killed during World War II. "We had no medical supplies," he recalls, "so it was easy to die."

Like many Japanese, he experienced competition early on. "From about age five, it starts," he continues. "There's a saying that if you sleep six hours, you'll fail. No chance. Sleep five hours, okay.

"There was very little time for play. Always very strong pressure until university entrance. When you enter university, it is as if spring has arrived, and the cherry blossoms are beautiful. We're mindful that, upon graduation, the pressure will begin again.

"A college major isn't particularly important, because Japanese university students seldom study that hard. We consider university life a chance to make friends. In several courses, I never attended a class. I met my professor for the first time at the final examination. Although this would be unusual in American universities, it's commonplace in Japan."

In 1959, Nakamura graduated from Hitosubashi University, a respected institution west of Tokyo that sends an impressive number of graduates to the top ranks of business. "Companies ask professors to recommend students, so when we see our professor for advice about a job, he may direct us to a suitable company," Nakamura explains. "Often that's where we go.

"Many Japanese students don't care what company they join. Students tend to feel that the big established companies are pretty much the same as far as opportunities and salaries are concerned. Initially, we didn't care much what company we joined, if we could eat and survive everyday.

"I got a telegram that I was welcomed at Daiwa. Things have worked out very well," he says, "but I can't say I really knew what I was getting into. I wasn't familiar with the other major securities firms like Nomura or Yamaichi which was the biggest back then.

"When I got into the securities business, it wasn't very respectable. Securities were for small chaps who speculated. Bankers were the ones who got respect. Companies depended on banks to provide almost all their funds.

"When you graduate from university, you may think you're important, but the big companies overwhelm you with tasks and physically exhaust you. There is great pressure.

"We are totally dedicated to doing a quality job and gaining market share. We work until ten, eleven at night and more, because it's a struggle. There is always more to do.

"What the companies do is make soldiers. This is why we have done so well against many other competitors. We encounter businesspeople, and soldiers are never defeated in competition with businesspeople. It was a John Wayne kind of thing."

Early in his career at Daiwa, Nakamura sold stocks door to door. He made a calling card with his picture on it, and on the back he wrote a couple stocks that he recommended. He noted the price. "In those days," he recalls, "almost all the stocks were going up. So a couple weeks after my initial call, I went back and asked people to check the prices on my card. I noted how much money they lost by not investing. It was an effective technique."

Nakamura developed systematic training for Daiwa's salespeople. He traveled around the country, calling on sales managers, looking for ways they could get more out of their people.

He joined the foreign department when it was headed by Yukio Hosoi. "At the time," Nakamura recalls, "the foreign department was a decoration, like a flower on your suit. It was nice to have international offices, but they didn't make any money. You'd send telexes, even though you had little business to report.

"Hosoi had ambitious ideas. He recognized that the Japanese economy was growing, international finance was changing, and we were minor players compared to the mighty investment banking houses in London and on Wall Street. He reminded his people of their previous mistakes, as he pushed them to do better. Within Daiwa, he promoted the growing importance of international finance.

During the mid-1970s, Nakamura was assigned to Daiwa's Paris office. "It's very important as a tourist office"—he laughs—"taking Japanese clients around to see the sights. I liked Paris. France is a charming country—good food, nice wines, beautiful women. Sometimes, we did some business. The French gave us a hard time, though. They joked that we were never eating properly.

"All this traveling has forced me to learn a number of languages—English, French, German, Italian, and Mandarin Chinese. I'm confident that, within two years, I can learn any language. We have to do it, because no one else speaks Japanese. When we do business abroad, we have to learn the language and ways of other people. You Americans seldom bother, because almost everywhere you see people struggling to learn your language."

He laughs at how easily people misunderstand one another. "When I was in London," he says, "I was asked by neighbors if Japanese wives aren't allowed to go outside. This turned out to be because my wife never appeared in our garden. Well, we had three young daughters, Madoka, Tsuki, and Midori. One got the mumps. As she recovered, the second one got the mumps, then the third. My wife did take a healthy child into the garden, but the sick ones complained so much that she decided to keep them inside until all recovered.

"Japanese misunderstand things, too. I remember a group of Japanese executives visited London on a November fifth, and they commented that Britain was finished as a country. Look at all the beggars! When I realized what they were talking about, I laughed: it was Guy Fawkes Day, commemorating a 1605 plot by disgruntled Catholics to blow up the Parliament, protesting their treatment under King James I. People take the day off, burn effigies of Guy Fawkes, and so on."

Nakamura is proud of what he has accomplished, but he misses the little pleasures that he sees Americans enjoying. "A Japanese manager generally has a poor-quality life," he says. "Relentless competition leaves you a harassed, overworked business soldier. You have practically no time for any family life or holidays. There's hardly any life outside the company's objectives, serving customers.

"Believe it or not, some Japanese managers engage in animated discussions about the social and personal problems which might result from too much free time. When faced with a little free time, Japanese managers suffer from the dread of the unknown.

"Japan may be the only country where officially granted holidays aren't used up by employees. Social pressures are such that it's virtually impossible to take holidays freely. It's not considered good form to enjoy oneself while others cannot. While, in principle, this ethic may have a lot of merit, it has some bad effects, too. Private pleasures, enjoyed by yourself or with your family, have little standing in Japanese society.

"Generally, job descriptions are lacking, and each worker has vague responsibilities. The result is the cultivation of job responsibility within a group. An individual has nothing to complete by himself. As long as the task assigned to the group remains incomplete, you can't leave. You always work late.

"The family, sometimes with a number of relatives, waits sadly night after night, hoping to share some time together. For the husband and wife, these occasions are important to keep a relationship alive and make the marriage meaningful. But this expectation is rarely fulfilled in the home of a Japanese manager. Divorce is more common, especially after children are grown up. Considering how hard a divorced woman's life can be in Japan, the figures are poignant testimony to barren marriages.

"I, too, was lost from home. For more than two years, I was involved with the company union. In addition to working late every night for the company, I'd spend Saturdays and Sundays with the union, talking about what we wanted—endless discussions about salaries, working conditions, everything. As a result, two children were born, and I wasn't there. Now my wife is in Japan seeing the children through college, and I am doing what the company has assigned to me, operating a trust bank in New Jersey. This is the plight of many international people."

"I have enjoyed my career," he says. "Always doing new things. I'm fortunate to have visited many countries and made many friends around the world."

Arrival of Euroyen

During the late 1970s, Japan was recovering from the oil shock that had throttled economic expansion and financial markets. Japanese financial executives were more confident about their ability to expand internationally. But currency controls limited what they could do. Their primary asset was established relationships with Japanese investors and borrowers, but neither were free to conduct business abroad.

These executives spent endless hours with Ministry of Finance officials, arguing that it was time to liberalize the yen. Officials resisted, because they feared that Japanese borrowers would rush into the Euromarkets. At the time, it was estimated that a Euroyen offering—any yen issue outside Japan—could be done for about a hundred basis points less interest than could a domestic Japanese offering. Officials needed a healthy bond market to absorb all the government bonds being issued to finance their deficits.

Moreover, officials worried that if they lost control of the yen, it would become more expensive. It was around three hundred per dollar, and a strengthening would make Japanese exporters less competitive on world markets.

Daiwa's Yukio Hosoi and Yutaka Onda were among those visiting the Ministry of Finance frequently. "As a first step, we encouraged liberalization of the domestic market," Onda explains. "That meant samurais—yen bonds issued in Japan by foreign borrowers.

"You can't get very far talking generalities, so we had to present the Ministry of Finance with a specific borrower interested in borrowing yen. The most appealing would be an unquestionably strong credit, like an international organization. After checking around, we learned that the European Investment Bank would be interested in borrowing about ¥10 billion for its annual lending programs to various European countries. They diversify their funding sources, and the Japanese market is one they wanted to tap.

"If we were just asking the Ministry of Finance to help us, they never would have cooperated," Onda continues. "We had to help them. Mr. Hosoi was especially helpful in answering questions about the likely impact of a new policy the officials were considering. They had to have confidence that we were offering a meaningful analysis, not just a pitch for our company."

Their patience was rewarded, for in 1977 the Ministry of Finance approved the first Euroyen bond. It would be for the European Investment Bank, lead-managed by Daiwa Securities. "That deal took six months to negotiate," recalls Koichi Kimura, the firm's managing director for international business. "I got a Euroyen ulcer."

Seven years later, the Ministry of Finance established standards for corporations that wished to issue Euroyen bonds. They had to have at least a single-A crediting and meet other tests of financial strength. About three hundred corporations met the requirements.

A Euroyen offering had many compelling advantages over bonds issued in Japan for companies that needed to borrow yen. The offering could go to market in about a week after submission of what's called a mandate letter to the Ministry of Finance, describing the participants and terms. A samurai bond takes seventy to ninety days, increasing the risk that market conditions may become less favorable. By tradition, a samurai issuer cannot receive better terms than the Japanese government does for its own bonds. Extensive documentation must be prepared and translated into Japanese before a samurai bond can be issued, but only the mandate letter is required for a Euroyen bond. While a non-Japanese financial firm could lead-manage a Euroyen issue, samurais must continue to be lead-managed by Japanese firms. All this means that a Euroyen offering saves about thirty basis points over a comparable bond issued in Japan.

In December 1984, Daiwa became the first Japanese firm to lead-manage a Euroyen bond for a corporation. They signed a ¥12.5 billion deal with Sears at 2 A.M., to beat Nomura's closing with Dow Chemical that same day.

Euroyen bonds appeal to Japanese investors who want higher returns than those available in Japan but don't want the foreign exchange risk of, say, a dollar bond. Since interest rates needed to attract Japanese investors tend to be lower than prevailing rates in the United States, Euroyen bonds also offered U.S. corporations an opportunity to cut their financing costs.

Few U.S. corporations wanted yen, since the United States isn't an aggressive exporter. So companies would enter into a currency swap, getting the dollars they needed, while limiting the risk that the yen will be more expensive, when they have to repay the principal.

Briefly, in a currency swap, one party agrees to exchange a principal amount of currency with another party. They also exchange interest payments. Then, at an agreed-on future date, they exchange the principal amounts back into their original currencies. The party with the weaker currency will pay a fee to the party with the stronger currency, based on the market situation when the swap was made.

When the Canadian government wanted to boost its reserves of U.S. dollars, it didn't do the obvious thing—borrow dollars. It issued ¥80 billion of bonds, then swapped these into $409 million. Canada got the dollar funds it needed for less than it would have cost borrowing directly. Nomura handled the underwriting.

With most institutions interested in swapping yen for their domestic currency, the main question is the availability of swap counter-parties. Usually, these are Japanese exporters with dollar receivables that must be converted into yen. Depending on market conditions, borrowing yen from Japanese lenders and swapping into dollars will cut total costs thirty to forty basis points.

In many cases, a borrower will do an interest rate swap as well as a currency swap. Take a borrower who can get fixed-rate funds cheaply but would be better off with floating-rate funds. This borrower could exchange its interest *payments*—not the principal—with a borrower in the opposite situation, preferring fixed-rate funds but able to borrow floating-rate funds more cheaply.

During the past three years, swaps became crucial for the Euromarkets, figuring in about 80 percent of the transactions. Usually swaps are arranged by banks. The field can be so complex that swap specialists earn $150,000 a year, plus bonuses.

But Euroyen bonds didn't really take off until the U.S. dollar headed south, and investors fled for stronger currencies like the yen. Liberalization by the Ministry of Finance gave the Euroyen market an additional kick. In May 1986, the Japanese Ministry of Finance announced it would allow non-Japanese banks to issue Euroyen bonds, enabling them to tap the huge market of low-cost yen funds. By borrowing yen and swapping into dollars, U.S. banks would save an estimated twenty-five to forty basis points over what money would cost in the U.S. market. The exact saving varies with a bank's financial strength and market conditions. By lowering their cost of funds, U.S. and other banks would be more competitive.

Euroyen bonds had emerged as a major factor in the European capital markets. They accounted for 21 percent of bond issues, more than any other currency except the U.S. dollar. The mighty deutsche mark ranked number three in the Euroderby.

Heaven and Hell

Competition inspires feverish innovation. A lot of it is intended to take advantage of changing relationships among various markets. Much financial innovation amounts to little more than reshuffling the bells and whistles on a basic bond offering. But periodically, an innovation comes along that has a significant impact. The Japanese, supposedly numbed by an educational system that stresses conformity and rote memorization, emerged as innovative competitors in the deregulated Euromarkets.

This was the case with dual-currency bonds in 1982. The idea, first used in the Swiss market, was to repay principal in a borrower's currency but make interest payments in the lender's currency.

Japanese securities firms adapted the idea with Japanese institutional investors in mind. The life insurance companies, for instance, compete with each other by offering better payouts to policyholders. Japanese law permits them to pay only from current income, not capital gains. They had a lot of 8 percent bonds maturing and wanted to reinvest at that rate, but the Japanese bond market was yielding about 6.5 percent. Because the dual-currency bonds are more risky than plain vanilla bonds, borrowers like Japanese manufacturers had to offer higher interest—8 percent—to attract Japanese investors. The issue was in yen, so the lenders didn't incur a foreign exchange risk. They were willing to assume the risk that a declining dollar would reduce the value of their principal, since they couldn't pay policyholders out from that anyway.

The securities firms used dual-currency bonds to establish relationships with prestigious multinational corporations. Nikko Securities, for instance, managed a dual-currency yen bond for Westinghouse, borrowing ¥12 billion and swapping yen into dollars. Westinghouse used forward contracts to lock in the future exchange dollar/yen exchange rate, so a rising yen wouldn't mean higher payments.

The deal saved Westinghouse fifty to ninety basis points over conventional domestic or Eurobond issues. By choosing an issue targeted at Japanese investors, Westinghouse expanded the market for its securities. There is a major drawback: because it's complex, the security is less liquid than simpler, more standard, widely understood securities. For this reason, it's harder to determine the current value of a dual-currency bond.

Japanese securities firms have had considerable success with warrants, which are options, attached to a bond, giving investors the right to buy related securities. Typically, a debt warrant applies to more of the borrower's bonds. An equity warrant applies to shares of the issuing company. Borrowers offer warrants to lower their borrowing costs. A straight debt warrant may save fifty to a hundred basis points. Nippon Oil issued a 4-percent bond with an equity warrant, considered equivalent to an 8-percent coupon on a plain vanilla bond. Equity warrants offer investors a less risky way to play in the wild Tokyo stock market.

Nomura Securities introduced what came to be known as "heaven and hell" bonds, starting with a $50-million, 10.75-percent issue for IBM Credit Corporation. These are indexed currency option notes. Like all bonds, they're issued at par, or $1,000 face amount. If, at maturity, the yen/dollar rate is 169, the bonds are redeemed at par. A weaker yen—with more yen per dollar—and the bonds would be redeemed above par. A stronger yen would mean investors get less principal.

Star Trek Bonds

Because of intense competition during the mid-1980s, many Euromarket deals were priced fifty to a hundred basis points below what they'd cost in the United States. IBM, Kodak, John Deere, Nabisco, Mobil, and other American companies rushed to take advantage of the Euromarket situation. Typical case: a $300-million issue for Rockwell, priced to the company at forty basis points below U.S. government guaranteed securities and seventy basis points below what comparable corporate issues yielded in the U.S.

While these low rates attracted borrowers, they weren't enough to compete for investors' funds, and some $5 billion of unsold securities accumulated in dealers' inventories. While the bonds earned interest, there was always a risk that interest rates would rise, sending prices tumbling. The dealers would face huge losses. "It's a mess," reported Hans Rudloff, deputy chairman of Credit Suisse First Boston, the leading Euromarket underwriter. He asserted that supply outstripped demand by five to one. Traders referred to the low-yield issues as "Star Trek" bonds, because "they were priced where no man dared to go."

Some Western bankers complained to the Ministry of Finance about kamikaze Japanese bankers and their hara-kiri bonds, allegedly issued below cost to gain market share, but officials simply replied that Western firms practiced price-cutting, too.

Bank Competitors

Japanese banks have lagged behind the securities firms in the Euro-market, but some are doing well. The most successful is the triple-A-rated Industrial Bank of Japan, headquartered in an angular beige marble downtown Tokyo building. It reports $193 billion of assets, with a market value about seven times greater than Citibank, and it's the only Japanese commercial bank among the top ten Euromarket lead-managers.

It's Japan's most blue chip bank, the equivalent of Morgan Guaranty Trust in the United States. Since it began in 1902 as a government-owned institution to finance heavy industry, and went private in 1948, the Industrial Bank of Japan has become perhaps the best-connected Japanese bank. Clients include 90 percent of the top two hundred Japanese companies. Though it isn't linked to any of the major industrial groupings, it does business with them all—Mitsubishi, Mitsui, Sumitomo, Fuyo, Sanwa, and DKB. It's the main bank for every regional public utility.

These connections put the Industrial Bank of Japan in a good position to cultivate clients for Euromarket offerings. Moreover, notes the deliberate, circumspect, Harvard-educated president Kaneo Naka-mura, the bank has extensive underwriting experience. "Before Japan adopted Article 65 of the securities law in 1947, barring commercial banks from the securities business," he explains in his mild British accent, "the Industrial Bank of Japan underwrote about 80 percent of Japanese corporate bond issues. Banks are still permitted to under-write Japanese government bonds and government-guaranteed bonds, and the Industrial Bank of Japan has 99 percent of these markets."

The bank has plenty of firsthand experience with Japanese institutional investors. "We're the largest issuer of securities in Japan, after the government," adds tall, genial managing director Hideo Ishihara, who heads the bank's international department. "Rather than taking deposits, we fund our operations by issuing debentures. They're bought by institutional investors, local banks, mutual savings banks, and credit unions, as well as individuals."

Japanese securities firms are wary of competition from the banks. Nomura president Yoshihisa Tabuchi warns that "Japanese commercial banks are not only providers of financial services but also major shareholders of very many companies. This could translate into a monopolistic situation if they were allowed to handle securities as well."

On the contrary, counters Ishihara. "It's the big securities firms that are using regulations to help protect their entrenched position and enforce high commission rates gouging customers." Ishihara notes that his bank faces some disadvantages compared to Nomura. "We'll never try to compete with Nomura's retail network reaching individual investors, but we'll provide good service for institutional clients in Japan, Europe, and the United States."

Ishihara, fifty-eight, became interested in Western culture while a student at Tokyo University. He headed the English Speaking Society. "I'm fascinated by beautiful English sentences," he says. "I'm an avid reader of books by many authors. Thriller writer Frederick Forsythe is a current favorite—not so much the story, but the precise style of writing."

After graduation in 1952, he joined the Industrial Bank of Japan because of its central role in financing reconstruction. The bank gives its people thorough training, and Ishihara was sent as a Fulbright Scholar to Duke University. He studied economics there for a year, then worked four months in Chemical Bank's international business department. At the time, Chemical Bank was among the most active banks in cultivating Japanese business relationships.

A decade later, Ishihara became involved with the bank's efforts to expand abroad. In 1962, he helped open a representative office in West Germany. Three years later, he was in London, helping to open a representative office there.

But because the bank had such a commanding position in the domestic Japanese market, it had less incentive to develop its overseas operations. Its very advantages handicapped the bank against more highly motivated competitors. No president of the bank had ever lived abroad. Top executives resisted the trend toward deregulation and securitization, believing the market wouldn't allocate scarce capital as well as a consortium of bankers did. In 1971, the Industrial Bank of Japan had only four international offices.

The pace quickened during the 1970s as the bank's industrial borrowers stopped growing and deregulation brought more intense competition. Ishihara returned to West Germany in 1972, heading that office. He established important links to the powerful Deutsche Bank. By 1976, he was back in London, running that office. He helped create IBJ International to build up the bank's Euromarket business.

Three years later, amidst the second oil crisis, Ishihara returned to Japan so he could run the bank's project finance group. He was involved with financing coal mines in China, uranium mines in Australia, and iron mines in Brazil. When Nissan wanted to build a $575-million auto-manufacturing plant in Smyrna, Tennessee, the Industrial Bank of Japan participated in the deal.

Ishihara and his wife Keiko have adapted enthusiastically to life in many countries. Their children have thrived, too. Their son Atsuo, twenty-seven, works for the Japanese trading company C. Itoh and is attending Harvard Business School. Their daughter Miki, twenty, is studying art at Sophia University after a year's exchange program in Pennsylvania.

The strong yen has battered the bank's traditional borrowers in coal, steel, shipping, and other industries, providing powerful incentives for the bank to accelerate its efforts abroad. The biggest casualty was Japan Line, Ltd. that resulted in a $475 million write-off in the fiscal year ending March 1987. The bank had to step in and rescue that company. "We can't depend only on established relations with our customers," Ishihara says. "We must come up with better deals."

Now the Industrial Bank of Japan has thirty-three offices abroad. It's in all the major money centers, as well as secondary markets like Bahrain, Bangkok, Guangzhou, Jakarta, Kuala Lumpur, Madrid, Mexico City, Panama, Paris, and Sydney.

During 1986, the bank lead-managed ¥108 billion worth of Eurobonds, up from ¥86 billion the year before. The market boomed, and the bank did almost that much volume during the first six months of 1987. The bank lead-managed Euromarket underwritings for American companies such as Anheuser-Busch, Eastman Kodak, Emerson Electric, Ford Motor Credit Corporation, and Morgan Stanley. International business contributes 25 percent of the bank's gross profit, compared with 15 to 20 percent at most other Japanese banks.

At a recent talk before the Tokyo University alumni club, Ishihara advised people to prepare for change. "The economy, your company, and career will become very different as times goes on. Just as in my case, where I joined the bank because of its domestic business, and I ended up spending years away from home. You never know where markets will lead you."

Money Speaks

The major American and European financial firms still have the advantage of capital markets experience and established relationships with borrowers. But inevitably the advantage passes to those with the money.

For the last few years, on Euroyen issues destined for the Tokyo market—so-called sushi bonds—British and American firms performed only nominal management functions. They didn't take any securities into their portfolios, as lead-managers normally do, because they didn't have a market for yen securities. The Japanese firms actually assumed the entire risk of placing such securities. But their names appeared on the public announcements only as comanagers.

"Firms like Credit Suisse First Boston got used to twisting our arm," says an investment banker with one Japanese firm. "They offered us comanagement on the condition that we buy a few million dollars' worth of bonds they couldn't get off their books."

A Japanese bond trader complains: "Whenever a Japanese house calls to buy, the price goes up. But if a Japanese house calls to sell, a lower price is quoted. Japanese houses are always treated like a stampeding herd."

By 1986, the Japanese demanded that they be named lead-managers if they were to assume the risks of placing an issue. Money was speaking. Now Japanese investment bankers lead-manage three-quarters of sushi bonds.

They owe their success to fire-breathers like Elwyn Wong, a dapper, thirty-year-old, Hong Kong-born, Cambridge-educated Chinese. After earning an M.B.A. at Columbia University, he worked for Banker's Trust trading U.S. Treasury bonds. "I became bored," he recalls. "You can have green hair, wear no clothes, and make $1 million a month, but it wasn't satisfying for me. I decided that while I could be a triple-B trader, I'd never be an A trader. I quit and went to Hong Kong.

"In 1982, I joined the British merchant banking firm S.G. Warburg, where I helped raise money for troubled companies and liquidate the ones which were beyond hope. A lot of shipping companies especially were hard hit by falling commodity prices. It was a mess."

Two years later, Wong met a stocky, opinionated Japanese maverick named Jeff Tanaka, who was involved with the Euroyen market. As a youngster, he was eager to see the world, so after World War II, his father gave him $400 and a steamship ticket for America. He decided this is where he wanted to be. After graduating from a small U.S. college, Tanaka worked for several years at an insurance company. Then he discovered the adventure of the securities business.

In 1973, he joined the New York office of Daiwa, the most internationally-minded Japanese securities firm. His outgoing personality helped him win assignments from American companies to raise Japanese capital. He has helped introduce many companies like Sears, Philip Morris, and Eastman Kodak to the Japanese market via investor presentations and Tokyo Stock Exchange listings. He was primarily responsible for arranging the first Euroyen offering by an American company, Sears. He has helped American companies raise funds in the Eurodollar, samurai and shogun markets. Presently, he's executive vice president for Daiwa's North American operations.

"As for myself," says Wong, "I couldn't expect a top-bracket firm to hire me, because they'd ask about my clients. All my Hong Kong clients were close to bankruptcy, if they hadn't actually gone under. Jeff Tanaka figured we could make money together, so I joined Daiwa.

"In this business, you must be willing to be beaten to a pulp. You call on prospective borrowers a dozen, twenty times, and always rejection. Endless reasons why a deal never happens. You can't break through entrenched relationships. When you develop a good idea, someone else gets a similar idea and beats you to market. But you've got to keep going on. Then one day, the sun and the moon and the stars are in position, and it happens. You make a deal.

"I remember calling on Ford Motor Company, which is among the last loyal clients. For decades, they did their financings through Goldman, Sachs, and most of the time they still do. But a Ford man named David Breni listened to me, and we raised ¥20 billion for them. Then we did a Eurobond raising another ¥20 billion for them. I did a deal with Honeywell—another ¥20 billion.

"Here I am: a Chinese married to an American woman, working

at a Japanese firm. My wife Kathleen does currency swaps at another firm, and we have a three-year-old daughter named Charlotte. But I don't see them much, because I'm off to work by six-thirty in the morning, usually I'm back home by eight, and before long I'm on the phone with Tokyo."

Zaiteku

Major Japanese companies have become controversial operators in the Euromarket. Their export business hurt by the rising yen, they've curtailed expansion plans. They continue to generate a lot of cash from their domestic business, but they're wary about spending it to buy other companies. This is seldom done in Japan.

Instead, they've pursued *zaiteku*, or financial engineering. It just means securities trading unrelated to their basic business. Often companies will take advantage of their strong credit ratings to borrow funds cheaply, then put it in investments that yield a little more. They trade far higher volumes than they actually need to finance trade or industrial needs.

Japanese trading companies started the zaiteku trend. Sumitomo was the first, establishing Sumitomo Corporation International Investment, a Luxembourg corporation, in 1984. It had $4 million of capital and $50 million total assets. Related corporations were set up in London, Panama, and the Cayman Islands. Following one strategy, Sumitomo Cayman issued $150 million of bonds for forty to fifty basis points below the London bank rate and loaned the proceeds to Sumitomo Panama, which, assisted by Sumitomo London, invested them in the Euromarket at fifteen to twenty basis points above the London bank rate.

However, Sumitomo incurred foreign exchange losses at its Luxembourg corporation. Its $50 million capital began with a yen loan from the parent company, a third of which was invested in deutsche marks and Swiss francs, which depreciated against the yen. "It will be satisfactory if the three offshore units can pay dividends at the end of each fiscal year," says Shuichi Koshio, director and general manager of Sumitomo's treasury operations.

Among the most sophisticated zaiteku players is Mitsubishi Corporation Finance, a London branch of that triple-A-rated Japanese trading company. Since it began operations in 1985, Mitsubishi has amassed a $1 billion investment portfolio of fixed-rate Eurobonds, floating-rate notes, U.S. Treasury bonds, equity warrants, and bonds convertible into equities. It's funded by borrowing from banks and issuing Euro-commercial paper and Eurobonds. Annual earnings are reportedly around $20 million.

Japanese manufacturers and other companies have pursued zaiteku, too. "About half the top five hundred Japanese companies are experimenting with some kind of financial innovation," says Nicholas Mather, a corporate finance representative at Paribas, the large French bank. "A year ago, fewer than one in five Japanese companies were involved, and the big trading houses dominated the action."

The activity is questionable for a couple of reasons. First, some people wonder if manufacturers are taking on more risks than they can handle. Sophisticated banks and securities firms have lost money doing the same things. Hugh Trenner of the British merchant bank Kleinwort Benson warns: "There's a big disparity between the top names in an industry and the rest. Generally, the best companies can pick and choose. But some of the lesser companies in depressed industries may be taking on larger risks as a short-term expedient to bolster profits."

Johsen Takahashi, chief economist at Mitsubishi Research Institute, reports a misadventure involving a company that borrowed $15 million for plant expansion. "While they waited to start the project, they bought Australian bonds for extra income. Well, they lost a third of their money within a few months. I'm skeptical about this whole zaiteku boom. Executives are starting to realize the pitfalls."

The most spectacular hit was taken by Tateho Chemical Industries, a company based in Ako, west-central Honshu. With annual sales of ¥6 billion (about $42 million), it's the leading producer of electro-fused magnesia, a key component of electric heaters. During the summer of 1987, it lost ¥28.6 billion ($197 million). This exceeded the company's net worth of ¥16.9 billion. Suddenly, Tateho faced default on ¥20 billion ($140 million) of bank loans.

Disclosure of Tateho's losses, on Wednesday, September 2, 1987, sent shock waves through world financial markets, because investors feared that far bigger companies might have unreported losses from financial operations. Fear gripped the Tokyo and Osaka stock exchanges. In London, securities of Japanese companies dropped more than 15 percent. "There was a state of panic," recalls Tony Beckwith, a trader at NatWest Investment Bank.

To avoid bankruptcy, Tateho president Shigeru Senzaki, fifty-seven, scrambled to renegotiate terms with its principal lenders, Toyo Kobe Bank and Chugoku Bank. By suspending principal payments, it's estimated, the company could recover within two years, if its basic business continues at present levels.

The Tateho debacle made front-page news in Japan. Tateho executives blamed the company's forty-year-old trader, Takaki Kobayashi, for unauthorized transactions. The riskiest was a ¥400-billion position in Japanese government bonds. Investors need put up only 3 percent of the value of these futures contracts, while they may be liable for unlimited losses. Kobayashi claimed he kept top management informed, and he blamed the company's broker, Nikko Securities. "When our purchases reached over ¥400 billion, we thought about decreasing this a bit and instructed Nikko to sell," he says. "But Nikko didn't sell. Instead they advised us to take other measures. In the end, we lost out on the timing." During the summer, interest rates moved up, and bond prices dropped.

As a result of this experience, Japanese companies seem to be more cautious. But until more find ways to expand internally or make suitable acquisitions, they'll probably continue as active participants in financial markets.

According to Waco Research Institute, the biggest zaitech players of 1988 were Toyota Motor, Matsushita Electric, and Nissan Motor. Analysts expect that Japanese corporations will make more capital available than ever before for zaitech operations, even as the widely publicized losses engender greater caution.

Japanese Losses

How have Japanese investors fared in the Euromarkets? Though the Euromarkets are huge, they're volatile. Sometimes, when investors become nervous, there's hardly a market at all. The Japanese have taken big hits.

Japanese banks are potentially big losers, because they hold 70 percent of floating-rate notes. About $160 billion are outstanding. Mostly issued by banks, these notes offer a variable yield linked to benchmark cost of London bank deposits. When the market developed during the early 1980s, floating-rate notes yielded more than the cost of funds at many banks, so asset-hungry banks were among the most eager investors. More and more issues hit the market, driving yields down to ten to twenty basis points—above the rate major London banks pay each other for deposits.

By late 1986, the market slumped, because of several developments. First came surging competition from mortgage-backed securities. As they yielded forty to sixty basis points above the London interbank rate, investors abandoned floaters to buy them. Moreover, the specter of default on Third World bank loans discouraged investors from buying any bank paper. Finally, bank regulators became concerned about the safety of the financial system as banks loaded their portfolios with paper from other banks. The prospect of new restrictions further dampened demand for the floating-rate notes.

In early 1987 the market collapsed. Some top-rated floating-rate notes dropped ten points in a couple of weeks—$1 million for each $10-million face amount. The number of market-makers plunged from about fifty to a half-dozen. Many market-makers, like Citibank and the Bank of Tokyo, answered their telephones only when it suited them. "The market functioned on the *Alice in Wonderland* belief that there would always be liquidity," says Archibald Cox, Jr., of Morgan Stanley International, London.

Japanese banks hold about half the perpetual floating-rate notes, another sector of the market that fell on hard times. Since 1984, banks have issued about $17 billion of these notes without any redemption date. They trade around endlessly and pay interest about twice a year. "The Japanese couldn't sell their bonds if they tried," declares Paul Dennison, a money-market specialist at Merrill Lynch Capital Markets.

From time to time, the U.S. government disrupts the Euromarket, warning Japanese and others how vulnerable they may be in that market. On June 29, 1987, the U.S. Treasury, always needing more money, announced it would discontinue a tax treaty with the Netherlands Antilles. Among other things, the treaty exempted bonds issued there from a 30-percent withholding tax. Some bonds dropped twenty points almost overnight.

There was an unexpected uproar from investors, and Treasury officials scrambled to reverse themselves. They announced that while they still wanted to drop the Netherlands Antilles treaty, they would seek legislation specifically protecting Eurobond investors. One Treasury official admits: "It became a nightmare. We had no idea there would be reverberations throughout the credit markets."

Euromarket Outlook

Japanese participation helps maintain the Euromarket as a vital alternative for companies that need to lower their financing costs and stay competitive. Fortunately, the Japanese are making substantial commitments that suggest they will be long-term players here.

All this competition means the Euromarket will continue to serve as a great laboratory for financial experiments. While most of the new securities may prove to be short-lived, the Euromarket will generate improved techniques to help maximize return while limiting risk.

As financial markets are deregulated further and become more international, we'll probably see new issues of securities offered simultaneously in Tokyo, London and New York. It isn't likely yet, since terms that are legal in one market and mutually appealing to issuers and investors may entail problems in another market. New York financial consultant Stephen Wechselblatt has suggested that such offerings, when they take place, might appropriately be referred to as sumos, because they'd almost certainly be very large.

Investment bankers complain about sashimi-thin profit margins, but intense Japanese competition is an important reason why borrowers should continue benefiting from perhaps the lowest financing costs anywhere.

A shakeout is underway to determine which firms can provide competitive services at the lowest cost. Some firms like Shearson Lehman Brothers and Salomon Brothers have announced cutbacks. More firms seem sure to cut back. Some will withdraw altogether from the Euromarket. This winnowing process is healthy as long as new firms are free to enter and challenge the leaders.

The Euromarket will probably account for a diminishing share of business as Japanese capital markets open up and expand. There's more money in Japan, and surely the Japanese would rather handle their transactions at home, when stifling regulations are ended.

As long as the yen remains strong, it will dominate Euromarket transactions. American policies to devalue the dollar further will undermine the position of American securities firms, while Japanese firms will gain in the Euromarket.

8

HOW'S TOKYO DOING?

During the past year, some xenophobes have mounted a new scare campaign. They allege that the Japanese triggered the October 1987 stock crash by abruptly pulling out of the bond and stock markets. This, it's asserted, shows that America must not become dependent on finicky foreign capital.

But the charges don't bear scrutiny. Certainly they weren't made by the Presidential Task Force on Market Mechanisms (the Brady Commission). According to their January 1988 report, proximate causes of the crash were "disappointingly poor merchandise trade figures, which put downward pressure on the dollar in currency markets and upward pressure on long term interest rates; and the filing of anti-takeover tax legislation, which caused risk arbitrageurs to sell stocks of takeover candidates resulting in their precipitate decline and a general ripple effect throughout the market. The market's decline created a huge overhang of selling pressure—enough to crush the equity markets in the following week."

A broader perspective suggests that the crash occurred because stocks simply became overpriced compared to bond yields. The Brady Commission noted that from the beginning of the global bull market in 1982 until the October 1987 crash, the nineteen largest equity markets gained 296 percent. "By the end of May [1987]," the Brady Commission reported, "it was becoming clear that on a valuation basis, there was diminishing justification for continued stock price increases." At that time, Wall Street analysts estimated the Standard & Poors 500 averages were 25 to 40 percent overvalued.

The October 1987 crash was global and didn't just affect Wall Street, where so many Japanese investors had bought stocks. In the year following the crash, both Japanese and American investors—especially individuals—cut back their positions on Wall Street. The volume plummeted, yet the averages recovered somewhat. At the same time, both Japanese and American investors switched funds to the Tokyo market, which surged to record highs.

The evidence suggests that both American and Japanese investors had similar reactions to the threatening news in the United States. Both were attracted to the more favorable environment in Japan.

If people imagine that cutting the U.S. off from foreign capital will reduce market fluctuations and the risk of losing money—well, there isn't much evidence to support that. Investors lose money everyday in transactions that didn't involve foreigners. On the contrary, the more participants in a market, the more effective it's likely to be.

What foreigners do is provide alternatives. The more foreign buyers there are in the United States, the more liquid the market, and the less U.S. companies have to pay for equity capital. Similarly, the Japanese stock market is an important alternative to the U.S. market.

On a more basic level, equity investors—foreign or domestic—provide an alternative to debt financing. When inexpensive equity capital is available, companies can finance their needs without taking on as much debt as they otherwise would. If regulations block equity investment—as is the case in most of the Third World—then the only options are assuming enormous debt burdens or doing without capital at all.

Influence of Institutions

The Japanese stock market may be wild sometimes, but it isn't as wild as it seems with prices often fifty times nominal earnings. The savvy Paul Aron, former vice chairman of Daiwa Securities America, insists that different accounting practices result in understated Japanese earnings and that Japanese depreciation is high by U.S. standards. The Japanese set aside reserves that in the United States would be counted as earnings. When Japanese financial statements are revised to reflect these differences, he says, the price-earnings ratios are similar to those of U.S. companies. So the rush into U.S. stocks is powered more by the strong yen and a need to diversify than by the situation on the Tokyo stock market.

Most Japanese investors focus on familiar names. Dai-Ichi Mutual Life, with 8 million policyholders and $35 billion of assets, has a $3.5-billion international portfolio. About 10 percent is in foreign equities. Vice President Minoru Yoshida reports they favor chemical, pharmaceutical, and technology stocks. Yoichi Kuwata, a fund manager at Nikko & Associates, which has an $8-billion portfolio, favors the stocks of major financial institutions.

The largest Japanese trust bank, Mitsubishi Trust & Banking, has $60 billion of capital and manages $8 billion of pension funds. They hold just $8 million of foreign stocks. "We're interested in blue chips," says managing director Tamotsu Hanada, "and we'd like to invest in smaller companies for capital gains. To minimize currency risk, we'll diversify our investments across Asia, Europe, and the United States."

Many Japanese institutions make portfolio decisions by committee, but there are some superperformers with uncharacteristic independence. Among the best-known is Keiichi Sawamoto, senior managing director of Sumitomo Mutual Life Insurance Company. After he gained total control over the portfolio during the mid-1970s, he began aggressive trading in major global markets. In 1978, for instance, he plunged into sterling bonds when the British pound was at 360 yen. Sawamoto closed out his positions two years later, with the pound at 560 yen.

Sawamoto resisted pressures from people within his company, who urged that he buy stocks in companies that were good prospects for buying group life insurance. A number of people feared the foreign exchange risks of investing overseas, but he proceeded anyway. He has traded positions in Britain, West Germany, Australia, and the U.S. Overall, he earned yields as high as 14 percent.

For all his aggressiveness as a trader, Sawamoto is an unassuming man. He says he smokes too much. He's an angler who, on his days off, relishes fly-fishing for trout.

Says Kotaro Asai, chief fund manager of Yasuda Trust & Banking: "Good investment in equity is essential, after the bond market passes its peak." The bank has $50 billion of assets. Its portfolio includes $600 million of foreign securities. About a third are equities— believed to be among the largest foreign equity holdings in Japan. "In our foreign investment portfolio, there is a possibility that equities could overtake bonds.

Big Four

The Big Four Japanese securities firms dominate the action in Japan. According to Nikkei Kinyu Nenpo research service, Nomura Securities handles 18.6 percent of stock transactions in Japan, followed by Daiwa's 12.1-percent share, Nikko's 11.3 percent, and Yamaichi's 10.3 percent. Nomura has more clout than may be apparent from these numbers. "Nomura decides they're going to move so many shares of a company," says a critical New York investor, "and damned if they don't do it."

The Japanese firms have additional clout because of trust funds they control. Nomura has $84.6 billion, Daiwa $52.7 billion, Nikko $51.7 billion, and Yamaichi $50 billion.

The Big Four buy shares of brand-name U.S. companies and market them aggressively back in Japan. During the past couple of years, Nomura has done well with such stocks as IBM, General Motors, General Electric, Exxon, Community Psychiatric Centers, and Chi-Chi's, the Mexican restaurant chain.

Nikko Securities bought about 400,000 shares of R.J. Reynolds Industries and 2.7 million shares of AT & T. Toshio Mori, chairman Nikko Securities International, reports that "some Nikko branch offices in Japan do more business in foreign than Japanese securities."

To take advantage of growing Japanese interest in U.S. stocks, Japanese securities firms promote listings on the Tokyo Stock Exchange. Listing costs a company $130,000 to $200,000 during the first year alone, because of required listing fees and financial reports. Annual charges may run $50,000, depending on the number of floor brokers a firm has. Many executives consider this a reasonable public relations move compared to other alternatives. A single full-page advertisement in the leading Japanese business daily, *Nihon Keizai Shimbun*, for instance, costs about $100,000.

While a listing isn't necessary—trading takes place via computerized communications networks comparable to the fast-growing National Association of Securities Dealers Automated Quotations (NASDAQ), which links brokers—a listing helps make a company more visible. A stock price is quoted in the newspapers, and a listing earns some goodwill by signifying the company's commitment to the Japanese market. "A listed company is more trusted," ventures Kiichi Oda, manager of the Tokyo Stock Exchange's foreign stock department, "because it has passed examination by the Ministry of Finance." As a result, tapping Japanese capital may be easier in the future.

To be sure, global stock markets are in their infancy. Perhaps the biggest concern is flow-back. Often, shares issued in a foreign market, such as Tokyo, tend to flow back to the domestic market, exerting a downward pressure on the price of the stock there.

Japanese securities firms compete fiercely for mandates to handle an American company's listing on the Tokyo Stock Exchange. While it generates only onetime fees, it's a door-opener that may lead to more business from a major company, and it contributes to the complex calculus of rank among securities firms. Daiwa leads the race, with twenty non-Japanese listings, such as Citicorp, IBM, ITT, Philip Morris, Sears, 3M, Proctor & Gamble, Eastman Kodak, McDonald's, Chrysler, Du Pont, and Pepsico. Nomura's seventeen non-Japanese listings include Dow Chemical, General Motors, BankAmerica, Walt Disney Productions, and American Express. Nikko arranged listings for nine non-Japanese companies, including Chase Manhattan, RJR Nabisco, Eli Lilly, and Exxon. Yamaichi arranged listings for Bell Atlantic, US West, and four others. Altogether, there are fifty-two non-Japanese companies listed on the Tokyo Stock Exchange, compared with fifty-nine non-U.S. companies listed on the New York Stock Exchange. Most companies listed in Japan have substantial operations there.

World's Largest Pachinko Parlor

The Tokyo Stock Exchange, a brassy high-tech facility in an angled granite building amidst Tokyo's Kabuto-cho district, is Japan's wildest roller coaster. In April 1987, it surpassed the New York Stock Exchange as the world's largest stock market, with total market value over $2.8 trillion. Average daily turnover in Tokyo typically exceeds 650 million shares and sometimes goes over a billion shares.

The Japanese stock market towers over every other country's. Its total market value is more than triple that of London, eight times bigger than Frankfurt, nineteen times bigger than Paris, and twenty-five times bigger than Sydney. Yet it's an exceedingly thin market. As much as 70 percent of all shares are held on a long-term basis by banks and companies that do business with each other. A stock holding shows respect and confidence. So relatively few of a company's shares are actually available.

Charles Elliot, who manages investment research for Goldman, Sachs (Japan) figures that thirty stocks account for about 70 percent of trading. This is better than a year ago, when about 90 percent of the trading was concentrated in just ten stocks. What makes the market devilish is that the high-volume stocks change continuously, depending on what the securities firms happen to be pushing.

When a stock is hot, it may trade as high as seventy times nominal earnings for a typical yield under 2 percent. By contrast, until the October 1987 crash, Big Board stocks traded around twenty times earnings, yielding about 5 percent.

The most extreme situation is Nippon Telegraph & Telephone, which went public in February 1987, part of the government's plan to privatize moribund nationalized companies and raise money for official coffers. NTT has a market value around $300 billion, more than IBM, Exxon, AT & T, General Motors, and General Electric combined.

For many, the NTT offering evoked a patriotic response. On February 9, 1987, the government issued 1.95 million shares—a small number considering the size of the company. They were priced at $7,820 apiece. Only Japanese could buy it, and even then just one per customer. Prices soared. At one point, the NTT shares sold for 270 times earnings, for a 0.3-percent yield. Some proud Japanese reportedly hung NTT stock certificates on their walls, showing that they owned a piece of Japan.

There's some sense behind the craziness. "Institutions that deal with NTT want to be able to tell them how much stock they own," explains Paul H. Aron, vice chairman of Daiwa Securities. "Potential suppliers to NTT hope to use this leverage for orders. They think it will be advantageous profitwise. Based on past experience, they have a high degree of conviction that it will. I think they're right. If I were a manufacturer of telecommunications equipment, I'd want to own some NTT. It opens the door in Japan. After all, you can't throw a stockholder out of the store. You must be polite to him."

In other cases, the securities houses helped the price of selected stocks. Nomura helped push up the price of Mitsubishi Heavy Industries stock from 420 to 670 in two months. Then, near the peak, Nomura issued convertible stock for the company. Soon afterward, the stock fell back around 400. "It's much more important to know what Nomura is doing than to understand Western analysis," says Hideo

Hayashide, equity investment manager for Nippon Life.

In recent years, so-called *tokkin*, or specified, funds have had a significant impact on the Tokyo market. Set up by corporations with idle cash, often because their growth has slowed, these funds don't need to make further capital investments. Since the tokkin funds are an arm's length from a company, they can be traded without incurring punitive taxes. An estimated $70 billion of tokkin funds are invested, reportedly in a small number of large-capitalization stocks. "It was getting to be dangerous," says Christopher Mitchinson, a director of Salomon Brothers' London office. "These people were pumping more and more money into fewer and fewer issues. The Ministry of Finance worried that things were getting out of control."

Often companies and institutional investors rush in and out of stocks, pushing prices up rapidly. When a Japanese woman reportedly died from acquired immune deficiency syndrome, pharmaeutical stocks soared, including those with little to do with AIDS research. There have been fads for telecommunications stocks, companies involving superconductivity, and so on. "Japanese investors move like a buffalo herd," says Keiki Yasuda, a general manager of New Japan Securities Co. Toyo Securities reports that clients commonly turn over their portfolios 250 percent a year. Sometimes, the turnover rate hits 1,000 percent.

Japanese money managers aren't held to the same standards as in the West. "No Japanese money manager tries to outperform the market," explains a British fund manager, "because they don't have to. Generally, Japanese equity managers are expected to generate a specific rate of return, usually about 8 percent. If they do, great. Never mind that the market was up 20 percent during the same period."

Reportedly there are many happenings that frustrate rational analysis of stocks on the Tokyo Stock Exchange. Sometimes stock is manipulated to favor friendly politicians. They're advised to buy certain stocks, and subsequently they have a nice run-up. Politicians bail out with funds for their next campaign, courtesy of the market.

The lack of short-selling in Tokyo leaves the market without the important discipline that is present in the U.S. Short-sellers, believing a stock will decline, borrow a desired number of shares from their broker, agreeing to return them later. They sell the stock, hoping to buy it back at a lower price. Their selling helps restrain a wild bull market. Their buying provides liquidity in a depressed market, when few investors may be willing to buy. The risk, of course, is that a stock continues rising, forcing a short-seller to buy stock back at a higher price.

When there's optimism on the floor of the Tokyo Stock Exchange, things tend to go wild. The Nikkei average of 225 stocks has tripled during the past five years. Would an earthquake provoke a crash? "It would be great for construction stocks," says a Daiwa analyst.

Often the Tokyo stock market is compared to pachinko, a popular Japanese pinball game played in city arcades. There's a lot of noise, a few people manage to make money, and more lose—rather like trading in New York.

"The Japanese stock market remains, above all, a local market," says Ronald Gould, head of trust banking at Barclay's Bank, Japan. "The marginal buyer is Japanese."

Despite its dangers for unwary investors, the dramatic volume on the Tokyo Stock Exchange is eloquent testimony to Japan's arrival as a world financial power. Few countries have created the conditions that enable a stock market to develop. Japan's market is growing up.

Gaijins in Tokyo

Dozens of American and European securities firms are expanding rapidly in Japan, hoping for a piece of the action. "We're afraid of missing the boat," says John A. Williams, president of Merrill Lynch Japan. In recent years, the major American securities firms have doubled and tripled their staffs.

Expansion was a long time coming. For years, foreigners, or *gaijins* as they're called, paid little attention to Japan. "We did a financing for Honda in the 1960s," recalls Roy Smith, a general partner of Goldman, Sachs, "but we didn't do anything else for quite a while. About fifteen years ago, we had a guy from Nikko Securities who was doing a kind of internship with us. He was in New York about eight months. As he was about ready to leave, he said I ought to know that Goldman, Sachs was missing big opportunities. Japan was growing rapidly, but hardly any American firms were cultivating potential clients. Certainly, we didn't have anyone in Japan. I discussed this with my partners, and I was elected to do something.

"In 1969, we set up a representative office. The first question was whether the Japanese had major companies. That was easy. They had a lot.

"It was evident, though, that the companies didn't need much investment banking, because they went to their traditional securities firms. So we'd call on the securities firms, offering our services if they ever needed to raise funds in the United States. There wasn't a great deal we could do, though, because a decade ago Japanese stocks were exotic for most Americans. Demand was limited.

"Meanwhile, the European markets became a blaze, and we expanded over there. The Japanese didn't become big players until the 1980s, when they started sending us their money. It's taken a long time and many experiments to become established in that market."

It costs plenty to be a top-bracket competitor. In 1986, Merrill Lynch, Goldman, Sachs, and Morgan Stanley were invited to join the Tokyo Stock Exchange, and they paid $5.1 million apiece for their seats. Seats on the New York Stock Exchange trade for about $500,000.

Tokyo seats cost more for several reasons. They're corporate, so each member can have many traders on the floor of the exchange. In New York, every floor trader must have an individual seat. Then, too, securities commissions are fixed at high levels in Japan, making membership a valuable franchise. Competitive, negotiated commissions make for slim margins in New York. Finally, the Tokyo Stock Exchange is limited to only ninety-three members.

There's also the cost of doing business in Tokyo. Junior executives command salaries over $125,000. Office rents exceed $100 a square foot, versus $65 for the most prestigious space Manhattan has to offer. Companies do a tremendous amount of entertaining.

Thus far, the leading foreign firm is Morgan Stanley International, which reports about twice as much stock market volume as runners-up Merrill Lynch or Jardine Fleming Securities, a Hong Kong firm. "We passed them in July 1986," says David Phillips, fifty-four, a savvy Japanese who heads Morgan Stanley's operations there. He has an American name, because he was adopted by an educational director of the U.S. Air Force.

Increasingly, American firms are hiring Japanese, to take advantage of their expertise and connections. "This may be Morgan Stanley," says Phillips, "but we're a Japanese company here. We want people to see that we're managed and supported by Japanese nationals. To understand the Japanese isn't easy. But it isn't easy to understand Morgan Stanley, either. I believe we have to bridge the gap between East and West."

Foreign firms don't pursue retail business, which calls for a large, costly network of branch offices. Rather, they aim at institutional investors, like the banks, trust companies, and insurance companies. To compete with the Big Four Japanese firms requires doing things Japanese-style: wining and dining every night on tatami mats in pricey Tokyo restaurants. "If my wife wasn't Japanese, I would have been divorced years ago," says Phillips. Morgan Stanley's clients include major Japanese companies like Hitachi, Ricoh, and Nippon Steel.

"Around here, relationships take a half-century to develop," says John Williams of Merrill Lynch, which has maintained a Tokyo office since 1961. "How do you get in the club? I'm not sure."

Neil Benedict, director of finance of Salomon Brothers, denied a seat on the Tokyo Stock Exchange during the initial go-rounds, is more cocky: "Regardless of long-term relationships, if you've got the best product for a prospective client, they'll see you. That's how we've broken through established relationships."

The trouble is that new financial products must be cleared with the Ministry of Finance. By the time everyone has talked about it, competitors have had time to develop their own versions. Being an innovator may count for little unless a firm has marketing muscle, as Salomon does.

Firms that don't belong to the Tokyo Stock Exchange must execute their orders through Japanese member firms, paying them 27 percent of the commissions. In return, the non-Japanese firms receive intelligence about the Japanese market. Once membership on the Tokyo Stock Exchange is granted, a non-Japanese firm becomes a direct competitor with the Japanese, and the flow of intelligence stops. "We cut ourselves off from the major brokers," says David Miller, general manager of Jardine's Tokyo office. On the other hand, having a seat on the exchange affords access to the doings there. "If Nomura places five million shares, we'll find out in seconds," Miller adds.

Foreign competition, particularly from American firms, puts pressure on the Japanese to deregulate their high fixed-rate commissions. Salomon Brothers, Goldman, Sachs, Morgan Stanley, and Merrill Lynch hammer at Japanese fund managers for their high commission costs. They urge saving money by trading blocks of stock in London or New York when the Tokyo Stock Exchange is closed, since brokerage commissions are deregulated in those markets.

"Japanese securities firms hate the very idea of block trading, offshore or on," says Jardine's David Miller. "They'll use every excuse—they're visiting, away from the office, whatever. They hate to take a phone call from an investor who may be asking about block trades." Yuichi Yoshimi, a Nomura manager, acknowledges: "We keep hearing about block trades from clients. Often, we're asked for bids and offers after the close. Usually, we don't do it, but the trend is that way."

There's considerable frustration dealing with the Japanese regulatory bureaucracy. Walter J. Burkett, former head of Merrill Lynch, recalls his experiences: "Having dealt with regulators in the United States, Britain, and Japan, I can say that the Ministry of Finance is toughest. Many gray areas.

"When meeting with a Japanese official, you must pay close attention, use honorific language, and avoid sitting too comfortably with your legs crossed. I was always advised to avoid discussing the issues directly. It was frustrating."

Says Morgan Stanley's Phillips: "Japanese markets may be more heavily regulated than American markets, but we can still do good business here. You just need more imagination and competitiveness."

Macho Trading

The Japanese securities firms are expanding rapidly on Wall Street. Nomura's offices at Continental Center, a glass tower overlooking the East River, are a jumble of new construction, as workers try to squeeze more people and telecommunications equipment into the present quarters. Every week, they hire more people. They're inquiring around the Manhattan real estate market for about four hundred thousand square feet of space.

Recently, Daiwa Securities moved into a hundred thousand square feet at World Financial Center, a magnificent granite complex on the Hudson River, where American Express, Merrill Lynch, Oppenheimer, and Dow Jones have established their headquarters. Already they're crowded.

Yamaichi Securities is expanding at Two World Trade Center. "New York has become the most important center of our overseas operations," says Takeshi Naito, chairman of Yamaichi America, a graduate of the University of California at Los Angeles. Yamaichi brokers are urged to pitch more "salesburgers," or catchy ideas, at their clients.

One play, known as macho trading, involves buying large volumes of a stock the day before its "ex-dividend" date. That's when you must be a shareholder of record to receive a dividend. A day later, the stocks drop by an amount that reflects the dividend, and they're sold back. "The play is appealing," explains Daiwa America chairman Takuro Isoda, "because dividends are 80-percent tax-free. U.S. corporations must hold a stock at least forty-six days to gain the exemption, but Japanese companies aren't restricted.

"Japanese life insurance companies do this since they can pass along only income to policyholders. They favor high-yielding stocks, such as utilities. American Electric Power, Philadelphia Electric, and Houston Industries are popular. Millions of shares may change hands within in an hour."

The Japanese expansion on Wall Street is hitting smaller securities firms that lack the capital to play ball in the global marketplace. Pricing is finer than it used to be.

International Man

The experience of Nikko shows how the Japanese are doing in the American market. Though hardly a household word, Nikko's $13 billion market valuation is more than double that of Salomon Brothers and triple Merrill Lynch's.

Started in 1918, Nikko has become a powerful department store of financial services. The firm underwrites stocks and bonds, distributing them through 110 domestic offices and twenty-one overseas offices in sixteen countries. Nikko represents Japanese investors buying U.S. securities. Worldwide, Nikko handled $139.1 billion of equity transactions in 1986.

Nikko's efforts in the United States are directed by Senior Managing Director Toshio Mori, fifty-four. He's a trim, amiable man who has worked here seventeen years. The year he graduated from Waseda

University, jobs were scarce. His uncle introduced him to Nikko Securities. Mori passed their examination and started work in the company's Osaka office. He sold government bonds and stocks of major companies such as Tokyo Electric, Hitachi, Kansai Electric, Sumitomo Bank, and Matsushita.

After three years, his boss advised that he prepare for future expansion overseas. At the time, in the 1950s, the United States had the most sophisticated securities markets, so Mori prepared for examinations as a registered representative there. He studied accounting, American securities practice, and—most difficult—conversational English. In 1959, he joined Nikko's Los Angeles office. Mori, his wife Toshiko, and their sons Toni and Haruki struggled with a new language.

For six years, he sold stocks to Japanese-Americans, mostly first generation. They had emigrated from prefectures in western Japan, like Hiroshima, Kumamoto, Kagoshima, and Wakayama, where unemployment was high. Once settled in Los Angeles, they formed social clubs of people from the same prefecture. "Once you met a few people, they'd introduce you to their friends, and before long you had a lot of clients," Mori recalls. "They were interested in the same stocks that were popular back in Japan."

He returned to Japan for a couple of years, then was off to New York in 1969. By then, the so-called Japanese economic miracle was becoming well known, and many American institutions were interested in buying Japanese stocks. Mori sold such stocks as Honda and Sony to Fidelity Fund, Investors Diversified Services, Prudential Insurance Company, and others.

By 1973, he was off to Paris, where, for six months, he and his family struggled with another language. "It's fun to work in Paris," he recalls, "once you learn the language. Sometimes the French may give you a hard time, but I discovered that when you become a friend, there's depth to the relationship. They're very nice people." He sold Japanese stocks to the major French banks, like Banque Paribas, Banque Pays, Societe Generale, and Credit Lyonnais.

He was back in New York by 1977, this time as branch manager. It was a quiet period, with both U.S. and Japanese economies recovering from the oil shock. Naomichi Toyama, the son of Nikko's founder Geniichi Toyama, was killed in a plane crash, and top executives decided they really didn't want to pursue international operations. They scaled back, just as the Euromarket was starting to boom.

Mori was rotated back to Japan, but returned to New York in 1981. While Nikko continued raising funds for Japanese companies by selling their stocks abroad, the times had changed. Japan regained its momentum as a premier exporter, and Japanese financial markets were being deregulated. Japanese capital started flowing to the United States.

Mori had some catching up to do, since competitors Nomura and Daiwa had expanded internationally during the years Nikko cut back. He hired mostly Americans and cultivated American customers. Now, while most of Nikko's equities business involves buying U.S. stocks for Japanese customers, about 70 percent of overall volume is with American customers. "Our aim is to become an international firm with strong roots in this country, like other successful foreign-owned firms such as Nestle, Seagram's, and Shell Oil," Mori says.

In 1986, Mori scored a coup by luring Stephen Axilrod, sixty, away from the Federal Reserve where he had served for thirty-four years. For the past decade, Axilrod was staff director of the Federal Open Market Committee which carried out the Fed's monetary policy. This Committee has immense influence on inflation and the economy. Every day, consulting with Federal Reserve Chairman Paul Volcker, Axilrod made decisions that involved trading currencies and government securities. He was a familiar figure to Wall Street investment bankers as well as central bankers around the world.

"I felt due for a little adventure," Axilrod says. "You've got to leave sometime. Better to leave with some adventure ahead of you than all of it behind you."

By joining Nikko as vice chairman, Axilrod gave them considerable credibility in the American market. His presence makes hiring superior American talent a lot easier. He also provides wide-ranging advice about doing business in the United States. For instance, the firm considered requiring everyone from the chairman on down to punch time clocks, a democratic way to handle the issue of overtime. Axilrod explained that the practice would backfire, particularly among salaried executives, who don't get overtime anyway.

"We're becoming a truly international company," says Mori. "Not a Japanese company or an American company. We're hiring much more on the basis of talent rather than nationality."

With all these years overseas, Mori's children have become international people. "We've helped each other, learning new languages and new ways in Los Angeles, New York, and Paris," Mori recalls. His twenty-two-year-old son, Toni, was born in California and graduated from Rikkyo University, Tokyo. He works for Meiji Life Insurance Company. His second son, Haruki, is twenty-one, studying at the Philadelphia College of Arts. "Often in Japan," Mori says, "it's important to attend a respected college, but for Haruki it doesn't matter, because he's interested in graphic arts. What counts there is that you develop an appealing portfolio."

Mori and his wife didn't want their children to forget their Japanese heritage. "Whenever they were outside playing with friends, working, whatever, they spoke English," he says, "but at home they had to speak Japanese. This way, they maintained their fluency. I have several friends whose children largely lost it abroad. I think it's important to stay in touch with the essence of our culture."

In recent years, Mori has directed a scholarship program where Nikko pays expenses for twenty students to visit Japan two months during the summer. They're selected from Harvard, Princeton, Yale, Brown, Georgetown, the University of California at Berkeley, and the University of Chicago.

Innovator

A lot of the financial conflicts between America and Japan have their roots in cultural differences. Few are able to bridge these as well as Tetsundo Iwakuni, an elegant investment banker who has worked for both Japanese and American securities firms. Iwakuni is a senior vice president of Merrill Lynch Capital Markets and former chairman of Merrill Lynch Japan. He's responsible for efforts to market American securities in Japan and to help Japanese companies in the United States.

Iwakuni, fifty-one, was born in Osaka where his father was a teacher. He died when Iwakuni was six. To avoid the World War II bombings, the family fled to Izumo, a picturesque country town where his mother was raised.

He set his sights on Tokyo University, passed the rigorous entrance examinations, and studied law—standard preparation for coveted posts in the Ministry of Finance or elsewhere in government.

"I applied for positions in the government and at Mitsubishi Bank. I also considered the securities business. The leading firm was

Yamaichi, but I didn't care for the name, which means "one mountain." I respected Nomura Securities, but it's a family name, and I didn't want to work for a family-owned firm where an outsider could rise only so far. Daiwa was a smaller firm, though the name is nice—it means "great peace." Nikko Securities has a good name, meaning "rising sun," and it was a larger firm.

"I went to see an acquaintance of mine who worked at Nikko. He was very smooth-talking. He described the firm's fast growth. He told me that if I did good work, my income would double in five years— almost inconceivable at the time. Now it's commonplace, but with large established companies, you may get 5-percent to 10-percent annual raises based on seniority.

"He asked me to seal a letter of preliminary acceptance with a *hanko*. That's a stamp carved in the end of a little ivory stick—your family name in Japanese characters. People use it to signify their approval of important documents. Well, I didn't have a hanko, so I refused. He asked me to mark the card with my fingerprint—no obligation—and I did that. He emphasized that I'd be free to change my mind about Nikko.

"But when I returned to my dorm, I felt obligated. After thinking about the prospects, I canceled my application for the government and for Mitsubishi Bank. I didn't go for any more interviews."

Iwakuni started in the bond department. Right away, he discovered ways to improve operations. "I knew people could gain tax exemptions by buying bonds from banks, and I thought the exemptions should be available through securities firms, too," he says.

"I analyzed the complex law governing our financial system and figured out a way securities firms could better compete with banks. The law was originally conceived to encourage small savers at commercial banks, but the way it was written it could apply to a securities firm. If each Nikko office formed a local savers' association, we could invite customers to join, and they could open tax-free, or *maruyu*, accounts. It was for bonds. Customers could buy, sell, and hold whatever bonds they wanted. Of course, they'd receive the full interest.

"Nikko implemented the idea in September 1959, and it proved to be tremendously popular. If I didn't create this, probably Nikko and other securities firms would have lost substantial numbers of customers to commercial banks, since ordinary securities accounts involved a 20-percent or 30-percent withholding tax."

Iwakuni became restless to introduce a new investment vehicle. "Japanese bought individual stocks and bonds," he explains, "but securities firms didn't have any distinctive products. So I explored the possibility of a bond fund. It would address the uncertainties and complexities of bonds: many people get confused, since bonds may sell above par or below par. But with a fund, you just check the single prevailing price.

"I decided that the unit should be a single yen. Before, a unit would be ¥5,000 or ¥10,000. You got interest only on full units. With a one-yen unit, any small saver could get prevailing interest on the entire investment. This was another effort to compete with commercial banks and trust banks, which paid interest on whatever amount of money customers deposited in their accounts."

Iwakuni was working in New York during the early 1960s when Nikko originated the Japan Fund, and he helped work out details with sponsors and lawyers. At that time, few Americans knew enough about Japanese companies to feel comfortable investing in them. But the idea of particpating in Japan's dramatic recovery, originally suggested by the late Naomichi Toga, was appealing. So the firm assembled the fund with stocks in major Japanese companies.

Iwakuni was assigned to Nikko's London office in 1967. During the next decade, he gained experience in Europe, Africa, and the Middle East. He organized syndicates of Arab investors to raise funds for Honda, Toshiba, and other Japanese companies.

Iwakuni served as the general manager of Nikko's Paris office branch, then transferred to London when in 1977, he was asked to head the Ginza branch in Tokyo. An assignment at this important branch was considered a step to becoming a board member. But in recent years, his daughters Mari and Eri had changed schools four times because of his career moves. They were teenagers trying to find themselves, and they didn't need another move.

Nikko executives insisted that he return to Japan after a decade in Europe. "They thought it was brutal to keep me away so long from Japan," he says, "and I think they were concerned about my future career. If I didn't return then, maybe I never would.

"During the eighteen years I was with Nikko," Iwakuni continues, "I always said yes. Go to New York, I said yes. Go back to Tokyo, I said yes. London to Paris, Paris to London, every time I said yes. Finally, in May 1977, I said no.

"People at Nikko were disappointed and angry. It was highly unusual for someone as senior as myself to leave. I explained that if I had the opportunity of going back to Japan three years earlier, when it was easier for my daughters to adapt, I'd have done it. They would have been eleven and nine, instead of fourteen and twelve."

Iwakuni left Nikko and joined the London office of Morgan Stanley. He did the most American thing, a job switch, for the most untraditional Japanese reason: his family. He observed Japanese etiquette that you don't join a Japanese rival. Foreign firm acceptable.

He scouted investment banking business for Morgan Stanley, moving back to Tokyo in 1981. By then, his daughters were old enough to take another move in stride. Iwakuni helped expand Morgan Stanley's operations, as American firms were beginning to tap the Japanese market.

Merrill Lynch had even more ambitious plans for Japan, and Iwakuni joined that firm as senior managing director in March 1984. Until then, Merrill Lynch Japan was a division of their European subsidiary. Iwakuni set it up as an independent entity. He established a pension plan in keeping with Japanese practice, so the firm would be more competitive in attracting and keeping a capable Japanese staff. He opened an office in Nagoya, the firm's third after Tokyo and Osaka—no other American securities firm has even this many Japanese offices. And he negotiated for Merrill Lynch to gain membership and listing on the Tokyo Stock Exchange.

Iwakuni helped cut deals with Japanese securities firms, to distribute Merrill Lynch mutual funds in Japan. With Nomura, Merrill Lynch marketed their Sci/Tech Fund in 1983 and their World Fund the following year. To expand their relationships, in 1985, Merrill Lynch marketed their Ginnie Mae Fund through Nippon Kongyo Kakumaru, the fifth-largest firm. Merrill's International Convertible Securities Fund was marketed in Japan jointly with Daiwa Securities in 1986.

"I spend a lot of time as a kind of ambassador," Iwakuni says. "When I'm in Japan, I hear a lot of criticism about the United States, and I speak up for America. Back in the United States, I have to deal with criticism of Japan. I speak up for Japan."

Iwakuni lives mainly in New York. "My wife Ginko didn't like all the moving. She wondered why we left Japan for London, but she came to love the city. When we moved to Paris, she didn't like it. But when the time came to go, she wanted to stay. Bottom line, she ends up happy anywhere."

Iwakuni's daughters are making their own mark in the United States. Mari, twenty-five, graduated from Stanford University and works for the investment banking firm First Boston. Eri, twenty-three, graduated from Harvard, having majored in education. She teaches in a Massachusetts private secondary school.

The Iwakunis spend part of every summer at their traditional-style three-story pine and cedar home in Tateshina, a hot springs resort town in Japan's Alps. "We just enjoy walking and reading and relaxing," he says.

Dreamer

Usually, Japanese financial companies compete by seeking clients among major American companies. The challenge here is to break through long-established relationships. Goldman, Sachs, for instance, has handled underwritings for Sears and Ford Motor Company going back a half-century. In some cases, the Japanese strategy is to bring brand-new players into the market. This is the mission of Sumiko Ito, thirty-five, a vice president of corporate finance at Nomura Securities.

Ito has concentrated her energies on emerging growth companies. She dreams of a phenomenal success like Morgan Stanley had when they handled the public offering for Apple Computer.

A lot of her work involves venture capital. She helped put together the Japan-American Venture Partnership, which has a $36-million portfolio of investments in fast-growing Japanese private companies such as specialty retailers and manufacturers of semiconductors and medical equipment. She recommends American companies that would be suitable for Nomura's venture capital subsidiary, Japan Associate Finance Company. Their portfolio exceeds $600 million.

Ito has become quite knowledgeable about biotechnology. She canvassed American companies and identified Plant Genetics of Davis, California as one of the most promising. Its principal asset is a tissue culture technology that produces virus-free seed potatoes and enables growers to boost their yields 20 percent to 30 percent. She arranged a 550,000-share initial public offering of the company. Meanwhile, Ito canvassed prospective Japanese investors, discovering that Kirin

Brewery wanted a significant stake in biotechnology. They provided a significant chunk of the $5-million offering.

Ito works with Robert Swanson, the founder and chief executive officer of Genentech, the leading biotechnology company, with $134 million annual revenues. She helped him arrange a whirlwind swing to meet more than a thousand Japanese investors, analysts, and brokers. Nomura channeled more than a million Genentech shares from the United States to Japan, and they reached a price-earnings multiple of 280—stellar even compared to the dizzy Tokyo Stock Exchange. Nomura participated in a $150-million Eurobond offering for Genentech.

Ito urged Leslie Wexner, chairman of The Limited, to have his firm listed on the Tokyo Stock Exchange. Though he doesn't have any stores in Japan, she argued that his company is likely to achieve a global profile. During the past five years, their gross sales and net income have grown about 50 percent annually. In 1986, the company reported $3.2 billion of revenues.

Wexner had other reasons to consider a Tokyo listing. He buys a significant amount of merchandise from Japan, and he's inspired by the phenomenal energy of the Tokyo retail scene. After more than a year of study, Wexner decided to proceed. He considered having the listing handled by another major securities firm which bid aggressively for the assignment, but he chose Ito and Nomura.

The Limited was listed on July 16, 1987, and since then it has averaged about 50 percent higher daily volume than on the New York Stock Exchange. Sometimes, Tokyo turnover is double that in New York. The Limited is the first large-scale U.S. growth company to get a Tokyo listing.

Ito's father, Hiroshi, was a conservative, hardworking man who worked in Tokyo for Fuji Bank. He wanted a wife from his home prefecture of Fukushima. Her mother, from Fukushima, was eager to get out of the country and make her way in the city. So the two were married.

Born in Tokyo, Ito displayed an independent spirit as a youngster. "I was always curious. I loved to read the classics of Japanese as well as English literature. My mother, Yoshiko, was worried that I tried to understand too much," Ito recalls. "She went to my teacher and asked if she should worry. Teacher said it's fine.

"In high school, I was involved with all the protests that were going on. We thought administrators were unfair to students, so we locked ourselves in the high school, stayed up all night, and smoked cigarettes. One of my classmates was the son of Daiwa Securities' vice chairman.

"There were many student riots back then—against the U.S.-Japan security treaty and against the building of Tokyo's Narita airport. We demonstrated in favor of returning Okinawa to Japan. I didn't always study much.

"The time came to declare my major interest. I told my father, Hiroshi, it was economics. He nearly fell off his chair. 'Nobody will marry you after you study economics!' he told me. 'How about Japanese classics? Japanese anthropology? Not economics.'

"Then he asked me what university I'd like to attend. I said Kyoto University, because it's antiestablishment. It's a freewheeling place which is an historic rival of Tokyo University. Kyoto is a beautiful city with more than a thousand years of history. A lot of high-tech companies there. My father said no. He urged me to find someplace closer to home, in Tokyo.

"Then I said Tokyo University. Tokyo University is like Yale, Harvard, and Princeton combined. It's where you must go if you want to enter the establishment. For a student, it's the biggest challenge there is.

"It's true that as a Tokyo University graduate, you'll lose your personality as far as people are concerned. If you kill your lover, the newspapers will say Tokyo University graduate kills lover.

"The rock musical *Hair* inspired me to really pursue Tokyo University. As you may remember, the actors and actresses were antiestablishment. It was a battle cry. I saw it on January 15th.

"Getting into Tokyo University requires passing tough examinations in Japanese, English literature, Japanese history, world history, and a scientific subject. My first examination was scheduled March 3, 1972.

"Beginning January sixteenth, I developed a strategic plan. I went to a bookstore which had the last five years' of examinations for Tokyo University. They told you what books to study. I followed a rigorous schedule where I broke the day into two-hour segments, alternating subjects. It might be Japanese history, sixth to the tenth century, eight to ten in the morning. Then Japanese classic literature, ten to twelve. I'd take a thirteen-minute break for lunch. Then I'd study two hours of biology. Then to world history, Japanese classics, and so on. I worked until dawn. My mother would bring me snacks like some noodles or hot soup. I lost five kilos in two months, but I got very good grades on every exam. Yet everyone was amazed that I got accepted.

"At Tokyo University, I worked hard as a student, though that's unusual. Most students work hard only if they're aiming for the Ministry of Finance. You need straight A's for that. But companies are suspicious if you get straight A's. They prefer a more well-rounded personality, someone who participated in a number of extracurricular activities.

"The male students didn't know what to do with me. They ignored the few women there—my class of four hundred had five women. The men preferred to date a woman from a prestigious women's college, where they teach you flower arranging. Certainly, they didn't want someone like me, who was interested in economics.

"I got along fine, though. I managed the men's handball club. We'd go out and drink all night. You forget you're a woman in that environment.

"But there were limits. The five of us women wanted to form a basketball team, so we went to the teacher. No—too much physical contact. We should play tennis or ping pong. We persisted, and eventually they let us play basketball.

"Though my father didn't always know what to do with me, he was supportive. My mother encouraged me to go as far as I could. They were proud when I graduated.

"I wanted to go into government service, preferably the Ministry of Health and Welfare. They had just started hiring economists, and I thought it might involve interesting issues. I prepared myself to discuss social security and other issues which they dealt with. I met someone in the personnel department and had a good conversation for a couple hours. But when it was over, he told me he wouldn't be asking me to come back.

"'Why not?' I asked. 'Don't you need economists? You don't like my attitude? You doubt my capability?'

"He replied: 'Our policy is to hire a woman every seven years. The last one we hired was two and a half years ago.'

"I was so upset. Total rejection.

"I called other people at the Ministry. Eventually, the deputy minister heard that an aggressive young girl was trying to get an interview. He figured, why not? Give her a chance. So I was invited to see him.

"Again I prepared to discuss the issues. He asked how I would handle young male subordinates—sometimes you have to take them drinking. Could I do that? I replied by talking about my experience managing the men's handball club.

"Another question: Assuming I were married, living in Tokyo, and my husband was assigned up north to Hokkaido, what would I do? You have to be clever answering that. I said I'd choose a wonderful gentleman for my husband, so he will understand whatever I would do, and he would be cooperative.

"They took me, and I stayed three and a half years. One benefit was an opportunity to study abroad. They had a scholarship from Swire and Sons, a London-based shipping company, that would cover expenses at Oxford, and off I went. I studied philosophy and economics. It was quite an international experience, because only about a third of the graduate students were British. The rest were from around the world.

"I learned how to get around in a foreign country. I learned spoken English—not in a class, but rather at parties and bars and the theater. I went to see a lot of plays. It was a struggle, and I felt stupid always talking in the present tense. Hardest of all was to express feelings and live like a human being.

"It was a satisfying experience. I had a boyfriend from Sweden. I could talk about basketball with Americans. I discussed world history with a high-ranking government officer from Senegal.

"On the other hand, I encountered few people who seemed to have much ambition. Many people, actually, hated to work. They didn't try to reach their office if the London subway was on strike.

"My second springbreak abroad, I visited America. I discovered healthy capitalism, where being aggressive was a good thing. I decided it was for me. I made arrangements to start work at Strategic Planning Associates, a Washington consulting group.

"After my two years in Britain, I wrote a five-page letter to the head of our personnel department. I told him I enjoyed Oxford very much, and I was grateful for the opportunity, but because of my career development purpose, I decided to resign the government and go to America. Well, the head of personnel was in tears reading the letter. It wasn't that he would lose face. It was more a matter of rejection to someone in the family. Why can't you stay? What's wrong with us?

"My parents were upset, too. Why, Sumiko, go to America where things are tough? Why give up all the prestige in the Ministry?

"I had to go. The job involved analyzing companies, and soon I realized I didn't know anything about American business. I was one of two people on the staff without an M.B.A. But increasingly, to understand the prospects for a multinational company, you had to analyze the competition from Japan. The firm was desperate for people who could do research on Japan. Just being Japanese was an advantage. That's what I did.

"Along the way, I developed an interest in investment banking. The idea of being a strategic and financial adviser to a company appealed to me. Strategic alliances between multinational companies were becoming more important, so that's what I decided to pursue.

"Nomura Securities was growing fast, and they needed people who could get along both in Japanese finance and American business, so I went to work there."

Ito is married to Donald Allison, a portfolio manager at the World Bank, Washington. They met while both were students at Oxford. Theirs is a commuter marriage, and they see each other on weekends. "We've done it, and everything's fine," she says.

A Piece of Wall Street

Few Americans take notice of the inevitable Japanese activity in the United States until the Japanese buy a sizable stake in a major company. Then people express indignation about the "selling off of America." There were shock waves on Wall Street when, in August 1986, it was announced that Osaka-based Sumitomo Bank wanted to invest $500 million for 12.5 percent of the respected Goldman, Sachs investment banking firm. Goldman, Sachs was the last major partnership on Wall Street—the rest had gone public or were acquired by the likes of American Express, Prudential Insurance, Sears, or General Electric. The Japanese would penetrate what was long an exclusive preserve of Europeans and Americans. The move needed what was expected to be a routine approval by the Federal Reserve.

Sumitomo Bank was hardly about to gain control. The Glass-Steagall Act and Bank Holding Company Act prevented it or any other bank here from underwriting securities. For their $500 million, Sumitomo couldn't get a single vote in Goldman, Sachs. They were entitled to their share of profits. They hoped some of their people could work at the firm and learn the securities business. Presumably, Goldman, Sachs could refer clients to Sumitomo Bank and vice versa.

All this was part of Sumitomo Bank president Ko Komatsu's grand strategy for becoming a global bank. As more traditional corporate customers cut their bank borrowings and raise funds in securities markets, it's urgent for all banks to acquire expertise in securities underwriting. This is difficult, because banks tend to be slow-moving, bureaucratic institutions. They're accustomed to developing long-term relationships with customers. The securities business, however, is transactions-oriented. What counts is the ability of an agile investment banker to devise the cheapest, quickest way to solve a specific problem. The corporate culture of an investment bank is very different than a commercial bank, even an unusually aggressive one like Sumitomo. Komatsu was skeptical that his people could grow successful investment bankers entirely from within.

Komatsu is widely respected as among the top bankers in Japan. Sumitomo Bank has among the lowest ratio of operating expenses to operating income of any Japanese bank. It registers the highest net profits and deposits per employee of the major Japanese commercial bank.

When Komatsu was a young naval officer during World War II, his ship was torpedoed in the Philippines. Most of his crew perished, but he survived for five hours in shark-infested waters until he was rescued. His associates believe the experience shaped his outlook: he's tough, demanding, but compassionate.

More than once, Komatsu has served the bank as a troubleshooter. Sumitomo's Bank of California operations were roiling with internal conflict during the early 1960s, and he was dispatched to restore order. The 1974–75 oil price hikes brought crisis at Ataka & Co., a Japanese trading company that had about $1 billion of loans outstanding to Sumitomo Bank. Komatsu resolved the worst problems with management and unions, then arranged a merger with C. Itoh, another Japanese trading company.

Among other things, he learned the importance of decisiveness. "Once something goes wrong," he says, "you have to take action. You don't need a long time to make a good decision."

In Osaka, if he goes out for an evening drink and a game of mahjong—he's an ardent player—he's usually back home by eight. "I like to say a few words to my wife," he says, smiling.

Komatsu was startled when in November 1986 the Federal Reserve announced their decision about Sumitomo's proposed investment in Goldman, Sachs. They approved it, but with severe conditions. Sumitomo Bank could not send any employees to learn the securities business at Goldman, Sachs. The two companies couldn't introduce clients to one another. Since Sumitomo Bank couldn't invest in any affiliate of Goldman, Sachs, plans for a London joint venture between the two firms would have to be scrapped. Sumitomo Bank would be allowed to invest as much as 24.9 percent in Goldman, Sachs, but under the circumstances it was unlikely that would happen.

Short-term, Goldman, Sachs cut a sweet deal for themselves. All investment banking firms are desperate for capital needed to compete in global markets. Goldman, Sachs boosted their capital reserves about 50 percent. They don't give up any voting stock. Nor do they need to share expertise with a potential competitor.

Long-term, though, the Fed's ruling looks like a self-inflicted blow against American financial companies. They're the most innovative in the world. They have more experience than anybody else in volatile, deregulated markets. But unless they're free to raise capital wherever it may be available, they won't keep up with their better-funded competitors in Europe and Asia.

Goldman, Sachs partners acknowledge that the $500 million they got from Sumitomo Bank won't be enough to stay alive in global markets. But they probably won't have much luck calling on Japanese banks again.

Tactfully, Komatsu says the Fed's ruling "was probably hammered out on the basis of extremely logical reasoning." One analyst, knowledgeable of Fed proceedings, guessed that suspicions of "inscrutable Japanese capital" triggered the harsh, restrictive ruling. Komatsu honored Sumitomo Bank's initial commitment and proceeded with the deal, chastened by the capricious playing field in the United States.

A number of powerful Sumitomo Bank executives, especially Chairman Ichiro Isoda, opposed many of Komatsu's policies, including the Goldman, Sachs deal and the takeover of troubled, scandal-plagued Heiwa Sogo Bank.

A mutual savings and loan institution, Heiwa Sogo was started by a former scrap-metal dealer named Eizo Komiyama, whose business did especially well during the Korean War. By opening new branches that served customers until 7 P.M., much longer than other banks, the business thrived. Somewhere along the way, the autocratic Komiyama viewed the funds as his own. He funded a number of family-held ventures that soured. Following his death, they spun out of control. Financial irregularities were discovered in 1984. Thirteen people were arrested.

Komatsu wanted the bank, because it looked like an easy way to gain a Tokyo branch office network—considering how difficult it is to buy land in that city. So, in 1986, Sumitomo Bank bought Heiwa Sogo. But the rescue operation cost more than Komatsu anticipated.

As a result, Sumitomo Bank fell from first to fourth place on the profitability ranking for Japanese commercial banks. Chairman Isoda wasn't pleased. Nor was he thrilled about the way things turned out at Goldman, Sachs.

In January 1987, Komatsu transferred Hisao Aoki and Ichiya Kumagai, the two senior managing directors responsible for managing those transactions, away from the firing line to positions in the bank's leasing and securities subsidiaries. Komatsu himself was ousted on October 1, 1987. It was an abrupt, unexpected departure, just a month before the end of his second two-year term. Gracefully, Chairman Isoda cited health reasons and gave Komatsu the honorary title of vice chairman.

Markdown at American Express

On April 15, 1987, American Express made a deal with Nippon Life, Japan's largest insurer, which has $108 billion of assets. For $538 million—$41.50 a share—Nippon Life acquired 13 percent of Shearson Lehman Brothers, American Express's investment banking subsidiary. As an insurance company, Nippon Life isn't constrained by the Glass-Steagall Act or Bank Holding Company Act.

The transaction does have to be reviewed by the Federal Deposit Insurance Corporation, but there's no reason to expect a hitch there. A letter from American Express chairman James Robinson III to Japanese finance minister Kiichi Miyazawa, who advocates Japanese financial companies expanding overseas, was delivered personally by Henry Kissinger.

In 1987, American Express went on to sell another 27 percent of Shearson to employees and the public. Suddenly, Shearson leaped ahead of Merrill Lynch and Salomon Brothers, with $3.5 billion of capital. They are well positioned to continue going head-to-head with their global competitors.

Nippon Life can benefit American Express a number of ways. They can help American Express expand their credit card operations in Japan, for instance. Nippon Life expects substantial benefits in return. All life insurance companies are under pressure from the major Japanese securities firms. Until recent years, these firms relied on the insurance companies to gather savings, then channel savings into securities investments. The securities firms would collect commissions on securities transactions. Now the securities firms are going direct to savers, offering them investment funds. Furthermore, the securities firms anticipate managing pension funds, currently restricted by the Ministry of Finance to life insurance companies and trust banks. Finally, the life insurance companies are reported to be dissatisfied with service they get on securities transactions.

The link may help give Nippon Life badly needed expertise to manage overseas portfolios—by one reckoning, the company had only a half-dozen money managers with international experience. Shearson Lehman Brothers manages $122 billion, and this is growing about 15 percent annually. They're especially strong in municipal finance.

Skeptics noted that Nippon Life paid a hefty premium for their stake: three times Shearson's book value. On the stock exchanges, most large, publicly owned U.S. securities firms sell for two or two and a half times book value.

Short-term, Nippon Life sat on a paper loss, for the stock declined as much as $10 within weeks. A U.S. money manager remarked that Nippon Life "got snookered by Jimmy three sticks."

Fairchild Fiasco

The biggest reactions to Japanese investment have come when an acquisition is involved, as in the 1986 case of Fairchild Semiconductor, the world's fourteenth-largest chip maker. Curiously, Fairchild isn't even a U.S. company. Nobody minded several years ago when management sold it to Schlumberger, the Paris-based oil services firm listed on the New York Stock Exchange.

Fairchild is a sick company. It has lost market share and recently reported losses in the millions. Fairchild's strength is a technology called emitter-coupled logic chips, which are used in mainframe and supercomputers. When no American firm made an offer to buy it, Fairchild president Donald W. Brooks sought a Japanese buyer whose financial strength and manufacturing capabilities could mesh with his company.

But there was a storm of protest when, in October 1986, it was announced that Fujitsu, the Japanese semiconductor maker, would pay $200 million to acquire 80 percent of Fairchild and combine it with San Diego-based Fujitsu Microelectronics. New York Federal Reserve chief Gerald Corrigan declared that "we've been had by the Japanese . . . and we're no longer willing to be their patsy." Ohio senator Howard Metzenbaum, an enthusiastic business-buster, snarled: "It's high time we dealt with the Japanese in a tougher manner." Secretary of Commerce Malcom Baldridge opposed the transaction on the grounds that it was the first step toward Japanese domination of the U.S. semiconductor industry. "Bad policy," he called the deal. He pledged to press for a new federal law that would limit foreign takeovers.

Fujitsu withdrew their offer in March 1987, and soon after that the Japanese cut back semiconductor production as requested by protectionists in Congress and the Reagan administration. But when shortages developed for certain chips, American semiconductor executives returned to Tokyo and begged the Japanese to expand production. The protectionists got what they asked for, and it hurt.

In September 1987, Schlumberger sold all of Fairchild to National Semiconductor, the eleventh-largest chip maker, for $122 million. The Fairchild and National Semiconductor combination ranks sixth in revenues behind Nippon Electric, Hitachi, Toshiba, Motorola, and Texas Instruments. But by being denied the benefits of Fujitsu's higher bid, Schlumberger's stockholders were the losers.

There's an intriguing afterthought to this story. Sources in Washington claim that after having made the initial agreement to invest in Fairchild, Fujitsu executives got access to the company's detailed financial records. Reportedly they were amazed to discover the company in worse shape than they had imagined, and they resolved that somehow the deal should be canceled.

But how? The Japanese are known for honoring their commitment, even when final terms go against them. They would lose face if they broke an agreement. So, these sources say, one of Fujitsu's lobbyists—and the Japanese retain the best—approached Commerce Department officials, expressing concern that the Fujitsu-Fairchild deal, if it went through, would be a threat to the interests of the United States. Protests escalated, and Fujitsu pulled out. Since they were acceding to American pressure, they maintained their honor as reliable business people.

Future Prospects

There's immense potential for future Japanese investment in U.S. stocks. Japanese banks, insurance companies, and securities firms control an estimated $500 billion of investment capital. Currently, only about 3 percent of this is invested in foreign securities.

A large number of Japanese companies are just starting to explore foreign stock markets. Some casualty insurers, for instance, have as little as 1 percent of their assets in foreign equities. Surely, this will go up as the companies become more sophisticated about international markets.

As mentioned already, if the Ministry of Finance agrees to let life insurance companies pay their policyholders out of capital gains as well as current yield, they'll gain greater leeway to invest a higher portion of their funds in stocks.

During the next five years, total Japanese investments in U.S. stocks could exceed $100 billion. While that's the equivalent of about six weeks' turnover on the Big Board, it's definitely important buying power.

Surely, Japanese investors would become more sophisticated here as everywhere else. This means they'll venture well beyond the Nifty Fifty blue chip stocks, with the result that more sectors of the U.S. stock market are likely to benefit from Japanese capital.

Japanese buying won't be steady, however. If the U.S. dollar continues to slide, many Japanese investors will become more wary about dollar-denominated assets, like stocks. Rising interest rates will make stock yields less appealing. A crash in the Japanese stock or real estate markets will force Japanese investors to pull back from the U.S. stock market. Their funds will be needed back home.

As the October 1987 stock crash demonstrated, financial markets are international. More Americans are aware that developments in one market affect what happens elsewhere. Increasingly, Americans will determine what's happening in Tokyo as they make their investment decisions.

9

ENDAKA SYNDROME

Foreign exchange markets are the most pivotal markets in the financial world. Very little trade or investment takes place when people can't get the currency they need. Only the most regulated, backward nations rely on inefficient barter.

Here, as in other markets, the more power governments try to assert, the less influence they actually have. Since regulations tend to increase the cost and risk of foreign exchange transactions, expanding the scope of regulations simply drives business offshore. Perhaps three-quarters of the more than 150 nations in the world are dictatorships; you can count on the fingers of one hand the number of places free enough for major foreign exchange markets to flourish. When a dictatorship wants to conduct international business, it must deal with one of these offshore markets. Hong Kong, for example, is China's window on the world, and its Bank of China is the largest banking institution there.

As other economies—most notably the Japanese—have expanded, and as the U.S. dollar has depreciated, its relative position has declined in the world. A reported 67 percent of central bank reserves are in U.S. dollars while less than 10 percent are in Japanese yen. A decade ago, 78 percent of central bank reserves were in U.S. dollars.

Thirty-eight percent of international bond transactions are in U.S. dollars while 14 percent are in Japanese yen. As noted already, the Japanese figure is artificial, because both Japanese borrowers and lenders conduct business in Europe to avoid costly regulations in Japan; as Japanese capital markets are deregulated, more and more borrowers as well as lenders will do their business at home.

About 70 percent of international trade is conducted in U.S. dollars. This percentage is going down. In the future, for example, more Japanese exports will probably have to be paid for in yen rather than U.S. dollars. A number of oil producers reportedly would prefer payment in yen, and that may happen before long.

Nonetheless, the huge size of the U.S. economy means a continued strong flow of U.S. dollar transactions. The U.S. dollar won't lose its dominant position anytime soon. Americans, however, will have to become more familiar with world currency markets and methods of protecting themselves against adverse fluctuations.

U.S. banks and British foreign exchange brokers continue to be the principal players in Europe, the United States, and most other markets. Japanese foreign exchange brokers are strong only in their home market.

The markets have expanded dramatically since the 1970s as foreign exchange barriers have come down, enabling companies and investors to move their funds where they can earn the highest, safest returns. Foreign exchange rates have become a highly sensitive barometer responding to volatile changes such as inflation, trade deficits, oil shortages, and political turmoil.

International foreign exchange trading surpasses $200 billion a day now. This is about double the size of the U.S. government bond market and almost forty times the average daily trading on the New York Stock Exchange.

Daily volume in London is about $90 billion, double the figures reported three years ago by the Bank of England. London thrives because it's a deregulated environment with abundant expertise and a strategic location. During the morning, London's trading hours overlap those in Asia and the Middle East. Afternoons, London traders talk to New York. There are more opportunities for transactions in London than the other major financial centers.

New York is the second most important foreign exchange market. The Federal Reserve Bank of New York estimates daily volume at $50 billion, up 92 percent from three years ago. The Bank of Tokyo has five thousand people handling business in New York.

Tokyo is coming on strong. During the past three years, volume has soared more than 400 percent to about $50 billion daily.

View From Tokyo

The sixty-three-year-old president of the Bank of Tokyo, Minoru In-ouye, is at the vortex of this tumultuous change. The bank is a powerful force in foreign exchange markets, particularly now that the yen is becoming more important. From his contemporary stone headquarters building in the Nihonbashi business district, Inouye manages more than $145 billion of assets. Over half the bank's business is denominated in foreign currencies, many, like the U.S. dollar, depreciating against the yen. Inouye is a cautious, suave, self-assured man seeking to negotiate a way through the thickets ahead.

"Japan is being transformed from a nation which relies on exports," he says, "to one which depends on a well-balanced combination of exports, capital, and technologies, as well as strong domestic demand. The new Japan will also be a nation in which its markets are open and accessible to foreign companies. These developments are redefining economic relationships within Japan and between Japan and other nations."

Since the Bank of Tokyo is Japan's principal foreign exchange bank, Inouye works closely with Bank of Japan's governor Satoshi Sumita, whose Roman-style fortress is across the street. Sumita is nicknamed "Kuma"—meaning "bear"—because he paces around and around his office silently when he's preoccupied with a decision. The son of a Japanese general and a graduate of Tokyo University, Sumita is a traditional Japanese who prefers speaking through an interpreter, but he collects French paintings and belongs to the wine society Commandre Bordeaux. He travels on commercial airlines without an entourage or ceremony.

Unlike predecessors who were meek and deferential toward Western finance officials, particularly those from the United States, Sumita is more blunt. He's an outspoken central banker, and he gets the spotlight that used to focus only on the likes of Bundesbank chairman Karl Otto Poehl or Federal Reserve chiefs Paul Volcker and Alan Greenspan.

For more than a hundred years, the Bank of Tokyo has enjoyed a special relationship with the Bank of Japan. The Bank of Japan deposits more currency reserves with the Bank of Tokyo than other banks, and the latter helps carry out Japan's foreign aid policy. It's widely considered a private extension of the central bank.

Consequently, market watchers try to monitor the foreign exchange operations of the Bank of Tokyo. When it's selling U.S. dollars heavily, for instance, a lot of people reconsider their dollar positions. Major purchases of yen could encourage more moves into that currency.

Despite their newfound financial power, though, the Japanese are worried. They're preoccupied with *endaka*—the strong yen. Coal, chemicals, textiles, shipbuilding, and other basic industries are in trouble.

Perhaps hardest hit is the steel industry. In 1986, Kawasaki Steel announced a program to cut five thousand jobs, about 20 percent of their work force. Sumitomo Metal Industries will cut six thousand, Kobe Steel six thousand, and Nippon Steel nineteen thousand jobs—about a third of their work force.

During 1986, Cannon, Japan's largest camera manufacturer, saw their pretax profits tumble 69 percent when the yen soared. Japanese exporters are closing factories and shifting production offshore to lower-cost labor markets, like South Korea and Taiwan. Japanese soap opera characters moan about love affairs disrupted by job transfers. In downtown Tokyo, electronic street signs display the latest yen/dollar exchange rate for passersby.

The Bank of Tokyo's foreign exchange traders look to the United States for clues. The bank's principal trading rooms have wall calendars marking the days and times when the latest results for U.S. unemployment, construction expenditures, wholesale prices, retail sales, retail prices, consumer credit balances, and the trade balance will be announced. No Japanese dates appear on these calendars. Foreign exchange traders don't anticipate that the Japanese trade surplus, for instance, will have a significant impact on the markets. They're concerned about the U.S. trade deficit.

There's little action during the hours before official economic data are released. Then, suddenly, the phones light up again, as corporations and individual investors scramble to adjust their currency positions.

Money Matchmakers

The Bank of Tokyo and other banks rely on brokers. By calling a single broker, a bank trader can find out right away what dozens, perhaps a hundred banks are bidding or offering for foreign exchange.

Japan's biggest foreign exchange broker is Tokyo Forex, on the sixth floor of a new building in Nihonbashi. There brokers sit around white masonite tables, one for each currency market—spot yen, spot Australian dollars, spot deutsche marks, spot British pounds, and spot "Swissy" (Swiss francs). Spot means the currency is offered for immediate delivery. At additional tables, brokers cover the market for future delivery of these currencies. Large tables serve major banks, where the minimum transaction is generally about $5 million. Smaller tables are for regional banks with minimum transactions around $1 million.

Each broker faces a couple of small, loud speakers and a dealing board with more than a hundred telephone buttons, each button representing a direct line to a bank. When a trader from Dai-Ichi Kangyo Bank, for instance, wants a spot dollar/yen quote, a certain button lights up, and the broker who covers that bank punches the button. Then the bank trader's voice crackles over the speakers. The broker shouts the bid or offer and writes it down on the tabletop in front of him with a black felt-tip marker.

Suppose the bank trader calls and asks the price for $10 million, dollar/yen. The broker might quote 10/20. At the present time, this means 145.1 yen per dollar to buy yen and 145.2 to sell. So the broker's spread is a tenth of a yen. The bank trader may hit the 10 bid or the 20 offer.

Sometimes banks use several brokers simultaneously, to mask their intentions. "Let's say five brokers were quoting 35/40," explains Peter McLachlan of the Tokyo Forex Group. "The market is 35/40, 35/41, 35/39, jumping around with small trades going through at 36/37, with bits and pieces trading—$2 million, then $5 million, and maybe $15 million at the price.

"Suddenly, along comes a big player, and he calls a broker. Says I'm a seller at 35, I've got $200 million to go, do what you can for me.

"If he hits everyone, then the entire market is 35 offered, because now they have the same one big guy offering everywhere. But you never know whether the bid at 35 involves different banks or the same bank on five different lines.

"Or take a bank who asks the size of the market, because he has $250 million to sell. A broker says he's 10-bid at 35. The bank calls another broker, who reports 35 bid, but only for about $5 million. The bids at 35/40 add up to only $15 million. If the bank whacks all those guys, and he still has $185 million to do, he doesn't know where the next bid is coming from. He may say I've got more than 5 to do at 35, how much can you do? I'll give you $25 million at 36, $25 million at 37."

Meanwhile, at the corner of each table is the "link man," who listens for the most attractive bids and offers relayed by link men in the company's trading rooms overseas. He shouts the best prices from his market to them. One moment, the best bid for a Tokyo offer may be elsewhere in the Tokyo market, and the transaction stays in Tokyo. A few seconds later, the best bid for another Tokyo offer may come from the link man, relayed from a client in New York, London, Bahrain, Zurich, Sydney, or somewhere else. It's an extraordinarily efficient market.

Two Traders

Japanese brokers are like traders almost anywhere. They have big egos. They love to trade, especially large positions. They get excited when they make money. They're depressed if they don't, although they may not show their emotions.

Take Kimotoshi Yasui, thirty-four, a trader with a polite, formal manner. He was born in Tokyo. His father, Yoshio, was a manager of a small company that produced gas meters. Yasui went to Dokkyo University, a relatively new institution north of Tokyo. One of his relatives had a friend at Tokyo Forex, and that sounded interesting. After graduation, he became a broker at the spot yen table.

Yasui handles transactions involving Dai-Ichi Kangyo Bank, Tokai Bank, Kiowa Bank, Mitsubishi Bank, Toyo Trust, and Fuji Bank. "If I had the Bank of Tokyo," he says, "I wouldn't be able to do much else, because of the tremendous volumes they buy and sell."

J. C. Okazawa, thirty-six, has developed a distinctly American style of foreign exchange trading. At Waseda University, Okazawa discovered French literature. He loved nineteenth- and twentieth-century writers like Stendhal, Zola, Camus, and Sartre. After two years, he became restless and dropped out, though he continued to read French authors whenever he could—increasingly, mystery writers like Georges Simenon.

Okazawa worked at a succession of jobs. For a while, he was behind the counter at a duty-free shop in the Ginza, Tokyo's most famous shopping district. He sold expensive items, like watches, cameras, and video equipment. Then he worked with the Tokyo Prince Hotel, where he became manager of the banquet department. He helped develop schedules, give job assignments, and handle emergencies.

In 1980, Okazawa saw a help wanted advertisement by the British money broker Ashley & Pierce in a Japanese newspaper. "That sounded like a possibility," he says. "I went for an interview, and a British guy explained the money market, but I didn't understand anything. Apparently, he thought I was aggressive enough that I could succeed."

Ashley & Pierce put him through a rigorous training program. He attended classes every morning for three weeks. They sent him to Singapore for further training. After six years, he sought wider opportunities at Tokyo Forex. "I like the excitement," he says. "It's better than keeping quiet."

Okazawa became something of a maverick. The Japanese, like the British, are loath to ask for business unless properly introduced. A foreign exchange broker may be called many times for quotes, yet not handle any transactions. The traditional Japanese practice would be to continue offering quotations and hope for a transaction eventually. But after providing several quotations, Okazawa asks when the caller will swing some business his way. "Why aren't we doing any business?" he'll say. He became a big hitter, handling as much as $300 million at a time.

International Connections

"My grandfather, Sakai Yanagita, started this company," explains Tokyo Forex president Kochi Yanagita, forty-seven. He's a handsome man over six feet, unusually tall for a Japanese. "My grandfather was from Kyushu, Japan's southernmost island. He was a very traditional Meiji-era man. He didn't graduate from high school, but he joined a company called Fujimoto Billbroker around the turn of the century, and he worked hard. They traded promissory notes issued by Japan's major companies. Principal buyers were banks and other financial institutions. When Fujimoto went out of business, my grandfather started on his own, in 1909. This became Tokyo Tanshi.

"My father, Tomoo Yanagita, now seventy-six, graduated from Keio University with a broad view of financial markets. After World War II, he recognized the need for more orderly foreign exchange markets was growing apace with Japan's growth. In 1952, he started Tokyo Forex, Japan's first foreign exchange broker. Because of exchange controls, there wasn't any international business. We grew by handling transactions among domestic banks.

"After I graduated from Keio University in 1964, I joined Mitsubishi Trust & Banking, where I analyzed the creditworthiness of Japanese companies. Until a few years ago, we didn't have any independent credit rating services like Dun & Bradstreet—each bank had to do its own homework."

Then came the "Nixon shock." On August 15, 1971, President Richard Nixon abandoned efforts to maintain fixed exchange rates. The Bretton Woods international monetary system, which the Allies fashioned after World War II, pegged major currencies to the dollar and the dollar to gold at $35 per ounce. As runaway federal spending vastly expanded the number of dollars in circulation, central banks had to buy more and more dollars if they were to preserve fixed relationships among currencies. When events gave people reason to lose confidence in the dollar, they'd switch into other currencies, and the U.S. government would announce a sudden devaluation. After a while, it became obvious that the promised monetary stability was an illusion.

Increasingly, investors shifted their funds around the world, seeking high, safe yields. As a result, foreign exchange trading grew to be fifteen to twenty times more than required to finance world trade. The flow of capital, not just trade, determined foreign exchange rates, inflation, the rise and fall of nations.

Meanwhile, U.S. regulations, especially Regulation Q, largely cut off the United States from international money markets. This political plum for the banks limited interest that could be paid on bank deposits, thereby saving them money. For years, domestic interest was fixed at 5 percent, while international interest rates climbed past 10 percent. Consequently, foreign investors didn't risk their funds in the United States when interest rates were higher elsewhere. Large U.S. investors, too, would go abroad, leaving their savings with the fabled Gnomes of Zurich.

American banks would have remained small, parochial players if they hadn't expanded overseas where they could attract deposits by paying competitive interest rates. They opened branches in London, Nassau, Grand Cayman, and elsewhere. This enabled Citibank, for instance, to continue serving General Motors when the latter planned a new manufacturing facility in West Germany. Hundreds of banks opened offshore branches.

A lot of these banks, particularly regionals, didn't have much experience with the huge volumes, speed, and volatility of international transactions. Banks needed much more sophisticated foreign exchange services to avoid being exposed to losing positions.

Concerned about a flow of funds out of the U.S., the federal government abolished many crippling regulations like Q by 1973. Massive amounts of capital flowed across borders, seeking the highest yields in the safest havens.

Bank defaults like that of Bankhaus I.D. Herstatt in West Germany and Franklin National Bank in the United States triggered shock waves through the international money markets. Instead of moving five points at a time, they'd move twenty or thirty points. "We faced an entirely new, international market," recalls Kochi Yanagita, "and my father asked me to help him at Tokyo Forex.

"We had a relationship with Morgan Guaranty Trust, and in 1973, they accepted me as a trainee at their London office so I could learn how things worked. I started as a broker. People shouting bids at you, prices changing from minute to minute, earnings based on daily production—all this was exhilarating.

"After about six months, I returned to Tokyo and worked as a broker. I did this for eight years. As international markets continued to expand, it was clear we'd have to open overseas offices if we wanted to remain a major broker. We decided we'd start close to home, where we could communicate easily. Hong Kong looked wild and risky. The Monetary Authority of Singapore helped minimize volatility in Singapore, so in 1981 I went there to open an office. I built it up to about 140 people within a couple years. It was a good experience managing a business.

"Further expansion, especially in the United States and Europe, would bring us face-to-face with the British foreign exchange brokers who did most of the international business. We didn't have enough expertise yet, so we explored the possibility of a merger or acquisition.

"We talked with people at Marshall's and Ashley & Pierce, but they wanted to buy us. So we approached Tullett & Riley, a smaller British firm with a good reputation."

Rugby and Money

Tullett's was started in June 1971 by Derek Tullett, fifty-four, a dapper, outgoing Englishman who was a director of the money broker Savage, Heath. Tullett was an ideal person to recruit and direct people for a risky new venture. He developed many contacts by playing rugby and training rugby teams in Surrey, where he lived. He met more people playing squash several times a week. He volunteered to do civic work for the City of London, reporting to the lord mayor.

His idea was to get in on the ground floor of the emerging Euro-dollar market, brokering deposits among banks. He recruited three fellow brokers as partners: David Riley, a tall, bearded broker who helped run the operation; Peter Doney, another weekend rugby enthu-siast, a quiet number-cruncher who handled the fine art of structuring complex deals with narrow margins; and Colin Probetts, an elegant gentleman who entertained clients and contacts almost every night.

Before the firm could conduct business, they needed six sponsors and approval from the Bank of England. Tullett was well known in the London financial community, so he lined up sponsors from major London banks like Barclay's and Standard & Chartered. They seemed to admire a nice chap striking out on his own.

It was more difficult persuading banks to give them direct phone lines, since this was an administrative bother and the banks were already connected with many other brokers. A direct line affords in-stant communications: you just pick up the phone, and a blinking light alerts a broker at the other end. No dialing necessary. "If you have to go through outside lines," explains Tullett, "you'll seldom get bids, because transactions will be done already by competitors with direct lines." The firm got underway with a twenty-five-hundred-square-foot office in the City of London. They had twelve 150-line dealing boards.

Tullett's served North American customers via a Toronto office, since it was the closest financial center to the United States, unre-stricted by U.S. exchange controls. Bay Street was a small market, but the five major Canadian banks were active in international markets. All the major British foreign exchange brokers opened offices in Toronto. The city might have become a major center, but the Canadian government erected barriers against competition from foreign banks. Protectionism doomed Toronto to second-rate status.

Toronto lost its opportunity fast after the New York market was opened to foreign exchange brokers in 1979. "Banks realized they were being picked off when they traded bank-to-bank internationally," explains Tullett's managing director Peter McLachlan, a burly, balding Canadian. "Because they didn't always realize how strong the market was, they'd sell too low. Or they'd overpay, not realizing the market had weakened. They wanted the fast deal and information which brokers can provide."

British brokers rushed to build their New York offices. "There was a total lack of experienced talent," recalls McLachlan. "Nobody seemed to have heard of foreign exchange, because it was something done in the back rooms of banks. Not yet very important. New York banks were mainly lending institutions run by the corporate loan department.

"We hired people who used to be cab drivers and friends of someone's father's cousin's nephew. Salaries doubled within a few years. I remember one guy was making $40,000 here, and another firm offered him $90,000 plus a car and company-paid parking space to join them. It wasn't that he was unusually good, but every firm needed skilled traders in a hurry.

"That we grew internationally made things more challenging. Sometimes, after we spent time training someone, and they worked out well they'd be assigned to another office which needed help. We'd have to start over again with a new person."

Tullett's built their operation to more than a thousand brokers worldwide. They established direct, twenty-four-hour lines linking world currency markets simultaneously. Pick up a phone, shout a bid to Australia, for instance, and brokers in Sydney, Bahrain, London, and Frankfurt heard it. Tullett's also served secondary foreign exchange markets in Toronto, Los Angeles, Brussels, Guernsey, Zurich, Kuwait, and Melbourne.

The gap in their network, Tullett realized, was Japan. The gap became more serious every month as Japan gained financial power. Clearly, a foreign exchange broker couldn't be truly international without a major presence there. But it's a tough market to penetrate, because of the language, established relationships, and traditional practices. Tullett recognized he needed to form a strategic alliance with a major Japanese foreign exchange broker.

So when Kochi Yanagida called, he was interested in talking about a deal. They had to work out an understanding not only between themselves but with the Bank of England. Officials there had seen British merchant banks lose their once mighty position in international finance. American banks, then Japanese banks, dominated the market. British firms held on only in insurance and money brokering. To help with the negotiations, Yanagida brought along Tatsuro Morita, president of Tokyo Tanshi, their affiliated company. He used to be a high official at the Bank of Japan, so he was accustomed to the protocol among central banks. Morita and Yanagida explained they wanted a strong presence in the London market, without necessarily controlling a British firm.

In July 1983, an agreement was reached: Tokyo Forex would buy 47 percent of Tullett's, and Tullett's would buy 20 percent of Tokyo Forex. Tokyo Forex would continue to do business in Tokyo under their name. Elsewhere, the venture would be known as Tullett & Tokyo Forex. Overnight, Tullett's gained entry to the Japanese market, and Tokyo Forex gained a sophisticated international network that included the United States. A hundred Tullett's brokers covered the New York market alone.

This deal triggered more alignments in the foreign exchange market. Ashley & Pierce bought 30 percent of Nittan, a Japanese discount brokerage house that had expanded into foreign exchange, and Nittan got about 5 percent of Ashley & Pierce. Marshall's bought 49 percent of Hattori, a small money broker. Harlow's, another British foreign exchange broker, bought into Ueda Tanshi. A new era of international competition was underway.

Meanwhile, other financial centers were expanding their reach. In New York, some foreign exchange traders start work by four in the morning, or nine London time, when markets open there. "We serve breakfast until seven-thirty," says McLachlan. "If you're not here by then, no breakfast. Arrive at a quarter to eight, and probably you'll be greeted with 'good afternoon'.

"We continue large-scale trading until about six, then pass on a lot of orders for execution in Los Angeles, which may continue trading until about eight their time. By then, Tokyo, Singapore, Hong Kong, and Sydney are trading, so positions can be passed to our offices in those markets."

London markets open earlier than they used to, so they can keep pace with events in the Middle East and Asia. Now Tokyo foreign exchange brokers are extending their hours, too.

Yen Speculators

In recent years, some of the most aggressive foreign exchange players have emerged from Japan.

One of the most unlikely gnomes is Shigeru Kita of Hanwa Koygo, a medium-size steel trading company. Kita has spent four decades dealing with steel bars and wires, but as that business slumped, he was agile enough to handle foreign exchange. From the trading room on the third floor of a building near the Tsukiji, Tokyo, wholesale fish market, he places $300 million to $500 million of foreign exchange orders a day. Now foreign exchange trading accounts for about 70 percent of the firm's profits.

Kita favors a distinctive technique for handling foreign exchange transactions, and traders are alert for signals that would reveal what he's doing. "Look!" shouts a bank trader in Tokyo, "Hanwa has switched to dollar buying!" The dollar notches upward.

Nomura Securities tries to keep a currency whiz named Hajime Yoshida away from outsiders, lest he become the target of corporate headhunters. He works on new kinds of Eurobonds that use yen swaps to help make them more appealing for both investors and borrowers. Inside Nomura, his biggest successes are referred to as Yoshida No. 1, Yoshida No. 2, and Yoshida No. 3. He's about thirty, but otherwise little is known about him.

After the May 1986 Tokyo meeting of finance ministers from seven major industrialized countries, wealthy Mideast investors approached New Japan Securities, asking for better ways to put their funds in yen. They conjured a complex Euroyen bond with swaps, designed to pay more on redemption in certain circumstances when the yen rises. Called Foreign Exchange–Interest Composite Index Bonds, they proved an immediate hit among Arab investors. Though it's exceedingly complex, Takuji Katayama, a gnome at rival Yamaichi Securities, figured out how to structure and price similar bonds within two hours. "We can unravel the secrets of almost any new financial product within a day," he says.

Other major foreign exchange speculators reportedly include C. Itoh and Nissho Iwai, major trading companies;, Nippon Oil; and

Osaka-based Sharp Electronics. Sharp, the most aggressive of the four, trades as much as $500 million daily.

What's Ahead

Freely floating exchange rates are here to stay. While central bankers may agree there should be some other world monetary system, their conflicting national interests lead them to insist on carving it up differently.

The trend toward fewer exchange controls and more freely floating rates will be hard to reverse, because too many people benefit from it. Almost instantly, freely floating exchange rates reflect expectations about world events and transmit vital price information everywhere, so people can see how they should plan. Higher yen exchange rates tell people to maximize yen income and reduce their yen obligations. On the other hand, with a depreciating U.S. dollar, people know to try and switch more obligations into dollars and minimize their dollar income, so they lose as little money as possible. This "dirty-float" system functions despite all the central bank interventions.

People have a strong stake in the floating system, too, because it's more stable than fixed-rate alternatives. World events are reflected incrementally, on a day-to-day basis. Because currency markets dwarf the biggest players, they're difficult to manipulate. Analysis of supply-and-demand forces may yield reasonable expectations. By contrast, a fixed-rate system means central bankers attempt to suppress markets and bottle up changes until they explode, as we saw during the 1960s and early 1970s. This is less predictable, more volatile and disruptive.

Foreign exchange markets will become more international as the trend toward deregulation continues. Trading hours will be extended to allow for more overlap among major markets.

The Japanese foreign exchange market will continue opening up. Foreign banks and currency brokers will become increasingly important in Japan.

Countries that attempt to hide behind exchange controls will stagnate in an economic backwater. They will have less incentive to adapt. Their companies will be handicapped in a competitive world.

The Japanese yen will gain importance commensurate with Japan's status as the second-largest economy in the world. The yen will play a greater role in trade. About 20 percent of Japan's exports to the

United States and 40 percent of exports to Asia are denominated in yen. Since the Japanese Ministry of Finance has recently legalized bankers' acceptances, those widely used instruments of trade finance can be negotiated in yen.

The volume of yen investment can be expected to rise. This is partially because of highly sophisticated swap technologies that enable borrowers and lenders to tap the most advantageous capital markets, wherever they may be, and convert the proceeds to the currency of their choice. Equally important, the Ministry of Finance has removed many barriers and permits virtually unrestricted growth of the Euroyen capital market.

About 5.5 percent of central bank reserves are in yen. Central bankers in the United States and Europe are pressuring Japan to liberalize the yen. It will become a more important reserve currency.

Financial institutions with a strong position in the yen market will gain the most. Primarily, this means the Bank of Tokyo and other major Japanese banks and foreign exchange brokers.

As the yen becomes more important in international finance, American companies will have to borrow more yen and cater to the needs of Japanese lenders. This will be a strange, uneasy experience for many American executives, since they've long been accustomed to borrowing dollars and letting foreign lenders worry about currency risks. In the future, American borrowers will assume more of those risks, and they'll have to become more skilled at protecting themselves.

10

$22,500 PER SQUARE FOOT

In 1986, a former Tokyo used-car salesman named Katoru Watanabe bet a bundle on Hawaii. He invested $232 million to buy the Kona Lagoon, Ala Moana, and Maui Marriott hotels. Then he plunked down $245 million more for the Hyatt Regency Waikiki. By the time he stopped to catch his breath, the fifty-two-year-old Watanabe had assembled a real estate empire with more than four thousand hotel rooms. It's valued at $750 million to $1 billion. "Hawaii is close to Japan, the economy is stable, and it's safe for investment," he says.

In recent years, the Japanese have had the most visible presence not just in Hawaii but in major cities on the mainland. According to Salomon Brothers, Japanese investors bought more than $7 billion worth of income-producing U.S. real estate in 1988. Most of this investment is in New York, California, and Hawaii, but Japanese investors are expanding their activity in other cities, such as Chicago, Atlanta, Boston and Washington. Among the most noteworthy transactions:

- Tower 49, a Manhattan office building, which Kato Kagaku, the world's largest sugar refiner, purchased for $301 million—at $500 per square foot, a record for an office building.
- Exxon Building, on Manhattan's Sixth Avenue, which Mitsui Fudoson bought for $610 million ($295 per square foot), the highest total price ever paid for a Manhattan office building.

- Arco Plaza, a Los Angeles office complex that Shuwa Investments purchased for $620 million, the largest all-cash U.S. real estate transaction ever.

- Tiffany Building, on Manhattan's Fifth Avenue and Fifty-seventh Street, which Dai-Ichi America Real Estate bought for $94 million, a record-high $940 per square foot for retail on any U.S. property.

- Hyatt Regency Maui, a hotel that sold to Kokusai Motorcars, Japan's largest taxicab and livery company, for $320 million, highest price ever for a hotel property.

Why Now?

Japanese investors favor the U.S. real estate market for several reasons. First of all, prime properties are available. The United States may be the most complex real estate market, with a seemingly endless number of submarkets. All kinds of properties turn over.

By contrast, opportunies are limited in Japan. Tokyo real estate prices skyrocketed 50 percent during 1986—often reaching $22,500 per square foot—but owners are reluctant to sell. If they ever did, they'd be hit with a land sales tax that goes as high as 80 percent. Tokyo office buildings are 98 percent occupied. The property turnover rate is estimated to be under 2 percent annually. A prospective buyer would be lucky to find one good building for sale.

Though Japan has about half the population of the United States, people must make do with about one twenty-fifth of the area. What's more, 85 percent of Japan is mountainous. Much of the remaining land is unavailable for commercial development. People keep little land holdings within their families for generations.

Once a building is up, tenants tend to stay, because they may have nowhere else to go. For example, the Marounuchi Building, downtown Tokyo headquarters for a number of Mitsubishi companies, was constructed in 1923. It endured the calamitous earthquake that year and the firebombing during World War II. Many original tenants continue to work there, and every year they gather for a party.

The Tokyo real estate market is so tight that foreign companies have great difficulty finding space. The Bank of China was out of luck until Mitsubishi Bank agreed to close one of its downtown branch offices and make the space available, hopefully gaining goodwill for its ventures in China.

American investment banks couldn't find space downtown, either. Salomon Brothers, Shearson/Lehman Brothers, Goldman, Sachs, and Citibank moved into Ark Hills, a spiffy new office-hotel-retail complex in Akasaka, near the American embassy. Foreigners occupy half the apartments—they're about 325 square feet and rent for $2,100 a month. Property billionaire Taikichiro Mori reportedly took two decades to assemble the property for that project—he had to outlive the owners.

From the Japanese standpoint, U.S. properties are a bargain because of the 40 percent decline of the U.S. dollar against the yen during the past three years. When the yen enters a down-cycle, Japanese investors won't be able to buy as much real estate in the United States. On the other hand, what they already have will gain value in terms of other currencies, like the yen.

U.S. property is also attractive because of comparatively high yields. According to Hideki Mitani, an economist with Goldman, Sachs, "Prime U.S. properties usually trade at values that equate to a first-year, cash-on-cash return of 6 percent to 9 percent. This compares to a typical annual return on Japanese real estate of 2 percent to 4.5 percent."

Moreover, U.S. real estate can be depreciated over a shorter period than Japanese real estate—thirty-one years versus sixty-five. This means substantially larger annual depreciation deductions on U.S. property.

The low cost of Japanese funds—several percentage points below U.S. interest rates—is another key factor stimulating Japanese real estate investment. The Japanese tax system encourages low-cost funds by taxing consumption and exempting much investment income, the reverse of the situation in the United States, where investment is heavily taxed. Japanese investors borrow yen, collateralized by their assets in Japan, then swap yen into dollars. Or they may borrow dollars, their aim is to have dollar liabilities that match the flow of dollars from rent rolls.

"Because little land is available, and the returns are low," says Hiroyasu Seike of Seiyo Corporation, "investing in Japanese real estate has become boring. Besides, there's increased risk of drawing a joker, after the sharp rise in land prices."

Long Learning Curve

"Before the Japanese make a commitment, they do an incredible amount of homework, and it takes a lot of time before they get to the table," explains Christopher McGratty, senior vice president of Tishman Realty and Construction, Manhattan. The firm is joint venture partner with Aoki Corp. in a convention hotel near Walt Disney World, Orlando, Florida, and with Japan Air Lines Development in a $70 million luxury hotel on Chicago's Riverfront Park.

Japanese interest in U.S. real estate didn't start yesterday. The Japanese have explored the market for years, most noticeably in Hawaii. All kinds of Japanese companies have made investments there. In 1954, Sumitomo Bank assisted in establishing Central Pacific Bank. Shizuoka Shimbun bought the *Hawaii Hochi* newspaper for $1.3 million in 1962. A year later, Kokusai Kogyo paid Sheraton $10.7 million for the Moana and Surfrider Hotels on Waikiki Beach. In 1974, wheeler-dealer Kenji Osano bought the Sheraton-Waikiki, Royal Hawaiian, and Sheraton-Maui hotels for $105 million. Then Meiji Mutual Life acquired controlling interest in Pacific Guardian Life Insurance Company. Suntory, the big Japanese distiller, built the Royal Hawaiian Shopping Center in Waikiki. Nittaku Enterprise Co. bought Spencecliff, a $40 million food service company with twenty-five restaurants, bake shops, and catering operations.

Meanwhile, during the 1960s, Japanese life insurance companies began analyzing mainland U.S. real estate. "Back then, I was with Equitable Life," recalls Kevin F. Haggarty, executive vice president of Cushman & Wakefield, the large commercial realty firm. "Coy Ecklund, who later became our chairman, encouraged exchanges between Japan and the United States. Many Japanese analysts came here for six months to two years, studying our investment policies. Since, like every major U.S. life insurance company, we had a significant portion of our assets in real estate, the Japanese observed how we handled real estate. Some of their analysts would spend time at our field offices, learning how to evaluate real estate, how it's financed, how our approval process works.

"Equitable cultivated relationships in Japan way ahead of the other U.S. life companies. This is why, when the Japanese were ready to move, Equitable has done more real estate joint ventures than anyone else. They've worked with Nippon Life, Dai-Ichi Life, Asahi

Life, Meiji Life, and so on. Equitable paid their dues, and the Japanese did their homework."

The Japanese needed time to understand U.S. real estate practice, which is very different than theirs. The most significant factor is that the real estate market there is premised on the scarcity of land.

Japanese landowners tend to have a longer view than Americans. Mitsubishi Estate is the largest landlord in Tokyo's Marunouchi business district, where sixty-eight Tokyo Stock Exchange companies have their headquarters. Mitsubishi Estate owns twenty-four buildings there—19 million square feet—and it hasn't sold a single property in a half-century. Back in 1890, Mitsubishi's predecessor company bought Marunouchi for the equivalent of $1 million when it was a meadow in front of the Imperial Palace, used as a military parade ground.

Capital gain just isn't part of traditional Japanese thinking, since they don't anticipate selling. "To the Japanese," says Hajime Tsuboi, chief executive officer of Mitsui Real Estate Development Co. Ltd., "the phenomenon of companies selling large landmark buildings is inconceivable. Mitsui Real Estate owns over a hundred buildings in Japan, and for the most part, we fully intend to hold those buildings forever. It's hard for me to imagine why Exxon would sell the Exxon Building, but it's a good catch for us."

Because of scarcity, Japanese real estate investors aren't accustomed to evaluating complex choices. "The idea of having alternative real estate investments is incomprehensible to many Japanese," says Haggarty. "Over there, if you're lucky, you come across one good piece of real estate. You don't sit there and contemplate a half-dozen options. If you own land, you hold it, because you never know whether you'll be able to buy more good land again."

Land accounts for about 80 percent of total value. Only about 20 percent is for the building on it. The situation is reversed in the United States, where about 20 percent of a property's value is for land. At least 80 percent of the value is in the building and the rental income it generates.

"Consequently," Haggarty explains, "ownership is straightforward. Japanese real estate is financed mostly with equity investment. Only about a quarter to a third of a deal involves debt. It's a direct obligation secured by your assets and your good name.

"They don't have mortgages where the lender has recourse only to the property and cannot put a lien on your other assets."

Japan has few investment vehicles. Convertible mortgages—which offer a lender the option of gaining an equity interest—aren't common. Nor do you find limited and general partnerships, popular real estate investment techniques in the U.S.

Finally, leasing practices are different in the United States. Typical Japanese office leases seldom extend more than three years. In major cities of the United States, the norm is more like five or ten years, and longer terms are common.

Eleven Kinds of Japanese Investors

There are at least eleven different kinds of Japanese investors in real estate. Among the players, each with somewhat different interests, are life insurance companies, development firms, construction companies, trust banks, long-term credit banks, city banks, trading companies, leasing companies, securities firms, cash-rich manufacturing companies, and high-net-worth individuals. There isn't a monolithic Japan Inc. in real estate or anywhere else.

Like U.S. life insurance companies and other major real estate investors, Japanese institutions determine the desirability of U.S. real estate by comparing yields to ten-year U.S. Treasury bonds, generally considered among the safest investments. Salomon Brothers estimates that the Japanese look for real estate to yield two to three percentage points more than Treasuries, including net income and capital gain at the end of perhaps a ten-year holding period. Many Japanese investors, however, deny that potential capital gains figures in their analysis, since they anticipate holding U.S. real estate indefinitely, as they do in Japan.

When Treasury interest rates declined in 1985, approaching the yields of prime real estate, Japanese real estate investors began to move. Almost all their major purchases on the Mainland have been made since 1985.

The 1986 Tax Reform Act created incentives for American property owners to sell. After December 31, 1986, annual depreciation deductions would be reduced as the depreciation period on a building was extended from nineteen to thirty-one years. The capital gains tax would jump from 20 percent to 28 percent. As properties came on the market, the Japanese stepped up to buy.

Since then, far fewer properties have become available, but the Japanese remain eager buyers. "As far as real estate is concerned, the Japanese aren't really tax-motivated, because they're gaining overall advantages here," says Arthur Mitchell, formerly an attorney with Coudert Brothers, Manhattan, and now chief executive officer of Pacific Investment Partners, also in Manhattan. He helps arrange U.S. acquisitions by Japanese companies and Japanese acquisitions by U.S. companies.

Generally, Japanese investors prefer downtown urban properties. "The Japanese understand the relationship of density and real estate values," says Jack A. Shaffer, managing director of Sonnenblick-Goldman, a mortgage banking firm that has handled many major transactions with Japanese investors. "The Japanese apply what they know in Tokyo: the greater the density, the greater the value of real estate. You need buying power, too, which is why they don't go to a denser metropolis, like Jakarta. Probably the Japanese understand midtown Manhattan as well as anybody else in the world now."

For Japanese life insurance companies, the top priority is safety. They tend to consider only central locations in major, diversified cities. Manhattan is the primary choice. There, a building has to be midtown, not downtown, because the downtown market is less diversified, and there's a steady exodus of office tenants from downtown to midtown. Moreover, Japanese requirements for midtown investments are quite specific: the most desirable addresses are from Third Avenue to Sixth Avenue, Forty-second Street to Fifty-ninth Street.

Some real estate companies are almost as concerned about safety as the life insurance companies. Look at Dai-Ichi Real Estate's purchase of the Tiffany Building. The 120,000-square-foot building cost $94 million, and it offers a meager 5.3-percent yield for the next twenty years without any potential for better returns. Dai-Ichi can't increase their yield by adding floors, because developer Donald Trump bought the air rights so his Trump Tower office-retail-residential complex next door could gain extra height. The Tiffany Building has potential only as a retail site. But there's minimum downside risk. Tiffany's, the carriage trade jeweler, is unlikely to go bankrupt or move. The location, Fifth Avenue and Fifty-seventh Street, is among the most prestigious in Manhattan.

After having bought the Tiffany Building, Dai-Ichi Real Estate bought the Manufacturers Hanover Building across the street, on the northeast corner of Fifth Avenue and Fifty-seventh Street. They expressed interest in the Crown Building on the southwest corner of Fifth Avenue and Fifty-seventh Street, but former Philippines president Ferdinand Marcos was one of its owners, so the Japanese passed. The situation is still unresolved.

Since the most desirable locations command the highest prices and offer the lowest yields, there are many aggressive Japanese investors willing to go elsewhere for better returns—typically over 7 percent. Some venture beyond the prime midtown Manhattan turf. Japanese construction companies, in partnership with local Manhattan developers, have demonstrated a willingness to participate in projects widely scattered around Manhattan.

In many cases, Japanese investors consider other cities. For instance, Mitsubishi Estate has developed an office building in Portland, Oregon, and condominiums in Atlanta, Houston, and Palm Beach. Nissei Realty bought the American Medical Association Building in Washington, D.C., in addition to properties in Chicago, Los Angeles, and San Francisco.

As yet, few Japanese investors have risked their money in the suburbs. Sumitomo Life Realty did pay $38 million for Burlington Business Center I, an office park outside Boston, but it's headquarters for Wang, an internationally known company. Thus far, only Japanese construction companies and trust banks representing private individuals have gone farther afield.

The most conservative Japanese investors want fully leased landmark office buildings constructed within the past two decades. The buildings must have A-grade elevators, heating, ventilating, and air conditioning systems. The Japanese prefer to avoid buildings with asbestos insulation, because of the cost and disruption involved with removing it. Some Japanese investors, notably the major life insurance companies, want a solid-looking building. They prefer a stone exterior to steel and glass—something that will look good in their annual reports. It helps if a building has some internationally known tenants.

Tokyo Connection

Rather than go it alone, Japanese investors prefer to find someone they trust to work with them in the vast American market. Nissei

Realty has worked with Dallas-based Trammell Crow and Houston's Gerald Hines, both of whom develop major office properties across the United States.

Manhattan attorney Arthur Mitchell has a hand in more Japanese-American joint ventures than just about anyone else. He serves Japanese clients like Matsushita, Nippon Electric, Sumitomo Life, Dai-Ichi Life, Yasuda Life, Mitsubishi Trust & Banking, Nomura Securities, and Daiwa Securities.

His knowledge of the Japanese goes back more than two decades. "My father is a medical doctor, and his hobby is traveling," Mitchell recalls. "So we traveled every summer. We visited Japan when I was fourteen, and again when I was seventeen. I thought Asia was the most exciting place in the world, and I decided I wanted to study abroad. I wasn't predicting that Japan would become a giant someday. I just thought it was more interesting than Western Europe."

Mitchell, thirty-nine, went to the University of California at Berkeley and spent his junior year in Japan. "I liked it so much that I decided to stay for another year," Mitchell continues. "I learned to speak, read, and write Japanese. I dreamed in Japanese. I was young enough to get the language under my belt, and I use it every day now."

One summer, while Mitchell was at Harvard Law School, he worked for Coudert Brothers, an international law firm based in New York. They sent him to Japan, and he spent three weeks at the Sumitomo trading company. "I learned a lot about how a Japanese company operates," he recalls. "I became familiar with international trade law.

"After graduation from Harvard, I studied Japanese law at Kyoto University for a year and a half under a Japanese government grant and worked part-time at Matsushita Electric—the Panasonic people. I helped with their contracts."

Mitchell continued to pursue his interest in Japan. "The Japanese are great collectors," he says. "Their traditional law is Chinese-based, because much of their formal culture came from China. They borrowed the writing system and legal system from China way back. After Admiral Perry went to Japan, the Japanese woke up and decided that to protect their independence, they'd have to strengthen themselves. They started shopping around for the most modern political system, educational system, medicine, science, and so on.

"They studied the constitutions of Germany, England, France, and the United States. Bismarck's Germany was considered the most advanced at that time, and they wound up with a German-based constitution and civil law. It was the most compatible with Japanese conditions. They lived with that system until World War II. Then General MacArthur came along and introduced an American-style constitution, American antitrust law, American tax concepts, American business and labor law. They have a mishmash, but it works.

"I discovered that the Japanese aren't inscrutable. They're inscrutable only if you don't understand them. There are many people like myself who have invested the time to understand. I handle Japanese business. If my Japanese clients give up real estate, I'm no longer in real estate. I'm in whatever they're in.

"I hear many complaints from Americans that the so-called playing field isn't level. Mostly, these complaints come from people who are concerned about protecting their market share here. Seldom do they have an serious interest in selling to Japanese companies. A few years ago, for instance, I came across a survey which reported that about eight hundred Americans were working in Japan with American firms, compared with sixty-five hundred Americans working in Europe with American firms and thirty thousand Japanese working in the United States with Japanese firms. Clearly, they're making much more of an effort to understand us than we make to understand them.

"With my interests, I made many friends in Japan, and they tend to stay your friends for years. People help you out, introduce you to other people. For instance, a business consultant named Yoshinori Takagi introduced me to a couple senior executives at Mitsubishi Trust and Banking, Japan's largest trust bank.

"One of my partners knew people at the highest levels of Cushman and Wakefield, the commercial real estate brokerage firm—people like Chairman Stephen Siegel and Executive Vice President Kevin Haggarty. They recognized that Japanese investors would become major players in U.S. real estate, and they wanted to do something.

"I told them a logical relationship would be with a Japanese trust bank, because Japanese trust banks have real estate brokerage licenses in Japan. Furthermore, they manage pension funds, which tend to have some real estate in their portfolios. Japanese trust banks participate in real estate developments. So they understand the business. The Cushman & Wakefield people said they were interested.

"I helped work out details of an agreement between Cushman & Wakefield and Mitsubishi Trust to pursue mutual business interests in the United States. The process took about six months, which is amazingly fast. Anticipate more time when a party hasn't yet decided what they really want. They face many alternatives, which may take time to analyze.

"In Japan, top executives—not necessarily the president—may make a decision, and then they spend time necessary to get everyone on board. They want to motivate those who will carry out a decision. Often, decisions are generated from below, and they move upward through the hierarchy, gaining the needed approvals.

"It's a lot different than the United States, where you shake hands with the president and have a deal. Or think you do. Of course, many deals with American companies fall apart in the documentation process."

Mitsubishi Trust & Banking signed their agreement with Cushman & Wakefield in June 1985. "We spent the next eight months in Tokyo conducting seminars," explains Kevin Haggarty. "We introduced them to the American real estate market, explained how mortgages, convertible mortgages, and mortgage-backed securities work here. We explained the implications of tax laws for real estate. Then we brought their people on tours to the United States, so they could understand the various Manhattan submarkets; Fairfield County in Connecticut; what Chicago is all about; what is Atlanta; a suburb of Atlanta; Tysons Corners versus Washington; Irvine versus Los Angeles; San Jose versus San Francisco.

"Eventually, they asked us when we were going to show them deals. So we started showing deals, and they got done." Thus far, Cushman has closed more than $1 billion of deals with the Japanese in New York, Washington, and Los Angeles.

"I believe many U.S. brokers haven't done deals with the Japanese," Haggerty says, "because they don't understand what the Japanese want. For instance, a broker makes a case for a property based on its projected internal rate of return. This number includes current yield plus an assumed capital gain down the line. The Japanese look at internal rate of return, mainly because they need to know how Americans think. But since few Japanese investors anticipate selling their buildings, internal rate of return won't sway them. They want cash-on-cash returns, generally over 7 percent.

"At one investment conference, I recall an American who stood up and told the Japanese that if they wish to invest here successfully, they'll have to change their culture. I couldn't believe someone would be that naive. All of us, including the Japanese, have alternatives. The Japanese can buy U.S. Treasury bonds without changing their culture, which has evolved over several thousand years."

Mitsubishi Trust turned out to be not only Japan's largest trust company but surprisingly savvy about U.S. real estate. President Takuji Shidachi is a personable man committed to expanding in the United States, particularly in real estate. He displays a detailed working knowledge of what's going on. The top real estate man is Akio Matsuyama, a smart, polished senior managing director. He's quick and decisive, belying all the stories about how slow the Japanese are. On the New York scene is Tatseo Wakabayashi, a young Japanese with a strong grasp of the overall U.S. real estate situation. He has traveled around the United States and worked on a number of major transactions.

Many more American real estate companies have formed working relationships with Japanese firms. For example, the brokerage firm Richard Ellis has advised Sumitomo Life Insurance Company on purchases in New York, Washington, and Boston. Williams Real Estate has handled transactions for Mitsubishi International, the Takenaka construction company, Tokyo Fire & Marine Insurance Company, and Orient Leasing. Equitable Life is a partner with Nippon Life in a Los Angeles property and with Daiei, Japan's largest retailer, in Honolulu.

Kumagai and Zeckendorf

Japanese construction companies like Shimizu, Takenaka, Toda, Maeda, Kajima, Ohbayashi, Aoki, Taisei, and Hasegawa Komuten expanded overseas during the 1970s, when oil shocks hit the Japanese economy. In Asia and the Middle East, these companies tackled massive projects like dams, waste-treatment facilities, power plants, and oil refineries.

As oil and other commodity prices tumbled during the early 1980s, many Third World countries couldn't handle their debts, and the international construction business turned sour. Japanese construction companies were stuck with millions' worth of unpaid bills.

So they looked for opportunities in the United States. There weren't many power plants or oil refineries going up, but real estate developers prospered with hotels, office buildings, shopping centers, and residential projects.

How could the Japanese builders enter the U.S. market? In Japan, they get a substantial flow of business from established relationships, but these wouldn't help in the United States. Low-cost labor isn't an issue, either, since construction would be done with American workers, mostly union.

Primarily, what Japanese construction companies bring to the table is financial strength. Typically, their shareholders include major Japanese banks who can be counted on as construction lenders. Shimizu, for instance, is backed by Dai-Ichi Kangyo Bank, largest bank in the world. Shareholders of Kajima Corporation include Sumitomo Bank, Sumitomo Trust & Banking, Sumitomo Life Insurance Company, Mitsui Bank, Kyowa Bank, and Nippon Life Insurance Company.

But financial strength isn't enough, since success in real estate depends so much on local factors. Volatile markets, supplier shortages, and labor problems could easily cripple a project. So the Japanese construction companies proceed only when they're doing a job for a Japanese client, like an automobile company that needs a manufacturing plant. Alternatively, they work with a U.S. developer who has a strong track record.

One of the most successful Japanese construction companies in the United States—with a couple billion dollars' worth of projects underway—is Kumagai Gumi. Perhaps surprisingly, it's not the industry leader. The firm's modest headquarters, in Tokyo's Yotsuya business district, is easy to miss, decidedly less imposing than that of such bigger firms as Kajima or Shimizu.

But Kumagai Gumi pioneered expansion overseas. It generates annual revenues of over $5 billion. In recent years, Kumagai has tripled their foreign order book, and they rank first among Japanese construction companies for worldwide contracts. Besides Japan, they operate in China, Indonesia, Singapore, Malaysia, Hong Kong, Australia, Hawaii, and Canada.

Kumagai Gumi is a low-key, traditional Japanese company that stresses harmony. Though it has about seventy-eight hundred full-time employees, mostly engineers, architects, and other professionals, and employs an average of twenty-eight thousand construction workers a day, it claims never to have experienced a work stoppage.

Yet Kumagai Gumi is unusually streamlined and adaptable.

Head office approvals which would take months at other Japanese firms come through within a couple weeks.

The firm goes back to Santaro Kumagai, who started his own engineering practice in 1902. By 1938, Kumagai's operation was big enough that it made sense to incorporate. Though Kumagai Gumi shares are listed on the Tokyo and Osaka stock exchanges, it's a tight-lipped, family-controlled enterprise.

The firm's ambition is to become the number-one contractor in the United States. It's pursuing that objective with a cautious strategy. President Taichiro Kumagai, fifty-three, is a quiet man who doesn't put his company's name out front. "We want to avoid frictions with America," he says. The aim is to work through local developers and let them deal with regulatory authorities, subcontractors, and construction unions.

Nor, as one might assume, does the company finance its U.S. projects with Japanese yen. Instead, it takes advantage of its strong credit rating to raise low-cost U.S. dollar funds via bond and commercial paper offerings in the United States as well as Europe. These funds go into projects as Kumagai Gumi's equity, and the construction financing comes from U.S. or Japanese banks—whoever is most competitive at the time. When a project is completed, Kumagai Gumi sells its interest and plows the proceeds into a new project.

The company had opened a West Coast U.S. office when Jack Shaffer of Sonnenblick-Goldman, the largest U.S. mortgage banker, was scouting the Orient for capital. His firm, which started in 1893 when Jacob and Emil Leitner began arranging mortgages in the Bronx, evolved into a supplier of debt capital—more than $3 billion annually—for developers across the United States. The firm financed the Manhattan skyline. It even represented the Shah of Iran when he purchased properties here. "It was amazing to see how Moslems and a Jewish company could work closely together," recalls Shaffer.

For a few years in the late 1970s, Sonnenblick-Goldman was owned by the investment banking firm Lehman Brothers, and Shaffer met Lehman associates Cyrus Vance, former secretary of state, and Richard Holbrook, former assistant secretary of state for Asian affairs. Later, when Arthur and Jack Sonnenblick and their associates bought the firm back from Lehman, the well-connected, onetime officials introduced Shaffer all over Asia.

He tried to raise funds in Hong Kong, but the entrepreneurial

Chinese preferred pooling capital from their families and handling things privately among themselves. The idea of selling real estate investment fund shares to small Chinese investors didn't go over, because they much preferred to have a little property of their very own where they could kick the bricks.

"About a half-dozen years ago," Shaffer says, "we got to Japan. We discovered the capital market there is more institutional than entrepreneurial. We found ourselves dealing with insurance companies, trust banks, and pension funds rather than individual businessmen."

Among the people he met, in 1984, were Kumagai Gumi chairman Jinichi Mita and president Taichiro Kumagai. They explained they had started to pursue projects on the West Coast of the United States, and they wanted to develop properties in the New York market. They'd appreciate advice.

A series of meetings followed as Sonnenblick and Kumagai people got to know one another. Arthur Sonnenblick met Richard Kitano, head of the company's U.S. operations, at the construction firm's Palo Alto, California, office. Sonnenblick partner William Stern talked with Kitano and others in New York.

Shaffer and his cohorts showed Kumagai a deal: Americas Tower, a forty-eight-story office building being developed by Joseph and Ralph Bernstein, young Manhattan builders. It would be on the west side of Sixth Avenue between Forty-fifth and Forty-sixth streets. While the site was too far west to be considered prestigious, it was in a well-established office corridor. Property values were rising, because there was little room on the East Side, and development was shifting west.

The building would be reminiscent of the Empire State Building, with setbacks and a crown of polished granite and stainless steel. Kumagai took the deal, providing funds and participating in the construction management.

By March 1985, Kumagai was ready for another deal. Shaffer suggested the Copley, which would be a $50-million, 162-unit condominium on Broadway and Sixty-eighth Street. It was a modest project, but a condominium was appealing, since it offered the prospect of getting one's money out as quickly as units sold.

The Copley was Kumagai's introduction to the hefty, six-foot, three-inch William Zeckendorf, Jr. He's a quiet man who has earned a reputation for pioneering projects. He likes to go into a problem neighborhood where property can be acquired for reasonable prices. Then he'll develop a project that, because of its size and classy design, may help spark a revival, so that his investment will appreciate.

As a teenager, Zeckendorf started working for Webb & Knapp, the real estate firm run by his flamboyant father, a charismatic supersalesman who cut deals across the North American continent as well as in Europe. He made a fortune when urban renewal subsidies were gushing.

William Zeckendorf, Jr., ventured out on his own during the 1970s. He limited himself to Manhattan so he could watch over the entire operation, doing mostly residential renovations. In 1981, Zeckendorf began his first development since the demise of Webb & Knapp. Until he met the men from Kumagai, he did everything: assemble parcels for a development site, determine the best use for it, work through architectural plans, and endure sometimes tumultuous zoning meetings where his plans were up for approval or rejection. As a deal came together, he arranged financing. Usually this meant recruiting a number of investors to provide the equity, then negotiating with a lender.

"Initially, Kumagai came in on deals which were already well along," Zeckendorf explains. "Kumagai was one among several investors who provided equity. They worked with me on construction, helping to select construction managers and observing how business is done in New York—among the toughest places to build in the United States, because of the regulations and unions."

One deal was Zeckendorf Towers, a proposed million-square-foot complex of condominiums and offices on the southeast corner of seedy Union Square, a site long vacant since the bankruptcy of the S. Klein discount clothing store. It was a dirty neighborhood, and there was crime in the park across the street. But the project is big enough and distinctive enough—Zeckendorf is gaining recognition for his sensitivity to fine design—that it might stimulate renovation in the area. Kumagai signed on.

In this and other transactions, Kumagai proved to be an unusually decisive Japanese company, making a commitment within two weeks, while major competitors might take six months. Chairman Makita, President Kumagai, and Senior Managing Director Motoo Otsuka would analyze the issues, make their decision, and it would be done.

"I realized that Kumagai could handle all our financing needs,"

Zeckendorf says. "They have a strong credit rating, and Sumitomo is their lead bank. The Long-Term Credit Bank of Japan does a lot of their business, too. Sometimes they arrange 100-percent debt financing and provide the lender some security with a bank letter of credit. We'd pay a fee and gain a little lower interest rate.

"Usually I talk with Hiro Sato, in charge of Kumagai's New York office, or with Richard Kitano at their North American headquarters out in California. They're nice, smart people. All on diet programs. Kitano is athletic, a sailor. He's a lot of fun. My wife and I have dinner with him and his wife quite often. We traveled to Japan together.

"They're good partners, because they rely on us to handle the real estate. They don't second-guess us. I don't think they second-guess the construction manager, either, though they certainly ask questions.

"I give them an outline of the financial terms, and they get on the phone with Tokyo. Or they'll write the message out, so it can be faxed over. Because of all their characters, they can't use teletype. It's very time-consuming, and they work late at night. If we go out to dinner in New York, they'll return to the office afterwards."

The biggest deal for Zeckendorf and Kumagai is a $550 million conversion of the old Madison Square Garden into six hundred fifty condominium units. "It's not exactly the Park Avenue of the West Side"—Zeckendorf laughs—"but there's a lot of redevelopment in the area."

Altogether, Kumagai and Zeckendorf have collaborated on seven deals around New York, including a hotel, condos, and offices. "Kumagai came along at the right time in my life, when I could give them a tremendous volume of deals," Zeckendorf reflects.

Says Kumagai senior managing director Koto Otsuka: "Rather than chase small profits by taking small risks, we are determined to go after big business."

Kamikaze Investor

Perhaps the most aggressive Japanese real estate mogul is Shigeru Kobayashi, sixty-one, who owns Shuwa Group. An astute, decisive, charming, and colorful man, he's perhaps as close to an American real estate entrepreneur as you're likely to meet in Japan. He travels first class and rides in a chauffeur-driven Mercedes. His headquarters building, in Tokyo's Akasaka district, where many of the embassies are, has a glitzy lobby with fountains and gold lighting.

Kobayashi greets visitors in a big, bright, white room more in keeping with American taste than Japanese. It's filled with American and European paintings and large porcelain dogs that could be wolf-hounds. Kobayashi isn't comfortable speaking English, preferring to speak to an interpreter who conveys his thoughts. He may understand more than he lets on.

He has more body language than a typical Japanese. He'll take off his suit jacket to show you blue and green striped suspenders he got as a gift. Most Japanese prefer to keep their jackets on, regardless of how hot it may be.

He's well-connected. He's on good terms with leading candidates for prime minister, reportedly making contributions to all of them. Around this room are photographs of him with Los Angeles mayor Tom Bradley and New York mayor Ed Koch. There's also a photograph of Los Angeles Dodgers manager Tommy Lasorda.

Often Kobayashi moves with an entourage of assistants. They take notes on the run—who should be called, what he wants done on various building projects. His assistants make sure everything he may need is taken care of. As Japanese, they're very aware of his high position.

Privately, Kobayashi observes Japanese norms. The big white room isn't actually his office. It's for show. Kobayashi works Japanese-style several floors below, at a modest desk on an open floor with everyone else.

His Western-style Tokyo residence is also surprisingly modest, on the top floor of an upper-middle class seven-story brick condominium. Kobayashi doesn't even have a penthouse. There are four other units as nice as his on the same floor. But it's within walking distance of his office. That does require some wealth.

Kobayashi is proud of his wealth—he amassed it without help from rich relatives. He doesn't have an aristocratic air at all. He conveys a working class feeling.

The son of a furniture manufacturer, he made a small fortune building ships after World War II. Business fizzled following the Korean War and, when he liquidated the company, he was amazed how much his real estate had appreciated. He began buying commercial property. In 1957, he built a modest building with shops and restaurants, in Tokyo's Ginza retail district, and an upscale residential building in Aoyama, near many of the embassies.

The 1971 "Nixon shock" made Kobayashi pessimistic about Japan, so he began buying foreign real estate, chiefly in Brazil and the United States. These were a bust—he lost ¥ 2 million.

As Japan's economy recovered, he began building more Tokyo office buildings—about sixty, with 4.8 million square feet in downtown Tokyo. He reports estimated gross annual revenues around $200 million from properties in Japan. He's Japan's fourth-largest property developer, ranked by income. With a net worth over $6 billion, he's one of the richest Japanese.

Kobayashi looks after the details of his business. First Boston investment banker Steve Chaum says: "As far as engineering, architecture, and infrastructure matters are concerned, Kobayashi's people are more thorough than most U.S. buyers."

Kobayashi is confident that the United States is a good place to buy property. "I had a vague feeling," he says, "that the company's future would be at the other side of the Pacific. My hunch was correct. No other country in the world can accept foreign people and investment as freely as the United States." At the company's U.S. headquarters in Los Angeles, Kobayashi's thirty-three-year-old son, Takaji, evaluates buidings offered for sale.

Kobayashi made a splashy debut during 1986, spending a reported $1.8 billion on nineteen office buildings in downtown Manhattan, Boston, and Los Angeles within a year. Among the best-known purchases were the Paine Webber Building in Boston and the ABC Building in New York. Kobayashi stunned the U.S. investment community when he bought Arco Plaza, Los Angeles, for $620 million cash.

After these major purchases, Kobayashi took out full-page advertisements in major newspapers across the United States. "A Landmark Year," banner headlines declared. "If you followed the Shuwa Group's 1986 acquisitions, stay tuned for future developments . . . the best may be yet to come." Kobayashi was looking for more sellers.

Kobayashi, perhaps more than any other Japanese investor, is criticized for overpaying. The prime example would appear to be the $175 million ($365 per square foot) he paid for the ABC Building. Reportedly, the next-lowest bid was under $100 million. In three years, ABC will move into new quarters elsewhere in Manhattan, and the building will be empty. At that time, Kobayashi will face high remodeling costs and the formidable challenge of renting space at rates that will justify their investment.

Kobayashi opened offices in Tokyo's Ginza shopping district, apparently to syndicate some of his U.S. properties. He may offer condominium interest in partial or entire floors. Skeptics suggest this may be a move to unload overpriced acquisitions. "U.S. real estate is a bargain compared to Japan," Yoshio Yamashita, Shuwa's vice chairman, says simply.

The U.S. properties have lost value as the U.S. dollar has declined, but yields are more than double those in Japan. Shuwa's revenue from leasing space in their U.S. properties now is believed to exceed revenues from Japan by about 10 percent.

For all his high-profile buying, Kobayashi maintains a lean U.S. operation: only about thirty people at offices in San Francisco, New York, Boston, and Los Angeles. Half are Japanese. They're told their U.S. assignment will continue at least a decade.

Kobayashi wants nothing less than to become the biggest real estate man anywhere. He wants to acquire more quality property than Albert and Paul Reichmann, whose Olympia & York is the biggest real estate company on the North American continent, with some 24 million square feet. There are reports Kobayashi is looking for property in London and Paris.

Will the Japanese Buy All Our Land?

Whether the Japanese continue paying high prices for U.S. real estate depends on their cash flows and alternative investments. For a while, Japanese investment in U.S. real estate seems sure to continue growing. Real estate remains a good inflation hedge, and tax laws haven't hit hard enough to drive investors elsewhere.

The Ministry of Finance is relaxing restrictions on the ability of life insurance companies to buy foreign real estate. They'll be able to move faster and structure deals with greater flexibility. These moves should contribute to more Japanese investment in U.S. real estate.

Japanese pension funds will become an important factor in the U.S. market. Before long, the Ministry of Finance is expected to relax regulations that forbid Japan's trust banks from investing pension funds in overseas real estate. "More than $100 billion are in Japanese pension funds," estimates Russell Lindner, an analyst of Japanese real estate investment. "If just 1 percent of that is invested in U.S. real estate, that's $1 billion which would surely have an impact." Japanese trust bank executives acknowledge their eagerness to take advantage of higher returns in U.S. real estate.

Probably other major Japanese companies will expand their investment here. Says Hajime Tsuboi of Mitsui Real Estate: "About 10 percent of funds we're using for real estate investment activities are invested in the U.S. The market value of our portfolio is ¥5 trillion, or about $35 billion. Perhaps 5 percent are held overseas. So our potential to make more investments in the U.S. is very high. It depends on the kind of opportunities we find."

We're likely to see new Japanese players on the scene, particularly large and medium-size Japanese industrial companies that aren't in the real estate business back home. Shuhei Sato, senior vice president of Sanwa Bank, New York: "Our large and medium-sized clients are knocking down our doors, asking us to help them find prime properties in the United States."

Large pools of capital will be raised from Japanese investors, then placed in U.S. properties. More American real estate companies like Balcor, the American Express syndication unit, will sell master limited partnerships to Japanese investors.

It's reasonable to expect that Japanese investors will invest more widely. "The Europeans are in Dallas, Charlotte, and the rest of the country," notes Steven Wheeler, managing director of Morgan Stanley, "because they've been here long enough and are sophisticated about real estate values. If you just buy property in Los Angeles and New York, it's like investing exclusively in the Dow stocks. The Japanese will see that they can make more money by diversifying on a regional basis."

Finally, Japanese investors will probably buy entire institutions with real estate portfolios. Look for a Japanese insurance company to buy a U.S. company and gain a property portfolio.

But the high yen is likely to curb Japanese trade surpluses and thus the investment funds available for recycling in the United States. Less money would be available for purchasing U.S. real estate.

Moreover, because of dizzy speculation in Japanese land, the Ministry of Finance is starting to lean on banks that provide loans for speculation. Until now, people could borrow virtually 100 percent of a property's current market value.

Furthermore, the government may enact higher taxes on farmland, which would encourage many rice farmers in dense urban areas to sell, making available substantial acreage for residential and office development. "Right to sunlight" regulations may be suspended. These have restricted high-rise construction in Tokyo.

Tokyo-based management consultant Kenichi Ohmae estimates that such measures would triple the amount of flatland that could be developed. Obviously, this would mean sharp downward pressure on Japanese real estate prices.

A lot of Japanese borrowers would be in trouble. Suddenly, they'd have to liquidate assets to raise enough collateral. U.S. assets, including real estate, would go on the market. It's a good bet to happen eventually.

Many Americans would miss Japanese capital. "We don't have much local money here," says Dr. Richard Joun, director of the Hawaii Department of Planning and Economic Development, "so we must import it to grow. If it isn't Japanese money, it'll have to be East Coast money or Saudi Arabian money. Money is money."

11

PROTECTIONISM AND DEPRESSION

Japan's emergence as the world's premier financial power has aroused an angry reaction in some quarters of the United States. Lane Kirkland, president of the American Federation of Labor and Congress of Industrial Organizations, blames Japan for many things: "Scores of industries, thousands of companies, and millions of workers are drowning under a flood of imports generated by foreign government initiatives and Washington's neglect. The effects are felt in every sector of the economy through plant closings, farm foreclosures, bankruptcies, and recession-level unemployment."

To many, like distinguished reporter Theodore H. White, Japan's financial success recalls its era of military conquest: "Today, 40 years after the end of World War II," White wrote in *The New York Times*, "the Japanese are on the move again in one of history's most brilliant commercial offensives, as they go about dismantling American industry. Whether they are still only smart, or have finally learned to be wiser than we, will be tested in the next 10 years. Only then will we know who finally won the war 50 years before."

Illinois congressman Dan Rostenkowski reports: "A lot of the anti-Japan feeling in Congress is based on jealousy about Japan's success as a global trader and anger over the failure of the Japanese to respond to some of our complaints."

Consider this outburst from Missouri senator John Danforth: "Do you think, as far as Japan is concerned, they view us as windbags,

215

crybabies who cry a lot but never do anything? If they have any sense they do, and I think they have some sense."

⟶ As the Japanese presence becomes more visible in this country, pressures grow to strike back with tough trade barriers. Businessmen, traditionally in favor of protectionism for their own industry, have become more vocal. The Business Roundtable, a lobby of Fortune 500 executives, favors political retaliation. Chrysler, Ford, and Motorola are among the best-known advocates of punishing our trade partners. "There's no longer a free-trade lobby," says Indiana senator Dan Quayle. "It just disappeared. That's one of the biggest changes in politics."

Do the Japanese Destroy American Jobs?

That old protectionist, Chrysler's Lee Iacocca, charges: "We know about the jobs lost; we can count them. The current level of imports is costing us conservatively 460,000 auto jobs, 370,000 apparel jobs, 280,000 in high-tech components, 130,000 in consumer electronics, 67,000 in machine tools, and 66,000 in steel. And these numbers don't include the ripple effect through the economy.

"The government's own rule of thumb is that for every billion-dollar increase in our trade deficit, twenty-five thousand American jobs are lost. This year, our trade deficit could be as much as $50 million worse than last year. That's a million and a quarter more jobs lost in just twelve months, directly attributable to the trade deficit."

Nonsense. When an American buys a Honda, dollars go to Japan. But the Japanese don't want dollars for their own sake. Most Japanese, like Americans and other people, prefer cash in their home currencies. Unless a Japanese company owes dollars or wishes to invest in dollar assets, probably it will convert dollar income to yen as quickly as possible, so it will avoid exchange rate losses. Then the dollars will flow to others who do want to invest in the American economy or buy American products.

Iaccoca objects, because Japanese customers aren't spending their dollars on his Chrysler cars. Why should they? The cars are too big for the Japanese market, the steering wheel is on the wrong side, and better-quality, more dependable and economical cars can be had elsewhere for less money. Japanese customers are using their dollars to buy soybeans, aircraft, hotel accommodations, sophisticated semi-conductors, U.S. stocks, and other things—and in the process, contributing to American jobs.

Iacocca's typical trade talk ends in a plea for protection, and that's where his argument collapses. Trade barriers are an incredibly expensive attempt to preserve jobs. "Voluntary" restraint agreements limiting export of Japanese cars to the U.S. cost taxpayers about $160,000 per auto industry job—about three times the maximum amount autoworkers earn. This exorbitant cost means that scarce capital is being drained from competitive sectors of the U.S. economy, subsidizing weak industries represented by powerful lobbyists.

After analyzing the impact of trade barriers in many industries, World Bank economists reached similar conclusions, as reported in their *World Development Report 1986*: "the cost per job saved exceeded the average labor compensation in each case. For each job saved in clothing, for example, the U.S. economy as a whole sacrificed about $169,600 to protect a worker earning about $12,600. Clearly, the resources wasted in the process could have been better used in other activities and in retraining and reallocating the affected workers. This example demonstrates that saving jobs is not a tenable defense of protectionism.

"Not only is protectionism very costly, it does not assist poorly paid workers. Indeed, it penalizes them. Import restraints are equivalent to a sales tax and often apply to necessities. When they do, they weigh heaviest on those who spend proportionately more of their income on these items: the poor."

That's not all. Trade barriers are net job destroyers. When the Congressional Budget Office analyzed the impact of a 15-percent steel import quota, they concluded that it saves twenty-six thousand jobs in the steel industry, at an astounding cost of $189,000 per job, making it one of the most expensive welfare programs. Quotas also destroyed about ninety-seven thousand jobs in steel-using sectors like the automobile industry. Net destruction: seventy-one thousand jobs.

"The greatest hazard is the destruction protectionism causes to U.S. manufacturers for whom steel is a significant part of their costs," declares F. Kenneth Iverson, chairman and chief executive of Nucor Corp., a Charlotte, North Carolina, steel producer. "Because the American steel industry is sheltered, world prices on some steel items are $100 to $200 a ton lower than in the U.S. This enables foreign manufacturers or American companies that move abroad to undersell domestic manufacturers. Automotive parts, oil rigs, farm implements, appliances, railroad parts, and numerous other products are examples of domestic products suffering under this handicap. In 1979, the imports of these downstream steel products were estimated at 5 million tons. In 1985, they reached an estimated 15 million tons.

"One steel analyst has projected that the increased imports of such products will cause a decrease in the domestic steel market of more than 1 percent a year. As this occurs, our steel industry will have to shrink even further. How ironic that protectionism will accomplish the very thing it is supposed to prevent."

Nucor, with 1986 sales of $755 million, has a headquarters staff of just seventeen. The company undercuts both domestic and foreign suppliers, because it fabricates steel products from scrap rather than smelting raw material. Nucor's profits have quadrupled during the past decade.

Those who advocate American trade barriers deserve much blame for the 9-percent loss of American manufacturing jobs during the past decade.

Japan's Unfair Trade Practices?

Some critics resent Japanese financial success because of the supposedly illicit way they earned their money. This is perhaps Iacocca's favorite line. "Japanese trade practices over the years," he declares, "have violated the closest thing we have in America to a state religion—fairness. Americans have begun to feel they are being had."

Yes, Japan is a challenging country for foreign sellers to penetrate. Success doesn't come as soon as one gets off the airplane in Tokyo. It's difficult to deal with Japan's complex language, byzantine distribution system, and established business relationships. Japanese bureaucrats are as stubborn and aggravating as any in Washington. The Japanese have their share of trade barriers, but these mainly hurt Japanese customers. They're forced to pay eight times the world price for beef and six times the world price for rice, thanks to powerful lobbyists like Mitsugu Horiuchi, seventy-year-old chairman of the Central Union of Agricultural Cooperatives.

But the Japanese market isn't closed. How can it be closed when

Japanese customers buy three times more foreign-brand goods per person than American customers do?

On the contrary, Japan is a very good market for companies that have taken the trouble to establish relationships and master the intricacies. "I established our company in 1972," explains Bill Totten of Ashisuto, a software developer. "Since that time, there hasn't been a single instance where the Japanese government hindered our operations. Although official approval is required for importing, if my secretary passes along the requisite materials to the officials, approval is granted.

"When we import a product and sell it in Japan, we translate instructions, labels, everything into Japanese. Our non-Japanese personnel speak some Japanese. But the foreigners who work for our competitors don't study Japanese. They don't do their job. Rather, they complain to the government. As a result, they leave the business for us. I'm happy indeed."

Or consider this. IBM employs about fifteen thousand people in Japan. Schick sells more razor blades than anyone else there. According to management consultant Kenichi Ohmae of McKinsey & Company, Nestle has 70 percent of the Japanese market for instant coffee. Coca-Cola is the best-selling soft drink in Japan. McDonald's, Polaroid, Seven-Up, Del Monte, Kentucky Fried Chicken, Adidas, Revlon, Pierre Cardin, Mister Donut, Max Factor, Chanel, Texas Instruments, and other foreign companies are all successful in Japan. The Japanese are the biggest customers for U.S. farm products. More than fifty thousand U.S. products are sold in Japan.

Altogether, foreign-owned firms report sales that are three times bigger than Japan's trade surplus. Digital Equipment scored tenfold gains in Japan during the last half-dozen years. U.S. affiliates in Japan ring up more than triple the sales of Japanese affiliates in the U.S. According to the *Economist*, the Japanese affiliates of foreign companies earn operating profits about a third higher than Japanese companies.

No question about it, Japan has gradually opened its markets. Japanese customers have quintupled their purchases of American goods during the past three years. Since 1982, U.S. telecommunications equipment sales to Japanese companies are up 38 percent. U.S. pharmaceutical products, up 41 percent. U.S. computers, up 48 percent. U.S. electronic parts, up 63 percent.

Meanwhile, the trend in the United States is toward protectionism. An estimated four hundred protectionist bills are introduced in each session of Congress. Pennsylvania senator John Heinz, for example, advocates a surcharge on everything that American customers want to buy from Japan. He brands Japan as "the best-known protectionist nation."

Missouri congressman Richard Gephardt got some publicity by proposing automatic trade barriers against countries, like Japan, whose trade surpluses U.S. officials may consider too big.

Illinois congressman Rostenkowski opposed Gephardt's proposals, promoting trade barriers of his own. "We have been chumps," he says, "and many of our trading partners, quite sensibly, have benefited from our generosity without opening their own borders."

The United States maintains trade barriers against thousands of imports. In recent years, the government has tripled the number of imports restricted by quotas. American customers must pay more of their earnings for screws, bolts, steel cookware, bicycles, bargain-priced porcelain, industrial fasteners, motorcycles, and hardened alloy tools. Since 1983, Washington has enforced quotas on 220 kinds of textile and clothing imports from twenty-three countries. Sugar quotas are tighter, forcing American customers to pay triple the world price of sugar. There's a 20-percent tariff on imported tobacco products. The 35-percent tariff on imported canned tuna costs American customers an estimated $91 million annually. New steel quotas restrict imports from Europe, Asia, and Latin America. U.S. officials have blocked imports of pizzas from Israel, noodles from South Korea, woodwind instruments from Italy, and carnations from Kenya. Washington even risked a trade war with our northern neighbor, slapping 35-percent tariffs on Canadian cedar shingles. Canada retaliated with tariffs on U.S. goods ranging from computers to oatmeal.

The United States forces customers to pay higher prices in other ways. The so-called "orderly marketing agreements" restrict production of commodities such as tin, ball bearings, and mushrooms. The government also penalizes American customers by enforcing senseless higher prices for cotton and peanuts.

Washington may pressure other governments to lean on their producers to adopt "voluntary restraints" that go on for years. Such restraints reduce imports and raise customer prices for cars, dairy products, and meat.

Don't forget those "Buy American" laws that deny American taxpayers the benefit of foreign-made products when they're better and cheaper. These laws determine what's acceptable in government procurement programs. For instance, Indiana restricts official purchases of lower-cost, superior-quality foreign steel and aluminum. California mandates the use of materials made in the United States. Often North Dakota requires that contractors "bid domestically produced material only." Kentucky discourages government agencies from purchasing foreign-made products. Idaho restricts the use of foreign products. Pennsylvania specifies that foreign steel and aluminum cannot be used if local officials determine that foreigners discriminate against American products. Massachusetts gives preferences to products made in the state. New York sets bid specifications that restrict access to foreign products. Federal "Buy American" laws enable government purchasing agents to order American products even when they cost as much as 6 percent more than foreign alternatives; with billions' worth of purchases, that 6 percent represents tremendous waste. The Defense Department awards domestic suppliers up to a 50-percent windfall over what a foreign supplier might charge. Guess who pays.

Overall, American trade barriers are comparable to those in Japan. Japanese tariffs are about the same as in the United States, according to the Institute for International Economics. The World Bank estimates that nontariff barriers like quotas and licensing are no more pervasive in Japan than in the United States. Agricultural imports are more restricted in Japan, while barriers to industrial imports are more pernicious in the United States.

"The United States today," asserts Harvard University economist Robert B. Reich, "is more protected against imports—and American manufacturers more subsidized—than any other advanced industrial nation."

Of course, there are many imaginative reasons offered for all these American trade barriers—protect jobs in politically powerful sectors, nurture infant industries, provide for national security, get even against foreign competitors, you name it. We've already reviewed some current favorites.

The point here is that American politicians have no moral ground to stand on when they demand righteous revenge against so-called unfair trade practices of Japan and other countries. These politicians are wallowing in their very own fever swamp of protectionism, which mainly hurts Americans.

Unfair Dumping?

Often, U.S. officials use "dumping" as an excuse to block trade.

Since 1921, the United States has had a so-called antidumping law, which directs customs officials to spring into action when they determine that foreign products are offered for "less than fair value"— meaning the price charged in the producer's home market. Officials are empowered to assess duties equal to the alleged dumping margin. In 1984, Congress authorized the President to withdraw trade "concessions" or restrict imports from countries that allegedly dump their products on eager American bargain hunters.

How curious. Dumping is Washington lingo for discounting, a popular American tradition. When supermarkets, clothing stores, car dealers, or anyone else want to raise cash and get more selling space for new goods, they have a sale. They offer customers a price advantage, so they'll take old, perhaps slow-moving inventory. Many outlets, of course, offer only discounted merchandise.

Some protectionists allege that the Japanese aren't just discounting, they're selling below cost. This line goes back at least a hundred years, when it was charged that John D. Rockefeller sold oil below cost to drive competitors out of business, then raised prices and cleaned up. But the evidence was flimsy, probably because that isn't a sound business strategy, and Rockefeller didn't make his fortune with dumb strategies. The bigger the producer, the bigger the losses with below-cost pricing. The notion of raising prices later doesn't work very well, because competitors can reenter most markets easily, and prices come down again.

Of course, below-cost Japanese pricing would be a bonanza for American customers. We'd gain terrific values and have money left over that could be invested or spent on other things we want, helping to generate American jobs in the process. Imagine: charitable Japanese companies subsidizing us! What a great idea!

But it's unlikely. If Japanese companies actually pursue a below-cost pricing strategy, then ambitious entrepreneurs would buy these Japanese bargains and sell them for immediate profit at market. It would be an obvious, irresistible arbitrage play. But juicy opportunities for arbitrage are hard to find and seldom overlooked very long in this competitive world.

A more plausible explanation for Japanese discounting: Japanese companies tend to produce many things less expensively, so they can squeak out a profit at prices that would mean losses for many American companies.

Rather than make costs competitive, a lot of American executives blame the Japanese for dumping and lobby for trade barriers that will hurt American customers.

Take the major U.S. steel companies. They may not be very good at producing competitive steel, and they may squander capital buying into businesses they seem to know little about, but they do know how to complain. In 1982, just seven U.S. steelmakers filed 132 cases of dumping complaints with the U.S. International Trade Commission, against European competitors. Result: European governments restricted their steel exports to about 5 percent of the U.S. market. The European steelmakers worked out a market-sharing arrangement. Economist Robert Crandall, at the Brookings Institution, estimated this adventure cost American customers about $1 billion. We're forced to pay the salaries of U.S. officials who make steel more expensive, handicap steel buyers like the American auto industry, bilk American customers, and help Europeans arrange cozy cartels.

Perhaps the most widely publicized recent dumping case involved semiconductors. Anticipating a boom for dynamic random-access memory chips (DRAMs), semiconductor manufacturers expanded their capacity beginning in 1980. The Japanese invested $9 billion in new factories, about a third more than U.S. companies. The market was swamped with chips as demand fell, partially because of slumping computer sales.

As advancing technology would make these chips obsolete, both Japanese and American companies discounted, giving customers a reason to take chips off their hands. Prices for a basic 256K DRAM, which stores 256,000 bits of information, dropped from $9.50 in 1985 to $2 by 1987. Such price cuts are commonplace with rapidly advancing technology in competitive markets.

U.S. semiconductor companies alleged the Japanese were selling chips below cost. But even if that were true, a company's cost has little relevance to customers. One can't afford to cover the mistakes of profit-seeking business executives who pay too much for their raw materials, guess wrong on the market, can't get quality products out the door, or encounter other problems. One's concern is to determine the best buys available.

The result was an oversupply of these chips. Values were low, since major chip-manufacturing facilities were being built in Korea, Taiwan, and Europe. Bargain prices were a boon for companies using chips to make computers and other electronic products.

Intel, National Semiconductor, Advanced Micro Devices, and other American semiconductor manufacturers lobbied the U.S. government to help gain profits that eluded them in the marketplace. Ac cordingly, U.S. trade negotiators pressured Japan's Ministry of International Trade and Industry to contrive a chip cartel. The aim: limit chip production and prop up chip prices in the United States. A cartel agreement was announced in July 1986. The Commerce Department announced minimum prices of $3 to $7.50 for 256 kilobit DRAMs, compared to average prices of $2.25 before the cartel. By making semiconductor chips more expensive, U.S. officials struck a blow against the U.S. telecommunications and computer companies and their customers.

But higher chip prices didn't mean much help for beleaguered U.S. semiconductor companies. The Japanese pressed forward to buy several of these companies, while NEC, Hitachi, and Toshiba expanded their own chip production in the United States. Twenty-six Japanese semiconductor companies entered joint ventures with thirty-six U.S. companies.

Cartels tend to be short-lived, undermined by conflicts among competing participants, and this semiconductor cartel was soon a shambles. Chip marketers bought chips in Japan and discounted them elsewhere in East Asia. American companies like Texas Instruments were reportedly selling chips below cartel prices. Korean companies, who weren't part of the cartel, sold chips for less than both American and Japanese companies.

American companies charged Japanese violations, and in March 1987, the Reagan administration imposed 100 percent tariffs on $300 million worth of Japanese portable computers, color TV sets, and power hand tools. This wasn't much in the overall scheme of things—we import more than $20 billion of Japanese electronics products annually—but the trade sanctions signalled a new get-tough attitude. Tokyo TV commentators described the acrimony as *kaisen zen-ya*—"the eve of war," an expression recalling the tensions leading up to Pearl Harbor.

The New York Times acknowledged: "A major and long-standing disadvantage for American chip-makers investing in new plants is that their cost of capital is at least twice that enjoyed by their Japanese competitors. That's not because Japanese chip-makers get subsidized loans. It's because the pension and tax systems in Japan strongly encourage saving over borrowing—the reverse of America's pattern—

and household savings are passed on at low rates to corporate borrowers.

"Besides the advantages America creates for them, Japanese manufacturers also have homegrown assets. Foremost is a highly trained and motivated work force."

The dumping issue is just a lot of hyperbole and hypocrisy. When the Japanese offer customers competitively priced products, politicians condemn it as dumping. But when the United States government dumps products below cost, like giving away free wheat, milk, and cheese to Egypt, and billions' worth of grain to India—we call it foreign aid. In 1986, the U.S. dumped more than $2.5 billion of food, contributing to depressed farm prices for impoverished Third World farmers.

The Folly of Trade Retaliation

U.S. politicians claim that trade retaliation—closing our market to foreigners—is an important lever to force open their markets. But the dirty secret is that this rarely ever works.

Those who have pursued U.S. retaliation can claim very few successes. Retaliation hasn't opened any important markets in Europe, the very most it has done is delay the closing of markets in Spain and Portugal. Officials in the U.S. Trade Representative's Office admit they've achieved zero success in the Middle East, zero in Africa, and zero in Latin America. Retaliation seems to have accelerated market openings in Taiwan and South Korea, but as these countries move toward democracy, governments there are becoming more responsive to local interests—and less responsive to U.S. trade officials. In terms of revenue growth, the biggest success for U.S. trade retaliation is the Japanese cigarette market.

Historically, trade retaliation has a horrifying record. Probably the first recorded case of trade retaliation involved a dispute between ancient Athens and its neighboring city of Megara; this led to the Peloponnesian Wars in which half of Athens was wiped out. Trade retaliation triggered economic wars and military conflict that undermined great powers such as Venice, Spain, and France. Trade retaliation and economic nationalism contributed to the outbreak of World War I. Afterward, incredibly, trade retaliation and economic nationalism accelerated in Europe, setting the stage for an even bloodier global conflict.

The great irony is that those nations that in the name of righteous retaliation have done the most to close their markets have stagnated and declined. Their industries have vanished from world markets.

What About the Trade Deficit?

Congressional oratory rings with anguish about the U.S. trade deficit. But this is a phony issue, because private, voluntary trade is mutually beneficial.

When a Japanese trading company buys $10,000 worth of Florida oranges, and an American wholesaler buys $25,000 of Japanese VCRs, everyone is better off. Some people gain the goods they seek, others get money. Yet added together, these transactions would contribute $15,000 to the U.S. trade deficit.

Similarly, each of us runs a continuous trade deficit with our local supermarket—we give them money, and we take home their goods. No one worries about this deficit, because we run a steady surplus elsewhere, namely with our employer. We provide services and get money. Life would become a nightmare if we had to find specific things our supermarket, doctor, lawyer, gas station, or other service providers want before we can get what we want.

"The same process occurs in trade between states," notes Lawrence J. Kotlikoff, chairman of the economics department at Boston University and research associate at the National Bureau of Economic Research. "In all probability, high-growth Massachusetts has been running large trade deficits with Texas and Mississippi, states that are suffering. Fortunately, we don't keep such statistics. If we did, some enterprising politician undoubtedly would try to erect internal trade barriers to stop Massachusetts from 'borrowing' from the rest of the country."

The trade deficit is a statistic that doesn't tell us how people are doing. For instance:

- The United States ran a trade deficit for much of the 19th century, as we became the world's greatest industrial power.

- We had a surplus during the Great Depression.
- The 1986 U.S. trade deficit, a record $166 billion, came amidst an unusually long economic expansion. The U.S. economy created over nine million new jobs during the past five years, more than Europe and Japan put together during the last decade. About 60 percent of new jobs are in the highest-paid occupations. Only 12 percent of new jobs are in the lowest-paid.
- Western Europe has maintained a trade surplus with the United States, yet they've lost more than two million jobs in the past decade.
- Japan incurred deficits almost every year from 1945 to 1965 when its economy boomed.
- As Japan's trade surplus has grown to $100 billion in recent years, its economy has slowed. Factories have closed, unemployment jumped.
- Improvident Argentina, Brazil, and Mexico together report trade surpluses in excess of $15 billion.

In itself, a trade deficit doesn't mean we're losing anything. Nor does a trade surplus mean we're winning. It's just a statistic that goes through cycles. "The trade deficit will end when Americans are no longer willing to borrow enough or foreigners are no longer willing to lend enough to finance it," explains economist Herbert Stein, senior fellow at the American Enterprise Institute. "These borrowers and lenders have a lot of their own money at stake and are at least as well informed and as well motivated as the government to decide when the deficit has gone too far."

In a recent report, the Institute for Research on the Economics of Taxation, Washington, adds: "The U.S. trade deficit has practically nothing to do with U.S. international competitiveness. U.S. international competitiveness is determined by the productivity and efficiency of American capital and labor relative to that of our competitors."

The trade deficit is not a crisis, as Missouri congressman Richard Gebhardt insists, calling for some protectionist panacea. There isn't a shred of evidence to suggest that eliminating the trade deficit would help save net jobs or enable American companies to be more competitive with the Japanese.

Protectionists like Gebhardt actually handicap American exporters they claim to help. The World Bank, in its *World Development Report 1987*, explains why: "Protection switches demand to products produced domestically. Exporting is then discouraged by both the increased cost of imported inputs and the increased cost of domestic inputs relative to the price received by exporters. This rise in the relative cost of domestic inputs may occur through domestic inflation or an appreciation of the exchange rate following the imposition of barriers to imports. In effect, protection puts a tax on exports."

Conclusions: "First, protecting one sector usually makes another worse off. Second, when export incentives are introduced alongside import restraints, the export incentives may do little more than offset the disincentive effects of import protection. Finally, the analysis implies that if export promotion is a goal of policy, the most direct means of achieving this goal may be import liberalization."

If politicians were really concerned about American competitiveness, they'd dismantle some of our export barriers, which prevent Americans from selling to foreign customers. The Trans-Alaskan Pipeline Authorization Act (1973) makes it illegal to export oil from the North Slope fields. If that law were repealed, exports to Japan would whack an estimated $10 billion to $15 billion off the U.S. trade deficit with Japan.

Public Law 94-373 prohibits the export of timber from federal land west of the 100th meridian—the Dakotas, Idaho, Oregon, Washington, and California.

The Export Administration Act (1979) restricts the export of technology deemed harmful to U.S. national security interests. The Commodity Control List cites more than a million products that need a license before they can be exported. The list includes plastics, synthetic fibers, computers, clocks, drugs, radio receiving equipment, and measuring devices—even though many of these products are readily available from other countries.

These laws make U.S. companies unreliable suppliers, so they discourage business, and Americans lose jobs. "The vigor with which U.S. regulations are now being imposed," a British aerospace executive wrote a U.S. supplier, "the risk of inadvertent non-compliance and possible cessation of supply from the U.S.—have all contributed to a close re-examination of our purchasing strategy." His company's policy, he continued, "is to select from U.K. or other European suppliers. . . . Consideration is also being given to Japanese equipment."

U.S. import and export barriers do their greatest harm to people in states such as Alaska, Arizona, California, Connecticut, Florida, Massachusetts, Michigan, New Hampshire, Ohio, Oregon, Rhode Island, Vermont, Washington, West Virginia, and Wisconsin where a significant number of jobs depend on exports.

Self-inflicted Blows

All these trade barriers are dangerous self-inflicted blows against America. They hurt us four ways.

First, they waste billions of dollars of precious capital. By forcing millions of Americans to pay more for things we buy, we squander opportunities to save and invest more productively. Maybe we could disregard this prodigality when we were number one in the world, but certainly we can't afford it anymore.

Second, trade barriers depress business. By raising prices, they lead to a falloff of demand in the protected industry. The higher the trade barriers, the more likely a protected industry will be priced out of the market. Recent U.S. trade barriers protecting cotton growers, for instance, are responsible for losing a lot of business to synthetic fibers. But the damage doesn't stop in a protected industry. When other industries buy protected products, as when the auto industry buys steel, their cost of doing business goes up, and they're under pressure to raise prices, which will cause a certain amount of their business to fall off. Protectionism helps accelerate market share gains by cost-competitive Japanese.

Third, trade barriers undermine American companies by denying them vital incentives to be competitive. No industry, not steel, nor automobiles, textiles or any other industry does its best behind protectionist walls. Executives often don't take the steps needed to improve quality and lower prices unless enough competitors are around to offer customers better value. Meanwhile, Japan and other countries excel by opening their markets, reinvigorating their industries, and gaining financial strength.

Fourth, protectionists risk triggering an international trade war, a cycle of restrictions that would mean a seriously reduced volume of world trade. That would mean a general decline of business and a horrendous loss of jobs—depression.

It's worth recalling how the infamous Smoot-Hawley tariff helped bring on the Great Depression. The 1929 stock crash happened while Congress was debating new trade barriers. The Dow Jones Industrial Average plunged from a high of 381 in September 1929 to 210. But by April 1930, the Dow recovered to 294. Industrial production stabilized. At this point, there was only a stock crash, no depression. A depression was avoidable.

On June 15, 1930, President Herbert Hoover announced he would sign Smoot-Hawley, the highest tariff in U.S. history, despite protests from 1,028 economists. Utah Senator Reed Smoot and Oregon Congressman Willis Hawley had started their adventure to bail out farmers, and it became a wild protectionist crusade. Congressmen boosted sugar tariffs, and western sugar beet growers cheered. Wheat farmers welcomed a higher tariff on wheat, since it penalized American consumers who bought cheaper wheat from Canada. Flaxseed farmers complained about competition from Argentina, so tariffs were slapped on imported flaxseed. California cotton growers won tariffs to help keep American consumers away from irresistible Egyptian cotton. As Smoot-Hawley gathered momentum, congressmen scrambled to pile on trade barriers against dairy products, leather, hides, silk, wool, woolen textiles, shoes, agricultural chemicals, meat, porcelain, surgical instruments, pocket knives, watches and much more.

Overall, Smoot-Hawley forced Americans to pay 59 percent more for 75 agricultural commodities and 925 manufactured products, squandering American resources at the worst possible time. The economy reeled from multiple blows, as Congress enacted crippling tax increases. Top rates jumped from 25 percent in 1930 to 69 percent by 1932, draining more resources away from productive enterprise, where they were desperately needed.

Smoot-Hawley triggered the collapse of trade. According to the Congressional Research Service, U.S. imports and exports fell more than two-thirds between 1930 and 1933. This contributed to the 50 percent drop in the gross national product and the sickening surge of unemployment which approached 30 percent. The Dow Jones Industrial Average skidded to 41 in April 1932.

Businesses went bankrupt, triggering loan defaults. This, in turn, brought on massive bank failures—more than 25,000 banks failed between 1930 and 1933. As a result, the money supply contracted one-third in these years. It was the kind of catastrophe that the Federal Reserve Board was created to prevent.

Congressional Quarterly declares: "the Smoot-Hawley Tariff Act of 1930 is universally regarded as a major mistake in trade policy and a central factor in the onset and depth of the Great Depression." *Wall Street Journal* Editor Robert L. Bartley: "If President Hoover had vetoed Smoot-Hawley, the Great Depression would in all likelihood have been an ordinary business correction despite the stock market crash." Further, historian Paul Johnson, author of *Modern Times*, says: "The Smoot-Hawley tariff, more than any other positive act of policy, spread the Depression to Europe."

American protectionists provoked a trade war where more than two dozen foreign governments hammered their economies with a succession of trade barriers. After Smoot-Hawley throttled the flow of Italian olive oil to America, the Italians retaliated by putting General Motors, Ford, and Chrysler out of business in their country. By 1931, tariffs on manufactured goods reached 18.2 percent in Germany, 22 percent in Switzerland, 27.7 percent in Austria, 29 percent in France, 32.8 percent in Yugoslavia, 41.8 percent in Italy, 42.6 percent in Hungary, 52 percent in Poland, 75.5 percent in Spain and 90 percent in Bulgaria. Agricultural tariffs were much worse: 42.2 percent in Switzerland, 53 percent in France, 59.5 percent in Austria, 60 percent in Hungary, 66 percent in Italy, 75 percent in Yugoslavia, 80.5 percent in in Spain, 82.5 percent in Germany, 102 percent in Finland, 110 percent in Poland and 133 percent in Bulgaria. In many cases, these tariffs represented a doubling of trade barriers within four years.

The Congressional Research Service reports that world trade was cut in half between 1928 and 1938. Unemployment hit 40 percent in Germany, and Hitler seized power amidst economic crisis. Totalitarianisn swept across Europe.

Noting how trade war exacerbated tensions in Asia, historian Goronwy Rees, author of *The Great Slump: Capitalism in Crisis*, reported that Smoot-Hawley "convince the Japanese public that American policy would not tolerate the legitimate expansion of Japanese trade." Subsequently, the Japanese Army High Command pursued military conquest in Manchuria.

"During the 1930s," says economist Murray L. Weidenbaum, director of the Center for the Study of American Business at Washington University, St. Louis, "the United States and many other countries followed 'beggar-thy-neighbor' trade policies that contributed to the worldwide depression. The Smoot-Hawley protectionist tariff epitomized this approach. The results for many companies were extremely negative. Firms that had relied on substantial foreign business were limited to the domestic market, which for some was inadequate for survival."

Likely impact of recent protectionist proposals? According to Nobel Prize economist Milton Friedman, some are so bad, they make "Smoot-Hawley look positively benign." He warns: "Unless the protectionist momentum is soon checked, the world may face another decade of beggar-thy-neighbor policies at a time when the web of international trade is far more closely knit than in the 1930s."

Unilateral Free Trade

The United States will regain much of its competitiveness and financial strength by letting Americans benefit from free trade. American companies will face inevitable adjustment to global competition, but the net gains will be overwhelming. This is true regardless what Japan, West Germany, Italy, Canada, or any other country chooses to do. If they continue their trade barriers, they'll hurt mainly their own people.

Similarly, if foreign countries subsidize companies that export to the United States, their taxpayers pick up the tab. American customers will save.

It would be a costly mistake for the United States to maintain trade barriers until foreign governments scuttle theirs, because we'll be the primary losers all the while. As the English sage William Beveridge quipped: "Just because other countries have bad harbors is no reason for us to sink rocks around our own coasts."

Leland Yeager, economics professor at Auburn University and author of *Trade Policy and the Price System*, explains: "Free trade is the common sense idea that it's better to obtain goods cheaply than expensively. Trade reduces the cost of goods. It raises the standard of living from available resources."

We can't hope to push the world toward free trade or any other system we may favor, as we did after World War II. We have more competition now, our currency is weak, and we're deep in debt to others.

The most likely policy to succeed would be the most radical: adopt unilateral free trade.

- Abolish quotas, tariffs and other barriers to imports from all countries, including Communist countries.
- Repeal anti-dumping and counter-veiling duty laws
- Notify all trading partners that we won't require them to limit exports to American customers under the various trade restraint agreements.
- Encourage the Japanese to abandon their so-called "voluntary" auto restraints and send American customers all the cars they want to buy.

Recall, for a minute, Britain's dramatic experience with free trade. In 1846, the failure of the Irish potato crop and ensuing famine prompted Britain to repeal virtually all its trade barriers. Parliament recognized that trade barriers tend to hurt the poor most. As a result of British free trade, starving people could gain the benefit of inexpensive food available on the world market.

Free trade, together with free movement of labor and capital, helped liberate phenomenal productive energy, and Britain prospered as never before. The standard reference *Abstract of Historical British Statistics* shows that from 1846 until the outbreak of World War I in 1914, Britain's industrial output expanded 362 percent. Imports soared 697 percent. Exports, 645 percent. According to one estimate, British entrepreneurs single-handedly accounted for almost a quarter of world trade. Britain enjoyed stability with the gold standard, and wholesale price indexes declined during the period, so these growth numbers really mean something.

"Britain dominated international finance with its banks and insurance companies," says Max Hartwell, economic history professor at the University of Virginia and author of *Industrial Revolution and Economic Growth*. "London provided a tremendous amount of the short-term as well as long-term credit for the world."

The crusading Englishmen Richard Cobden and John Bright hailed free trade as among the most effective measures to promote peace among nations, and they were right. For about twenty-five years, Europeans prospered as trade barriers came down in France,

Holland, Belgium, Germany, and other countries. The nineteenth century was the most peaceful period in modern history, and free trade made an important contribution, because it reduced the range of possible disputes among governments. No one was denied advantageous trading opportunities or cut off from vital resources.

In 1870, German chancellor Otto von Bismarck ushered in an ominous European trend back toward protectionism and war, but Britain held fast and continued to reap the benefits of free trade. By 1914, Britain was the world's wealthiest country and the biggest capital exporter, with $20 billion worth of foreign investments—130 percent more than France and 230 percent more than Germany. Britain had more financial power than any other country before or since, including the United States at its zenith after World War II.

In recent years, there have been many cases where those who adopt free trade realize dramatic gains. For example, in 1965 the United States and Canada signed a pact to lower auto-related tariffs between the two countries. Since then, according to Canadian deputy prime minister Don Mazankowski, the volume of automobiles exported from Canada to the United States has expanded from $2 billion to $64 billion. The number of auto-related jobs in Canada is up from 80,000 to 130,000.

Hong Kong, a free-trade mecca, is among the most dynamic economies. With a population of only 5.5 million and, like Singapore, no natural resources except a harbor, it's one of the world's top five financial centers. According to the *World Bank Atlas*, Hong Kong's per capita income of $6,220 is 203 percent higher than Malaysia's, 199 percent higher than Mexico's, 1,073 percent higher than Indonesia's, 1,906 percent higher than China's and 2,388 percent higher than India's, all of which are highly protectionist countries with abundant natural resources. Altogether, Hong Kong offers people a better standard of living than one hundred thirteen countries for which data is available. Per capita, Hong Kong imports 246 percent more American products than Europeans do. Foreign investment is welcome, and over 900 American companies have invested $6 billion in Hong Kong. Hong Kong continues to grow at a sizzling 12 percent annually.

In 1986 and 1987, the World Bank reviewed the experience of forty-one Third World countries and reported the contrast between those pursuing relatively free market policies versus those enforcing protectionism and government control of the economy. The former, which the World Bank refers to as "outward-oriented," include Hong

Kong, Singapore and South Korea, with trade barriers ranging from zero to 20 percent. On the other side are strongly "inward-oriented" countries like Bangladesh, Bolivia, Dominican Republic, Ethiopia, Ghana, India, Madagascar, Peru, Sudan, Tanzania, and Zambia, where high trade barriers deny their poor people the benefit of inexpensive, good-quality imports. Nigeria's trade barriers, for example, have pushed their consumer prices up 80 percent. Trade barriers force poor people in the Philippines to pay 99 percent more for things, and in Chile the damage is 217 percent.

Results, published in *World Development Report '87*, are dramatic. "The figures from the period 1963 to 1985 suggest that the economic performance of the outward-oriented economies has been broadly superior to that of the inward-oriented economies in almost all respects. Growth rates of gross domestic product show a clear descending pattern from the strongly outward-oriented to the strongly inward-oriented economies. The more effective policy for most developing countries is outward orientation."

The report continues: "Governments often adopt an inward-oriented strategy to promote industrialization. . . But it seems that countries have industrialized faster under outward orientation . . . average annual growth of manufacturing value added was highest in the strongly outward-oriented group and lowest in the strongly inward-oriented group . . . Industry provides more of the jobs in the outward-oriented economies than it does in the inward-oriented ones . . . Moreover, employment has grown faster in the outward-oriented economies.

"It is well known that the protection associated with inward-oriented policies imposes economic costs, not least on the country that puts the policy into effect . . . The advantage of an outward-oriented strategy over an inward-oriented strategy is that it promotes the efficient use of resources. The gains from this go well beyond the ones which are revealed by conventional analyses of the costs of protection . . . By dismantling [trade barriers], entrepreneurs could direct their energies away from unproductive activities, such as lobbying for changes in regulations. Further gains derive when firms achieve economies of scale: in an outward-oriented regime, the size of the domestic market does not limit the output of exporting firms.

"With global liberalization, the industrial and developing countries would together gain about $64 billion annually which is more than double the level of official development assistance coming from the Organization of Economic Cooperation and Development. *The main beneficiaries of unilateral liberalization are the liberalizers themselves."* [emphasis added]

Despite higher U.S. trade barriers, foreign competition has disciplined American management to adapt, and it has achieved higher productivity and profits. U.S. manufacturing productivity has increased more than 30 percent since the 1982 recession, and total manufacturing output is up a third. In every year but one, the U.S. manufacturing sector has surpassed Japan.

"The gains are especially dramatic in industries like textiles, mining, and forest products," says Joe Cobb, senior economist with the Congressional Joint Economic Committee. "The big old steel companies are foundering, but a lot of small steel mills are opening in the United States. These results suggest the far greater gains we could expect if our trade barriers were abolished altogether."

By adopting unilateral free trade, America would conserve capital, become more adaptable and competitive. American companies would become stronger, and American customers would be able to save more as a result of intensified competition and lower prices. This decisive step would enable us to help regain our role as a business leader and set an inspiring example for the world.

12

HOW AMERICA CAN BE MORE COMPETITIVE

We handicap ourselves with policies that increase the cost of capital, generate economic instability, and undermine the strength of American financial companies. We, not the Japanese, are responsible, so it's within our power to improve our competitive situation.

Among the most serious handicaps is the huge amount of capital siphoned away from the private, productive sector by government, most of which goes for consumption. Whether funds are siphoned by borrowing or taxing, they're unavailable for private investment. Raising taxes to balance the federal budget means little if the total drain on the economy is the same. Investment capital remains harder to come by than if government spending, taxes, and borrowing were lower. Capital is more expensive for American companies, and they have difficulty competing with Japanese companies, which enjoy a lower cost of capital.

Currently, federal spending accounts for almost a quarter of the gross national product, and it's headed up. Until about fifteen years ago, most federal spending was specifically appropriated. Then, during the 1970s, major programs were transformed to entitlements, guaranteeing benefits to whoever qualified. The major entitlements include Social Security, civil service pensions, military pensions, Medicare, Medicaid, and farm subsidies.

Altogether, in 1986 entitlements consumed $445 billion—more than half the federal budget. They account for 80 percent of nondefense spending. Federal entitlements exceed the total U.S. investment in new manufacturing plants, civilian research and development, plus roads, bridges, and other public facilities.

Politicians claim entitlements help the poor, but actually most recipients are middle class. About 85 percent of entitlements are disbursed without a means test. At most, according to some experts, perhaps 20 percent of recipients would be considered poor.

In 1986, the federal government siphoned $26 billion away from the productive sector to subsidize mainly big farmers. The result is warehouses bulging with grain, cheese, and other foodstuffs that customers don't want.

Senior citizens are among the most visible beneficiaries of entitlements, yet their poverty rate is the lowest of any age group, about 3 percent. While income may be down and health costs up for senior citizens, they have some savings, their children are out on their own, and about 80 percent have paid off their home mortgages. The biggest chunk of entitlements—$271 billion—goes for Social Security and Medicare. An estimated 75 percent of current recipients collect as much as five to 10 times more money than they ever contributed.

Civil service pensions don't help poor people, either. Pension terms provide recipients with triple the benefits of the most generous private pension plans. Benefits are set at 56 percent of preretirement compensation; retirement may be at age fifty-five; and disability standards are easy, enabling about a quarter of recipients to collect compensation for disability. When bureaucrats retire from government, a substantial number get private-sector jobs, anticipating a second pension. On average, retired bureaucrats report $35,000 of annual income.

Military pensions, too, are for the middle class. These programs yield six times the benefits of the best private pension plans. Benefits range from 50 percent to 75 percent of preretirement compensation. Though military personnel don't contribute toward their pensions, they're likely to spend more time collecting payments than they ever worked. After retiring and collecting their pension, typically at age forty-one, former military personnel may collect Social Security and get another job, where they may qualify for a private pension. These people are triple-dippers.

Government pensions are ticking time bombs, because they depend on a continuous stream of tax transfers from working people. These pensions aren't like private plans, where each individual pays his or her own way. The pension-age population is growing faster than the work force supporting the pensions. Now the unfunded liabilities for Social Security, Medicare, and federal pensions is a stupefying $10 trillion.

The government distributes more than $120 billion as means-tested assistance targeted at the poor. Noncash benefits like medical benefits, housing subsidies, and food stamps have zoomed fourteenfold during the past two decades. Despite means tests, an estimated 42 percent of recipients reported total income more than 150 percent above the poverty line.

"The main problem created by the growth of government spending," says economist Paul Craig Roberts of Georgetown University, "is the transformation of the United States from a free society in which private property rights are respected to a state where productive people have only a residual claim on what's left of their income and savings after all levels of government are finished redistributing it to the politically deserving.

"As scholars increasingly document, when governments make redistribution of income more important than the production of income, people reallocate their energies from economic to political action. The enormous growth in special-interest lobbies, which many members of Congress lament, parallels the growth in the proclivity of government to take from some and give to others."

Overall, federal entitlements have expanded twice as fast as defense spending and economic growth. Because 78 percent of entitlements are indexed, they'll continue to grow automatically if Congress and the President do nothing.

Federal spending has outpaced federal receipts, which have held steady between 18 and 20 percent of the gross national product. Hence, our chronic budget deficits. During the past two decades, the federal government reported a budget surplus only once.

The 1986 federal deficit, about $150 billion, was equal to about 90 percent of private-sector savings. "Should a recession come," warns William C. Freund, economist at the New York Stock Exchange, "the deficit could easily mount to $250 billion or $300 billion or more."

None of this includes off-budget programs like the Federal Financing Bank, Postal Service Fund, Strategic Petroleum Reserve Account, Rural Electrification and Telephone Revolving Fund, Rural

Telephone Bank, and the U.S. Railway Association. Add about $75 billion more to federal outlays.

Runaway spending has accelerated federal borrowing. During the past five years, federal debt has doubled, to nearly $2 trillion. The tab for interest on the debt exceeds $136 billion—an amount that approaches the present deficit. Each 1 percent rise in interest rates means an additional $5 billion of federal interest costs. Interest is among the fastest-growing government costs, lurching up more than 18 percent annually. At some point, it's feared, the government will have to borrow money just to pay interest, and we may stumble toward a runaway inflation.

To be sure, there's nothing wrong with borrowing as such. American companies borrowed heavily from foreign investors, chiefly the British, during the nineteenth century, and they helped finance construction of our railroads. In the 1950s, Japanese companies relied on foreign capital to rebuild their industrial plant. In these cases, money was borrowed for productive investment that would provide the means of paying it back.

But the federal government borrows for consumption, which yields zero return. All this federal borrowing means less productive investment. Today, federal borrowing takes about half of funds raised in U.S. capital markets. Consequently, interest rates are higher than they would be otherwise, many private borrowers are crowded out of capital markets, and the U.S. investment rate is the second-lowest in the industrialized world.

It's no wonder we spend less than the Japanese on productive equipment. Japanese factories have been rebuilt and refurbished many times since World War II. The average Japanese plant is eight to ten years old, versus American plants that average sixteen to eighteen years old. Japanese companies have twice as much investment supporting each worker, compared to American companies.

A bigger share of Japan's gross national product goes for research and development. During the past decade, the Japanese have produced 300 percent more patents, while American patent production dropped 10 percent. At the Massachusetts Institute of Technology, more professorships are endowed by Japanese companies than by American companies.

Because we're consuming more than we're producing, we're ever more dependent on the willingness of Japanese and other foreign investors to continue providing funds. Warns investment banker Peter G.

Peterson: "Nearly two thirds of our net investment in housing and in business plant and equipment would not have occurred without dollars saved by foreigners."

We can't take foreign investments for granted, because dollars are less attractive than they used to be. "For a currency that has fluctuated as widely as the dollar has over the past fourteen years, this risk is obviously considerable," says economist Stephen Marris at the Institute for International Economics. "The limits on the ability of the United States to go into external debt are likely to be determined more by people's willingness to incur exchange rate risk than by their assessment of its liquidity position or creditworthiness as a sovereign borrower.

"Because of the dollar's role as the world's leading currency," he notes, "foreigners are already exposed to an exchange risk on a large existing stock of dollar-denominated assets which do not, at the end of the line, represent claims on the United States, but on other countries that have issued liabilities denominated in dollars. As long as things go well, there is an advantage in being the issuer of the world's leading currency. Increasing demand for working balances and wealthholding in dollars provides a more or less automatic source of finance. If things go wrong, it is a different matter. People will try to sell off dollar-denominated assets that originated outside the United States and for which the United States is in no way responsible. The United Kingdom learned this lesson from bitter experience."

Increasingly, our indebtedness restricts options for Washington policymakers. To help finance federal spending with Treasury bonds, interest rates must be high enough to attract investors, including the Japanese. But high interest rates risk a U.S. recession. Federal Reserve governor Preston Martin warns: "You simply cannot frame targets for interest rates, credit, or monetary aggregates without looking over your shoulder at whether Japanese investors took a good piece of the last Treasury auction."

Former Fed chairman Paul Volcker: "The stability of our capital and money markets is now dependent as never before on the willingness of foreigners to continue to place growing amounts of money in our markets."

Zbigniew Brzezinski, who was assistant to the President for national security affairs, observes that America's indebtedness "will clearly place American global leadership in the greatest jeopardy. The United States will be hard put to exercise effective economic leadership, and its capacity to sustain its role as the principal defender of the free world will be severely undermined. If history is any guide, there can only be three outcomes to the emerging financial dilemma: war, bankruptcy, or inflation."

How to Cut the Capital Drain

If less capital is siphoned away for government consumption programs, and instead it becomes available for the productive sector, American companies will become far more competitive than they are now. They'll be more productive, generate more jobs, and give better service at less cost for customers. Here are six specific recommendations:

1. Establish an immediate federal budget freeze.

This means spending no more nominal dollars than were spent the previous year. Don't adjust the dollars for inflation. The freeze should be continued indefinitely, so that even if nothing else is done, over the years the government will become smaller relative to the private, productive sector of the economy.

A budget freeze shouldn't be confused with what's widely referred to as "budget cuts." The 1974 Congressional Budget Act requires the Congressional Budget Office to monitor federal spending against a yardstick called the "current services baseline." It projects future federal spending based on the current spending rate, inflation adjustments, changes in various laws, and other factors. Politicians talk about a "budget cut" if spending is less than the "current services baseline," even though they spent more of your money than last year.

Thus, in the current session of Congress, politicians wrestled with each other and the President about how to achieve $23 billion of spending "cuts." Actually, spending went up $47 billion. This compared with the "current services baseline" of $70 billion.

Congress and the President tout a modified Gramm-Rudman-Hollings deficit reduction law, whereby two-thirds of the budget is protected from the budget cutters' ax. The President exempted military pay, military pensions, his Strategic Defense Initiative, and some major military procurement programs. Congress exempted Social Security, much of Medicare, farm subsidies, Medicaid, welfare, food stamps, student loans, civil service pay, and pensions.

A meaningful spending freeze must apply to the grand total of federal outlays—farm subsidies, Social Security, defense, pork barrel construction projects, everything. No exemptions. If one scheme gets more money, it must be taken out of another program.

2. Don't make any direct benefit payments without a means test.

This would mean phasing out the hodgepodge of programs— from farm subsidies to Social Security—that transfer a significant chunk of taxpayer earnings to various politically powerful voting blocs without a means test. Ended, too, would be a wide range of subsidies to private companies and government enterprises.

There are many practical proposals for handling the phaseout process. For instance, economist Joe Cobb of the Congressional Joint-Economic Committee argues that Social Security tax increases should be channeled into private 401(K) private retirement plans, helping to provide for the retirement of working people.

All these government programs should be replaced with a single safety-net welfare program, where funds are disbursed exclusively on a means-tested basis.

Since only a small fraction of special interest programs actually trickle down to the destitute, a means-tested welfare program in itself will help slash government spending several hundred billion dollars.

With a means-tested welfare program, an individual would receive safety-net payments regardless of whether he or she happens to be over sixty-five, a farmer, textile worker, or something else. On the other hand, just because one is a farmer, for instance, is no reason to be subsidized at taxpayers' expense.

A means-tested welfare program should be set up in a way that minimizes the loss of incentives toward self-sufficiency. For instance, when a person on welfare works and earns $1, they shouldn't lose a full $1 of welfare, since there would be no point working. Better: lose perhaps 50¢ of welfare for each $1 of income, so that people will be better off working.

Applying a means test would still mean we'd have an entitlement program, but it would be a fraction the magnitude of the present morass, and it could be handled simply: Congress appropriates the same number of dollars as were spent the previous year, and if by year end it becomes apparent that more people than expected met the means test, then the shortfall is funded with a supplemental appropriation. The means test itself could be adjusted, if it's being abused.

3. Slash the cost of government operations.

Perhaps because people tend to be less careful with other people's money than with their own, government is an exorbitantly expensive conduit for funds. There's a huge amount lost as funds are siphoned away from the productive sector, processed through Washington, and passed on to a favored voting bloc. Cutting the cost of government operations will help lessen the drain of resources away from the productive sector.

Consider the potential savings that would be realized by sensible cash management methods. The federal government spends or collects almost $971 million each working hour. Yet officials don't have systems in place to monitor their cash position. Billions are lost, because officials don't have much incentive to apply elementary cash management techniques that are commonplace in private business—like depositing checks immediately, not paying bills until they're due, and minimizing cash in non-interest-paying accounts.

Evidence of immense waste seems to appear in every government department. The Social Security Administration's financial systems are a mess—some 138 million Social Security tax payments, worth $89 billion, are in a suspense file, because officials don't know which individuals should be credited. It costs the Army about $4.20 to process each payroll check, quadruple the cost in the private sector. The Defense Department pays $91 for 3¢ screws, $100 for 25¢ compressor caps and $114 for 9½¢ silicon electric cells. The federal government has eighty thousand pages of instructions for procurement, yet a survey of twenty-five major Pentagon weapons programs shows they come in 223 percent above original estimates. The General Services Administration's recovery rate on overcharged freight bills is a fifth that of the private sector. U.S. government employees take 15 million trips a year, and their rate for prepaid "no-shows" on commercial airlines is three times greater than that of private citizens. Federal employees claim 160 percent more sick days than workers in the private sector. Federal employees take an additional 120 percent more time off. Incredibly, the government doesn't know the total unfunded liabilities of its pension system, though two plans alone exceed $1 trillion.

The best analysis of potential savings is the Grace Commission's forty-seven-volume report, issued in 1984. It developed 2,478 specific recommendations that could save an estimated $424 billion within three years and $1.9 trillion per year by the year 2000. That's a lot of money to take away from productive investment.

One can grow a little numb amidst all the numbers, but they're provocative. According to Grace Commission analysts, cutting out waste would contribute to a 31 percent decline of government spending, 5 percent higher government revenues, a 14 percent lower inflation rate, 23 to 37 percent lower interest rates, 60 percent more business investment, 64 percent higher growth of industrial production, and 2 million more people employed.

4. Cut personal income tax rates to a maximum 15-percent flat rate and abolish deductions, including home mortgage interest. Set the minimum taxable income high enough to exempt poor people—perhaps $12,000 for a family of four.

Based on Treasury Department analysis, a 15-percent flat-rate tax would raise about as much revenue as comes now from current high tax rates and all the deductions that survived the 1986 Tax Reform Act. It shouldn't be surprising that a flat-rate tax could be in this low range, because total federal income taxes are only about 11 percent of total personal income in the United States. If federal spending were cut sharply, as it should be, personal income taxes could be cut further, to a rate approaching 5 percent.

Cutting personal taxes would improve work incentives and stimulate the economy without distortions induced by the tax code. Generally, the lower the tax rates, the stronger the incentive for people to concentrate on maximizing income rather than avoiding taxes. Recall our recent experience with capital gains taxes. In 1978, they were cut from 49 to 28 percent. They were cut again in 1981, to 20 percent, and it remained there for five years. While the capital gains tax rate dropped 60 percent during the 1978–85 period, capital gains tax revenues soared 184 percent. This was double the gain registered by the gross national product and the Dow Jones Industrial Average.

A sharply reduced personal income tax rate would give the United States important competitive advantages over Japan, where the top rate remains at a confiscatory 70 percent. The most optimistic reforms being discussed would bring it down only to 50 percent.

5. Abolish the capital gains tax.

It comes on top of the personal income tax, since funds committed to an investment were taxed when earned initially. Investment income, if any, is subject to the personal income tax as it's realized.

High capital gains taxes discourage vital investments. In 1969, U.S. federal capital gains taxes increased to 49.125 percent, and venture capital investment plummeted. It reached a nadir in 1977, when tax rates on ordinary income and long-term capital investment were close.

Then, in 1978, with passage of the Steiger Amendment, capital gains taxes were cut to 28 percent. In a single year, the funds raised by venture capital firms soared from $39 million to $600 million, more than 1,400 percent. Within three years this grew to $1.4 billion, quadruple the 1977 level.

In 1981, the capital gains tax was lowered again, this time to 20 percent. By 1986, venture capital investment was reported at $2.9 billion, a sevenfold gain compared to 1977.

When capital gains taxes are lowered, it's easier for new entrepreneurial ventures to raise funds from equity markets. In 1978, there were 45 initial public offerings, which raised $249 million. By 1980, 237 companies came to market and raised $1.4 billion. The venture capital market continued to expand, and in 1986, 717 initial public offerings generated $22.4 billion of fresh capital.

In many of the world's most successful economies, people recognize the wisdom of abolishing a capital gains tax. Neither Japan nor the fast-growing Pacific Rim countries of Hong Kong, Singapore, Malaysia, Taiwan, or South Korea have a capital gains tax. Nor do Belgium, the Netherlands, or Italy. Long-term capital gains are tax-free in West Germany.

"Abolishing the capital gains tax will increase the return on capital," says Dr. Norman Ture, president of the Institute for Research on the Economics of Taxation and author of *The Effects of Tax Policy on Capital Formation.* "Consequently, there will be greater incentives to save, both among households and businesses."

6. Abolish the corporate income tax.

It's utterly counterproductive. American corporations need more capital so they can make investments essential for growth and jobs. Yet the corporate income tax depletes 34 percent of a corporation's earnings. Moreover, earnings distributed as dividends are hit again by the personal income tax. By lowering the return on capital, the corporate income tax further reduces the volume of funds available for investment.

Generally, the higher the tax on capital, the greater the after-tax return must be to justify investment. Since there aren't many business opportunities that offer extremely high returns, higher corporate income taxes correspond with a drastic reduction of total investment.

The corporate income tax exists only as a convenient way for government to gather revenue. Like any cost of doing business, corporate income taxes are passed on to customers via higher prices for goods and services.

"Washington would lose surprisingly little revenue by abolishing the corporate income tax, because its importance has declined during the past three decades," notes economist Joe Cobb. "The corporate income tax yields only about a fifth as much revenue as the personal income tax."

But the corporate income tax does considerable damage to the economy. The depreciation provisions of the corporate income tax code penalize capital investment. If a company makes a $10 million outlay for new equipment this year, for instance, $10 million cannot be deducted this year. For tax purposes, the company is restricted to deducting a little at a time over five, ten, or twenty years, depending on the kind of equipment. Yet a dollar in hand today is worth a lot more than a dollar that won't be available for twenty years.

Less capital investment means fewer jobs. Available jobs will be less productive, and they'll pay less, since the value of a job depends significantly on the capital a person has to work with. So the corporate income tax penalizes American workers.

Since long-term investments have the longest depreciation schedules, the tax code makes them riskier than they already are. Thus, business executives are encouraged to delay or put off altogether as many long-term investments as they can. The corporate income tax favors short-term thinking, widely blamed for handicapping American companies as they race with Japanese and other foreign competitors. Abolishing the capital income tax would encourage executives to make investments on their business merits, without being distracted by tax complications.

Perhaps hardest hit by the corporate income tax are smaller and middle-market entrepreneurial companies, which generate important innovations and all the net new jobs in our economy. They desperately need capital to grow. But because these companies tend to be riskier than big, established corporations, they must yield higher returns to attract capital. By lowering the return on capital, the corporate income tax restricts their growth. Abolishing the corporate income tax would provide a powerful stimulus for these companies.

The corporate income tax contributes to unnecessarily high interest rates, because investors need to be compensated for the lower return on capital. "If the capital gains tax were abolished, interest rates could conceivably come down a full point from their current level around 10 percent," says economist Ture, who served as an under secretary of the Treasury for tax policy. "This would mean billions of dollars saved for American borrowers. Billions more would be saved if other taxes like the capital gains tax and personal income taxes were cut."

Abolishing the corporate income tax would result in a huge, immediate contribution to American savings. "Corporations tend to retain about 70 percent of earnings," notes Gregory Ballentine, partner in the Big Eight accounting firm Peat Marwick Main, "so instead of paying out more than $100 billion in taxes as they do now, American corporations would have about $70 billion more each year for investment.

"Because corporations would become much more profitable than they are now, stock would be more attractive. If the corporate income tax were abolished, we'd see corporations raise more capital via new stock issues. Conversely, since interest wouldn't offer the advantage of tax deductions, corporations would probably borrow less. Debt ratios would come down, and American companies would be stronger than they are now."

Free Movement of People

Sharply lower personal income taxes would almost certainly prove to be a powerful magnet helping attract more prime talent to the United States from around the world. The abolition of corporate income taxes would be especially appealing to entrepreneurs.

We would be in a position to gain immense competitive advantages as foreign entrepreneurs, financiers, scientists, inventors, engineers, artists, and others establish roots here. We'd perhaps become more aware that our most important natural resource is an energetic, resourceful people.

In his congressional testimony on a bill that became the 1986 immigration law, Johns Hopkins University history professor John Higham recalled "the prominence of the foreign-born among American inventors, entrepreneurs, and technicians in new, high-risk industries such as textile manufacturing in the early nineteenth century, investment banking at mid-century, and moviemaking in the early twentieth century. Innovation flourishes under the stimuli of mobility and cultural diversity, which have been the basic parameters of the American immigrant experience"

But the present maze of immigration restrictions would squander our magnificent opportunity. Immigration quotas should be abolished, and we should reopen our borders for unlimited numbers of healthy people who show they have some personal assets and skills that will enable them to make a contribution here.

Throughout our history, immigration laws have reflected little more than xenophobic hatred and often jealousy of foreigners. It's unbecoming of a great nation like the United States to discriminate against individuals just because they happen to be born somewhere else on the planet.

Certainly, we have plenty of room for more people in the United States. Even along the Boston/New York/Washington corridor, there's substantial open space. The United States is among the least densely-populated countries.

Some places are crowded, of course, but they hardly justify ethnic discrimination. As experience in relatively clean, low-crime Tokyo shows, many urban problems cannot be blamed on crowding. In any case, population density is an issue that tends to sort itself out naturally, as people move away from places that are too expensive or otherwise undesirable.

It's a vicious myth that foreigners create unemployment. Because they tend to lack business connections and fluency in English, often they start with jobs that Americans no longer want. In New York, for example, a high percentage of taxi drivers and cooks are immigrants from places like Greece, Iran, and Vietnam. Enforcing tough restrictions against immigrants deprives western fruit and vegetable growers of labor they need, so precious food rots on the vine.

The 1986 *Economic Report of the President* reports a survey of findings: "Studies that take a broad view of the labor market have found no significant evidence of unemployment among native-born workers attributable to immigration. Any direct effects of immigration on domestic employment have either been too small to measure or have been quickly dissipated with job mobility. Although existing studies may not be conclusive, the evidence currently available does not suggest that native-born American workers experience significant labor market difficulties in areas that have attracted immigrants. Several studies, moreover, have shown that the presence of immigrants in labor markets is associated with increased job opportunities overall, including job opportunities for native-born minority groups.

"The experience of the Los Angeles labor market in adjusting to a growing concentration of unskilled immigrant labor is instructive. One study estimated that more than a million foreign-born persons settled in Los Angeles County between 1970 and 1983. During the early 1980s, the foreign-born in Los Angeles represented close to a third of the total population. Job growth in the area was strong and the new immigrants were quickly absorbed into the labor market. New immigrant workers accounted for some 70 percent of the net growth in employment in the 1970s. Job gains by native-born workers were predominantly in white-collar occupations that expanded rapidly. Job growth among immigrants was concentrated mainly in unskilled jobs. Wage growth was lower than the national average for workers in manufacturing, particularly unskilled manufacturing. In jobs outside manufacturing, however, including jobs in services and retail trade, wage growth was higher than the national average. This study also showed that the unemployment rate in Los Angeles, which had exceeded the national average in 1970, fell below the average by the early 1980s."

"Perhaps the most striking pattern among American ethnic groups," says Stanford University economist Thomas Sowell in *Ethnic America*, "is their general rise in economic conditions with the passage of time. Progress is so generally taken for granted in the United States that it is necessary to realize that it is not automatic. In many parts of the world, people still live at an economic level not much above that of their ancestors. But in addition to absolute rises in living standards, political representation, and longevity, American ethnic groups have typically also risen in relative terms. Italian Americans who earned less than half the national income in the early twentieth century now receive more than the national average. The poverty-stricken Jews of the late nineteenth century now earn more than any other ethnic group, including Anglo-Saxons. There are wide variations in the rates of progress among American ethnic groups, but progress itself is pervasive."

America would be decidedly poorer without the capital, jobs and products generated by foreign-born American entrepreneurs like John Jacob Astor, Pierre Samuel du Pont, Andrew Mellon, Meyer Guggenheim, Henry Lehman, Adolphus Busch, William Colgate, Herbert H. Dow, James J. Hill, Alfred Fuller, Alexander Graham Bell, Andrew

Carnegie, Samuel Goldwyn, Louis B. Mayer, John Dessauer, Helena Rubenstein, Joseph Hirshhorn, Elizabeth Arden, Rupert Murdoch, Anthony Rossi, and An Wang.

Immigration laws not only deny American companies valuable ethnic talent, they impose serious costs as well. The 1986 immigration law requires employers to keep more records and increases the risk of being caught by conflicting regulations. Even paperwork violations could cost thousands in fines. Employers who persist in hiring so-called illegals could be jailed for up to six months. Economists at the Federal Reserve Bank in Dallas estimate the 1986 immigration law will increase the cost of goods and services in the United States by $20 billion to $60 billion each year.

Abolishing American immigration laws would probably present the Japanese with their most painful challenge, because they have a long history as a homogenous people.

Very few foreign residents in Japan ever really gain social acceptance. *Gaijin*, meaning "foreigner," remains a pejorative word. The Japanese continue to treat their Korean minority as second-class citizens. The Japanese discomfort with foreigners has kept away all but a small number of Southeast Asian refugees. Most Japanese seem reluctant to depart from their tradition of ethnic purity, and this will mean incalculable losses as prime talent contributes to other countries, particularly the United States.

Monetary Stability

The government should promote stable money. This would be an honest, fair policy enabling everyone to make future commitments with more confidence than now. American companies could be more competitive if money were stable, because they wouldn't be distracted by as much volatility in the business environment.

Many politicians advocate an inflation policy, believing it will help the poor generally and debtors in particular. This is nonsense. Inflation is a cruel tax that hurts the least skilled, poor people who have little bargaining power. Often their wage rates lag behind consumer prices, which is why strikes and riots are decidedly more frequent during high inflation. Further, inflation robs purchasing power from the elderly who must survive on fixed incomes.

Sometimes inflation is promoted—incredibly, in a *New Yorker* magazine series—as a social welfare program to benefit debtors at the expense of lenders. At best, though, it's a clumsy effort, since wealthy investors and corporations rank among the biggest borrowers.

In any case, it's a myth that inflation necessarily benefits debtors. Lenders aren't dummies. They demand interest rates to compensate for anticipated depreciation of their money. Wealth is transferred from lenders to debtors only if the inflation rate is greater than anticipated. To accomplish this, monetary authorities must practice deceit and instability, tricking lenders into accepting interest rates that won't cover inflation losses.

The charade can continue for a while, but when lenders conclude that a particular market is a hopeless loser, because of volatile inflation or any other reason, they'll take their money to safe havens elsewhere. Consequently, everyone will be denied the benefit of their savings and investment. As a social welfare policy, volatile inflation tends to be short-lived and self-defeating. In South America, which is plagued with chronic inflation, the volume of flight capital leaving the countries approaches the volume of bank loans to the same countries.

Volatile monetary policy is dangerous. It undermines the economy. If continued long enough, it can lead to runaway inflation which makes people so desperate that they'll demand a strong ruler to take charge. Result: dictatorship, as has happened in France, Germany, Chile, Argentina, Brazil, and other countries.

What's needed is to regain reasonable control over the money supply. If it happens faster than anticipated, then people supposedly helped by the inflation policy become victims. Farmers, for instance, who borrowed money to buy more farm land or corporations that borrowed for business expansion.

Vastly preferable to the agony of inflation and deflation is stable money. It requires stable bank reserves. The Federal Reserve exercises two kinds of control here. First, indirect control by adjusting the discount rate that it charges for loaning money to commercial banks. According to the *1982 Economic Report of the President*, the discount rate is most likely to promote monetary stability if it's set at a consistent premium to market money rates. Consistency would minimize variable incentives for banks to borrow at the Fed's discount window. A premium would discourage borrowing.

Second, the Fed has the power to control bank reserves directly by buying and selling government securities held by banks. Buying these securities injects cash into the banking system. Selling securities to banks withdraws cash. Bank reserves should be maintained at a level consistent with long-term price stability.

But the Fed has failed to maintain stable money. "Throughout its history, the Federal Reserve has proclaimed that it was using its powers to promote economic stability," says Nobel laureate Milton Friedman. "But the record does not support the claim. On the contrary, the Fed has been a major source of instability." Friedman's massive *A Monetary History of the United States* documents experience before and after the Federal Reserve was established in 1914.

Since then, recessions have become more frequent than they used to be, and they tend to last longer. We've had persistent inflation since 1940, something unheard of in our history. Before 1914, U.S. inflation was a wartime phenomenon, and prices declined afterward. Friedman notes: "The blind, undesigned, and quasi-automatic working of the gold standard turned out to produce a greater measure of predictability and regularity—perhaps because its discipline was impersonal and inescapable—than did deliberate and conscious control exercised within institutional arrangements intended to promote monetary stability."

The Federal Reserve Board adds to whatever instability there is in the world, because it enables seven governors to tinker with a complex economy. They don't gain any unique wisdom by donning a Federal Reserve hat. Their information isn't any better than what the rest of us have, nor do they get it any earlier. They make impressionistic guesses based on conflicting data. Since they're human, they're bound to make mistakes, and because of their power, the mistakes reverberate throughout the world. Disaster is always a possibility.

Although on October 6, 1979, the Federal Reserve announced it would abandon efforts to control interest rates and instead would aim to assure steady monetary growth, its performance continues to be volatile. During the first quarter of 1985, for instance, the Fed accelerated growth of the monetary base at about a 20 percent rate and continued at this high level for a year. Because people still remembered disinflation of the early 1980s, inflationary expectations were low. The increased quantity of money didn't produce higher consumer prices. Instead, it flowed into financial markets, particularly the stock market, and the bull market boomed. But by 1987, the Fed had cut monetary growth to a 10-percent rate, then 3-percent. Shutting down the flow of money was a major factor contributing to the October 1987 stock crash.

To prevent future monetary disasters, we must recognize that the monetary system is so complex that it can't be managed on a discretionary basis by a few people. They'll continue to make dangerous mistakes, as central economic planners have for more than four thousand years. "The United States would have been far better off had the Federal Reserve System never been created," Friedman declares.

Ideally, the Fed should be abolished. It wasn't set up in 1913 to manage the money supply, and it certainly isn't needed for that now. The United States, like most countries, has had dismal experience with central banks. On the other hand, the United States became a major economic power during the nineteenth century without a central bank. Hong Kong prospers without a central bank—two local banks issue private banknotes, and competition helps keep them sound.

The Fed's original purpose was to provide insurance for the financial system. But this function is handled by the Federal Deposit Insurance Corporation and the Federal Savings and Loan Insurance Corporation. We don't need the Fed for insurance.

Nor is it needed to finance the federal government, since it buys a relatively small portion of total federal debt. In any case, we'd achieve a beneficial curb on federal spending by eliminating the Fed as a source of easy money.

Since abolishing the Fed would be too radical for most people, at least Federal Reserve monetary policy should be tied to some external constraint. Unpredictable, discretionary monetary management should be replaced with an automatic monetary rule, an idea Friedman proposed more than three decades ago. He recommended increasing the monetary base by an amount equal to average output, perhaps 3 percent to 4 percent annually. It's a relatively stable number. As a result, a major source of volatility would become predictable. "Of course," he says, "the Fed cannot achieve a precise rate of growth from day to day or week to week. But it can come very close from month to month and quarter to quarter.

"The Federal Reserve Board could be replaced," he continues, "with a simple statement that every Monday at 10:00 A.M. the government agent will buy a certain specified amount of bonds, one-seventeenth of 1 percent of the outstanding high-powered money. Then close up shop and go home." Friedman says this routine administration of the money supply could easily be transferred to the Treasury Department.

Alternatively, monetary policy could be linked to gold or an index based on a "basket" of strong currencies and gold, such as Treasury Secretary James Baker discussed at a 1987 conference of the International Monetary Fund. This idea, which has been kicked around for quite a few years, has the disadvantage of being vague and thereby inviting the kind of discretionary policy that contributes to instability.

A primary aim of this and other monetary rules is to provide independent discipline for the financial system. To regulate the system as well as print the money involves a perennial conflict of interest. "There shouldn't be insider trading in monetary policy," says economist Cobb, who contributes to *The Wall Street Journal.*

With a firmly applied, specific, stable monetary rule, individual sectors of the economy would continue to go through cycles of good times and bad, but there would be less likelihood that the whole economy would experience a crisis. Private individuals and companies would be more able to make meaningful long-term plans.

Better Protection for American Assets

We should make it easier for Americans to protect their savings. Because it's difficult for Americans to store savings in a currency other than the U.S. dollar, we're vulnerable to having a substantial chunk of savings wiped out when the dollar declines.

We should begin by ending the Federal Reserve policy that makes it illegal for U.S. banks to take foreign currency deposits or extend foreign currency loans with domestic customers. If you believe that the U.S. dollar is likely to lose value against the Japanese yen, Swiss franc, or any other currency, the only way you can open an account in one of those currencies is to visit a foreign bank. This is inconvenient for people who live away from money centers like New York, Chicago, and Los Angeles, where foreign banks are concentrated. An American bank would be reluctant to open a foreign currency account for you unless you're engaged in international transactions. Scuttling this regulation will give individuals and companies the flexibility to deal in the strongest currency, so they'll better preserve their assets.

Americans would be in an even stronger position if legal tender laws were repealed. These enhance the monopoly of the U.S. dollar in the United States and make it harder for Americans to protect themselves when the value of the dollar is manipulated.

The legal tender laws require that government notes be accepted for all debts, public and private. If you have a contract that provides you'll be paid in dollars, and the dollar loses substantial value, you're stuck. You can't reject the dollars you're offered, on the grounds that they're worth less than what you bargained for. Americans will be better able to build up assets if they're free to insist on value-for-value exchanges.

These changes would intensify pressure on the United States to maintain the value of the dollar. When Americans across the country see the dollar declining, they'd be able to limit their losses and seek refuge in a stronger currency. Probably more Americans would diversify their holdings among several major currencies. If the dollar continued depreciating enough, eventually it would be driven out of circulation like any bad product in a competitive market where customers have choices.

There's nothing radical about all this. Multinational American companies have managed assets in many currencies for decades. Dealing in more than one currency, like learning another language, is common among people in Europe, East Asia, and elsewhere. Now it's time that Main Street, America, have these options, too.

Lower-cost Corporate Finance

American companies pay needlessly high costs to raise capital, because competition is restricted. The Glass-Steagall Act (1933) excludes banks from most securities underwriting, creating privileged turf for securities firms.

By repealing Glass-Steagall, banks could compete freely for securities business, and financing costs would drop. Edward I. O'Brien, president of the Securities Industry Association, concedes as much, though he minimizes the savings.

Look at municipal finance. Banks can underwrite general-obligation bonds of state and local governments, but they aren't permitted to underwrite state and local government-revenue bonds.

Result: general-obligation bonds involve 50 percent lower underwriting costs than revenue bonds.

According to National Governors Association estimates, state and local governments would save about $500 million in annual borrowing costs if banks were permitted to compete for muncipal bond underwritings.

While commercial banks are excluded from corporate securities underwriting in the United States, they're free to compete with securities firms on the Euromarket. Underwriting costs are about a third less there than in the United States. One noteworthy effect of Glass-Steagall is to export corporate underwriting jobs from the United States to Europe.

The Glass-Steagall Act was enacted on the mistaken notion that abuses by banks caused the Great Depression. In fact, as ample empirical analyses have demonstrated, the primary causes of the Depression were militant protectionist trade barriers followed by steep tax increases and the failure of the Federal Reserve Board to stop the catastrophic one-third drop in the money supply.

"Congress passed the Glass-Steagall Act," says Emory University economist George Benston, author of *Perspectives on a Safe and Sound Banking System*, "because banks allegedly engaged in self-dealing, abused their trust to foist defaulted Peruvian bonds on the public, took positions in securities privately to the detriment of the public—and failed at their appointed tasks because of such abuses.

"But a close reading of the Glass-Steagall hearings show there's no evidence any of this actually happened. There were many unsupported allegations. A lot of the headlines focused on the way First National City Bank President Charles Mitchell and Chase Bank President Alfred Wiggins handled their personal finances. They don't seem to have done anything wrong, but they were financial giants no one had ever questioned before, and the adversary questioning was brilliant. Congress wanted scapegoats."

There's some evidence that diversification by banks into the securities business and securities firms into the banking business would help strengthen both. "Many studies show that reported cash flows of commercial banks and securities firms tend to complement one another," says Benston. "This suggests it would be less risky for firms to combine these two kinds of cash flows"

It's true that bank underwriting would involve a potential conflict of interest, particularly with trust department clients. But securities firms face conflicts of interest, too, between their department that represents clients issuing securities and their department representing securities investors. Usually, securities firms manage this inherent conflict. When an issuer or investor isn't satisfied, they'll take their business someplace else.

Smaller American companies probably would be major beneficiaries if Glass-Steagall were abolished. Their current financing options are limited mainly to bank loans and equity infusions from friends or venture capitalists. Smaller companies can't tap domestic as well as international equity markets as easily as the Fortune 500 can.

Smaller companies would be better able to raise capital for growth. Now banks have a perverse incentive to push loans—that's all they're permitted to provide. Without Glass-Steagall, banks would be able to offer companies whatever makes the most sense, debt or equity. Bankers have specialized knowledge to evaluate the soundness of smaller companies, which Wall Street securities firms lack. So bankers are in an ideal position to help develop regional equity markets. They might even be good at it.

To further lower corporate financing costs, the McFadden-Act (1927) should be repealed. This restricts the ability of nationally chartered U.S. banks to compete in any U.S. market.

Because of the McFadden Act, nationally chartered banks are subject to the same restrictions as state-chartered banks. In some states, for instance, state banks aren't permitted to have more than one branch, while elsewhere state banks may be limited to a county. There are fourteen thousand banks in the United States, but most enjoy a local cartel, with customers denied the benefits of unlimited competition.

By repealing the McFadden Act, nationally chartered banks could open branches anywhere. The poorest-served markets would offer the most lucrative opportunities.

To survive, state-chartered banks would have to adapt, expand, and improve their customer services. Suddenly, the restrictions of a state charter would be a handicap they couldn't afford, and most would switch to national charters. Local banks that already did a good job serving their customers would have the least to worry about. Laggards would close down or merge with other banks. When weaknesses are flushed out, the result would be stronger banks, because they'd be able to attract deposits from a wider region and diversify their loan portfolios in more industries, rather than bet the bank on a few like energy, agriculture, and real estate.

Smaller companies across the United States would gain more accommodating, less expensive financial support. Obviously, this would improve their prospects to stay competitive.

How to Strengthen American Banks

In recent years, American banks have absorbed billions' worth of loan losses on loans to Third World countries, real estate operators, energy companies, and farmers. Perhaps most major American money center banks have had their credit ratings downgraded. To strengthen their financial position and stand a chance against strong Japanese banks, American banks must raise more capital.

Perhaps the most readily available source would be investments by nonbank companies. Industrial companies like IBM, Ford, and General Electric have huge reservoirs of capital, far more than the largest American banks. Yet vital capital infusions are blocked by the Bank Holding Company Act (1956, 1970). It must be repealed.

In West Germany and many other countries, nonbank companies are free to buy banks. There's extensive cross-ownership among banks and industrial companies. The West German banking system, for instance, is strong and innovative. West German banks pay interest on all their checking deposits. They were among the first to introduce money market accounts.

There's no economic reason to prevent nonbank companies from buying banks. The restriction serves only to shelter bank managements who might become acquisition targets.

Many states are moving in the right direction, according to Robert 0. Quinn, economist with the Federal Reserve in Washington. Recognizing the need to help local banks raise more capital, thirty-six state legislatures and the District of Columbia have passed laws to permit some interstate bank acquisitions. In many cases, such as Georgia, these may take place within a region, like the Southeast. But ten states, Massachusetts and Rhode Island among them, permit banks from any state to acquire banks within their state. Another dozen states will drop regional restrictions and permit acquisitions from anywhere within three years. By 1991, banks with an estimated 75 percent of U.S. deposits will be free to combine with other banks.

Repeal of state restrictions, plus repeal of the Bank Holding Company Act, McFadden Act, and Glass-Steagall Act would result in a very different banking system. Instead of fourteen thousand banks, there may be a few thousand or only a few hundred survivors, but they'd be more diversified, better-financed, and much stronger. We'd probably have about the same number of branch offices, as banks joined hands in stronger units.

Local cartels would be gone, and there would be more competition, benefiting individual and corporate customers everywhere. Since financial markets would be more fluid, competitors would be free to move in where they see opportunities to offer valuable service.

Bonanza for Customers

As you can see, more open-market American policies will help assure that American customers benefit from quality services and lower prices that Japanese financial companies offer. America will be better off, because the savings realized will translate to desperately needed capital. That means greater growth and more jobs.

At the same time, open-market policies will unshackle American companies so they can serve us better than they do now. It's crazy for the American government to deny American companies free access to the capital, talent, goods, and services they need.

While thoughtful cooperation among countries is always important, none of the measures I've recommended depends on others. The recommendations can be implemented unilaterally, without waiting for anyone else. On the contrary, the sooner the recommendations are implemented, the sooner America will be reinvigorated, and that means opportunities for people everywhere.

It doesn't really matter whether Citicorp or any other American financial company is the biggest in the world. But it's important that these institutions be capable of providing what their customers need. If they don't, Japanese and others will.

APPENDIX 1

FOREIGN INVESTMENT IN THE UNITED STATES

How extensive are foreign holdings? Despite all the headlines about foreigners taking over America, reported foreign holdings are actually small when compared with the total assets in the United States.

Total holdings

Total assets in the U.S.	$30.0 trillion
Total held by foreign investors	$1.5 trillion
Percentage held by foreign investors	5%

Source: Federal Reserve Board

U.S. government securities

Total U.S. government securities	$2,600 billion
Total held by foreign investors	$334 billion
Percentage held by foreign investors	12.8%

Source: U.S. Treasury Department, *U.S. Budget*

Corporate equities

Total U.S. corporate equities	$3,066 billion
Total held by foreign investors	$193 billion
Percentage held by foreign investors	6.29%

Source: Federal Reserve Board, *Quarterly Levels,* Third Quarter 1988

Land
Total acres in the U.S.   2.2 billion
Total owned by foreign investors   12.5 million
Percentage owned by foreign investors   1%

Source: U.S. Agriculture Department, *Foreign Ownership of U.S. Agricultural Land through December 31, 1987*

Stocks and Bonds
Total value of financial assets $12.275 billion

Source: Salomon Brothers

U.S. Investment Overseas Surpasses Foreign Investment in the U.S.
(*$US billions*)

As you can see, U.S. companies make a considerably higher volume of direct investments abroad than foreign companies make in the United States.

	U.S. direct investment abroad	Foreign direct investment in the U.S.
1980	215	83
1981	228	109
1982	208	125
1983	207	137
1984	212	165
1985	230	185
1986	260	220
1987	309	261

Source: U.S. Commerce Department, Department of Economic Analysis
Note: Commerce Department data includes corporate acquisitions over $1 million and land purchases over 200 acres. An unspecified amount of data is suppressed to protect confidentiality.

10 Most Popular Countries Among U.S. Investors
(1987)

Country	Book value of investment ($US millions)
Great Britain	44.67
West Germany	24.45
Switzerland	19.97
Bermuda	18.22
Japan	14.27
Netherlands	14.16
France	11.47
Australia	10.98
Brazil	9.95
Italy	8.49
All countries	308.79

Source: U.S. Commerce Department, *Survey of Current Business,* August 1988

U.S. Direct Investment Income From Overseas Exceeds Foreign Direct Investment Income in the U.S.
($US millions)

Year	U.S. investment income from abroad	Foreign investment income from U.S.
1985	33,202	6,079
1986	38,407	5,279
1987	52,308	19,504

Source: U.S. Department of Commerce, *Survey of Current Business,* August 1988

U.S. Rate of Return From Overseas Investments Exceeds Foreign Investors' Rate of Return in U.S.
(1987)

Industry	Foreign rate of return (%)	U.S. rate of return (%)
Petroleum	7.6	12.7
Manufacturing	5.5	23.4

U.S. Rate of Return From Overseas Investments Exceeds
Foreign Investors' Rate of Return in U.S. (cont.)
(1987)

Industry	Foreign rate of return (%)	U.S. rate of return (%)
Other	1.6	16.4
All industries	4.4	18.4

Source: U.S. Department of Commerce, *Survey of Current Business*, August 1988

How Shareholders Benefit From Foreign
Direct Investment in the U.S.

This summary shows how dramatically U.S. shareholders benefit when an acquisition is permitted to go through. U.S. shareholders do a little better when the acquirer is foreign.

Conversely, you see that when an acquisition is thwarted, U.S. shareholders lose a significant amount of money.

Premium over market price realized by U.S. shareholders from U.S. acquirers	43%
Premium over market price realized by U.S. shareholders from foreign acquirers	46%
Average change in stock price a month after a prospective acquirer (foreign or domestic) was blocked	−10%

Source: Federal Reserve Bank of Boston, *New England Economic Review*, November/December 1988

Biggest Foreign Investors in the U.S.
(1988)

This table shows that the biggest direct sources of foreign investment in the United States are our allies, not our adversaries.

Country	Acquisition value ($US billions)
Great Britain	81.9
Netherlands	52.0

Biggest Foreign Investors in the U.S. (cont.)
(1988)

Country	Acquisition value ($US billions)
Japan	44.8
Canada	22.5
West Germany	20.1
Total value of foreign direct investment in U.S.	261.9

Source: U.S. Commerce Department, *Survey of Current Business,* June and December 1988

Most Active Foreign Investors in the U.S.
(Number of acquisitions)

This table shows that when a U.S. company is sold to a foreign investor, it's almost always European. In terms of the number of companies purchased, the Japanese aren't as high as one might expect, based on their dollar volume of purchases.

Country	Acquisitions Past 10 years	1987
Great Britain	640	78
Canada	435	28
West Germany	150	15
France	113	19
Japan	94	15
Switzerland	86	9
Netherlands	81	9
Australia	68	17
Sweden	63	9
Italy	31	6
Total for top 10 countries	1,761	205
Total for all countries	1,967	220

Source: Federal Reserve Bank of Boston, *New England Economic Review,* November/December 1988

Key U.S. Sectors Favored by Foreign Investors, 1987
($US millions)

Country	Total	Manufacturing	Real estate
Great Britain	5,849	5,800	49
Japan	5,280	980	2,125
West Germany	4,127	4,026	30
Australia/NZ	2,418	1,330	293
Switzerland	1,332	948	26
Latin America	1,296	377	65
Middle East	737	460	50
Netherlands	161	41	88
All countries	30,543	16,270	2,861

Source: U.S. Department of Commerce, *Survey of Current Business,* May 1988

Market Entry Strategies Favored by Foreign Investors in the U.S.

This data, compiled from surveys, suggests that Japanese investors tend to establish new operations more frequently than investors from other countries.

The percentages below add up to less than 100; the gap is accounted for by firms that use a combination of strategies to enter the U.S. market.

Country	New operation	Acquisition	Joint-venture
Japan	88.3	3.7	1.3
Netherlands	55.7	18.9	4.9
Switzerland	71.7	18.5	2.2
Sweden	73.1	5.1	3.9
France	70.9	9.5	4.7

Source: National Governors' Association, *Foreign Direct Investment in the United States,* July 1987

How Foreign Investors Reinvest in the U.S.

Wholesaling	81%
Petroleum	78%

How Foreign Investors Reinvest in the U.S. (cont.)

Manufacturing	68%
Average for all industries	37%

Source: U.S. Commerce Department, *Survey of Current Business*, June 1988

Which U.S. Industries Have Gained the Most Capital From Foreign Direct Investment?
(1986)

Note that the following data doesn't include banking.

Industry	Assets from foreign sources ($US millions)
Nonbank finance	247,328
Manufacturing	190,476
Insurance	87,897
Wholesale trade	86,612
Petroleum	76,839
Real estate	67,751
Retail trade	29,629
Services	19,248
Mining	12,242
Transportation	4,244
Construction	3,013
Agriculture	2,417
Telecommunications	1,927
Forestry and fishing	298
Total non-bank assets provided by foreign investors	829,921

Source: U.S. Department of Commerce, *Survey of Current Business*, May 1988

Manufacturing Job Growth Financed by Foreign Direct Investment

Growth between 1980 and 1986	+22%
Change in total U.S. manufacturing employment during this period	−6.4%

Source: U.S. Department of Commerce, Bureau of Economic Analysis

Which U.S. States Have Gained the Most Jobs From Direct Foreign Investment?
(1986)

State	Number of jobs
California	298,796
New York	241,933
Texas	211,633
New Jersey	154,763
Pennsylvania	150,182
Illinois	143,863
Ohio	138,147
North Carolina	115,975
Georgia	107,367
Florida	94,812
Michigan	81,834
Massachusetts	71,545
Tennessee	69,559
Virginia	69,385
South Carolina	66,641
Wisconsin	63,406
Indiana	54,143
Louisiana	51,026
Maryland	49,487
Missouri	46,164
Connecticut	43,496
Kentucky	37,238
Minnesota	35,712
Delaware	34,785
Washington	35,534
Arizona	34,485
West Virginia	32,404
Colorado	30,993
Alabama	31,507
Oklahoma	26,900
Maine	21,130
Oregon	18,586
Hawaii	18,680
Iowa	18,488
Arkansas	18,399
New Hampshire	16,486
Mississippi	15,938
Kansas	14,642
Rhode Island	11,301
New Mexico	11,245

Which U.S. States Have Gained the Most Jobs From Direct Foreign Investment? (cont.)
(1986)

State	Number of jobs
Utah	9,912
Nebraska	7,523
Nevada	7,370
Alaska	7,122
Vermont	6,591
Wyoming	3,121
Montana	2,910
Idaho	2,755
North Dakota	2,768
South Dakota	1,780
Total	2,840,462
Proportion of U.S. work force	7%

Source: U.S. Department of Commerce, *Survey of Current Business*, May 1988

Which U.S. Industries Have Gained the Most Jobs From Foreign Direct Investment?
(1984–86)

Industry	Number of jobs
Manufacturing	1,399,602
Retail trade	578,798
Wholesale trade	304,515
Services	245,559
Insurance	73,941
Nonbank finance	52,629
Construction	51,314
Transportation	46,557
Real estate	34,715
Mining	29,269
Telecommunications	14,351
Agriculture	11,098

Source: U.S. Department of Commerce, *Survey of Current Business*, May 1988

Who Tends to Pay Better:
U.S. or Foreign-Owned Companies?

Average annual wage at U.S. companies	$18,000
Average annual wage at foreign-owned companies in the U.S.	$22,000
Pay raises at U.S. companies, 1980–1986	39%
Pay raises at foreign-owned companies in the U.S., 1980–1986	279%

Sources: U.S. Department of Commerce, *Survey of Current Business;* U.S. Treasury Department internal staff document on compensation at foreign vs. domestic companies

APPENDIX 2

WORLD FINANCIAL MARKETS & INSTITUTIONS

World's 50 Largest Investors
(1986 ranking by assets under discretionary management)

Rank	Investor	Assets managed ($US millions)
1	Union Bank of Switzerland (S)	150.0
2	Prudential Insurance (US)	145.1
3	American Express (US)	140.0
4	Swiss Bank Corporation (S)	130.0
5	Credit Suisse (S)	120.0
6	Metropolitan Life (US)	103.2
7	Equitable Financial Cos. (US)	102.7
8	Merrill Lynch Asset Management (US)	81.1
9	Aetna Life & Casualty (US)	71.8
10	FMR Corp. (US)	65.1
11	Algemeen Burgerlijk Pensioenfonds (N)	63.0
12	Bankers Trust (US)	59.1
13	Nomura Group (N)	58.0
14	TIAA/CREF (US)	54.3
15	Wells Fargo Investment (US)	53.6
16	Travelers Insurance Cos. (US)	52.0
17	Sumitomo Trust & Banking (J)	51.5
18	J.P. Morgan & Co. (US)	50.6
19	Nippon Life (J)	49.0
20	Daiwa Securities Group (J)	48.0

World's 50 Largest Investors (cont.)
(1986 ranking by assets under discretionary management)

Rank	Investor	Assets managed ($US millions)
21	Post Office Life Insurance (J)	48.0
22	Sears Roebuck Group (US)	48.0
23	PNC Financial Corp. (US)	47.8
24	Mitsubishi Trust & Banking (J)	46.7
25	Swiss Volksbank (S)	45.0
26	Cigna Corp. (US)	44.1
27	John Hancock Financial (US)	42.0
28	Nikko Securities Group (J)	42.0
29	Allmana Pensionsfonden (SW)	41.0
30	Kemper Financial (US)	40.0
31	Putnam Cos. (US)	39.9
32	State Farm Group (US)	38.6
33	Yamaichi Securities (J)	38.0
34	Mitsui Trust & Banking (J)	38.0
35	The New England (US)	37.2
36	Scudder Stevens & Co. (US)	35.0
37	Prudential Corp. (UK)	34.6
38	Dreyfus Corp. (US)	33.2
39	New York Life Insurance (US)	33.0
40	General Electric (US)	32.6
41	Franklin Distributors (US)	32.1
42	Toyo Trust & Banking (J)	31.5
43	Manufacturers Hanover (US)	31.0
44	Capital Group (US)	30.0
45	Robert Fleming Holdings (UK)	29.6
46	Caisse des Depots et Corp. (F)	29.3
47	Thorndike, Doran, Payne & Lewis (US)	29.0
48	Dai-Ichi Mutual Life (J)	28.7
49	Mellon Bank Group (US)	27.8
50	Sumitomo Mutual Life (J)	27.1

Source: *Euromoney*, September 1987
Abbreviations: (F) France, (J) Japan, (N) Netherlands, (S) Switzerland, (SW) Sweden, (US) United States, (UK) Great Britain.

World's 50 Largest Banks & Securities Firms
(1988 ranking by market value)

As far as market value is concerned, the world's 25 largest banks are all Japanese. They tend to be substantially less profitable than U.S.

banks, but they have the wherewithal to finance major acquisitions if that's what they choose to do.

Rank	Company	Market value ($US billions, 12/30/88)
1	Industrial Bank of Japan (J)	85.96
2	Sumitomo Bank (J)	79.94
3	Fuji Bank (J)	75.20
4	Mitsubishi Bank (J)	71.29
5	Dai-Ichi Kangyo Bank (J)	70.85
6	Sanwa Bank (J)	60.20
7	Nomura Securities Co. (J)	57.08
8	Long-Term Credit Bank (J)	36.88
9	Mitsui Bank (J)	33.85
10	Tokai Bank (J)	33.73
11	Mitsubishi Trust & Banking (J)	33.50
12	Sumitomo Trust & Banking (J)	28.19
13	Bank of Tokyo (J)	26.00
14	Daiwa Securities Co. (J)	24.73
15	Nikko Securities Co. (J)	21.32
16	Mitsui Trust & Banking Co. (J)	20.01
17	Taiyo Kobe Bank (J)	18.12
18	Nippon Credit Bank (J)	17.56
19	Yamaichi Securities Co. (J)	17.34
20	Daiwa Bank (J)	16.37
21	Yasuda Trust & Banking (J)	15.70
22	Toyo Trust & Banking (J)	12.86
23	Kyowa Bank (J)	12.39
24	Bank of Yokohama (J)	11.50
25	Saitama Bank (J)	11.34
26	Deutsche Bank (FRG)	11.29
27	American Express Co. (US)	11.10
28	Union Bank of Switzerland (S)	9.47
29	Citicorp (US)	8.18
30	Barclays Bank (UK)	8.13
31	Banco Biblao-Vizcaya (SP)	8.00
32	Swiss Bank Corp. (S)	7.48
33	Shizuoka Bank (J)	7.39
34	National Westminster Bank (UK)	6.99
35	Hokkaido Takushoku Bank (J)	6.97
36	Credit Suisse (S)	6.61
37	Chiba Bank (J)	6.61
38	Banco Santander (SP)	6.63
39	JP Morgan & Co. (US)	6.25
40	Hokuriku Bank (J)	5.78
41	Joyo Bank (J)	5.53

World's 50 Largest Banks & Securities Firms (cont.)
(1988 ranking by market value)

Rank	Company	Market value ($US billions, 12/30/88)
42	Nippon Kangyo Kakumaru Securities (J)	5.31
43	Dresdner Bank (FRG)	5.16
44	Hachijuni Bank (J)	5.08
45	New Japan Securities (J)	5.00
46	Societe Generale (F)	5.03
47	Ashikaga Bank (J)	4.89
48	Bank of Fukuoka (J)	4.76
49	Lloyds Bank (UK)	4.74
50	Toronto-Dominion Bank (C)	4.65

Source: *Euromoney*, 2/89
Abbreviations: (C) Canada, (F) France, (FRG) West Germany, (J) Japan, (S) Switzerland, (SP) Spain, (UK) Great Britain, (US) United States.

World's Top 50 Banks
(1987 ranking by total assets)

Rank	Bank	Assets ($US billions)
1	Dai-Ichi Kangyo Bank (J)	289.72
2	Sumitomo Bank (J)	271.39
3	Fuji Bank (J)	264.33
4	Mitsubishi Bank (J)	246.51
5	Mitsubishi Trust & Banking (J)	238.82
6	Sanwa Bank (J)	234.69
7	Sumitomo Trust & Banking (J)	225.50
8	Caise Nationale du Credit Agricole (F)	214.38
9	Industrial Bank of Japan (J)	205.21
10	Citicorp (US)	203.51
11	Yasuda Trust & Banking (J)	197.14
12	Mitsui Trust & Banking (J)	196.55
13	Norinchukin Bank (J)	186.18
14	Mitsui Bank (J)	184.04
15	National Westminster Bank (UK)	182.88

World's Top 50 Banks (cont.)
(1987 ranking by total assets)

Rank	Bank	Assets ($US billions)
16	Banque Nationale de Paris (F)	182.67
17	Tokai Bank (J)	170.15
18	Deutsche Bank (FRG)	169.88
19	Credit Lyonnais (F)	168.34
20	Barclays Bank (UK)	164.30
21	Mitsui Bank (J)	164.04
22	Toyo Trust & Banking (J)	156.19
23	Societe Generale (F)	153.02
24	Bank of Tokyo (J)	145.15
25	Long Term Credit Bank of Japan (J)	142.61
26	Dresdner Bank (FRG)	130.46
27	Union Bank of Switzerland (S)	125.52
28	Compagnie Financiers de Paribas (F)	122.28
29	Swiss Bank Corporation (S)	114.39
30	Industrial & Commercial Bank of China (PRC)	114.38
31	Hong Kong & Shanghai Banking (HK)	107.36
32	Commerzbank (FRG)	102.26
33	Chase Manhattan Corp. (US)	99.13
34	Bayerische Hypotheken-und Weschel-Bank (FRG)	94.61
35	BankAmerica Corp. (US)	92.83
36	Banca Nazionale del Lavorno Group (I)	92.40
37	Nippon Credit Bank (J)	92.35
38	Midland Bank Group (UK)	90.68
39	Westdeutsche Landesbank Giroz (US)	89.88
40	Kyowa Bank (J)	87.20
41	Algemene Bank Nederlands (N)	84.87
42	Lloyds Bank (UK)	84.05
43	Credit Suisse (S)	83.91
44	Bayerische Landesbank Girozentrale (FRG)	83.04
45	Industrial & Commercial Rabobank (N)	81.86
46	Daiwa Bank (J)	81.32
47	Amsterdam Rotterdam Bank (N)	80.97
48	Deutsche Genossenschaftsbank (FRG)	80.57
49	Weschel-Bank (FRG)	79.85
50	Chemical New York Corp. (US)	78.19

Source: *Euromoney*, 6/88
Abbreviations: (B) Brazil, (C) Canada, (F) France, (FRG) West Germany, (HK) Hong Kong, (I) Italy, (J) Japan, (N) Netherlands, (PRC) Mainland China, (S) Switzerland, (UK) Great Britain, (US) United States.

Profitability of Major International Financial Institutions
(1986 income before taxes)

Company	$US millions
Nomura Securities	4,360
National Westminster Bank	1,872
Citicorp	1,700
Barclays Bank	1,657
J.P. Morgan & Co.	1,166
Phibro-Salomon	795
Merrill Lynch	773
Manufacturers Hanover Corporation	443
First Chicago Corporation	390
Union Bank of Switzerland	356

Source: annual reports, consolidated results for year ending December 1986, except for Nomura Securities, whose fiscal year ended September 1987.

10 Most Profitable Foreign Banks in Japan
(Fiscal year ending March 1988)

Bank	Pre-tax profit (¥Japanese millions)
Bankers Trust (US)	4,316
Chemical Bank (US)	2,312
Morgan Guaranty Trust (US)	2,257
Irving Trust (US)	2,119
Korea First Bank (RK)	1,936
Banque Paribas (F)	1,521
Hongkong & Shanghai Banking (HK)	1,470
First National Bank of Chicago (US)	1,419
First Interstate Bank of California (US)	1,359
Banque Nationale de Paris (F)	1,234

Source: Peat Marwick
Abbreviations: (F) France, (HK) Hong Kong, (RK) South Korea, (US) United States.

How Japanese Banks Lower Borrowing Costs for U.S. Municipalities
($US billions)

The volume of municipal bond offerings peaked in 1985. Lower volumes since then are largely the result of unfavorable changes in the

How Japanese Banks Lower Borrowing Costs
for U.S. Municipalities (cont.)
($US billions)

tax laws. Japanese banks, with high credit ratings and competitive pricing, serve about half the market for letters of credit that reduce borrowing costs for U.S. municipalities.

Year	Total volume municipal bonds	Letters of credit	Japanese letters of credit	% of LOC
1980	$48.054	$0.071	$0.000	0.0
1981	47.126	4.959	0.000	0.0
1982	77.815	6.849	0.558	8.1
1983	83.594	7.333	0.084	1.1
1984	102.485	18.403	4.806	26.1
1985	216.793	38.726	16.053	41.5
1986	147.964	15.310	8.810	57.5
1987	101.500	15.900	7.500	47.1
1988	114.700	17.600	9.400	53.4

Source: Securities Data Company, Inc., New York

Surprising Trend in California Banking

High-visibility Japanese acquisitions of California banks have created the impression that the state is being overrun by foreigners. Yet the percentage of foreign bank holdings in California has actually declined during the past five years.

In part, this is probably because California banking assets have grown along with the economy. Also, a number of the Japanese acquisitions involved British rather than U.S. sellers.

Total banking assets in California, 1983	$278.5 billion
Portion held by foreign investors	18.2%
Total banking assets in California, 1988	$295.9 billion
Portion held by foreign investors	13.8%
Total California banking assets held by foreign investors, 1988	$35 billion
BankAmerica assets, 1988	$82.6 billion
Security Pacific National Bank assets, 1988	$47.3 billion

Source: California State Banking Department

How Japanese banks fare in California

- They pay above-average costs to attract funds.*
- They raise only about 10 percent of their funds through their parent companies in Japan.*
- They offer loans for 25–50 basis points (a quarter to half a percentage point) less than other banks.**
- About 60 percent of foreign-owned bank assets in California are Japanese.**
- Practices vary widely. For instance, at Sanwa Bank, 98 percent of employees and almost 100 percent of customers are American. At Sumitomo Bank, more than 60 percent of employees are Asian, and it tries to help Asian-American entrepreneurs.**

Sources: *Federal Reserve Bank of San Francisco. **Independent Bankers Association of America.

World's Largest Life Insurance Companies (cont.)
(1987–1988 fiscal year)

Below are the major Japanese life insurance companies, ranked several different ways. If the yen continues to appreciate against the U.S. dollar, then Japanese firms will head the asset ranking as well as the insurance-in-force and premium income ranking.

	Insurance in force	
Rank	Company	$ US billions
1	Nippon Life	1,799.5
2	Dai-Ichi Life	1,558.4
3	Sumitomo Life	1,192.1
4	Prudential Life	644.9
5	Metropolitan Life	569.4

	Premium Income	
Rank	Company	$ US billions
1	Nippon Life	35.6
2	Dai-Ichi Life	24.2
3	Sumitomo Life	22.4
4	Metropolitan Life	13.9
5	Prudential	13.3

World's Largest Life Insurance Companies (cont.)
(1987–1988 fiscal year)

Rank	Total assets Company	$ US billions
1	Nippon Life	144.9
2	Prudential	108.8
3	Dai-Ichi Life	99.7
4	Metropolitan Life	88.1
5	Sumitomo Life	83.2

Sources: *Best's Insurance Management Reports*, 7/11/88 and 7/18/88; Nippon Life, *Summary of Overseas Investments*, 2/89 for 1987–1988 fiscal year; Sumitomo Life; Dai-Ichi Life; yen figures converted at the rate of 126 per US dollar.

How Major Stock Markets Compare in Turnover
(1987)

This was the year Tokyo surpassed New York.

Market	$ US millions of turnover
Tokyo	1,873,268
New York	1,837,482
Osaka	259,018
London	166,616
Frankfurt	85,973
Paris	69,038
Sydney	43,461
Singapore	3,959

Source: Respective stock exchanges, year ending December 1987

How Major Stock Markets Compare in Capitalization
(1987)

Market	$ US million total market value
Tokyo	2,515,552
New York	2,216,311
London	589,686
Frankfurt	276,185

How Major Stock Markets Compare in Capitalization (cont.)
(1987)

Market	$ US million total market value
Paris	177,863
Sydney	131,563
Singapore	17,887

Source: Respective stock exchanges, year ending December 1987

10 Companies With the Largest Market Capitalization on the Tokyo Stock Exchange
($US billions)

The general public may know Japan best for its manufactured goods such as cars and consumer electronics, but financial services companies dominate Japanese equity markets, as you can see from this table.

Company	Market capitalization
Nippon Telegraph & Telephone	63
Sumitomo Bank	56
Fuji Bank	53
Dai-Ichi Kangyo Bank	53
Tokyo Electric Power	51
Mitsubishi Bank	47
Industrial Bank of Japan	44
Sanwa Bank	43
Nomura Securities	37
Toyota Motor	37

Source: Tokyo Stock Exchange

112 Foreign Companies Listed on the Tokyo Stock Exchange

A listing on the Tokyo Stock Exchange is one way for a company to gain visibility in Tokyo and make it easier to raise funds on this, the world's largest equity market. Despite the strong yen, an increasing number of foreign companies are listed. There have been a few delistings, mainly because of mergers. Here's the current roster:

112 Foreign Companies Listed on the Tokyo Stock Exchange (cont.)

Company	Date listed	Sponsoring broker
Dow Chemical (US)	12/18/73	Nomura
Citicorp (US)	12/18/73	Daiwa
First Chicago (US)	12/18/73	Daiwa
Chase Manhattan (US)	9/20/74	Nikko
IBM (US)	11/27/74	Daiwa
ITT (US)	12/16/74	Daiwa
General Motors (US)	12/20/74	Nomura
BankAmerica (US)	12/22/75	Nomura
Rotterdamsch Beleggings-Consortium NV (N)	12/8/76	Nomura
Sears, Roebuck (US)	6/29/84	Daiwa
Walt Disney Productions (US)	6/27/85	Nomura
Security Pacific Corporation (US)	9/4/85	Nomura
National Australia Bank (A)	9/6/85	Nikko
Telefonica (FRG)	10/4/85	Nikko
Philip Morris (US)	10/16/85	Daiwa
3M (US)	10/17/85	Daiwa
Dresdner Bank (FRG)	10/24/85	Daiwa
American Express (US)	11/14/85	Nomura
Bell Canada Enterprises (US)	11/19/85	Nomura
Union Bank of Switzerland (S)	12/24/85	Nomura
Cable & Wireless (UK)	4/2/86	Nomura
Westpac Banking (UK)	5/9/86	Nomura
Toronto-Dominion Bank (C)	5/13/86	Nomura
Procter & Gamble (US)	5/28/86	Daiwa
British Telecom (UK)	5/30/86	Nomura
McDonald's (US)	7/3/86	Daiwa
Waste Management (US)	7/22/86	Nikko
Barclays PLC (UK)	8/1/86	Nikko
Eastman Kodak (US)	8/26/86	Daiwa
Canadian Imperial Bank (C)	9/9/86	Daiwa
Smithkline Beckman (US)	9/17/86	Nomura
Chrysler (US)	9/19/86	Daiwa
Commerzbank (FRG)	10/1/86	Yamaichi
Du Pont (US)	10/2/86	Daiwa
Royal Bank of Canada (C)	10/30/86	Daiwa
RJR Nabisco (US)	10/30/86	Nikko
BTR (UK)	11/5/86	Daiwa
Northern Telecom (C)	11/12/86	Nomura
Pepsico (US)	11/13/86	Daiwa
Merrill Lynch (US)	11/18/86	Merrill
Eli Lilly (US)	11/20/86	Nikko
FPL Group (US)	12/9/86	Nomura

112 Foreign Companies Listed on the Tokyo Stock Exchange
(cont.)

Company	Date listed	Sponsoring broker
AGA (SW)	12/10/86	Yamaichi
Volvo (SW)	12/12/86	Nomura
Exxon (US)	12/16/86	Nikko
Weyerhauser (US)	12/17/86	Daiwa
Ameritech (US)	12/18/86	Daiwa
Bell Atlantic (US)	12/18/86	Yamaichi
US West (US)	12/19/86	Yamaichi
Royal Trust (C)	12/19/86	Nikko
Standard Chartered Bank (UK)	12/22/86	Yamaichi
Brunswick Corporation (US)	2/4/87	NKK, Merrill
Pacific Dunlop (US)	2/25/87	Nomura
Pharmacia (SW)	2/26/87	Daiwa
Glaxo Holdings (SW)	6/17/87	Nomura
NCNB Corporation (US)	7/1/87	Nomura
Georgia Pacific (US)	7/9/87	Nomura
The Limited Inc. (US)	7/16/87	Nomura
Lonrho Public Limited Co. (UK)	7/22/87	Nomura
Borden (US)	8/25/87	Nomura
British Petroleum (UK)	8/28/87	Nomura
PPG Industries (US)	9/4/87	Daiwa
Marriott (US)	9/17/87	Daiwa
American International Group (US)	9/18/87	Nikko
Potomic Electric Power (US)	9/29/87	Yamaichi
J.P. Morgan (US)	9/30/87	Nomura
Anheuser Busch (US)	10/6/87	Nomura
Nynex (US)	10/29/87	Daiwa
Abbott Laboratories (US)	10/30/87	Daiwa
General Electric (US)	11/10/87	Nomura
AT&T (US)	11/17/87	Nomura
BellSouth (US)	11/26/87	Yamaichi
Rockwell International (US)	11/30/87	Daiwa
Grumman (US)	12/4/87	Daiwa
K Mart (US)	12/8/87	Nomura
Southern California Edison (US)	12/11/87	Daiwa
Swiss Bank Corporation (S)	12/15/87	Daiwa
Lincoln National (US)	12/15/87	Nikko
Squibb (US)	12/16/87	Nikko
American Family (US)	12/17/87	Nomura
Avon Products (US)	12/17/87	Nomura
Foreign & Colonial Investment Trust (UK)	12/18/87	Yamaichi
Occidental Petroleum (US)	12/18/87	Daiwa
Allied-Signal (US)	12/21/87	Nomura

112 Foreign Companies Listed on the Tokyo Stock Exchange (cont.)

Company	Date listed	Sponsoring broker
Transamerica (US)	12/22/87	Daiwa
Peninsula & Oriental Steamship Co. (UK)	12/22/87	Nomura
Goodyear Tire & Rubber (US)	1/7/88	Daiwa
Archer Daniels Midland (US)	1/19/88	Nomura
Globe Investment Trust (UK)	2/4/88	Nikko
Dun & Bradstreet (US)	2/5/88	Nomura
Credit Suisse (S)	2/18/88	Yamaichi
Broken Hill Proprietary (A)	4/12/88	Daiwa
Hewlett-Packard (US)	5/24/88	Daiwa
Dixons Group PLC (UK)	5/31/88	Daiwa
Elders IXL Ltd. (A)	6/28/88	Yamaichi
Scott Paper Company (US)	7/15/88	Yamaichi
Knight-Ridder Newspapers (US)	9/13/88	Daiwa
Ford Motor Company (US)	9/20/88	Daiwa
British Gas Ltd. (UK)	9/29/88	Nomura
Philips (N)	9/30/88	Nomura
Aegon (N)	10/4/88	Nikko
Satchi & Satchi (UK)	10/13/88	Nomura
National Westminster Bank (UK)	10/18/88	Nomura
Mobil (US)	10/19/88	Nomura
Bayer (FRG)	10/26/88	Nomura
Motorola (US)	11/10/88	Daiwa
Volkswagen (FRG)	12/2/88	Daiwa
Imperial Chemical (UK)	12/8/88	Nomura
Fisons (UK)	12/12/88	Nomura
General Electric (F)	12/20/88	Nomura
GKN Public Ltd. (UK)	12/23/88	Daiwa
Paribas (F)	12/23/88	Yamaichi

Abbreviations: (A) Australia, (C) Canada, (F) France, (FRG) West Germany, (N) Netherlands, (S) Switzerland, (SW) Sweden, (UK) Great Britain, (US) United States.
Source: Tokyo Stock Exchange

20 Largest Stock Offerings in Japan
($US millions)

Company	Issue amount	Date
Dai-Ichi Kangyo Bank	942.8	9/87
British Petroleum	939.1	11/87

20 Largest Stock Offerings in Japan (cont.)
($US millions)

Company	Issue amount	Date
Fuji Bank	822.6	10/87
Toyota Motor	740.4	7/81
Sanwa Bank	724.7	9/87
Mitsubishi Bank	659.7	8/87
Toshiba	609.6	9/81
Sumitomo Bank	559.6	9/87
British Telecom	519.2	12/84
NEC	468.4	2/84
Fujitsu	453.5	8/84
Kyocera	437.8	2/84
British Gas	398.2	12/86
Mitsui Bank	396.7	12/87
Long-Term Credit Bank	375.0	7/87
NEC	368.3	5/82
Nippondenso	348.3	12/82
Tokyo Broadcasting System	331.7	8/87
Kansai Electric Power	302.6	12/82
Tokyo Electric Power	298.1	9/81

Source: Nomura Securities

20 Largest Stock Offerings by Foreign Companies in Japan
($US millions)

Company	Issue amount	Date
British Petroleum	939.1	11/87
British Telecom	519.2	11/84
British Gas	398.2	12/86
Union Bank of Switzerland	266.0	12/85
Commerzbank	197.2	9/86
Barclays Bank	195.0	5/87
Bell Canada Enterprises	189.0	3/86
Dresdner Bank	145.7	10/85
Westpac Banking	139.7	4/86
NCNB	112.8	6/87
Cable and Wireless	105.3	12/85
Lonrho	102.4	6/87
Toronto-Dominion Bank	98.6	4/86
Telefonica	89.7	10/85

20 Largest Stock Offerings by Foreign Companies in Japan (cont.)
($US millions)

Company	Issue amount	Date
Telefonica	70.2	4/87
American Express	68.7	11/85
National Australia Bank	57.5	9/85
Swiss Bank Corporation	54.5	12/87
AGA	46.3	11/86
Peninsula & Oriental	42.6	12/87

Source: Nomura Securities

20 Eurobond Book Runners
(firms which lead-managed the largest volume of securities)
(1988)

This is one of the key rankings of performance among financial companies competing in the Euromarket. As the yen has strengthened and gained importance in international transactions, Japanese firms have come to dominate the Euromarket.

Rank	Book runner	No. issues	Total ($US millions)
1	Nomura	135	17,678.65
2	Credit Suisse/First Boston	83	13,953.91
3	Deutschbank	85	12,285.48
4	Daiwa	81	9,541.96
5	Yamaichi	61	7,272.12
6	Nikko	61	6,866.59
7	Merrill Lynch	36	6,562.52
8	Paribas	46	6,026.77
9	Industrial Bank of Japan	51	5,617.80
10	J.P. Morgan Securities	34	5,602.78
11	UBS Securities Ltd.	47	5,445.21
12	Bankers Trust	49	5,339.91
13	Salomon Brothers	32	5,064.68
14	Warburg Securities	23	4,541.33
15	Goldman Sachs	26	3,962.28
16	Morgan Stanley	32	3,945.15
17	Dresdner Bank	24	3,800.96

20 Eurobond Book Runners (cont.)
(firms which lead-managed the largest volume of securities)
(1988)

Rank	Book runner	No. issues	Total ($US millions)
18	Commerzbank AG	31	3,475.40
19	Swiss Bank Corporation	26	2,852.61
20	Hambros Bank	46	2,683.64
	Totals	1,534	175,365.47

Source: International Financial Review, London

20 Largest Euroyen Bond Offerings
(May 1977 to December 1987)

Issue amount

Borrower	($US millions)	(¥ billions)	Date
Italy	2,241	300	10/87
Denmark	971	130	12/86
Denmark	747	100	1/87
Canada	598	80	1/86
Canada	598	80	6/86
Canada	598	80	6/87
GM Acceptance Corp.	448	60	8/86
Norway	448	60	10/86
Tokyo Electric Power	448	60	2/87
Norway	448	60	3/87
Kansai Electric Power	448	60	4/87
Tokyo Electric Power	448	60	11/87
Belgium	411	55	11/87
Dow Chemical	374	50	12/84
Fannie Mae	374	50	2/85
Fannie Mae	374	50	8/85
Sallie Mae	374	50	8/85
World Bank	374	50	7/86
NTT	374	50	8/86
NTT	374	50	12/86

Source: Nomura Securities

World's Top 20 Investment Banking Firms
(in mergers & acquisitions)
(1988)

As if to show that money isn't everything, Japanese firms don't even show up on this list. They excel at selling large volumes of securities into the Japanese market, and they offer cost-competitive services elsewhere, especially in Europe.

But mergers and acquisitions require entrepreneurial resourcefulness, plus considerable time to develop relationships with buyers as well as sellers. The old-line British firms didn't do it overnight, and neither did the U.S. firms, both of which dominate here.

The Japanese do have a presence through minority holdings: Sumitomo Bank owns 20% of Goldman Sachs, and Nomura Securities has 20% of Wasserstein-Perella.

Firm	Value of transactions ($US billions)	Number of transactions
Morgan Stanley (US)	86.00	121
Goldman Sachs (US)	84.89	167
First Boston (US)	71.23	142
Shearson Lehman Hutton (US)	63.05	223
Merrill Lynch (US)	52.47	134
Wasserstein-Perella (US)	38.92	25
Salomon Brothers (US)	38.14	138
Drexel Burnham Lambert (US)	36.25	165
Schroder Group (UK)	36.23	156
SG Warburg (UK)	27.27	99
Security Pacific Group (US)	21.20	106
Barings (UK)	21.08	60
Kleinwort Benson (UK)	21.08	98
Kidder Peabody (US)	17.91	70
Lazard Brothers (US)	17.12	69
Morgan Grenfell (UK)	15.94	105
County NatWest (UK)	13.01	78
Robert Fleming (UK)	10.67	73
Samuel Montagu (UK)	9.91	79
Bear Stearns (US)	9.86	68
NM Rothschild (UK)	8.86	65

Source: *Euromoney*, 2/89

Investment Banking Firms With the Most Experience Where a U.S. Deal Involves a Japanese Buyer
(1988)

Firm	Value of transactions ($US billions)	Number of transactions
First Boston (US)	2.63	2
Industrial Bank of Japan (J)	2.58	6
SG Warburg (UK)	2.13	1
Shearson Lehman Hutton (US)	.46	5
Dillon Read (US)	.32	2
Bank of Tokyo (J)	.20	4
Kidder Peabody (US)	.02	2

Source: *Euromoney*, 2/89

APPENDIX 3

JAPANESE WEALTH & INVESTMENT

Comparing Vital Statistics for Japan and the U.S.

	Japan	U.S.
Population*	121.5 million	241.6 million
Area†	145,856 square miles	3,618,770 square miles
Gross national product (GNP)‡§	$2.5 trillion	$4.7 trillion
Per capita GNP*	$12,800	$17,400
Central government expenditures as a share of GNP*	17%	24.5%
Central government revenues as a share of GNP*	12.6%	19.5%
Central government budget deficit as a share of GNP*	3.4%	2.6%
National debt as a percentage of GNP‡§	51.8%	52.8
Labor force: portion of population 15–64 years old*	68%	66%
Portion of workers on farms*	11%	4%
Portion of workers in industry*	34%	31%
Portion of workers in services*	55%	66%
Average annual inflation rate, 1980–1986*	1.6%	4.4%
Life expectancy at birth*	78	75

Sources: *"World Bank, *World Development Report 1988.* †*The World Almanac 1989.* ‡Japanese Ministry of Finance. §*Statistical Abstract of the United States.*

20 Japanese Billionaires

Yoshiaki Tsutsumi, 54, Tokyo	$21 billion	Seibu Railway, Prince hotels, real estate
Taikichiro Mori, 84, Tokyo	$16 billion	Real estate in Tokyo's Minato ward
Shigeru Kobayashi, 61, Tokyo	$6 billion	Real estate development & investment
Keizo Saji, 68, Tokyo	$3.4 billion	Suntory, distiller
Eitaro Itoyama, 46, Tokyo	$2.4 billion	Chairman of Shin Nihon Kanko Kogyo (hotels)
Yoneichi Otani, 72, Tokyo	$2.3 billion	Hotel New Otani and TOC (hotels and real estate)
Seijiro Matsuoka, 94, Tokyo	$2.1 billion	President of Matsuoka Industries, art & real estate
Konosuke Matsushita, 93, Tokyo	$2 billion	Matsushita (world's electronics manufacturer)
Rinji Shino, 79, Tokyo	$2 billion	Real estate & art
Masatoshi Ito, 64, Tokyo	$1.8 billion	Ito-Yokado (retail chain), 7-Eleven stores, and Denny's Japan
Renichi Takenake, 77 Toichi Takenake, 45, Tokyo	$1.5 billion	Real estate & trade
Hirotomo Takei, 70, Tokyo	$1.4 billion	Chairman of Chusen (real estate)
Shoji Uehara, 59, Tokyo	$1.3 billion	32% of Taisho Pharmaceutical
Kanichiro Ishibashi, 68, Tokyo	$1.2 billion	Chairman of Bridgestone Corp., major tire producer
Takeo Shigemitsu, 65, Tokyo	$1.2 billion	President of Lotte confectionery
Yohachiro Iwasaki, 86, Tokyo	$1 billion	Chairman of Iwasaki Sangyo (resorts)
Shinichi Kobayashi, 79, Tokyo	$1 billion	Chairman of Paroma group (gas boiler manufacturer)
Genshiro Mawamoto, 56, Tokyo	$1 billion	Marugen, Tokyo real estate
Kiyofumi Moroto, 76, Tokyo	$1 billion	President, Moroto Forestry with 7,500 acres
Masao Nangaku, 68, Tokyo	$1 billion	President of Minami group (home electric appliance retailing)

Source: Forbes, 7/27/87

We Aren't the Only Pebble on the Beach

Many Americans seem to believe the Japanese will be stuck with whatever restrictions and penalties Washington may impose on foreign investors, imagining that they have nowhere else to go.

Yet Japanese companies have made more than $70 billion of direct investments in over 30 countries. They have plenty of alternatives and are surely comparing the relative advantages and disadvantages as circumstances change. The following is a partial list of countries where Japanese companies hold controlling interest in a subsidiary:

Australia	India	Portugal
Brazil	Indonesia	Singapore
Canada	Italy	Spain
Costa Rica	Malaysia	Switzerland
France	Mexico	Taiwan
Great Britain	Peru	Thailand
Hong Kong	Philippines	West Germany

Sources: annual reports for Honda, Matsushita, Sony, Toyota and other companies

Japanese Direct Investments by Industry
(total worldwide)

These results provide an overview of Japanese direct investments worldwide, ranked by current importance.

Industry	1985 ($ US millions)	Since 1951 ($ US millions)
Finance	$3,805	$10,859
Commerce	1,550	12,677
Transport	1,240	5,900
Real estate	1,207	2,533
Services	665	4,686
Transport machinery	627	3,373
Mining	598	11,756
Electrical machinery	513	3,747
Steel, non-ferrous metals	385	5,190
Machinery	352	1,971
Chemicals	133	3,982
Construction	94	798
Foodstuffs	90	1,091

Japanese Direct Investments by Industry (cont.)
(total worldwide)

Industry	1985 ($ US millions)	Since 1951 ($ US millions)
Fisheries	42	442
Textiles	28	2,083
Lumber, pulp	15	1,120
Agriculture	12	780
Others	751	10,660
TOTAL	$12,107	$83,648

Source: Nihon Keizei Shimbun

Major Japanese Industries Investing in the United States

Industry	1985 export value ($US millions)	Change from previous year
Automobiles	$19,223	+24.6%
Tape recorders, VCRs	4,948	+11.5%
Automobile parts	2,475	+30.3%
Photocopiers	1,399	+17.1%
Records, tapes	773	+29.9%
Office machines	748	+18.5%
Construction machinery	604	+40.4%
Ships	504	+38.2%
Machinery	433	+37.1%
Toys	317	+62.9%

Source: Ministry of Finance

Japanese Direct Investment & U.S. Jobs

Although many American companies continue to manufacture overseas, more and more Japanese companies are manufacturing in the United States. They employ an estimated 260,000 Americans at more than 450 plants. There are several reasons: the declining dollar makes U.S. direct investments economical, Japanese executives fear the U.S. government will erect higher trade barriers, and companies can more

Japanese Direct Investment & U.S. Jobs (cont.)

easily adapt to a market when they have a major presence in it, rather than just exporting from afar.

In the following partial list of Japanese direct investments, companies are ranked by number of jobs created. Companies creating less than 100 jobs not included. The sampling mainly goes through the end of 1987.

Owner	Factory location	Product	Jobs
NKK Corp.	Many locations	Steel	12,000
NEC	Many locations	Computers	10,000
Dainippon Ink & Chemicals	Many locations	Inks & chemicals	9,900
Matsushita	Many locations	Consumer electronics	8,000
Fujitsu	Many locations	Mainframe computers	6,000
Sony	Many locations	Consumer electronics	6,000
Mitsubishi Heavy Industries	Many locations	Pulp/paper making machinery	5,000
Honda	Marysville, OH	Automobiles	4,750
Kokusai Kogyo	Honolulu	Hotels	4,500
NEC	Many locations	Computers	4,078
Kyocera	San Diego, CA	Ceramics	3,620
Mazda	Flat Rock, MI	Autos	3,400
Nissan Motor	Smyrna, TN	Autos, trucks	3,100
Toyota	Georgetown, KY	Automobiles	3,000
Toshiba	Many locations	Electronics	2,790
Toyota/GM	Fremont, CA	Automobiles	2,700
Minebea Ltd.	3 locations	Ball bearings	2,650
Mitsubishi/Chrysler	Bloomington, IL	Automobiles	2,500
Marubeni Corp.	Many Alaska locations	Canned/frozen fish	2,450
Mitsubishi Electric	Many locations	Computers, communications	2,350
Nissan	Smyrna, TN	Automobiles	2,000
Alcoa Fujikura	Many locations	Auto parts	1,800
Fujitsu	Many locations	Integrated circuits	1,730
Subaru-Isuzu	Lafayette, IN	Autos, trucks	1,700
Okabe Co., Ltd.	Rockford, IL	Industrial fasteners	1,500
Tsuzuki Spinning	Many locations	Textiles	1,450
Sumitomo Rubber	2 NY locations	Radial tires	1,435
Fanuc Ltd.	2 locations	Controls	1,430
Canon	Many locations	Cameras	1,400
NKK Corp.	Torrance, CA	Aluminum bars	1,400
Suntory	Many locations	Soft drinks	1,375
Kirin Brewery	Many locations	Soft drinks	1,345

Japanese Direct Investment & U.S. Jobs (cont.)

Owner	Factory location	Product	Jobs
Sumitomo Bakelite	3 locations	Flexible circuits	1,300
Ricoh Co.	Many locations	Copier parts	1,285
Bridgestone	LaVergne, TN	Tires	1,100
Fujisawa Pharma-ceutical	Orlando, FL	Injectable drugs	1,100
Nippon Piston Ring	Muskegon, MI	Auto parts	1,100
Canon	2 locations	Copiers	1,090
Tokyo Seat Co.	Many locations	Seats & covers	1,070
NTN Bearing Co.	2 locations	Bearings	1,000
Ricoh	West Caldwell, NJ	Cameras	1,000
Toyo Menka Kaisha	Many locations	Cottonseed oil	1,000
Hitachi Ltd.	Many locations	Electronics	940
Jujo Paper	Longview, WA	Newsprint	880
American Shizuki	Ogallala, NE	AC/DC capacitors	850
Kawasaki Steel	Fontana, CA	Galvanized steel	850
Mitsubishi Foods	Ponce, PR	Canned fruit & fish	850
TDK	Many locations	Components for TV sets, tapes, microwave ovens	840
Sharp Corp.	Memphis, TN	Color TV sets	830
Mitsui & Co.	Many locations	Canned fish, feed	805
Alpha Therapeutic	Los Angeles, CA	Blood products	800
Tachi-S	2 locations	Auto seat covers	800
Shin-Etsu Handotai Co.	Vancouver, WA	Silicon ingots	790
Calsonic Corp.	2 locations	Auto air conditioning	750
Onoda Cement	2 locations	Cement	750
Rohm Co., Ltd.	2 locations	Integrated circuits	720
Hitachi Metals	San Jose, CA	Magnets	700
Victor Co.	Tuscaloosa, AL	Video tapes	700
Tokyo Rope	Danville, KY	Steel tire cord	680
Hitachi Zosen	Many locations	Stamping presses	650
Toshiba	Lebanon, TN	TV sets	650
Nichiro Gyogyo	3 locations	Canned/frozen fish	640
Oki America	Hackensack, NJ	Software, semiconductors	600
Ryobi Ltd.	Chandler, AZ	Weed trimmers	600
Sakata Corp.	Many locations	Printing ink	580
Alps Electric	Garden Grove, CA	Computer keyboards	575
Sanyo Electric	2 locations	Computers, stereo speakers	550
Murata Mfg. Co.	State College, PA	Ceramic capacitors	532
Kawasaki & Nissho Iwai	Yonkers, NY	Subway cars	500
Mitsubishi Corp.	Many locations	Primary copper	500
TDK Corp.	Shawness, OH	Magnets	490

Japanese Direct Investment & U.S. Jobs (cont.)

Owner	Factory location	Product	Jobs
Tsubakimoto Chain	3 locations	Sprockets, conveyor chains	465
Hitachi Chemical	2 Georgia locations	Chemicals	450
Kawasaki Heavy Industries	Lincoln, NE	Motorcycles	450
NGK Insulators	Baltimore, MD	Electrical insulators	400
Nippondenso Co.	Battle Creek, MI	Auto parts	400
NOK Corp.	LaGrange, GA	Oil/mechanical seals	400
Nippon Senso	Many locations	Specialty gases	400
Kobe Steel	Boonton, NJ	Auto air bags	365
Sankei Giken Kogyo	Marysville, OH	Auto seats	360
C. Itoh	Many locations	Metal products	355
Minebea	Princeton, IN	Electric motors	355
Daishowa Paper	Port Angeles, WA	Groundwood paper	350
Yamaha Corp.	2 locations	Musical instruments	350
General Co.	Arvada, CO	Typewriter ribbon cartridges	330
Mitsui & Co.	Etiwanda, CA	Steel bars	320
Tokai Seiki	Rancho Cucamonga, CA	Disposable cigarette lighters	320
Sumitomo Corp.	Auburn, NY	Steel bars	315
Kohkoku Chemical	Everett, WA	Polyvinyl chloride film	310
Alaska Pacific Seafood	Kodiak, AK	Frozen fish	300
American Koyo Bearing	Orangeburg, SC	Ball/tapered bearings	300
Komatsu Ltd.	Chattanooga, TN	Earth moving equipment	300
Yamaha Motor	Newnan, GA	Golf carts	300
Yoshida Kogyo	2 locations	Fasteners	290
Anja Engineering	Monrovia, CA	Writing instruments	280
Takihyo Co.	New York, NY	Women's clothing	280
Hirata Press	St. Paris, OH	Auto parts	260
Alyeska Seafood	Dutch Harbor, AK	Boiled fish paste	250
Dai-Ichi Seihan Co.	Honolulu, HI	Bakery products	250
Terumo Co.	Elkton, MD	Blood collection tubes	230
Yokogawa Electric	Newnan, GA	Strip chart recorders	210
Advantest Corp.	Buffalo Grove, IL	Semiconductor test equipment	200
Chuo Kagaku	San Bernadino, CA	Plastic containers	200
Hitachi Metals	St. Marys, OH	Auto wheels	200
Kanto Seiko	Lewisburg, TN	Auto parts	200
Morinaga Milk	San Jose, CA	Baby food	200
Naigai Chikusan	Sidney, OH	Meat processing	200
Nihon Radiator Co.	Shelbyville, TN	Auto air conditioners	200

Japanese Direct Investment & U.S. Jobs (cont.)

Owner	Factory location	Product	Jobs
Nippon Columbia	Madison, GA	Compact discs	200
Pentel	Torrance, CA	Writing instruments	200
Seiko Epson	El Segundo, CA	Quartz watches	200
Tabuchi Electric	Jackson, TN	Microwave transformers	200
Sanden Corp.	Dallas, TX	Clutches	185
Asahi Glass	Bellefontaine, OH	Auto safety glass	180
Namco KK	Milpitas, CA	Video games	170
Toshiba Ceramics	Many locations	Quartz/pyrex apparatus for semiconductor cos.	170
Mitsui Mining & Smelting	Hoosick Falls, NY	Cooper foil	165
Oyo Corp.	Houston, TX	Geophysical equipment	160
Sumitomo Metal Industries	Little Rock, AK	Welded steel tubes	150
Ogihara Iron Works	Plymouth, MI	Auto body stampings	120
Mitsubishi Corp.	2 locations	Plastic pipes	115
Mitsubishi Electric	San Fernando, CA	Audio/visual mixing consoles	110
Fujitec Co.	Lebanon, OH	Elevators	100
Kanto Seiki Co.	Lewisburg, TN	Auto dashboards	100

Source: Japan Economic Institute, *Japan's Expanding U.S. Manufacturing Presence*, December 1988

Overview of Japanese Real Estate Investment

During 1988, Japanese real estate investment in the United States seems to have declined 7 percent from 1987. In part, this reflects Japanese government efforts to curtail real estate speculation, especially at home. There's also been a lot of criticism of flamboyant bidding, and it has probably contributed to more caution among publicity-shy Japanese investors.

Real estate companies account for about 35 perent of U.S. real estate purchases. Insurance companies, about 25 percent. Construction companies, about 12 percent.

As in past years, Japanese investors concentrate on office buildings (about 58 percent of investments) and hotels (30 percent). Only about 2 percent of investments were in retail projects.

Overview of Japanese Real Estate Investment (cont.)

Here's what the numbers look like for major markets and investment categories:

Location	Office ($US billions)	Hotel ($US billions)	Other ($US billions)	Total ($US billions)	Percentage of total
New York	5.0	0.2	0.4	5.6	25.1
Los Angeles & Orange County	3.5	0.4	0.9	4.8	21.6
Hawaii	0.3	2.7	0.4	3.4	15.3
Chicago	1.0	0.4	*	1.4	6.3
San Francisco	0.6	0.6	*	1.2	5.4
Texas	0.4	*	0.5	0.9	4.0
Atlanta	0.5	*	*	0.5	2.2
Washington, DC	0.5	*	*	0.5	2.2
Boston	0.4	*	*	0.4	1.8
Other	0.5	1.0	0.3	1.8	8.1
Multi-state	0.2	1.1	*	1.3	5.8
Multi-investment funds				0.5	2.2
Total	12.9	6.4	2.5	22.30	100.0

Source: Salomon Brothers, *Japanese Investment in U.S. Real Estate: Caution Tempers Aggressive Buying*, February 22, 1989

Major Japanese Purchases of Real Estate in the United States

Because Japanese real estate investors have favored so-called "trophy type" properties—good quality buildings at prime downtown locations—they've achieved a visible presence here.

At the same time, you can see this list covers a tiny portion of the market, and comparatively few are trophies. The Japanese aren't about to take over.

This listing shows the range of Japanese interests: the cities, types of buildings, and financial commitments. Note how the Japanese like to cut their risks by entering into joint-ventures with experienced American real estate investors.

Arizona

The Crossings, a 1,023-acre master-planned community at Superstition Highway and Ellsworth Road, Mesa, March 1987: Taiyo Investments U.S.A., $500 million. New construction.

Camelback Esplanade, Phoenix, 1987: Shimizu Land Corp., $200 million.

Scottsdale Princess Hotel, 600-room resort, Scottsdale, February 1987: Japan Development Corp. (America), $90 million.

Westcourt in the Buttes, a 300-room resort, Tempe, February 1987: Shimizu General Corporation, Mitsui & Co., Westcor Co. and Fred Cox, $35 million.

California: Los Angeles and vicinity

Beverly Hilton, 578-room hotel, November 1987: an unnamed Japanese investor, price believed to exceed $100 million.

1000 Wilshire Boulevard, 450,000 square foot office building, March 1987, Sumitomo Life Realty, $145 million.

New Otani Hotel & Garden, 1987: Kajima International.

Los Angeles Hilton, 1987: an unnamed Japanese investor, $170 million.

California Bank Building, 1987: Toshiu Corp., $11.3 million.

Shopping center, 1987: Kataoka & Co., $15 million.

La Colonnade, 1987: Chivoda Trading Co., $16 million.

I. Magnin Building, 1987: to an undisclosed Japanese investor for $7.5 million.

The Enclave, 1987: Chitaka International Foods, Hollywood, $7.5 million.

100 Wilshire Boulevard, 1987: Asahi Urban Development Corp., Santa Monica, $70 million.

626 Wilshire Boulevard, office building, December 1986: Toyo Real Estate, $25.75 million.

California: Orange County

Hutton Center, complex with eight-story office building and two restaurants, April 1987: Tobishima Development Co., 22 of 46 acres for $26 million.

1900 McArthur Boulevard, April 1987: Shuwa Investments, $40.6 million.

Downey Savings and Loan Association headquarters building, Costa Mesa, April 1987: Shuwa Investments, $28 million.

Taco Bell Building, Irvine, April 1987: Shuwa Investments, $64 million.

Westerly Place, Newport Beach, 1987: Shuwa Corp., $25.5 million.

1825 Over Road, Santa Ana, 1987: Hasegawa Komuten, $46.4 million.

California: San Diego and vicinity

Complex with 30-story office building and 497-room hotel, July 1987: Emerald Hotels, subsidiary of Tokyu Group, joint venture with Shapery Enterprises, $115 million. New construction.

Avondale Center, La Jolla, 1987: Shimizu Construction, $155 million.

California: San Francisco and vicinity

Robert Dollar Building, 87,000 square foot office tower at 311 California Street, April 1987: Kugaya Shoji, a Tokyo real estate company, $21.45 million.

111 Sutter Street, 22-story, 273,000 square foot office building, December 1985: Orient Finance Company, Ltd.

101 California Street, 1987: Nippon Life Insurance Co., $560 million.

Citicorp Center Building, 41-story office tower, October 1985: Dai-Ichi Mutual Life Insurance Company, half-interest for $100 million.

15-story, 400,000 square foot office building, San Jose, June 1986: Toda America, $70 million.

California: other

Office building, Ontario, 1987: Matsubara Construction, $8 million.

Almond orchard, Pixley, 1987: Hokuriku Coca Cola Bottling Company, $1.2 million.

2700 Vgnacio Road, Walnut Creek, 1987: Mitsui Fudosan, $16.3 million.

Office building, 1987: Yoshida Kosan Co., Palm Springs, $6 million.

Indian Wells complex of 2,500 homes, hotels, retail center, convention facility, five golf courses, tennis courts, Palm Springs, December 1986: Mitsubishi Jisho $1.25 billion. New construction.

Colorado

Pavilion Towers, Aurora, 1987: Chiemori Kogyo Co., $12.8 million.

District of Columbia

U.S. News & World Report Building, July 1987: Shuwa Investments, $80 million ($480 per square foot). This building was developed in 1983 by Mortimer Zuckerman, Boston-based owner of the magazine which leased back the building for 25 years.

Judiciary Center, April 1987: Kondobo USA Inc., for an undisclosed sum. Main tenant is Department of Justice.

One Thomas Circle, office building, April 1987: Asahi Mutual Life Insurance Company with Prudential Insurance Company of America, 50-50 deal for $24.7 million.

1155 21st Street, N.W., office building, April 1987: Meiji Mutual Life Insurance Company together with Equitable Life Assurance Society, a 50-50 deal.

1101 Vermont Avenue, N.W., American Medical Association Building, April 1987: Nissei Realty Inc., $37 million.

1750 K Street, N.W., 150,000 square foot office building, April 1987: Sumitomo Life Realty Company, $30 million.

1101 Pennsylvania Avenue, a 14-story, 795,000 square foot office building, February 1987: Kokusai Kogyo Company provided $175 million of financing and bought a 15 percent interest. New construction.

Judiciary Center, 1987: Kondo Beseki, $86 million.

Land, 1987: Kumagai Gumi, $7.3 million.

2025 M Street, NW, 1987: Dai-Ichi Mutual Life, $46.4 million.

Florida: Miami and Dade County

World Trade Center, 33-story office tower, January 1987: JDC (America) Corporation, $42 million, New construction.

Calusa Country Club, S. Dade County, 1987: Nichon Kowa Co., $5.5 million.

Florida: Orlando

Sheraton Hotel and Holidy Inn Crowne Plaza, 2,300 rooms altogether, Walt Disney World, 1986: Aoki Corporation of America with Metropolitan Life Insurance Company and Tishman Realty & Construction, $265 million.

Hawaii: Hawaii Island

Mauna Kea resort, February 1988: to a partnership between Aoki of Japan and the Bass Brothers of Fort Worth, Texas, for $315 million. This property originally developed by the Rockefellers.

Mauna Lani Bay Hotel, 351-room hotel, January 1987: Tokyu Group, 50-50 with Dai-Ichi Seimi America, $103 million.

Mauna Lani Bay Hotel, and 80-unit Mauna Lani Terrace, February 1983: Mauna Lani Resort, $72 million.

Francis Brown Golf Course, July 1981: Mauna Lani Resort, Inc., $6 million.

40 acres in Kona, May 1973: Taiyo Fudosan, $6 million.

3,095 acres in South Kohala, September 1972: Orchid Island Resorts Corp., $12 million.

Hawaii: Kauai
Sheraton-Kauai Hotel completed expansion on function room, 1986, for $1.3 million.

Kauai Beach Villas, December 1981: Hasegawa Komuten, $40 million.

Kauai Gem of Hawaii store, June 1981: Kawaii Seiyo, Ltd., $300,000.

Sheraton-Kauai Hotel with 152 rooms, March 1972: Ohbayashi-Gumi, Ltd., $4 million.

Hawaii: Maui
Hyatt Regency Maui, 815-room, 18.4-acre resort, April 1987: Kokasai Motorcars Co., $319 million, largest ever paid for a hotel.

Maui Hyatt Regency, 850-room hotel, January 1987: Kokusai Jidosa, $300 million.

Maui Marriott, 720-room hotel, January 1987: Azabu USA Corp., $150 million.

Kona Lagoon Hotel, 462-room property, May 1986: Otaka, $10.3 million.

Lahaina Cannery Shopping Center, 120,000 square foot center, 1986: Hawaii Omori Corp., $16 million.

Kaanapali Alii, 264-unit condominium, September 1982: Hawaii Omori Corp., $100 million.

Makena Golf Course, September 1981: Seibu Hawaii, $6 million.

Kaanapali Shores Resort, 463-unit hotel and condominium complex, April 1980: Hasegawa Komuten, $35 million.

1,000 acres in Makena, July 1973: Seibu Fodosan, $7.5 million.

Hawaii: Oahu

Amfac Center, Honolulu, early 1988: Mitsui Real Estate Development, $140 million ($295 per square foot). This was about two and a half times what the previous owner paid in 1984.

Ala Moana Americana, 1,200-room hotel, January 1987: Azabu USA Corp., $65 million.

Hyatt Regency Waikiki, 1,234-room hotel, September 1987: Azabu USA Corp., $245 million.

Ko Olina Resort, a 1,105-acre master-planned development, January 1987: Kumagai Gumi, joint ventured with Chris Hemmeter and Herbert Horita, $3.1 billion. New construction.

1500 Kapiolani Building, an office and retail complex adjacent to KGMB-TV studios, December 1986: Kanto Building, $15.7 million.

Sultan Building, at 939 Kapiolani Boulevard, December 1986: Nihon Lancre, Ltd., $3 million.

Royal Islander Club & Hotel, 12-story, 101-room hotel, December 1986: Chitose Group, $6.2 million.

5571, 5577 and 5599 Kalanianaole Highway, December 1986: Japan Development Co., $2.4 million.

5603 Kalanianaole Highway, 48,000 square feet of vacant land, December 1986: Aiki Ono $1.7 million.

Pioneer Plaza, 22-story office building in Honolulu, December 1986: Yamate Shoji, $44 million.

Ala Moana Americana Hotel, 1,250-room property, October 1986: Azabu USA, for an undisclosed sum.

Hawaiian Regent Hotel, 1,346-room Waikiki property, October 1986: Otaka Inc., $207.7 million.

Quality Inn, 451-room Waikiki property, October 1986: Matsuzato Hawaii, $27 million.

Sherry Waikiki Hotel, 100-room property at 334 Lewers Street, August 1986: Genichi Sugiyama, $5.5 million.

Kaiser Foundation Hospital site, July 1986: Seibu Railway Co., $24.5 million. Company will build the Waikiki Prince Hotel with local developer Jack Myers.

Mililani Golf Course with 172 acres, May 1986: Sports Shinko, $16 million.

Atkinson Center, a mini-shopping complex on a 15,000 square foot property, April 1986: Kaijima Chemical Industries, $2.7 million.

Honolulu Sake Bakery, 1986: company not disclosed, $2.8 million.

Kapiolani Commercial Center, 1580 Makaloa Street, Honolulu, 1986: Yamate Shoji, $16.5 million.

Sheraton-Waikiki Hotel, renovations completed 1986: company not disclosed, $50 million.

Holiday Inn Waikiki, 636-room hotel, February 1985: Otaka Inc., $50.3 million.

HK Building, April 1985: Toho Kikaku Co., $15 million.

Liliuokalani Gardens, 382-unit Waikiki condominium, March 1984: built by Hasegawa Komuten for $44 million.

456-room luxury hotel on Kalia Road, January 1984: Halekulani Corp., subsidiary of Mitsui Fudosan, $57 million.

Ala Moana center, largest shopping center in Honolulu (60 percent interest), 1984: Daiei Inc., $330 million. Transaction included Kaahumanu Shopping Center on Maui and several thousand square feet of Oahu office space. Equitable Life Assurance Society bought the remaining 40 percent interest in these properties.

Central Pacific Plaza, 22-story building, February 1983: $34.7 million.

Halekulani Hotel plus about 190,000 square feet of Waikiki property, November 1980: $24 million.

HK Building, eight-story office tower, August 1980, $10.5 million. Hawaiian headquarters for Japanese developer Hasegawa Komuten.

Kaseko Hawaii, 740-unit condominium, November 1979: Hasegawa Komuten, $40 million.

Hawaiian Regent Hotel, 650-unit wing, April 1979: Tokyu Corp., $33 million.

Pacific Monarch, 216-unit resort condominium, April 1979: Hasegawa Komuten, $12 million.

Hawaiian Monarch, 44-story Waikiki hotel, spring 1979: company not disclosed, $22 million. Subsequently some units sold to individuals.

Royal Kuhio, 39-story, 385-unit Waikiki condominium, August 1976: company not disclosed, $30 million.

Sheraton-Waikiki, Sheraton-Maui and Royal Hawaiian hotels with almost 3,000 rooms, July 1974: Kenji Osano, $105 million. Osano died in 1986.

Makaha Inn and Country Club, 200-unit property, April 1973: Hawaii Daiichi Kanko, $21 million.

Surfrider Hotel, 430 rooms, May 1969: Kokusai Kogyo, $10 million. New construction.

Princess Kaiulani Hotel, August 1963: Kokusai Kogyo Corp., $8.7 million.

Illinois: Chicago

Nikko Chicago Hotel, February 1987: Nikko, hotel subsidiary of Japan Airlines, a joint venture with Tishman Realty & Construction, $75 million.

1 Prudential Plaza, 41-story, 1.1 million square foot office building; and 2 Prudential Plaza, a planned 64-story, 940,000 square foot office building, February 1987: Nissei Realty, $180 million for a 50 percent interest.

Avondale Center, 1987: to an unidentified Japanese investor for $47.5 million.

Two Prudential Tower, 1987: Nippon Life Insurance Co., for an undisclosed sum.

Prudential Plaza, 1987: Nippon Life Insurance Co., for an undisclosed sum.

101 North Wacker Drive, 1987: Dai-Ichi Mutual Life, for an undisclosed sum.

Massachusetts: Boston

Paine Webber Building, 20-story, 300,000 square foot office tower, December 1986: Sumitomo Trust Bank, $107 million.

Burlington Business Center I, office park headquarters for Wang Corporation, 1986: Sumitomo Life Realty, $38 million.

Nevada: Las Vegas

Dunes Hotel & Casino a 1,200-room hotel on a 163-acre site, August 1987: Masao Nangaku, $157.7 million. Hotel filed for bankruptcy in 1985, with debts around $148 million.

Park Hotel & Casino, November 1987: Katsuki Manabe, for an undisclosed sum.

Aladdin Hotel, 1986: Ginji Yasuda for an undisclosed sum.

New York: Manhattan

Citicorp Center, office tower at Lexington Avenue and 53rd Street, October 1987: Dai-Ichi Mutual Life Insurance Company, $670 million ($430 per square foot) for a two-thirds condominium interest, in the 23rd to 59th floors. Citicorp and Dai-Ichi will own the land beneath this building jointly. Citicorp reported a $270 million after-tax gain.

399 Park Avenue, also a Citicorp building, October 1987: Dai-Ichi Mutual Life Insurance Company, one-third condominium interest, in the 17th to 39th floors. Citicorp and Dai-Ichi will own the land beneath this building jointly. Part of same transaction as Citicorp Center.

Mobil Building, a 42-story office tower at Lexington Avenue and 42nd Street, August 1987: Hiro Corporation, $260 million, owned by the Honzawa family of Tokyo. Hiro acquired the ground lease as part of the deal, from the Goelet family, old New York landlords. Mobil will be moving headquarters to Fairfax, Virginia.

666 Fifth Avenue, a 41-story office building, June 1987: Sumitomo Realty & Development, for $500 million ($365 per square foot). The seller, Integrated Resources, had bought the building a year earlier for $320 million.

Algonquin Hotel, 59 West 44th Street, April 1987: Aoki Corporation, $29 million. The new owner promised not to disturb the ambiance of this famous literary watering hole.

30 Wall Street, a 118,000 square foot office building, April 1987: Tozai Real Estate Company, $31.6 million. Headquarters for Seamens Bank for Savings.

Americas Tower, 1987: Kumagai Gumi, for an undisclosed sum.

461 Fifth Avenue, 1987: Mitsui Real Estate Development, for an undisclosed sum.

Tower 49, 12 East 49th Street, a 44-story office building, December 1986: Kato Kagaku, the world's largest corn syrup refiner, for $301 million ($500 per square foot, record for a Manhattan office property).

Exxon Building, the company's 54-story 2.2 million square foot headquarters at Rockefeller Center, December 1986: Mitsui Fudosan, for $610 million ($277 per square foot), the highest price for a single building.

Tiffany Building at Fifth Avenue & 57th Street, November 1986: Dai-Ichi Real Estate Company, for $94 million ($940 per square foot). Return to buyer: 5.3 percent.

ABC Building, Sixth Avenue at 53rd Street, September 1986: Shuwa Corporation for $175 million ($365 per square foot). American Broadcasting Company leasing back space for three years, assuring 8 percent return during that period, then moving to new headquarters elsewhere in Manhattan.

Belgravia, a 21-story condominium at 124 East 79th Street, 1986: Hiro Enterprise Co., for $105 million. Seller was Donald Trump. Hiro adding 27 floors of office space.

451 Fifth Avenue, a building site at 40th Street, 1986: Mitsui Fudosan building a 26-story, 200,000 square foot office tower.

Essex House, 450-room hotel on Central Park South, $175 million, 1986: Nikko, the hotel operating subsidiary of Japan Air Lines, which also owns hotel properties in Chicago and San Francisco. Seller was Marriott Corporation.

Manhattan Tower, 101 East 52nd Street, a 35-story, 270,000 square foot office building, 1986: Sumitomo Life Realty, which acquired a 49.9 percent interest from the British developer, London & Leeds.

655 Fifth Avenue: Hiro Corporation, for an undisclosed sum. Major tenant is Japan Air Lines.

650 Madison Avenue: Hiro Corporation, for an undisclosed sum. Major tenant is Bank of Tokyo

New York: other

David's Island, a 2,000-unit luxury housing project, New Rochelle, November 1986: Kumagai Gumi arranged $46 million of financing and will participate in construction.

North Carolina: Raleigh

One million square foot office-warehouse complex, October 1986: Aoki Corporation, $13.5 million. New construction.

Texas: Dallas

53-story, 1.3 million square foot office building, January 1987: Nissei Realty and Equitable Life Assurance Society, 50-50 deal for $40 million.

Dallas Market Center, 1987: Dai-Ichi Mutual Life, $200 million.

Office building, 1987: Matsushita Kosan Co., $6 million.

Texas: other

Shoreline Plaza, office building, Corpus Christi, 1986: KG Land in a joint venture for $60 million.

Virginia

Five-story, 122,000 square foot office building, 330,000 square foot shopping center and 208-room hotel, Norfolk, August 1986: Dai-Ichi Mutual Life Insurance Company, a 50-50 deal for Morgan Guaranty Trust, $80 million.

Washington: Seattle

AT&T Gateway Tower, office building, December 1986: KG Land, $165 million. New construction.

12-story office building at First and Stewart Streets, December 1986: Konoike Construction Company, C. Itoh & Co. and Prescott Development Company, joint venture partners in $12 million project.

Mill Creek residential development, November 1986: United Development Corp., owned by Tokyu Group and Ohbayashi-Gumi Ltd.

APPENDIX 4

HOW TO TAP
JAPANESE CAPITAL

As you've seen in this book, Japanese lenders and investors expand the range of financing choices available in the U.S. market. Price competition from the Japanese helps lower financing costs.

Moreover, good relations with a Japanese lender or investor can prove invaluable if you contemplate distribution, licensing, manufacturing, or other business in Japan. The linking of complementary skills—domestic or foreign—can help raise living standards all around.

But before you can even think about trying to borrow some Japanese money, sell equities or other assets to Japanese investors, look at your business the way outsiders see it—a risky proposition. In the past, it's true, some exuberant Japanese financiers threw money at buildings, for example, but times have changed. They've become more skeptical, cautious, sophisticated. This isn't a sucker's game anymore, if it ever was. Opportunities are out there for those who can offer mutually beneficial deals.

Term loans. Although the biggest Japanese banks tend to concentrate on Fortune 500 business, middle-market borrowers—loans under, say, $2 million—have a number of options. Regional offices of major Japanese banks may be worth contacting. Smaller Japanese banks seldom compete for Fortune 500 business, so they may be sources for middle-market loans. When a Japanese bank acquires a middle-market lender, as in California, it continues serving that clientele. See the accompanying list of bank offices.

Japanese leasing companies make a lot of corporate loans. In some cases, it amounts to half their business. They're worth contacting, too.

The Japanese are overwhelmingly concerned about safety. They prefer to do business with well-established, creditworthy individuals and firms. The Japanese want at least as much reassurance as anyone else who's being asked to put their money at risk.

To maximize your changes of a loan at attractive terms, you must prepare thoroughly. This means marshalling as much material as possible to help provide assurance about the stability of your market, the track record of your company, your cash flows, and so on. Expect a lot of detailed, technical questions. The Japanese will independently check out your claims and references.

The Japanese have a reputation for slow decisionmaking, but this has improved considerably in recent years as more loan underwriting officers have moved to the United States. Once a bank has become comfortable with your company, loan decisions shouldn't take any longer than at a U.S. bank.

Equity capital. A listing on the Tokyo Stock Exchange may be part of a strategy to help major companies expand into Japan. A listing on the Tokyo Stock Exchange definitely helps a company gain acceptance as part of the community.

But a listing doesn't come cheap. Initial costs for lawyers, accountants, transfer agent, public relations firm, printing house and Exchange fees run about ¥30.5 million (about $250,000); if there's a new public offering, costs may approach ¥50 million (about $400,000). Then there's a fee based on the number of shares issued and outstanding. For a company with about 100 million shares, the fee would be about ¥450,000 ($3,600).

To qualify for listing, a company must meet these requirements:

- Incorporated and continuously in business for at least five years
- Earned before-tax profits of at least ¥10 billion ($US 80 million) during each of the past three years
- Have shareholder equity during the previous year of at least ¥10 billion ($US 80 million)
- Paid dividends for the past three years

- Listed in the country of origin on a recognized exchange for at least two years
- Have liquidity in the home market
- Have at least 1,000 shareholders already in Japan
- Impose no restrictions on transferability of shares
- Made no false statements in financial statements and related documents during the past three years

The listing process starts about a hundred days before the anticipated date of listing and the start of trading.

You need the services of a Japanese lawyer, especially for application forms, disclosure forms, and negotiations with the Tokyo Stock Exchange. Koichi Takeuchi, for example, with the Tokyo firm Nagashima & Ohno, has worked on listings for Exxon, McDonald's, Chrysler, Eastman Kodak and Northern Telecom.

You should have someone in Tokyo available to answer whatever questions may come up when documents are prepared and reviewed. It isn't enough to rely on the telephone or the fax machine.

Overall, Japanese authorities don't require anything that isn't disclosed in the U.S. They are sensitive about potentially disruptive developments such as an acquisition, management turnover, or serious write-offs.

Authorities are also wary of management policies which could put Japanese investors at a disadvantage. For example, having more than one class of shares that involve preferential and inferior voting rights would cause concern.

Among the supporting documents that must be translated into Japanese are the annual report, proxy statements, the equivalent of an SEC 10-K, and 10-Q forms.

A Japanese securities firm is essential for marketing the shares. Nomura has handled more listings than any other firm, followed by Daiwa, Nikko and Yamaichi. They don't charge for their work to help a stock get listed; their payoff is in sales commissions generated after listing.

The sponsoring securities firm can help satisfy certain regulations, such as the requirement that a company have at least 1,000 shareholders already in Japan. The securities firm buys shares on the New York, London, or some other exchange, and then sells them to customers in Japan. The Big Four firms have enough sales clout that this shouldn't be an issue.

Examination by the Tokyo Stock Exchange should be completed within two months. If there are any problems, a company will be advised to withdraw its application quietly.

Once approved, the application goes to the Ministry of Finance. At that time, it's made public. Final approval comes in about 20 days.

Thus far, corporate giants have dominated the foreign company listings. But many observers expect that as Tokyo builds its data bank about foreign companies, and as more foreign companies orient themselves to the international market, the size of listed companies will come down and more companies will be able to raise equity capital in Tokyo.

Venture capital. It is the most expensive kind of capital. The Tokyo venture capital market is tiny compared to the market in the United States, so it wouldn't make sense to go there for financial reasons alone. If U.S. venture capitalists have all turned thumbs down on a proposed deal, don't expect the Japanese to go for it. They're becoming quite sophisticated. You'd be better off figuring out some way to make a deal competitive.

Japanese venture capital may be a good idea when a U.S. company needs a Japanese connection to do business in Japan or elsewhere around the world. As it happens, your most likely prospects aren't primarily interested in financial considerations either. Rather, they're companies looking for an investment which will help further their strategic objectives. In fact, it's unlikely that you'll raise Japanese venture capital without working out an agreement for joint research, manufacturing, or distribution.

You'll need a *nakodo*, or go-between. Partly, this is because the right venture capital investors are hard to locate anywhere, especially in a distant country where you may not speak the language, have connections, or have sufficient knowledge of business practices. The prospective Japanese investor wants assurance, too, since venture capital risks are high. Japanese venture capital investors must trust you and have confidence in you before they'll talk business.

Where do the go-betweens come from? Tak Yamamoto, for example, worked for IBM in Japan and Los Angeles before establishing his firm in Menlo Park, California. Yoriko Kishimoto, whose Japan Pacific Associates is in Palo Alto, California, developed contacts through her work at Nomura Research Institute.

To find a good go-between, contact a U.S. company that used one for raising Japanese venture capital or finding a Japanese buyer. Make sure that a go-between's contacts are appropriate for your needs. For example, some go-betweens have worked mainly in financial services; they may have few contacts among Japanese consumer companies, and if you have a consumer product, you'd probably be best off with another go-between.

Alternatively, a number of Japanese securities firms and trading companies serve as go-betweens. Nomura Securities, for instance, has some people who do this. So does Marubeni America and C. Itoh & Co., among others. The minimum transaction size varies from firm to firm; in some cases it's as low as $100,000.

Very large transactions are handled by U.S. investment bankers who also help structure, finance, and close the transactions. They work through their Tokyo offices as well as their preferred go-betweens.

Expect to pay a retainer plus a percentage of money raised. It can take a year from the time you start a systematic search for prospects until a transaction closes. Many deals are concluded within a few months, but don't count on it.

There's a common tendency for U.S. companies to be either paranoid or overly trusting when they approach a Japanese investor. Both attitudes can get you in trouble. Take the same precautions as you would if you were entering a joint venture with a big U.S. company such as IBM or Digital Equipment. Retain experienced counsel to help structure a deal which will protect your interests.

Real estate. With more and different kinds of Japanese investors entering this market, there's plenty of money available.

But U.S. vacancy rates are relatively high, there's a glut of properties. Not many are top quality. As noted earlier, Japanese investors want prestige buildings. Generally, this means a good location, financially strong tenants, an attractive stone exterior, high quality mechanical systems. They aren't crazy about cheap-looking steel-and-glass boxes, even though Tokyo is full of them.

Japanese bankers can be excellent contacts, since many clients back in Japan want to invest in U.S. real estate but lack the knowledge. A banker may serve as a prospect's advisor throughout a transaction.

A few real estate brokerage firms—such as Manhattan's Pacific Investment Partners and Cushman & Wakefield—have much experience selling to Japanese buyers. They routinely cultivate prospective buyers.

Although Japanese business people are wary of lawyers, there are some U.S. lawyers who know a lot about selling to the Japanese. Ko-Yung Tung, a Chinese-born, Japanese-raised lawyer with O'Melveny & Myers (a large firm based in Los Angeles), has worked on some of the largest transactions, including the $500 million sale of Manhattan's Tower 49 to the Japanese sugar refiner Kato Kagaku and the $670 million sale of interests in two Citicorp buildings to Dai-Ichi Mutual Life. O'Melveny & Myers's real estate office is in New York.

Your principal advisor should be someone experienced in the intricacies of real estate finance, preferably with Japanese buyers, because it can make or break a deal. The trick is to satisfy the buyer's business and tax situation with yours, while providing as much protection as possible from adverse foreign exchange fluctuations.

When dealing with a prospective Japanese buyer—or anyone else overseas—it's a good idea to document the obvious. In your initial presentation, provide current details about the local economy, vacancy rates in your segment of the market, new construction coming on stream, the age of your building, mechanical systems, tenant roster, cash flow—everything. These details are especially important for international buyers, since basic information is harder to come by.

There have been horror stories of Japanese investors being burned, so expect detailed questions about asbestos and tax liabilities such as real estate transfer "fees."

A Directory of Major Japanese Financial Service Companies

This is a partial listing.

The highest-ranking office is the head office, usually in Tokyo. Some banks have their head office in Osaka, in which case their highest-ranking Tokyo office is called headquarters.

Overseas offices may be branches, representative offices, or agencies. Branches are the highest-ranking, and that's where the top managers and loan underwriting officers are located. In the U.S., the highest ranking office is usually in New York, so those offices are listed first.

But don't try to take your business to the top people in a Japanese company. Most follow the so-called *ringi* system where business proposals tend to originate somewhere among middle-level people and work their way up through the organization as they gain approvals. A consensus has to develop before a high-ranking executive is likely to sign off on it.

Individual officers aren't listed here, since they're rotated so often.

Bank of Tokyo

Tokyo headquarters
6-3, Nihombashi
Hongokucho 1-chome
Chuo-ku
Tokyo 103, Japan
(03) 245-1111

New York branch
100 Broadway
New York, New York 10005
(212) 766-3400

Chicago subsidiary office
69 West Washington Street,
  Room 910
Chicago, Illinois 60602
(312) 236-3120

Honolulu branch
Davies Pacific Center
Suite 2110
841 Bishop Street
Honolulu, Hawaii 96813
(808) 521-9811

Houston representative office
2 Houston Center, Suite 1104
Houston, Texas 77010
(713) 658-1021

Los Angeles branch
Bank of Tokyo Building, Suite
  200
640 West Sixth Street
Los Angeles, California 90017
(213) 972-5333

Miami branch
2100 Ponce de Leon Boulevard
Coral Gables, Florida 33134
(305) 445-2100

Portland branch
411 South West Sixth Avenue
Portland, Oregon 97204
(503) 222-3661

San Francisco branch
350 California Street
San Francisco, California 94104
(415) 445-0400

California First Bank headquarters
350 California Street
San Francisco, California 94104
(415) 445-0400

Seattle branch
1111 Third Avenue
Seattle, Washington 98101
(206) 382-6000

*Washington, D.C. representative
  office*
1825 K Street, N.W.
Suite 703
Washington, D.C. 20006
(202) 463-0477

Bank of Yokohama

Yokohama head office
47 Hon-chuo 5-chome
Naka-ku
Yokohama, Japan
(045) 201-4991

New York branch
One World Trade Center
New York, New York 10005
(212) 775-1700

Chuo Trust & Banking Co., Ltd.

Tokyo head office
7-1 1-chome Kyobashi
Chuo-ku
Tokyo 104, Japan
(03) 567-1451

New York branch
One World Trade Cener
New York, New York 10048
(212) 938-0200

Dai-Ichi Kangyo Bank

Los Angeles office doubles as head office for Dai-Ichi Kangyo Bank of California.

Tokyo head office
1-5, Uchisaiwaicho
1-chome
Tokyo 100, Japan
(03) 596-1111

Chicago branch
Mid-Continental Plaza
111 South Wabash Avenue
Chicago, Illinois 60603
(312) 782-5400

New York branch
One World Trade Center, Suite
  4911
New York, New York 10048
(212) 466-5200

Houston representative office
1001 Fannin, Suite 3860
Houston, Texas 77002
(713) 654-5055

Atlanta representative office
Georgia Pacific Center, Suite
  4050
133 Peachtree Street
Atlanta, Georgia 30303
(404) 523-0327

Los Angeles branch
770 Wilshire Boulevard
Los Angeles, California 90017
(213) 612-6400

San Francisco representative office
101 California Street, Suite 2775
San Francisco, California 94111
(415) 788-8448

Dai-Ichi Mutual Life Insurance Co.

Tokyo head office
1-13-1 chome Yuraku-chuo
Chiyoda-ku
Tokyo 100, Japan
(03) 216-1211

Los Angeles head office
611 West Sixth Street
Los Angeles, California 90071
(213) 624-7759

Dai-Ichi Securities

Tokyo head office
1-6 Nihonbashi-Muromachi
Chuo-ku
Tokyo, Japan
(03) 244-2845

New York representative office
33 Whitehall Street
New York, New York 10005
(212) 344-1060

Daiwa Bank

Osaka head office
21, Bingomachi 2-chome
Higashi-ku
Osaka 541, Japan
(06) 271-1221

New York branch
140 Broadway
New York, New York 10005
(212) 480-0300

Los Angeles agency
555 South Flower Street
Los Angeles, California 90071
(213) 489-3600

Daiwa Bank Trust Company
75 Rockefeller Center
New York, New York 10019
(212) 399-8500

Daiwa Securities

Tokyo head office
6-4 Otemachi, 2-chome
Chiyoda-ku
Tokyo 100, Japan
(03) 243-2111

Chicago branch
Two North La Salle Street
Suite 625
Chicago, Illinois 60602
(312) 845-9666

New York subsidiary office
One World Financial Center
Tower A, 200 Liberty Street
New York, New York 10281
(212) 945-0100

Los Angeles branch
333 South Grand Avenue
Suite 3636
Los Angeles, California 90071
(213) 628-0201

Diamond Lease Company Ltd.

Tokyo head office
7-2, Yaesu 2-chome
Chuo-ku
Tokyo 104, Japan
(03) 274-0731

New York representative office
780 Third Avenue
Suite 4202
New York, New York 10017
(212) 752-5710

Greenwich main office
2 Soundview Drive
Greenwich, Connecticut 06830

Fuji Bank

Note that almost all offices also have representatives from Fuji Bank & Trust Company.

Tokyo head office
5-5, Otemachi 1-chome
Chiyoda-ku
Tokyo 100, Japan
(03) 216-2211

Houston agency
2 Houston Center, Suite 2800
909 Fannin Street
Houston, Texas 77010
(713) 759-1800

New York branch
One World Trade Center, Suite 6011
New York, New York 10048
(212) 839-5600

Los Angeles agency
333 South Grand Avenue, 25th Floor
Los Angeles, California 90071
(213) 680-9855

Atlanta representative office
Cain Tower, Suite 801
229 Peachtree Street, N.E.
Atlanta, Georgia 30303
(404) 688-4992

Miami representative office
Southeast Financial Center, Suite 2950
200 South Biscayne Boulevard
Miami, Florida 33131
(305) 374-2226

Chicago branch
33 North Dearborn Street, Suite 1730
Chicago, Illinois 60602
(312) 621-0500

San Francisco agency
601 California Street
San Francisco, California 94108
(415) 362-4740

Seattle representative office
Seattle-First National Bank
  Building
Suite 4333
1001 4th Avenue
Seattle, Washington 98154
(206) 624-4757

*Heller International Corporation
  headquarters*
200 North LaSalle Street
Chicago, Illinois 60601
(312) 621-7000

New York head office
One World Trade Center, Suite
  8067
New York, New York 10048
(212) 839-6800

Hachijuni Bank, Ltd.

Nagano head office
178-8, Okada
Nagano, Japan
(0262) 27-1182

International Department
2-1 Marunouchi 2-chome
Chiyoda-ku
Tokyo, Japan
(03) 214-8282

New York representative office
One World Trade Center, Suite
  8129
New York, New York 10048
(212) 466-0882

Hokkaido Takushoku Bank, Ltd.

Sapporo head office
7, Nishi 3-chome
Odori, Chuo-ku
Sapporo 060, Japan
(011) 271-2111

*International Banking Division
  office*
3-13 Nihonbashi 1-chome
Chuo-ku
Tokyo 103, Japan
(03) 272-6611

New York branch
One World Trade Center, Suite
  3841
New York, New York 10048
(212) 466-6060

Chicago representative office
One First National Plaza, Suite
  2750
Chicago, Illinois 60602
(312) 236-9525

Houston representative office
One Houston Center, Suite 1708
Houston, Texas 77002
(713) 759-0330

Seattle branch
800 Fifth Avenue, Suite 3880
Seattle, Washington 98104
(206) 624-0920

Los Angeles agency
333 South Grand Avenue, Suite
  3522
Los Angeles, California 90071
(213) 620-9100

Hokuriku Bank, Ltd.

Toyama head office
2-26, Tsutsumicho-dori 1-chome
Toyama, Japan
(0764) 23-7111

New York branch office
One World Trade Center, Suite
  8463
New York, New York 10048
(212) 524-9771

Foreign Department
1-5, Nihonbashi Muromachi
  3-chome
Chuo-ku
Tokyo, Japan
(03) 241-7771

Hyakujushi Bank, Ltd.

Takamatsu head office
5-1 Kamei-chuo
Takamatsu, Kagawa 760, Japan
(087) 831-0014

New York office
One World Trade Center
New York, New York 10048
(212) 524-0848

Industrial Bank of Japan

Tokyo head office
3-3, Marunouchi 1-chome
Chiyoda-ku
Tokyo 100, Japan
(03) 214-1111

Atlanta representative office
235 Peachtree Street, N.E.
Suite 1500
Atlanta, Georgia 30303
(404) 524-8770

New York branch
245 Park Avenue
New York, New York 10167
(212) 557-3535

Chicago branch office
70 West Madison Street, Suite
  1800
Chicago, Illinois 60602
(312) 855-1111

Houston representative office
Citicorp Center, Suite 2780
1200 Smith Street
Houston, Texas 77002
(713) 651-9444

Los Angeles agency
800 West 6th Street
Los Angeles, California 90017
(213) 628-7241

San Francisco representative office
555 California Street, Suite 5010
San Francisco, California 94104
(415) 981-3131

Washington, D.C. representative office
1700 Pennsylvania Avenue, N.W.
Suite 550
Washington, D.C.
(202) 393-8383

Juroku Bank, Ltd.

Gifu head office
8-26, Kandamachi
Gifu, Japan
(0582) 65-2111

International Division office
4-15, Nihonbashi Honcho
Chuo-ku
Tokyo, Japan
(03) 242-1621

New York representative office
One World Trade Center, Suite 8353
New York, New York 10048
(212) 466-1600

Kyowa Bank

Tokyo head office
1-2, Otemachi 1-chome
Chiyoda-ku
Tokyo 100, Japan
(03) 287-2111

New York branch office
One World Trade Center, Suite 4673
New York, New York 10048
(212) 432-6400

Chicago representative office
115 South LaSalle Street
Chicago, Illinois 60603
(312) 726-6707

Los Angeles agency
635 West Seventh Street
Los Angeles, California 90017
(213) 626-6266

San Francisco representative office
One Montgomery Street, Suite 1120
San Francisco, California 94104
(415) 989-2800

Long-Term Credit Bank of Japan, Limited

Tokyo head office
2-4 Otemachi 1-chome
Chiyoda-ku
Tokyo, Japan
(03) 211-5111

Dallas representative office
1960 Americas Tower
2323 Bryan Street
Dallas, Texas 75201
(214) 969-5352

New York branch
140 Broadway
New York, New York 10005
(212) 248-2000

Los Angeles agency
444 South Flower Street
Los Angeles, California 90071
(213) 629-5777

Chicago representative office
30 South Wacker Drive, Suite
  2805
Chicago, Illinois 60606
(312) 454-9023

Mitsubishi Bank

Tokyo head office
7-1 Marunouchi 2-chome
Chiyoda-ku
Tokyo 100, Japan
(03) 240-1111

Houston representative office
1001 Fannin Street, Suite 2210
Houston, Texas 77002
(713) 658-1160

New York branch
One World Trade Center, Suite
  8527
New York, New York 10048
(212) 524-7000

Los Angeles agency
800 Wilshire Boulevard
Los Angeles, California 90017
(213) 621-1200

Chicago branch
115 South LaSalle Street, Suite
  1200
Chicago, Illinois 60603
(312) 269-0430

*Mitsubishi Bank of California
  headquarters*
800 Wilshire Boulevard
Los Angeles, California 90017
(213) 621-1200

Mitsui Bank

California offices also have representatives from Mitsui Manufacturers Bank. The head office is in Los Angeles.

Tokyo head office
1-2, Yurakucho 1-chome
Chiyoda-ku
Tokyo 100, Japan
(03) 501-1111

New York branch
277 Park Avenue, 45th Floor
New York, New York 10172
(212) 644-3131

Atlanta representative office
230 Peachtree Street, N.W.
Suite 2360
Atlanta, Georgia 30303
(404) 523-9831

Chicago branch
30 South Wacker Drive, Suite
  2112
Chicago, Illinois 60606
(312) 782-3114

Houston representative office
3940 InterFirst Plaza
1100 Louisiana
Houston, Texas 77002
(713) 225-5261

Los Angeles agency
515 South Figueroa Street, Suite
  400
Los Angeles, California 90071
(213) 680-2900

San Francisco representative office
301 California Street
San Francisco, California 94104
(415) 765-0814

Seattle branch
900 4th Avenue, Suite 1610
Seattle, Washington 98164
(206) 622-0330

New Japan Securities International, Inc.

Tokyo head office
1-17-10 Nihonbashi
Chuo-ku
Tokyo, Japan
(03) 273-2311

New York subsidiary office
One World Trade Center
New York, New York 10048
(212) 839-0001

Nikko Securities

Tokyo head office
3-1, Marunouchi 3-chome
Chiyoda-ku
Tokyo 100, Japan
(03) 283-7418

New York office
200 Liberty Street
One World Financial Center
New York, New York 10281
(212) 416-5400

Chicago branch
One South Wacker Drive
Suite 3230
Chicago, Illinois 60606
(312) 726-7037

Los Angeles branch
800 Wilshire Boulevard
Los Angeles, California 90017
(213) 626-7163

San Francisco branch
Bank of America Center
555 California Street
Suite 5020
San Francisco, California 94104
(415) 981-3120

Nippon Credit Bank

Head office
13-10 Kudan-kita
1-chome, Chiyoda-ku
Tokyo 102, Japan

Los Angeles agency
800 Wilshire Boulevard
Suite 1400
Los Angeles, California 90017
(213) 629-5566

New York branch office
245 Park Avenue
New York New York 10167
(212) 984-1200

Nippon Kangyo Kakumaru Securities Co., Ltd.

Tokyo head office
2-35 Kabuto-chuo, Nihonbashi
Chuo-ku
Tokyo, Japan
(03) 639-7511

New York head office
World Financial Center
New York, New York 10281
(212) 587-7600

Nomura Securities

Tokyo head office
9-1, 1-chome
Nihonbashi, Chuo-ku
Tokyo 103, Japan
(03) 211-1811

Chicago branch
Three First National Plaza
Suite 4488
70 West Madison Street
Chicago, Illinois 60602
(312) 372-0786

New York main office
Continental Center
180 Maiden Lane
Suite 3701
New York, New York 10038
(212) 208-9300

Honolulu branch
190 South King Street
Suite 2760
Honolulu, Hawaii 96813
(808) 538-3837

Los Angeles branch
523 West Sixth Street
Los Angeles, California 90014
(213) 626-9301

San Francisco branch
Bank of America Finance Center
Suite 4777
555 California Street
San Francisco, California 94104
(415) 788-0700

Norinchukin Bank

Tokyo head office
8-3, Otemachi 1-chome
Chiyoda-ku
Tokyo 100, Japan
(03) 279-0111

New York branch
One World Trade Center, Suite
    8025
New York, New York 10048
(212) 432-6886

Orient Leasing Co., Ltd.

Tokyo headquarters
World Trade Center Building
2-4-1, Hamamatsu-cho
Minato-ku
Tokyo 105, Japan
(03) 435-6641

Orient-U.S. Leasing Corporation
Wilshire-Grand Building
Suite 1460
Los Angeles, California 90017
(213) 622-9936

New York office
780 Third Avenue
New York, New York 10017
(212) 308-2650

Saitama Bank

Tokyo head office
1-3-1 Kyobashi
Chuo-ku
Tokyo, Japan
(03) 276-6611

Chicago branch
Three First National Plaza
70 West Madison Street
Chicago, Illinois 60602
(312) 782-4185

New York head branch
44 Wall Street
New York, New York 10005
(212) 248-2690

Los Angeles branch
Pacific Financial Center
600 West 6th Street
Los Angeles, California 90017
(213) 629-3121

Sanwa Bank

Osaka head office
10, Fushimimachi, 4-chome
Higashi-ku
Osaka 541, Japan
(06) 202-2281

Tokyo headquarters
1-1 Otemachi 1-chome
Chiyoda-ku
Tokyo 100, Japan
(03) 216-3111

New York branch
200 Park Avenue
New York, New York 10166
(212) 949-0222

Atlanta agency
Georgia-Pacific Center, Suite
    4750
133 Peachtree Street, N.E.
Atlanta, Georgia 30303
(404) 586-6880

Boston representative office
100 Summer Street, 29th Floor
Boston, Massachusetts, 02110
(617) 654-2930

Chicago branch
39 South Lasalle Street
Chicago, Illinois 60603
(312) 368-3000

Houston representative office
Entex Building
1200 Milam
Houston, Texas 77002
(713) 654-9970

San Francisco agency
300 Montgomery Street
San Francisco, California 94104
(415) 772-8200

*Golden State Sanwa Bank head
    office*
300 Montgomery Street
San Francisco, California 94104
(415) 772-8200

Sumitomo Bank

Osaka head office
International Banking Division
22, Kitahama 5-chome
Higashi-ku
Osaka, Japan
(06) 227-2111

*Tokyo Foreign Business
    Department*
3-2, Marunouchi 1-chome
Chiyoda-ku
Tokyo, Japan
(03) 282-5111

New York branch
One World Trade Center, Suite
    9651
New York, New York 10048
(212) 553-0100

Atlanta representative office
Georgia-Pacific Center, Suite
    1100
133 Peachtree Street
Atlanta, Georgia 30303
(404) 521-1185

Chicago branch
Sears Tower, Suite 7117
233 South Wacker Drive
Chicago, Illinois 60606
(313) 876-0525

*Los Angeles International Banking
   Division*
First Interstate Tower, Suite 1700
707 Wilshire Boulevard
Los Angeles, California 90017
(213) 688-7511

*San Francisco International
   Banking Division*
365 California Street
San Francisco, California 94104
(415) 445-8000

Sumitomo Bank of California
365 California Street
San Francisco, California 94104
(415) 445-8000

Seattle branch
4600 Seattle-First National Bank
   Building, Suite 1001
Fourth Avenue
Seattle, Washington 98154
(206) 625-1010

Taiyo Kobe Bank

Kobe head office
27, Naniwa-cho
Chuo-ku
Kobe 650, Japan
(078) 331-8101

New York branch
350 Park Avenue
New York, New York 10022
(212) 750-1050

Los Angeles agency
444 South Flower Street
Los Angeles, California 90071
(213) 629-3939

Seattle branch
900 4th Avenue
Seattle, Washington 98164
(206) 682-2312

Tokyo Leasing Co., Ltd.

Tokyo head office
Nottochi Building, 5th Floor
4-1, Kasumigaseki 1-chome
Chiyoda-ku
Tokyo 100, Japan
(03) 581-5541

New York representative office
780 Third Avenue
New York, New York 10017
(212) 832-0808

Wako Securities (America), Inc.

Tokyo head office
6-1 Nihonbashi, Koamicho
Chuo-ku
Tokyo, Japan
(03) 667-8111

New York branch
One World Trade Center
New York, New York 10048
(212) 432-0971

Yamaichi Securities

Tokyo head office
4-1 Yaesu, 2-chome
Chuo-ku
Tokyo 104, Japan
(03) 276-3181

Chicago branch
30 South Wacker Drive
Suite 3903
Chicago, Illinois 60606
(312) 930-9133

Yamaichi International (America)
Inc.
Two World Trade Center
Suite 9650
New York, New York 10048
(212) 912-6400

Los Angeles branch
333 South Hope Street
Los Angeles, California 90071
(213) 626-0401

Yasuda Trust & Banking Co., Ltd.

Tokyo head office
2-1, Yaesu 1-chome
Chuo-ku
Tokyo 103, Japan
(03) 278-8111

Chicago representative office
3 First National Plaza, Suite 5660
70 West Madison Street
Chicago, Illinois 60602
(312) 704-2288

New York branch
One World Trade Center, Suite
8871
New York, New York 10048
(212) 432-2300

Los Angeles representative office
Citicorp Plaza, Suite 3990
725 South Figueroa Street
Los Angeles, California 90017
(213) 624-4864

Atlanta representative office
285 Peachtree Center Avenue,
N.E.
Suite 2104
Marquis Two
Atlanta, Georgia 30303
(404) 584-7807

Zenshinren Bank

Tokyo head office
8-1, Kyobashi 3-chome
Chuo-ku
Tokyo 104, Japan
(03) 563-4111

New York representative office
One World Trade Center, Suite
8007
New York, New York 10048
(212) 524-6811

English Language Publications to Help You Keep Informed About Developments in Japanese Finance

There's so much reporting about Japanese business that it makes sense to list only those publications providing extensive coverage.

Business Tokyo, Tokyo, monthly.
U.S. office:
1270 Avenue of the Americas
New York, New York 10020
(212) 757-2135

Corporate Finance, London,
monthly. U.S. office:
Reed Publishing
205 East 42nd Street
New York, New York 10017
(212) 867-2080

Economist, London, weekly. U.S.
office:
10 Rockefeller Plaza
New York, New York 10020
(212) 759-1259

Euromoney, London, monthly.
U.S. office:
Reed Publishing
205 East 42nd Street
New York, New York 10017
(212) 867-2080

Financial Times, London, 6 days
a week.
U.S. office:
14 East 60th Street
New York, New York 10126
(212) 752-4500

Global Investor, London, monthly.
U.S. office:
Reed Publishing
205 East 42nd Street
New York, New York 10017
(212) 867-2080

Japan Economic Journal, Tokyo,
weekly.
U.S. office:
1221 Avenue of the Americas
New York, New York 10020
(212) 512-6666

Japan Financial Report, Tokyo,
biweekly.
C.P.O. Box 857
Tokyo, Japan
(03) 423-4366

Tokyo Financial Letter, Tokyo,
  biweekly. U.S. office:
1221 Avenue of the Americas
New York, New York 10020
(212) 512-3600

Wall Street Journal, New York,
  daily.
200 Liberty Street
New York, New York 10281
(212) 416-2000

INDEX